Vandana

CORP
GOVER

CW00503223

Corporate Governance

R. K. Aggarwal
Principal
Seth G. L. Bihani S.D.P.G. College
Sri Ganganagar (Rajasthan)

S.S. Aggarwal
Head, Department of Accounting and Finance
Seth G. L. Bihani S.D.P.G. College
Sri Ganganagar (Rajasthan)

Dr. H. K. Singh
Lecturer, Department of Accounting and Finance
Seth G. L. Bihani S.D.P.G. College
Sri Ganganagar (Rajasthan)

A.P.H. PUBLISHING CORPORATION
4435-36/7, ANSARI ROAD, DARYA GANJ
NEW DELHI-110 002

Published by
S. B. Nangia
A.P.H. Publishing Corporation
4435-36/7, Ansari Road, Darya Ganj
New Delhi-110 002
☎ 23274050
email : aphbooks@vsnl.net

2011

Typesetting at
NEW APCON

Printed at
Balaji Offset
M-28, Navin Shahdra, Delhi-110032

CONTENTS

CHAPTER-1

Creating a Better India Through Corporate Governance: Transparency and Accountability

Meenakshi Mandal

B.B.A.L.L.B 6th Semester (3rd Year)
KIIT LAW SCHOOL, Bhubaneswar: 751024, Orissa

"Corporate Governance is concerned with holding the balance between economic and social goals and between individual and communal goals. The corporate governance framework is there to encourage the efficient use of resources and equally to require accountability for the stewardship of those resources. The aim is to align as nearly as possible the interests of individuals, corporations and society."

-Sir Adrian Cadbury in 'Global Corporate Governance Forum', World Bank, 2000[1]

INTRODUCTION

Corporate governance is about ethical conduct in business. Ethics is concerned with the code of values and principles that enables a person to choose between right and wrong. In this regard, managers make decisions based on a set of principles influenced by the values, context and culture of the organization. Corporate governance is a key element in improving the economic efficiency of a corporate.[2] The basic objective of corporate governance is to maximize long-term shareholder value and serve the interests of all the stakeholders. The main issues in corporate governance are transparency and accountability.[3] Good corporate governance ensures that their Boards are accountable to the shareholders.[4] The shareholders, the supplier of resources, the consumers, the employees, the local community and society at large are affected by the way an enterprise functions. According to the Declaration issued by the International Seminar on Social Responsibility of Business, a business enterprise has to be socially very responsive so that a social balance may be struck between the opposing interests of these groups. The concept of social responsibility assumes that the business has not only economic and legal obligations but also certain other social responsibilities too.[5]

BACKGROUND OF CORPORATE GOVERNANCE

The idea of corporate governance, as it stands today in India, has been shaped by the prevailing socio- economic environment. Significantly it was the economic liberalization of the country that gave an impetus to development of the standards of corporate governance in India.

PRE-1991 ERA

Post-independence and until the early 1990s, the Indian economy was largely socialistic, with public or government ownership and control in all major sectors and industry. The few industries that were privately owned were heavily regulated by the state. Another characteristic feature of the companies in the pre-1991 era was that the ownership of a number of companies was family –held. So the number of shareholders was limited and commercial decisions of the company were taken by keeping the larger interests of the family mind so, the issue of transparency and disclosures of the decision-making process was not so keenly felt.[6]

LIBERALIZATION OF THE INDIAN ECONOMY

The first recorded attempt by the Indian Government to reform the financial sector is in the Chakravarty Committee Report of 1985, following which the Narasimha Committee Report of 1991 laid down the basis for financial reforms in India. This report aimed at removing direct Government control on the capital market and suggested to replace it by a regulatory framework based on transparency and disclosure surprised by an independent regulator.[7]According Kumarmanglam Birla Committee three key constituents of corporate governance are the shareholder, the Board of Directors and the Management they also recognize the role and responsibility as well as their rights in the terms of good corporate governance which is based on transparency, accountability. According to Naresh Chandra Committee ' Report of the Committee on Corporate Audit and Governance' one of the cores of corporate governance is designing and putting in place disclosures, monitoring oversight and corrective systems that can align the objectives of the two sets of players as closely as possible and hence, minimize agency costs. According to Narayan Murthi Committee on 'Report of the SEBI Committee on Corporate Governance' commented on Corporate Governance that a corporation is a congregation of various stakeholders, namely, customers, employees, investors, vendor partners, government and society. A corporation should be fair and transparent to its stakeholders in all its transactions.[8]

BENEFITS OF GOOD CORPORATE GOVERNANCE

Investors primarily consider two variables before making investment decisions- the rate of return on the invested capital and the risk associated with the investment. Good corporate governance practices reduce this risk by ensuring transparency, accountability, and enforceability in the marketplace.[9] The pivotal role in any system of corporate governance is performed by the board of directors[10] by framing suitable business strategies, monitoring the activities of company's management, and prescribing the measure for sustainable growth of the company in a transparent fashion.[11]Business is a major social institution and as such, it is importantly involved in social values. The idea of social responsibility is that the decision-makers are obliged to take actions which protect and improve the welfare of the society as a whole along with their own interests. It builds a better quality of life, thus harmonizing organizational actions with society's wants. The idea is that the businessman acts in a manner that will accomplish social benefits along with the traditional economic gains which the firm seeks men and women to engage in business, the business in return make contributions to the society, because it is what society demands from it.[12] It also helps the shareholder to make informed decisions about valuation, ownership and voting of shares. It also helps improve public understanding of structure and activities of the enterprise, corporate policies and performance with reference to environment and ethical standards.[13] So to create a better India transparency and accountability in every level is required.

TRANSPARENCY AND ACCOUNTABILITY IN CORPORATE GOVERNANCE

Transparency[14] means accurate, adequate and timely disclosure of relevant information to the stakeholders. Without transparency, it is impossible to make any progress towards good corporate governance. The company is a trustee of the investors, money and this responsibility in turn demands full disclosure. Corporations in India must learn to work with transparency and impeccable integrity as these are the essential ingredients to maximize their wealth and the wealth of the nation.[15] A company is not only accountable towards its shareholders but also the society as a whole.[16]

VARIOUS ASPECT OF TRANSPARENCY

- **Access:** the information should be accessible to all.
- **Relevance:** information should be according to the needs of the user.
- **Quality:** Qualities ensure compatibility of information over time. So it should be useful, fair, reliable, timely, complete, consistent and presented in clear and simple terms.
- **Reliability:** the source of data and methodology used for gathering information should be disclosed to enhance its reliability.

RESULT OF LACK OF TRANSPARENCY AND ACCOUNTABILITY

If the promoters fail to fulfil the essential requirement of Corporate Governance then fraud, corruption, bribery comes into picture. India has faced many scams like, Harshad Mehta's scam, most recent incident Satyam Scandal, etc.

SCANDAL IN SATYAM

"Satyam" it is a Sanskrit word which means the truth and for that the company had won the coveted Golden Peacock Global Award for Excellence in Corporate Governance for 2008[17] but after one year, it appears with the biggest frauds in India's corporate history. B. Ramalinga Raju, Founder & CEO of Satyam Computers announced that his company had been falsifying its account for years. The balance sheet and books of account recorded a fictitious amount of money which had been audited by PriceWaterhouseCoopers (PWC).The entire episode of attempt to purchase of Maytas by Satyam was nothing but making mockery of the concept of corporate governance in India, ie. Fairness, transparency and accountability have failed here. This case is an eye opener of the extent to which the independent directors are really performed well their role.[18]

LEGAL FRAMEWORK

Article 19(1) (g) provides every citizen has the right to know. The Ministry of Corporate Affairs (MCA) is the main authority for regulating and promoting efficient, transparent and accountable form of corporate governance in the Indian corporate sector. It is primarily concerned with administration of the Companies Act, 1956 and related legislations as well as convenient compliance of regulations with transparency and accountability in corporate governance.[19] Disclosure is the key mechanism for achieving transparency and enabling informed decisions which are the hallmarks of Corporate Governance. To make the Government company transparent, Section 619 of the Companies Act is there and according to Section 219 of the Companies Act, 1956, Shareholders have a right to receive copies of balance sheet and auditors' report. According to section 211 of it, the balance sheet and profit and loss account should give true and fair view of the state of affairs of the company.[20]In America, in response to the Enron, WorldCom, and other corporate crises and accounting scandals, the Sarbanes-Oxley Act of 2002 was passed. Congress stated that the objective behind passing this Act was to "protect investors by improving the accuracy and reliability of corporate disclosures made pursuant to the securities laws. Back home in India, the need for strengthened norms for Corporate Governance is also felt. The revised clause 49 of the Listing Agreement is, therefore, most timely and provides much needed disclosure requirements and issue of certificate of compliance.[21]

Under clause 49(iv) of the Listing Agreement, every listed company is required to make certain disclosures on a periodic basis. The same is presented in a tabular form below. This is in addition to disclosures that are required to be made under the provisions of the Companies Act of 1956.

- **Basis of related party transactions:** According to Clause 49(iv) (A) Directors occupy a fiduciary position in relation to the company. Hence they should ensure that their personal interests do not conflict with the interests of the company.

- **Accounting treatment:** According to Clause 49(iv) (B) of the Listing Agreement, Accounting Standard has been prescribed the Institute of Chartered Accountants of India in respect of accounting practices and for preparing and presenting financial statements.[22]

- **Risk management:** According to Clause 49(iv) (c) of Listing Agreement, a company is required to lay down procedures to inform Board members about the risk assessment and minimization procedures. This disclosure should be made to the members of the Board of Directors.

- **Proceeds from public issues, right issues, preferential issues, etc.:** According to Clause 49(iv) (D) a company raises money from the public by way of public issues, rights issues etc. at the time of making the issue, the purpose of raising the money is disclosed to the public so as to enable them to decide whether the project/ purpose for which the money is proposed to be utilized, is the project in which they want to invest.

- **Remuneration of directors:** According to Clause 49(iv) (E) it is important for the shareholders to be informed of the remuneration of the directors of the company. The Kumaramangalan Committee was of the view that the company must have a credible and transparent policy in determining and accounting for the remuneration of the directors.

- **Management :**According to Clause 49(iv) (F) of the Listing Agreement, There has to be a periodic review of the management's implementation process of the policies and strategies of the Board, by the shareholders so that in case any mid-course corrections are required in the policy, strategy or implementation process, the same can be made.

- **Shareholders:** According to Clause 49(iv) (G) of the Listing Agreement, the shareholders are the owners of the company. Therefore, it is necessary that all the fundamental corporate events relating to changes in directorship, company news-financial or otherwise, grievance redressal mechanism and share transfer/ transmission mechanism are communicated to the shareholders.[23]

SUGGESTION

India has written law regarding Corporate Governance still India has faced several scams and it indicates that the laws are not properly executed. So something more is required to execute it properly. Hence, there is a greater need to increase awareness among entrepreneurs about the various aspects of corporate governance. There are some of the areas that need special attention, namely:-

- Quality of audit, which is at the root of effective corporate governance;
- Role of Board of Directors as well as accountability of the CEOs and CFOs;
- Quality and effectiveness of the legal, administrative and regulatory framework; etc.

It is necessary to provide the corporate desired level of comfort in compliance with the code, principles and requirements of corporate governance; as well as provide relevant information to all stakeholders regarding the performance, policies and procedures of the company in a transparent manner. There should be proper financial and non-financial disclosures by the companies, such as, about remuneration package, financial reporting, auditing, internal controls, etc.[24] It is suggested that in the light of the experience of the Act in the US, some reforms should be introduced in India for achieving corporate excellence and accountability. For example, There should be an enactment of laws on the pattern of the Corporate and Criminal Accountability Act, 2002 and White Collar Crime Penalty Enhancement Act, 2002 for investigation and prosecution white collar corporate crimes. There should be greater self-discipline and emphasis on codes of ethics and social responsibilities on the part of companies. In the ultimate analysis the society has created business institution for its welfare and it has to discharge its duties and responsibilities as good corporate citizens.[25]

CONCLUSION

In the wake of high profile corporate scandals and a rising concern over yet increasing risk of corporate fraud and issues around financial statement, it is now necessary to step away from the traditional approach and focus on establishing a cohesive system, delivering two important qualities: transparency and accountability. As companies grow in size and complexity they need to take into account several requirements – internal monitoring controls, corporate governance, and external reporting activities - that are able to function as a synergistic whole. Moreover, as one increases their stakeholder base the expectation level also rises from regulators as well as the society at large. It is paramount that companies adopt and implement a code of conduct that re-enforces the culture of transparency in business transaction.[26]

BIBLIOGRAPHY

Books

- Indrajit Dube, Corporate Governance, LexisNexis, Butterworths Wadhwa, Nagpur, 2008
- Renu Jatana& David Crowther ,Corporate Social Responsibility,Deep & Deep Publications Pvt. LTD, New Delhi, 2007
- The Institute of Company Secretaries of India ,Corporate Governance, 7th ed. 2008
- V.Sithapathy & ,Taxmann's Corporate Governance Practice & procedures, , 2006
- Corporate Governance, Amarchand Mangaldas &Suresh A. Shiroff & Co. Wolters Kluwer (India) Pvt Ltd, New Delhi, 2009
- Dr. C.L.Bansal ,Taxmann's Corporate Governance,Reader, College of Vocational Studies, University of Delhi, 2005

END NOTES

1. "Enhancing Transparency and Accountability in Indian Corporates", https://www.in.kpmg.com/SecureData/aci/.../Enhancing_Transparency.pdf, last accessed in January, 2011
2. V.Sithapathy & ,Taxmann's Corporate Governance Practice & procedures, p 5 (2006)
3. RAVISH BHATEJA,CORPORATE GOVERNANCE, www.aoc-india.co.in/pdf/ETHICS-IPCC-1-RAVISH%20BHATEJA.pdf, last accessed in January, 2011

4. V. Sithapathy & Taxmann's Corporate Governance Practice & procedures, p. 5 (2006).

5. Renu Jatana & david Crowther ,Corporate social responsibility, 339, (Deep & deep Publications Pvt.Ltd, New Delhi.

6. Amarchand Mangaldas &Suresh A. Shiroff & Co. Wolters Kluwer (India) Pvt Ltd, Corporate Governance, 26 (New Delhi, 2009).

7. Amarchand Mangaldas &Suresh A. Shiroff & Co. Wolters Kluwer (India) Pvt Ltd, Corporate Governance, 26 (New Delhi, 2009).

8. Indrajit Dube, Corporate Governance,14 (LexisNexis, Butterworths Wadhwa Nagpur, 2008).

9. Amarchand Mangaldas &Suresh A. Shiroff & Co. Wolters Kluwer (India) Pvt Ltd, Corporate Governance, 3 (New Delhi, 2009).

10. Indrajit Dube, Corporate Governance,14 (LexisNexis, Butterworths Wadhwa Nagpur, 2008).

11. Indrajit Dube, Corporate Governance, 20 (LexisNexis, Butterworths Wadhwa, Nagpur, 2008.

12. Renu Jatana & David Crowther, corporate social responsibility, 341(Deep & Deep Publications Pvt. LTD, New Delhi, 2007.

13. Dr. C.L. Bansal, Taxmann's Corporate Governance, Reader, College of Vocational Studies, 275 (University of Delhi, 2005).

14. Transparency: openness,. clarity, lack of guide and attempts to hide damaging information. The word is used of financial disclosures, organizational policies and practices, lawmaking and other activities where organization interaction with the public, Black's Law Dictionary, (6th Ed., 1990).

15. RAVISH BHATEJA,CORPORATE GOVERNANCE, www.aoc-india.co.in/pdf/ETHICS-IPCC-1-RAVISH%20BHATEJA.pdf, last accessed in January, 2011.

16. A.N. Tiwari, Transparency and Accountability in Administration, Orissa Review August - 2004.

17. Businesswire India, "Satyam receives Golden Peacock Global Award for Excellence in Corporate Governance" http://www.financialexpress.com/news/satyam-receives-golden-peacock-global-award-for-excellence-in-corporate-governance/364843/, last accessed in January, 2011.

18. Ms. Hemlata Manglani & Mr. Sumit Srivastava, "Corporate Governance: Necessity for Companies (Comparative Analysis of Infosys and Satyam)", http://www.indianmba.com/Faculty_Column/FC1068/fc1068.html, last accessed in January, 2011

19. Business Gov .In ,http://business.gov.in/corporate_governance/companies_laws.php, last accessed in January, 2011

20. Advisory Group on Corporate Governance, "CORPORATE GOVERNANCE IN INDIA: CURRENT STATUS & RECOMMENDATIONS", rbidocs.rbi.org.in/rdocs/Publication Report/Pdfs/20024.pdf, last accessed in January, 2011

21. Maheshwari and Co., "AN ANALYSIS OF REVISED CLAUSE 49 OF THE LISTING AGREEMENT", www.maheshwariandco.com/articles/Clause%2049.pdf, last accessed in January, 2011

22. V.Sithapathy &, Taxmann's Corporate Governance Practice & procedures, 5 (2006)

23. Corporate Governance, Amarchand Mangaldas & Suresh A. Shiroff & Co. Wolters Kluwer (India) Pvt Ltd, 108(New Delhi, 2009)

24. Business Gov .In http://business.gov.in/corporate_governance/suggestions_opinions.php last accessed in January, 2011

25. NARESH KUMAR, CORPORATE EXCELLENCE AND ACCOUNTABILITY UNDER THE SARBANES – OXLEY ACT, 2002 — LESSONS FOR INDIA, www.icsi.edu/.../CORPORATEEXCELLENCEANDACCOUNTABILITY-NARESHKUMAR.doc, last accessed in January, 2011

26. KPMG IN INDIA, "Enhancing Transparency and Accountability in Indian Corporates", https://www.in.kpmg.com/SecureData/aci/.../Enhancing_Transparency.pdf.last accessed in January, 2011

CHAPTER-2

Corporate Governance in Insurance Companies

Aishwarya Padmanabhan

IVth year, Law Student, B.A.LLB (Hons.), National University of Juridical Sciences (NUJS, Kolkata, West Bengal

Corporate Governance is understood as a system of financial and other controls in a corporate entity and broadly defines the relationship between the Board of Directors, senior management and shareholders. In case of the financial sector, where the entities accept public liabilities for fulfillment of certain contracts, the relationship is fiduciary with enhanced responsibility to protect the interests of all stakeholders. The Corporate Governance framework should clearly define the roles and responsibilities and accountability within an organization with built-in checks and balances.

The importance of Corporate Governance has received emphasis in recent times since poor governance and weak internal controls have been associated with major corporate failures. It has also been appreciated that the financial sector needs to have a more intensive governance structure in view of its role in the economic development and since the safety and financial strength of the institutions are critical for the overall strength of the financial sector on which the economic growth is built upon. As regards the insurance sector, the regulatory responsibility to protect the interests of the policyholders demands that the insurers have in place, good governance practices for maintenance of solvency, sound long term investment policy and assumption of underwriting risks on a prudential basis. The emergence of insurance companies as a part of financial conglomerates has added a further dimension to sound Corporate Governance in the insurance sector with emphasis on overall risk management across the structure and to prevent any contagion.

The Insurance Regulatory and Development Authority (IRDA) has outlined in general terms, governance responsibilities of the Board in the management of the insurance functions under various Regulations notified by it covering different operational areas. It has now been decided to put them together and to issue the following comprehensive guidelines for adoption by Indian insurance companies. These guidelines are in addition to provisions of the Companies Act, 1956, the Insurance Act, 1938 and requirement of any other laws or regulations framed there under. Where any provisions of these guidelines appear to be in conflict with the provisions contained in any law or regulations, the legal provisions will prevail. However, where the requirements of these guidelines are more rigorous than the provisions of any law, these guidelines shall be followed.

The objective of the guidelines is to ensure that the structure, responsibilities and functions of Board of Directors and the senior management of the company fully recognize the expectations of all stakeholders as well as those of the regulator. The structure should take steps required to adopt sound and prudent principles and practices for the governance of the company and should have the ability to quickly address issues of non-compliance or weak oversight and controls. These guidelines therefore amplify on certain issues which are covered in the Insurance Act, 1938 and the regulations framed there under and include measures which are additionally considered essential by IRDA for adoption by insurance companies.

The guidelines accordingly address the various requirements broadly covering major structural elements of Corporate Governance in insurance companies including Governance structure, Board of Directors, Control functions, Senior management, Disclosures, Relationship with stakeholders and finally, Whistle blowing policy.

GOVERNANCE STRUCTURE

Currently, the private insurers in India are yet to go public and get their shares listed on the stock exchanges. The composition of the Boards of the Public Sector Undertakings in the insurance sector is also laid down by the Government of India. It is relevant to observe here that the Corporate Governance requirements of companies listed in the Stock Exchanges have evolved over time and are outlined in Clause 49 of the Listing Agreement of the Stock Exchanges. As the listing requirements are available in public domain they are not being repeated. The Indian insurance companies are as yet unlisted but the Authority advises all insurers to familiarize themselves with Corporate Governance structures and requirements appropriate to listed entities.

VARYING STRUCTURES OF THE BOARD

Subject to the above, the insurance companies presently could have different structures with the Board of Directors headed by a Full-Time or Part-Time Chairman with distinct executive and oversight responsibilities among the other Directors and Senior Management. It is expected that whatever form is taken, the broader elements of good Corporate Governance are present.

BOARD OF DIRECTORS

Composition

- The Insurance Act stipulates that the insurance companies in India would be public companies and hence, would require a properly constituted Board.

- Insurers should ensure that the Board comprises of competent and qualified Directors to drive the strategies in a manner that would sustain growth and protect the interests of the stakeholders in general and policyholders in particular.

- It is expected that the shareholders of the companies elect or nominate Directors from various areas of financial and management expertise such as accountancy, banking, insurance, economics etc., with qualifications and experience that is appropriate to the company.

- The Board of Directors is required to have a significant number of "Independent Directors" (as generally understood). The optimum contribution of Independent Executive and Non-Executive Directors enhances the quality of business judgment and benefits the shareholders and policyholders. At a minimum, where the company has a non-executive Chairman, at least fifty percent of the directors should be independent and in other cases at least one third of the directors should be independent. This is especially important in respect of insurance companies under conglomerate structure and where there is potential scope for transfer of risks and conflicts of interests that affect the group entities.

- Similarly, where the Chairman of the Board is non-executive, the Chief Executive Officer should be a whole time director of the Board.

- As a matter of prudence, not more than one member of a family or a close relative as defined in the Companies Act or an associate (partner, director etc) should be on the Board of an Insurer.

- Procedures concerning election, re-election, removal and retirement of members of the Board of Directors should be set out and documented.

FIT AND PROPER CRITERIA

In line with the international and domestic norms, the Directors of insurance companies have to meet the "fit and proper" criteria. The criteria to be satisfied, at a minimum, would relate to integrity demonstrated in personal behaviour and business conduct, soundness of judgment and financial soundness. The Insurance Act prohibits (i) a life insurance agent to be the Director of the life insurance company; and (ii) the common directorship among life insurance companies. Currently, the fit and proper requirements seek to ensure that the Director should not have come under adverse notice of the laws and regulations or of any professional body. With a view to ensuring that the Directors comply with the above requirement, a due diligence enquiry should be undertaken on the person to be appointed as Director or for the continuance of the existing Directors only after obtaining a declaration from the proposed/existing Directors in the format given in Annexure 2, at the time of their appointment/re-appointment.

The Directors are also required to enter into a Deed of Covenant as per the format placed at Annexure 3, with the insurance company, duly approved by the Board, pursuant to their terms of appointment to ensure that there is a clear understanding of the mutual role of the company and the Board in Corporate Governance.

The company can establish several Committees to undertake specific functions depending on the size and level of the complexity of the operations. Typically, the Committees that assist the Board are Audit Committee, Risk Management Committee, Nominations Committee, Remuneration Committee, Investment Committee and Asset-Liability Management Committee. However, the Authority advises insurers that it is mandatory to establish Audit; Investment; Risk Management; Policyholder Protection; and Asset Liability Management (in case of life insurers) Committees that have a critical role in strengthening the control environment in the company.

SENIOR MANAGEMENT

CEO & OTHER SENIOR FUNCTIONARIES

The Chief Executive Officer of the company and other key functionaries are responsible for the operations and day to day management of the company in line with the directions of the Board and the Committees set up by the Board. Section 34A of the Insurance Act, 1938 requires prior approval of the Authority for appointment, re-appointment or termination of the Chief Executive Officer and the Whole Time Directors. The Authority expects the CEO to be responsible for the conduct of the company's affair in a manner which is not detrimental to the interests of the policyholders and is consistent with the directions of the Board. The Board should, therefore, carry out effective due diligence to establish that the new incumbent is 'fit and proper' before recommending the name for Authority's approval. The Insurance Act also prohibits the CEO of a life insurance company from being a Director in any other insurance company/ bank/investment company.

ROLE OF APPOINTED ACTUARIES

IRDA has brought out detailed Regulations on Appointed Actuary vide IRDA (Appointed Actuary) Regulations, 2000, detailing the procedure for his appointment, qualifications, powers along with his duties and obligations. The Regulations also stipulate that prior approval of the Authority shall be taken for eth appointment of the Appointed Actuary. In brief, it is reiterated that

(a) A procedure for appointment of Appointed Actuary should be put in place.

(b) The Appointed Actuary should qualify and satisfy the 'Fit & Proper' criteria.

(c) The insurer shall clearly set forth the Actuary's responsibilities and any advisory role vis-à-vis the Board or the management as well as his/her rights and obligations. These shall be in addition to the duties of the Appointed Actuaries as specified in the IRDA Regulations and any other directions of IRDA in the matter.

DISCLOSURE REQUIREMENTS

The prescriptions on financial disclosures in the financial statements are laid down in the IRDA (Preparations of Financial Statements) Regulations, 2002. In addition, the Authority is in the process of finalizing additional disclosures to be made to it and generally to the public at large at periodical intervals. Once these disclosure requirements are finalized, all insurers would be required to ensure compliance thereof.

RELATIONSHIP WITH STAKEHOLDERS

A stakeholder is any person, group or organization that has a direct or indirect stake in an insurer.

The stakeholder can affect or be affected by the insurer's actions, objectives and policies. The key stakeholders in case of an insurer include shareholders, employees, policyholders and supervisors. Other stakeholders could include creditors, service providers, unions, rating agencies, equity analysts and the community at large.

In case of a situation arising whereby there is a possibility of conflict of interests, the board plays an important role and balances and resolves the conflicting objectives. The board must be guided by clear and understandable principles. It must ensure protection of the interests of both current and prospective policyholders.

In assessing the governance practices in place, the IRDA would:

- Seek confirmation that the insurer has adopted and effectively implemented sound corporate governance policies and practices;

- assess the fitness and propriety of board members;
- monitor the performance of boards;
- assess the quality of insurers' internal reporting, risk management, audit and control functions;
- evaluate the effects of the insurer's group structure on the governance strategies and assess the adequacy of governance processes in the area of crisis management and business continuity.

The IRDA would, at periodic intervals, also bring to the board's and senior management's attention problems which have been detected through supervisory activities.

REPORTING TO IRDA

Insurers should examine to what extent they are currently complying with these guidelines and initiate immediate action to achieve compliance (where not already in compliance) within a period of six months from the date of these guidelines. Where such compliance is not possible for any specific reason, the insurer should write to the IRDA for further guidance. Each insurer should designate an officer as the Compliance officer whose duty will be to monitor continuing compliance with these guidelines.

WHISTLE BLOWING POLICY

The insurers are well advised to shall put in place a "whistle blowing" policy; where by mechanisms exist for employees to raise concerns internally about possible irregularities, governance weaknesses, financial reporting issues or other such matters. These could include employee reporting in confidence directly to the chairman of the board or of a committee of the board or to the external auditor.

The Policy illustratively covers the following aspects:

- Awareness of the employees that such channels are available, how to use them and how their report will be handled
- Handling of the reports received confidentially, for independent assessment, investigation and where necessary for taking appropriate follow-up actions

- A robust anti-retaliation policy to protect employees who make reports in good faith

The appointed actuary and the statutory/internal auditors have the duty to 'whistle blow', i.e., to report in a timely manner to the IRDA if they are aware that the insurer has failed to take appropriate steps to rectify a matter which has a material adverse effect on its financial condition. This would enable the IRDA to take prompt action before policyholders' interests are undermined.

CONCLUSION

Regulation acquires significance in sensitive areas like financial transactions, where chances of mismanagement, deception, fraud, etc., are more possible. If such malpractices do occur, the common man would stand to lose the most as he would be unaware of the intricacies of financial transactions. Hence, some sort of governance, regulation and supervision is essential in such financial services such as insurance.

Further, in common with other financial services, insurers are repositories of public trust and accept money from the insured in return for a promise of payment at some future date or on the occurrence of some certain event. An insurance company can fulfill this commitment only if it has adequate professional capability, is financially soundly managed, holds adequate reserves to meet the requirement of funds with reference to the nature of term of liabilities and invests its large corpus of funds carefully and judicially.

Collaborations with foreign companies which are globally experienced and larger in size are no guarantee that all such companies will behave well. Reckless rate wars, undercutting, unhealthy links with industrial houses and a disregard for prudential norms are not totally unknown in other markets. Hence, the need to regulate strictly. Accordingly, they are subjected to close regulation by the state in all countries, with the objective of ensuring that their business is run fairly, is conducted by competent persons, and protects the legitimate interests of the insuring public.

In case of Insurance Companies, Insurance Regulatory Development Authority (IRDA) has been entrusted with the regulatory responsibility to protect the interests of the policyholders and public interest and accordingly would like to ensure that appropriate governance practices are in place in the insurance companies for maintenance of solvency, sound long-term investment policy and assumption of underwriting risks on a prudential basis, particularly as the insurance companies are yet to be listed.

The IRDA thus, outlined in general terms, governance responsibilities of the Board in the management of the insurance functions under various Regulations notified by it covering different operational areas.

CHAPTER-3

Better Corporate Governance is the Key of Better India

1. R.P. Verma, (B.Ed., LL.M.)

2. Miss. Jayantika Bihani, (B.Com I Year)

A State is governed by its constitution and a Corporation is by its memorandum. The both have legal existence and get recognition through their strategies of governance. governance is the activity relating to decisions that define expectations, grant power or verify performance. It consists a specific part of management or leadership process. In India such management or leadership is represented by a 5 years voting based government.

Corporate governance refers to processes, customs and policies of a corporation. According to **Milton Freidmann**, "Corporate Governance refers to the conduct of business in accordance with owner or shareholders' desires conforming to the basic rules of society embodied in law and local customs". According to **J. Wolfenshon**, former President of World Bank "Corporate Governance is about Promoting corporate fairness, Tranparency and Accountability."

CERTAIN MODELS OF CORPORATE GOVERNANCE

When shareholder elect the Board of Directors. They play advisory role and control the affairs.

- Where shareholders do not directly control the governance mechanism. Half of the members on the supervisory board are elect by the labour unions while the remaining are elected by the shareholder. In such model the employers are not just stake holders, but they also have a say in the governance mechanism.

- Where the financial institution have a major say in the governance mechanism. The shareholder appoint the members of the board with the consent of the banks.

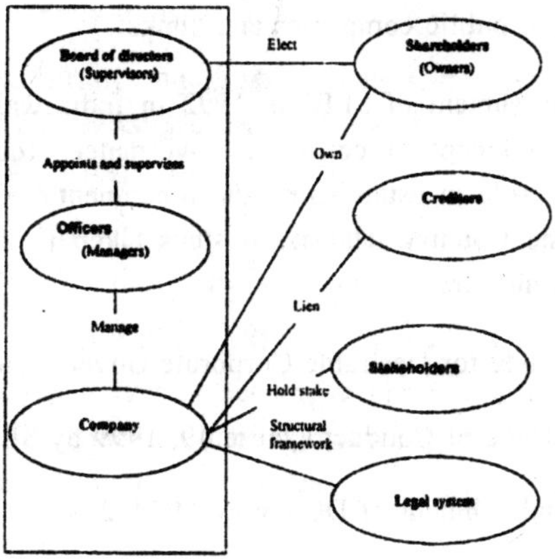

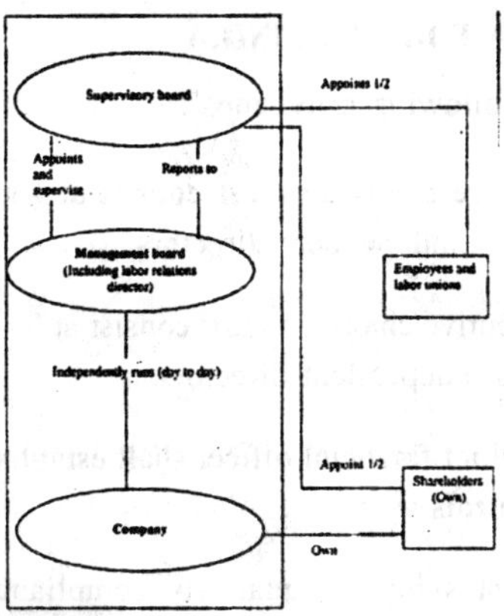

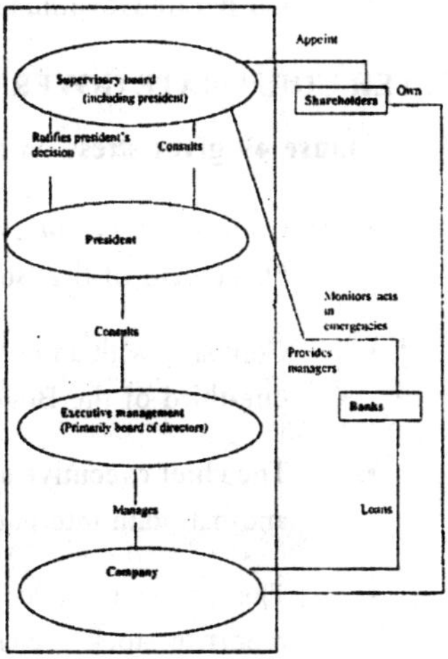

CORPORATE GOVERNANCE IN INDIA

In India corporate governance practices are a set of structural arrangements that are emerging in free market economics to align the management of companies with the interest of their shareholders and other stake holder and society at large.

The Indian corporate governance is a mix of the Anglo American and German models. There are three types of corporations in India named private companies, public companies and banks.

The establishment of SEBI in 1992 in India was a first positive step to develop concept of corporate governance. Today, it has been playing a crucial role in establishing the fundamental rules of corporate governance in the Country. The major steps taken in India to establish corporate governance are

- A code for Desirable Corporate Governance 1998 by CII
- A Code of Conduct Clause 49, 1999 by SEBI
- Establishment of DCA now MCA 2002
- Compulsion of provisions of clause 49, 2006
- Corporate Governance Voluntary Guide Lines 2009 by MCA

BETTER CORPORATE GOVERNANCE BETTER INDIA

Clause 49 gives stress on the following provisions :

- Company with an executive chairman must consist at least 50 percent of the Board as independent directors.
- Company with a non-executive chairman must consist at least one-third of the Board as independent directors.
- The chief executive and chief financial officer shall establish and maintain internal controls.
- The company listed must submit a quarterly compliance report to stock exchange in the prescribed form.
- One of the directors must be financially literate

Corporate Governance Voluntary Guidelines 2009 : MCA has ensured Corporate governance by providing the following guidelines.

- There should be fifty percent non executive directors who do not take part in day to day operations of company
- Vacancies of the board should be filled in within reasonable period of time
- Board meetings should be regularly held at least four times in a yeas with a maximum gap of three months.
- The primary role of the board of directors should be that of trusteeship
- For good governance the office of chairman of the Board and CEO should be separated.
- The directors should be able, competent and committed to values.
- Every company should clearly state and declare the rights, duties, responsibilities and remuneration of all the directors and other managerial personnel.
- There should be fix limit on number of directorship, in case of Managing Director or Whole Time Director it should be restricted to seven and for other directors may be restricted to Fifteen.
- The remuneration of all the directors should be based on the recommendation of the Remuneration Committee. The remuneration package should be disclosed to the shareholders in the Annual Report of the company.
- The directors should be supplied with all the information well with in time that is necessary for discharging their duties efficiently and effectively.
- Every company should establish a Sound Auditing System. The board should appoint an internal auditor who should not be an employee of the company. Appointment of a statutory auditor is mandatory for every company.

- Every company should lay down a code of conduct for all its directors and other managerial personal. Such code of conduct should be published on the website of the company.
- Every company should have a sound system of disclosures and reporting to ensure transparency of its operation.
- Every company should establish a whistle blowing mechanism for employees to report concerns about unethical behaviour, fraud or violation of the company's code of conduct or ethics policy.

According to the above guidelines the MCA has provided us clear progressive course of better governance. The main stress for better governance in India. **We must ensure the following requirements**

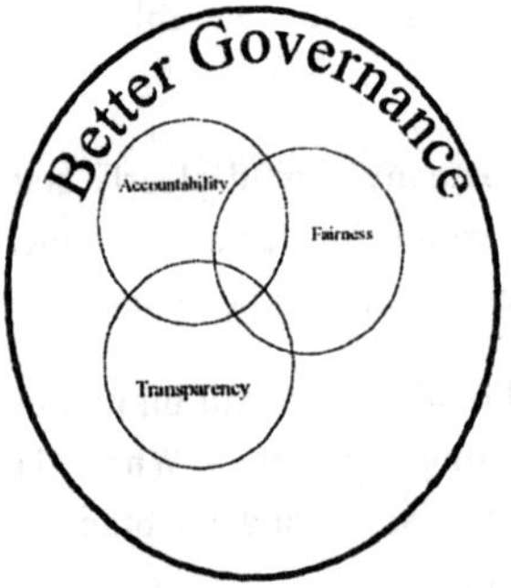

- **Accountability**
- **Transparency**
- **Fairness**
- **Responsiveness**
- **Inclusive and equitableness of acts**
- **Efficient and effective working**
- **Compliance with law**
- **Participation of all the stakeholders**
- **Whistle blowing mechanism**

CHAPTER-4

Corporate Governance in India: Past, Present and Suggestions for the Future

Dr. M.L.Sharma

Director Academic, Bihani Education Trust, Sriganganagar (Rajasthan) India

Prof. R.K.Agarwal

Principal, Bihani S. D. P. G. College , Sriganganagar (Rajasthan) India

Dr. P.C. Acharya

Professor in Department of Hindi, Bihani S. D. P. G. College , Sriganganagar (Rajasthan) India

INTRODUCTION

Former World Bank President James Wolfensohn "has equated the importance of the governance of corporations to that of the governance of countries." According to the Organisation for Economic Co-operation and Development ("OECD"), "Corporate governance deals with the rights and responsibilities of a company's management, its board, shareholders and various stakeholders." The spectacular collapses of Enron and WorldCom in the United States, where shareholders lost a combined $245 billion, and the collapse of Italian dairy giant Parmalat in Europe, have transformed corporate governance from an afterthought to the cornerstone of any firm's or country's long-term success.

Corporate governance in a developing-country setting takes on additional importance. Good corporate governance is vital because of its role in attracting foreign investment. The extent of foreign investment, in turn, shapes the prospects for economic growth for many developing countries. This Note presents an in-depth inquiry into corporate governance in one such developing country, India. While India's corporate-governance framework is advanced for a developing country, it still can be significantly improved

MEANING OF CORPORATE GOVERNANCE

Corporate Governance in general is a mechanism to maximize the wealth of owners, which can be achieved by optimum utilization of resources and maximization of return in given economic environment by managing the organization in more transparent and participating was. Corporate Governance has been seen by many as a combination of corporate ethics, corporate transparency, as well as corporate accountability.

Corporate Governance is strongly affected by the relationship among the participants in the governance system like individual shareholders, employees, suppliers etc. Though, the role and relationship among these participants are focused through law, regulation the voluntary adaptation in Corporate governance mechanism play the most crucial role promoting and protecting the interest of shareholders and policy holders.

WHY CORPORATE GOVERNANCE?

Investors primarily consider two variables before making investment decisions—the rate of return on invested capital and the risk associated with the investment. In recent years, the "attractiveness of developing nations" as a destination for foreign capital has increased, partly because of the high likelihood of obtaining robust returns and partly because of the decreasing "attractiveness of developed nations." The lure of achieving a high rate of return, however, does not, by itself, guarantee foreign investment; the attendant risk weighs equally in an investor's decision-making calculus. Good corporate-governance practices reduce this risk by ensuring transparency, accountability, and enforceability in the marketplace.

Also, sound corporate-governance practices enable management to allocate resources more efficiently, which increases the likelihood that investors will obtain a higher rate of return on their investment. Finally, leading indices show that developing countries that have good governance structures consistently outperform developing countries with poor corporate-governance structures. Thus, in an efficient capital market, investors will invest in firms with better corporate-governance frameworks because of the lower risks and the likelihood of higher returns. At a macro level, if firms in developing countries attract investment, they will stimulate growth in the local economy. If they "cannot attract equity capital, they are doomed to remain on a small, inefficient scale," and they will be unable to stimulate growth in their host country.

HISTORY OF CORPORATE GOVERNANCE IN INDIA

A. Pre-Liberalization

When India attained independence from British rule in 1947, the country was poor, with an average per-capita annual income under thirty dollars. However, it still possessed sophisticated laws regarding "listing, trading, and settlements." It even had four fully operational stock exchanges. Subsequent laws, such as the 1956 Companies Act, further solidified the rights of investors.

Scholars believe that "takeover threats act as disciplining mechanism to poorly performing companies" because as the stock price of poorly governed firms decreases (because disgruntled investors discard stock), the firms become susceptible to hostile-takeover attempts. Thus, "the fear of a takeover ... is supposed to keep the management honest." However, until recently, hostile takeovers were almost entirely non-existent in India, and therefore, the poorly governed Indian firms had little to worry about in terms of following corporate laws once they had raised capital through their initial public offering. Thus, corporate governance in India was in a dismal condition by the early 1990s.

B. Post-Liberalization

In 1999, in a defining moment in India's corporate-governance history, the Indian Parliament created the Securities and Exchange Board of India ("SEBI") to "protect the interests of investors in securities and to promote the development of, and to regulate the securities market." In 1998, the Confederation of Indian Industry ("CII"), "India's premier business association," unveiled India's first code of corporate governance. However, since the Code's adoption was voluntary, few firms embraced it. Soon after, SEBI appointed the Birla Committee to fashion a code of corporate governance. In 2000, SEBI accepted the recommendations of the Birla Committee and introduced Clause 49 into the Listing Agreement of

Stock Exchanges. Clause 49 outlines requirements vis-a-vis corporate governance in exchange-traded companies. In 2003, SEBI instituted the Murthy Committee to scrutinize India's corporate-governance framework further and to make additional recommendations to enhance its effectiveness. SEBI has since incorporated the recommendations of the Murthy Committee, and the latest revisions to Clause 49 became law on January 1, 2006.

THE CURRENT STATE OF CORPORATE GOVERNANCE IN INDIA

From the beginning of 1980s, situations have changed in India. There have been wide-ranging changes has taken place in both the laws and the regulations in the field of corporate law and the capital market. As a result of several scams in India a need has arisen to bring reforms, in response to that, reforms began in 1991 in India. The most important event in the field of investor protection in India was the establishment of Securities and Exchange Board of India (SEBI) in 1992.

Corporate governance reform in India has focused primarily on the "role and composition of the board of directors." Each of the three sets of recommendations (the CII Code recommendations from 1997, the Kumar Mangalam Birla Committee recommendations from 2000, and the Murthy Committee recommendations from 2003) has advanced a more nuanced and sophisticated understanding of corporate governance in this respect. For example, while the CII Code was silent on the financial-literacy levels expected of directors, the Murthy Committee recommended that companies train their "Board members ... in the business model of the company as well as the risk profile of the business parameters of the company."

SUGGESTIONS FOR FUTURE

The following are some suggestions to be implemented based on the recommendation of various committees :

Board of Directors: The measure of the board is not simply whether it fulfils its legal requirements but more importantly, the board's attitude and the manner it translates its awareness and understanding of its responsibilities. An effective corporate governance system is one, which allows the board to perform these dual functions efficiently.

Audit Committee: The need for having an audit committee grows from the recognition of the audit committee's position in the larger mosaic of the governance process, as it relates to the oversight of financial reporting.

Disclosures of Remuneration Package: All elements of remuneration package of all the directors i.e. salary, benefits, bonuses, stock options, pension etc. has to be disclosed to shareholders.

Accounting Standards and Financial Reporting: Reporting on accounting based on accounting standards. Reporting should include consolidated accounts in respect of all its subsidiaries in which they hold 51% or more of the share capital. Segment reporting is a must where a company has multiple lines of business. It is important that financial reporting in respect of each product segment should be available to shareholders and the market to obtain a complete financial picture of the company.

CHAPTER-5

E-GOVERNANCE IN INDIA

Dr Seema Mahlawat

Associate Professor, SBMIMSAR, Asthal Bohar, Rohtak

Dr Rana Zehra Masood

Faculty Member ,Aligarh Muslim University, Aligarh

INTRODUCTION

E-Governance is not a new name now days. It has flourished its fragrance to major cities of many countries, but still rural areas are not getting full benefits upto its extent. E-Government (from electronic government, also known as e-Gov, digital government, online government or in a certain context transformational government) refers to government's use of information technology to exchange information and services with citizens, businesses, and other arms of government. E-Government may be applied by the legislature, judiciary, or administration, in order to improve internal .The primary delivery models are Government-to-Citizen or Government-to-Customer (G2C), Government-to-Business (G2B) and Government-to-Government (G2G) & efficiency, the delivery of public services, or processes of democratic governance. Government-to-Employees (G2E).While e-government is often thought of as "online government" or "Internet-based government," many non-Internet "electronic government" technologies can be used in this context. Some non-internet forms include telephone, fax, PDA, SMS text messaging, MMS, wireless networks and services, Bluetooth, CCTV, tracking systems, RFID, biometric identification, road traffic management and regulatory enforcement, identity cards, smart cards and other NFC applications; polling station technology (where non-online e-voting is being considered), TV and radio-based delivery of government services, email, online community facilities, newsgroups and electronic mailing lists, online chat, and instant messaging technologies. There are also some technology-specific sub-categories of e-government, such as m-government (mobile government), u-government (ubiquitous government), and g-government (GIS/GPS applications for e-government).There are many considerations and potential implications of implementing and designing e-government, including disintermediation of the government and its citizens, impacts on economic, social, and political factors, and disturbances to the *status quo* in these areas.In countries such as the United Kingdom, there is interest in using electronic government to re-engage citizens with the political process. In particular, this has taken the form of experiments with electronic voting, aiming to increase voter turnout by making voting easy. The UK Electoral Commission has undertaken several pilots, though concern has been expressed about the potential for fraud with some electronic voting methods. E-Governance is a process of reform in the way Governments work, share information, engage citizens and deliver services to external and internal clients for the benefit of both government and the clients that they serve. Government shares information technologies such as Wide Area Networks (WAN), Internet, World Wide Web, and mobile computing reach out to citizens, business, and other arms of the government to: improve delivery of services to citizens, businesses and employees. Engage citizens in the process of governance through interaction Empower citizens through access to knowledge and information and make the working of the government more efficient and effective results in enhanced transparency, convenience and empowerment; less corruption; revenue growth.

E-GOVERNANCE IN PRESENT SCENARIO

When a common citizen accesses the Government repository of information, he finds a process many times which are confusing and uncoordinated, cumber some and complicated when more than one organization are involved and require same kind of information multiple number of times in different formats at multiple locations. Government agencies also have to enter the same data repeatedly at different places even department are computerized but duplication of data and effort increases cost and complexity for citizen availing their services. The inconsistent and incompatible data, thus generated at different departments hinders government effort to detect frauds. The effort put within an isolated department as part of e-governance initiative, reaps sub-optimal benefits and finally results in no substantial speed or efficiency gain. If we talk about E-government services, perhaps no legacy of the President's Administration is more important to the average citizen than the E-government initiative to make government services and information available on the Internet.

Hansdehar, a small Haryana village with a population of about 2,000 people, is now part of the worldwide web. Or, to put it more precisely, Hansdehar has a website (www.smartvillages.com) of its own that serves as a window to the village and its activities. The website really marks a significant step in what it is probably the first village among the 6.38 Lakh villages in India (2001 Census) to have a website of its own. Importantly, the initiative to build such a website came neither from the state government, nor from the private sector. Rather, it's the brain-child of Kanwal Singh, the village boy who went on to work for the e-governance division of the Haryana Electronics Corporation. Singh says the website is part of his plans to bring about development in Hansdehar. He would like to concentrate on education and employment, with the website listing illiteracy and unemployment as two problems dogging Hansdehar. Having collated basic statistical details—its area, number of voters, crops cultivated, etc.—Singh hopes his fledgling project, launched just about a month ago, will encompass other villages too as he plans to put them as well on the worldwide web. But for now, it is Hansdehar's website that's drawing e-mails from across the globe. There's one from South America offering assistance in rain-water harvesting, another one from New Zealand offering to start an English literacy project, while a third wants recipes for the local cuisine. Much as the government cries itself hoarse about the importance of e-governance and the need to make the life of citizens easier through it, Hansdehar's example shows that it can begin at a basic level, like having a website Or at least providing Internet connectivity to more and more areas, particularly in the rural belt. In Uttranchal, There is a village in Uttarkanshi district named "Darkaan". This village have only 60 houses. It is situated at height of 6500 feet from the sea level. There is no means of transport to reach there, except by foot. But still it came into the lime light of press, because e-government policies were first implemented in that village. A NGO named "Rural Litigation Enlightenment" and an ICT consultant company have undertaken to work to establish e-governance in Uttranchal. They have undertaken the project work to provide that village e-government benefits. This is Uttranchal's small but important step. By the way, Uttranchal's name is not in list if those states, which have achieved milestone in the field of e-government. Yet Uttranchal govt have started so many projects which aim at providing e-government services to the people.

CURRENT PROBLEMS IN IMPLEMENTATION OF CORPORATE GOVERNANCE

Citizens do not have much interest in selling tender forms through Kiosks, because it proves cheaper to photocopy the form than go for online printouts. It's true that citizens are ready to invest money for government services, but the major interruption in this work is lack of administrative model. Another problem which adds to this sphere is that people are not getting complete information.

Lack of appropriate infrastructure like shortage of power, inconvenient atmosphere of computerization are major source of interruption for G2C services. These are main factor for the inefficient functioning of G2C services. Transaction related portals require proper data input and it can work successfully on when all the government data are interconnected, just like West Bengal's state wide area network under which they have connected all states 18 district offices and other subdivision initially. Now they are working toward rural e-government to connect all the societies at punchayat level by which we can get all the information regarding panchayat administration. This panchayat kiosk will provide all information regarding agriculture, health related services to the people. In order to create G2C environment, the first prerequisite is to put all the necessary information on the net, but without data warehouse, it seems impossible. For successful working of all transaction based occupation, it is necessary to provide security to deposition job.

Efficient government purchasing: Governments are the largest purchasers in all economies, and for both moral a political reasons they should buy goods and services in the best way possible. One dollar paid in excess of the best possible price is a dollar less to provide health care, social security or public housing.

- E-Procurement in Andhra Pradesh: The Government of Andhra Pradesh has set up an E-Procurement Marketplace, linking government departments, agencies and local bodies with their vendors, in a bid to reduce the cost of doing business with government, and the inherent corruption associated with manual procurement processes.
- Chile's Government Procurement E-System: E-procurement has produced increased transparency and has begun to

generate highly significant savings for the Chilean government.

- Philippine Customs Reform: Using an "off-the-shelf" software package, the Philippines Customs Bureau has developed an on-line system that lessens the cost of trade for businesses, reduces opportunities for fraud, and helps the Bureau to maximize revenue collection.

- Empowering through Information: Information is a critical ingredient for development and the more information that the poor possess, the greater their sense of empowerment. Empowered citizens can more readily hold governments accountable. With greater information the poor also are better able to organize and take actions to improve their quality of life.

- Colombia's Government Portal: The government of Colombia made a serious commitment to e-government in 2000-01, mandating that all federal government agencies develop an Internet presence, and creating a unit in the Office of the President to assist and monitor their progress... The centrepiece of this initiative is the State of Colombia Portal (PEC).

- Empowering Dairy Farmers through a Dairy Information and Services Kiosk: Automation of the milk buying process at 2,500 rural milk collection societies, and the extension of the co-op database through the creation of a Dairy Information Services Kiosk (DISK).

- Gyandoot: Community-Owned Rural Internet Kiosks: A government-to-citizen Intranet gives marginalised tribal citizens the opportunity to access knowledge and a number of government services with minimum investment.

- Kothmale Community Radio/Internet Project: Expanding the Knowledge Base: The Internet has the potential to offer a new set of tools for rural development. However, it does not require special efforts to create appropriate access models for those who can afford Internet access nor have the language capacity to understand the content. The Kothmale Community Radio Internet project is an access model that reduces these barriers and empowers marginalized communities in rural areas

- Improved services for business: Many government services and regulations are aimed at businesses (domestic and international), not everyday citizens.

In increasingly competitive markets, the quality and efficiency of these interactions has received growing attention.

- Beijing's Business E-Park: The Zhongguancun E-Park allows businesses in the hi-tech park to apply for a license, file monthly financial reports, submit tax statements and conduct 32 other "g to b" and "g to c" functions online. The system has greatly increased government transparency and efficiency, and reduced the opportunities for corruption.

- Philippine Customs Reform: Using an "off-the-shelf" software package, the Philippines Customs Bureau has developed an on-line system that lessens the cost of trade for businesses, reduces opportunities for fraud, and helps the Bureau to maximize revenue collection.

- Vietnam's Tale of Two Cities: Hanoi and Ho Chi Minh City each launched Web development projects for business service agencies in 2000. The two websites are designed to serve as the first point of contact for potential investors, especially foreign investors.

- Village Information Kiosks for the Warana Cooperatives in India: The stated goal of the Warana "Wired Village" project is not only to increase the efficiency and productivity of the sugar cane cooperative, but also to provide a wide range of information and services to 70 villages around Warana. The project aims at giving villagers access to information, in their local language, about crops and agricultural market prices, employment schemes from the government of Maharashtra, and educational opportunities.

FUTURE CHALLENGES

Past research has largely been descriptive. There has been a lack of critical examination of process of strategizing; choice of applications; process of design and implementation. Often a supply side view is taken. Outcome and impact on clients, agencies and society is not assessed. With hardly any project where impact has been assessed systematically, successes/failures have often been reported on the basis of anecdotal evidence. The workshop papers presented many different perspectives on pro-poor e-Governance. The conclusions as have been reported in this paper point to an overall lack of serious concern for the poor and vulnerable in the design and implementation of e-Governance programs. There were many rich ideas that were presented but there was a certain lack of convergence in terms of the way forward. Given that e-Governance and e-Government is in an early stage in many countries of the region, the way forward can at best define the first steps that can be taken. In the concluding sessions of the workshop the participants suggested the following steps.

1. Each country should define as to which sections of the population constitute the vulnerable group that needs to be targeted. Their geographical spread needs to be mapped. Participatory approaches need to be used in developing e-Government programs and plans, so that the needs of the poor are well articulated and can be reflected in the choice of applications and their design.

2. Existing national e-Government programs and e-Government projects should be audited in a systematic way to determine the potential and actual impact on poor and the vulnerable. A Tool Kit can be designed for the purpose of carrying out such an audit.

3. Policy-makers need to be sensitized to the fact that the digital divide will be further exacerbated unless e-Government specifically focuses on the poor and the vulnerable and that e-Government has the potential to deliver significant benefits to the vulnerable/poor.

PROJECT KIOSK

There are many projects which are working for promoting e-government in rural areas also. Ashok Jhunjhunwala of IIT-Chennai developed rural kiosks. It requires investment of around 15 Crores. Through this kiosk, villagers could use internet, can consult agricultural experts with help of video conferencing for agriculture related problems. In additional they have also developed Rural ATM. Any ATM cost about 10 lakhs, but this one would cost mere Rs 50,000. Under this scheme they have also developed such a Diagnostic Kit by which Physician at distant places could examine their patients. That's why In India, which have more than 6000 villages and 1400 villagers of each village require such a technique to be connected to e-government

CONCLUSION

In India there are almost 6000 city centres. If we try to practise e-government practises through these city centres then it could be proved beneficial to citizens, but bringing al these city centres on line would be a cumbersome task to do. According to survey, we need 57000 manpower to generate application for 30,000 departments whose work expanding on the 89,000 sites. It is expected to have installation cost worth $89 Crore. But the need of hour for government is to concentrate not only on software and hardware, but to implement this strategy with honesty. Experts sates that it better to first create strong administration , to bring all government employees under confidence, only then we can think to bring e-governance, to connect each and every person to this e-Governance world and to provide basic facilities to the citizens while sitting at home .

CHAPTER-6

Role of Business Ethics in Corporate Governance

Prof. H.N.Kumawat

Professor in Department of EAFM, Bihani S. D. P. G. College, Sriganganagar (Rajasthan) India

Prof. Vinay Goyal

Professor in Department of Accountancy and Business Statistics, Bihani S. D. P. G. College, Sriganganagar (Rajasthan) India

Anil Goyal

M.Phil., Sriganganagar (Rajasthan) India

ABSTRACT

Ethical Corporate Governance (also called Ethical Governance) has very much become a buzzword these days, just about every company thinks its a good idea and may even proclaim to follow it, but what exactly is it, and how can we know for a sure that a company is practicing what it preaches?

Ethical Corporate Governance refers to the processes and policies that a company has in place to deal with issues concerning how it is administered and conducts day to day business. It is important to remember that companies exist primary to create a product or service, which is used to generate profit. However, that intention must be balanced with controls that ensure a company pursues profit without crossing over the line into the realms of unethical behaviour.

Key Words: corporate governance, business ethics, ethical issues, provisions of companies act relating to business ethics

INTRODUCTION

Former World Bank President James Wolfensohn "has equated the importance of the governance of corporations to that of the governance of countries." According to the Organisation for Economic Co-operation and Development ("OECD"), "Corporate governance deals with the rights and responsibilities of a company's management, its board, shareholders and various stakeholders."

MEANING OF BUSINESS ETHICS

A few years ago, sociologist Raymond Baumhart asked businesspeople, "What does ethics mean to you?" Among their reply were the following: Ethics has to do with what my feelings tell me is right or wrong. Ethics has to do with my religious beliefs. Being ethical is doing what the law requires. Ethics consists of the standards of behavior our society accepts

Business ethics also relates to the behaviour of manager. It can be defined as an attempt to ascertain the responsibilities and ethical obligations of business professionals. Here the focus is in people, how individuals should conduct themselves in fulfilling the ethical requirements of business?

DEFINITION OF BUSINESS ETHICS

According to Kotler, "that companies must adopt and disseminate a written code of ethics, build a company tradition of ethical behaviour, and hold their people fully responsible for observing the ethical and legal guidelines. A code of ethics is a formal document that states an organization's primary values and the ethical rules it expects its employees to follow. It has been suggested that codes should be specific enough to give employees the spirit in which they are supposed to do things, yet loose enough to allow for freedom of judgement."

According to Parekh Deepak, "Do not do something that you would be ashamed of, if it becomes public." It is not too difficult to achieve this reality. There is no pillow as soft as a clear conscience.

NATURE OF BUSINESS ETHICS

On the basis of meaning and definitions we can conclude that:

1. Business ethics is a rule of business conduct
2. Business ethics is a way to apply economic and social principles of ethics in commercial transactions

3. It creates business environment
4. It is known as ethical code of business
5. It regulates an organization in a disciplined manner.

ETHICAL ISSUES IN CORPORATE GOVERNANCE

Ethical Corporate Governance refers to the processes and policies that a company has in place to deal with issues concerning how it is administered and conducts day to day business. It is important to remember that companies exist primary to create a product or service, which is used to generate profit. However, that intention must be balanced with controls that ensure a company pursues profit without crossing over the line into the realms of unethical behaviour. On the basis of ethical approach in corporate governance the following issues are concerned:-

ETHICAL ISSUES IN STRATEGIC MANAGEMENT

Ethical issues such as setting vision, senior manager's remuneration, implementing strategic change, changes in organization ownership and global strategic operation question the management to what extent such decisions are proper. In such a scenario managers make use of ethical decision model, to make a right decision and while taking decisions an organization should know the principles that enable an ethical approach to take strategic decisions.

ETHICAL ISSUES IN PURCHASE MANAGEMENT

The purchasing function has been disregarded for a long time, but now it is being scrutinized closely because of its interaction with suppliers and external market. Through this point it is that the importance of the purchasing function and the impact just-in-time has on achieving product quality through long-term contract and fair prices. Ethical issues in purchasing- favoritism accepting of gifts by suppliers, disclosing confidential information were also discussed. Purchase managers often favor suppliers who are also good customers. Thus developing a mutually beneficial relationship.

ETHICAL ISSUES IN HUMAN RESOURCE MANAGEMENT

The attitude of a business towards its employee's acts is a litmus test for its ethical character. The relationship between the business and its employees is based on the employment contract. According to this principle an organization should hire a person who is expected to contribute the maximum towards enhancing long-term owner value. According to the principle of ethical selection factors like age, gender, religion and nationality are irrelevant for hiring a person.

BUSINESS ETHICS AND ENVIRONMENT

Environmental Ethics is concerned about moral basis of environmental responsibility. This concern in turn gave rise to three approaches: Anthropocentrism approach, axiological approach and eco-centric approach. The first approach focuses on the utility that human beings can derive by protecting the environment. According to the second approach it is moral responsibility of human beings to protect animals. The last approach is a blend of first and second approach, which states environment has to be influenced by taking such activities, which are aimed at preserving environment.

ETHICAL ISSUES IN FINANCE

The attitude of a business towards its employee's acts is a litmus test for its ethical character. The relationship between the business and its employees is based on the employment contract. According to this principle an organization should hire a person who is expected to contribute the maximum towards enhancing long-term owner value. According to the principle of ethical selection factors like age, gender, religion and nationality are irrelevant for hiring a person.

PROVISIONS OF COMPANIES ACT RELATED TO BUSINESS ETHICS

Ethics among shareholders, owners, directors and management are a necessary element for companies in the 21st century to adequately meet their objectives, to the degree that Ethics are a key requisite in guaranteeing and balancing the rights and interests of all stakeholders involved: employees, clients, shareholders, suppliers and business partners and the society at large. - Ethics presuppose rigorous compliance in and by the company with applicable legislation, as well as with the Articles of Incorporation and Regulations for internal operations, where they exist. Ideally, the Board of Directors is responsible for drawing up the Code of Ethics for the company and the General Shareholders' Meeting for approving that Code. Should, however, the Board also proceed with approval, that decision must be ratified by the Shareholders' Meeting.

DIRECTORS AND MANAGEMENT

In the exercise of their administrative and management functions, they should:

- Carry out their activities in a professional, ethical and responsible manner.
- Comply and demand compliance with the Code of Ethics of the company and, to that end, make the Code known and establish appropriate mechanisms to guarantee application.
- Provide external and internal auditors of the company with all such information and explanations as maybe required to carry out their work.
- Facilitate the transparency of and control over their remuneration in such a way that it is guaranteed to be appropriate to their level of responsibility and performance and to the characteristics of the company.
- Maintain as confidential the background, data and documents to which they have access by virtue of their functions in the company, even when they no longer carry out such functions.
- Make payment and comply with debts incurred by the company without unjustified delay or breach, and collect on balances due with the diligence required in each case.
- Prepare and maintain in place a succession plan for key positions within the company, to ensure that continuity of the company does not depend on the presence of any given director or manager.
- Choose their collaborators and subordinates in accordance with the principles of merit and capacity, looking only to fulfil the interests of the company.

CHAPTER-7

ECO-FRIENDLY GOVERNANCE IN INDIAN BANKS THROUGH GREEN BANKING

Raghu Dutt Kaushik* and Ritu Sharma**

**Department of Economic Adminstration and Financial Management*
Seth G.L. Bihani S.D.P.G. College, Sri Ganganagar (Rajasthan)
Email:raghusgnr@gmail.com

***Department of Commerce, JNV University, Jodhpur (Raj.)*

INTRODUCTION

The term "Green Banking" is being heard more often today as more Americans look for ways in which they can help the environment. While green banking can encompass a wide variety of banking services or policies, many banks are actively promoting their online banking services as a form of green banking. The environment and the banking industry can both benefit as more bank customers start to use the online banking services that are available. Benefits of online banking include less paperwork, less mail and less driving to branch offices by bank customers, which all have a positive impact on the environment. Interestingly, online banking can also increase the efficiency and profitability of a bank. A bank can lower their own costs that result from paper overload and bulk mailing fees if more of their customers use online banking. Green banking also can reduce the need for expensive branch banks.

WHY GREEN BANK IS NECESSARY

Banks can do much more to help the environment than just promote online banking. A truly green bank can reduce their carbon footprint by building more efficient branches, implementing more energy-efficient operational procedures, offering transportation services for their employees and carefully screening their lending in environment-sensitive industries. Banks can also support eco-friendly groups, offer green lending and raise money for local environment initiatives. Banks that go to these significant lengths to be eco-friendly are a little more difficult to find than the banks that claim to be green by merely offering online services. Banks that offer rate incentives on CDs, money market accounts, online savings accounts and checking accounts for online banking also help the green banking cause by rewarding online banking customers. It take a little bit of an incentive to convert some people away from paper statements and branch banking.

Green Mortgages: Green mortgages allow home buyers to add as much as an additional 15% of the price of your house into your loan for upgrades including energy-efficient windows, solar panels, or water heaters. The savings in your monthly energy bills can offset the higher monthly mortgage payments and save you money in the long run. The Energy Efficient Mortgage (EEM) is a type of HUD-approved green mortgage that will credit you for your home is energy efficiency in the mortgage itself. Banks offering these green mortgages will give qualified-HUD borrowers the opportunity to finance cost-effective, energy-saving improvements to their house. If you are undertaking an energy-saving house project, shop around for a bank that will offer a great deal on a green mortgage.

Green Credit Cards: A green credit card allows cardholders to earn rewards or points which can be redeemed for contributions to eco-friendly charitable organizations. These cards offer an excellent incentive for consumers to use their green card for their expensive purchases. Imagine the millions of dollars that could be raised for environmental groups if green credit cards really took off.

GREEN BANKING IN INDIA

India is on a higher growth trajectory for last one and half decade and the industrial sector plays the most important role in India's growth story. However, Indian industry faces the challenges of controlling environmental impact of their business i.e. reducing pollution and emission of their clients. Though government has been trying to address the issue by framing environmental legislations and encouraging industry to follow environmental technologies and practices, they would not be enough given the poor track records of enforcement, public awareness and inability to derive competitive advantage by producing eco-friendly products.

Incidentally, India's is the world's sixth largest and second fastest growing country in terms of producing green house gases. Delhi, Mumbai and Chennai are the three of the world's ten most polluted cities. The major polluting industries in India are (a) primary metallurgical industries namely zinc, copper, steel etc. (b) paper and pulp (c) pesticides/ insecticides (d) refines (e) fertilizers (f) tanneries (g) sugar (h) textiles (i) chemicals/pharmaceuticals, etc. The banking operation and investment by financial institutions should take care of environmental management of these polluting industries by improving the overall environment, the quality and conversation of life, level of efficiency in using materials and energy, quality of services and products. In this context, the role of banking sector, which is on major financing sources to the Industries, assumes high importance.

The environmental regulations in India can be broadly classified into two broad categories i.e. command and control regulations and liability law. The command and control regulations are ex ante regulations that are designed to dissuade environmentally damaging projects. This regulation is implemented by setting industry specific pollution standards, scrutinizing the projects and granting/denying permissions by the concerned authorities like Ministry of Environment and Forest. The liability laws are ex post in nature and are implemented by enforcing authorities through imposing fines, closing down the defaulting industries etc. However there is no law and rule in India that can hold banks responsible for scrutinizing investment projects before financing and for the environmental damage created by its client. Once legal framework for the environmental pollution standards are formulated in India, the polluting industries either have to close down or have to make necessary investment to comply with the standard. In this process these industries will loose their competitiveness in the international market, which would directly affect Indian economy and the banking sector.

Thus in the present context, it is equally important for banks to guard themselves against the conversion of the now performing assets into non-performing one in the future. Realization of these facts by banks will certainty make them fast adopt the concept of Green Banking. The industries, which are ill-equipped to control pollution now, are the possible polluters of future. A day may come, when legislation may take a hard stance against these environmental culprits and may order the closer of these units. Almost 150 SSI units around Agra and Delhi were forced to close down for their non-compliance to the mandated environmental standards12. In such an eventuality, the industries cannot be rescued from becoming the non-performing ones, as the banking institutions continue to overlook these aspects.

Besides, the public is gaining consciousness of the multifarious problems associated with pollution. So, the public will resort to protest, strike, and agitation to stop the misuse of the environment or in a simple fashion consumers may reject the products produced by the polluting units. Before 1986, there was no provision for public to file a suit against the polluting units but now the citizens are also permitted to file suits. The present green consumerism is more concerned with the quality of the products more than the quantity. In future, market will reward those industries or the companies, which emerge as the efficient users of the energy and raw materials and will penalize the less efficient one. Further, the investors in the stock market are equally aware of environmental pollution and would take a stand against those industries/institutions that do not comply with pollution norms (Gupta, 2003; Goldar, 2007). So the preferences of the investors will dry up in the case of polluting units and market capitalization will go down significantly. Thus, financial institutions should help developing the right instruments to meet the needs of industry to control environmental impact.

As far as Green Banking in India is concerned, the banking and financial institutions are running behind the schedules compared to global trends. None of our banks or financial institutions has adopted equator principle even for the sake of records. None of them are signatory to the UNEPFI.

Today the products of the countries violating the human rights or the child labor law are denied entry into the US or the European markets. So it would not be surprising when the export of the domestic polluting industries gets a severe jolt if they continue degrading the environment. For the first time, the WTO ministerial talks in Seattle had in its agenda the issue of Environment. The fall of demand of the product of the units because of green consumerism will make the units suffer and in turn affect the quality of the assets of lending institutions. The major blow will be to the performances of the public sector banks in India. Because most of the SSIs are within the fold of these banks and SSIs are likely to be worst hit in strict environmental regime.

Therefore, banks need to be more careful in India about the environmental aspects of their clients and products because (1) future of exports and product market are going to go through stringent environmental rules and eco-friendly product will have better market. (2) increased demand for pollution controls equipments will require more financial assistance from banks. (3) Reserve Bank of India (RBI) may follow environmental guidelines for the banks in the lines of IFC and Asian Development Bank etc (4) recent announcement of the government to use economic instruments for environmental control may include Banks in future (4) big investment projects supported by international organizations like the World Bank and ADB require Environmental Impact Assessment (EIA). Therefore the banks should begin implementing procedures like (1) assessment of risk due to environment (2) Environmental audit management (3) assessment of credit requirement and loan follow up before investing on different projects. However, since banking sector is profit driven, it needs incentives and governmental support to assist environmental protection which is beneficial for the whole economy and society and also to the banking sector itself in the long-run. For the medium and large-scale industries, the lending institution should finance only those units, which are envirônmentally clean. A unit can be said to be environmentally clean only when its pollution level is within the permissible level fixed by the pollution control board or any certified agency.

For this measure to succeed the pollution control agencies are required to play an important role by supplementing the banks efforts to control pollution. National Environmental Policy (NEP) in 2006 brings out clear policies, principles and also rules to implement environmental rules and regulations. Though, NEP is silent about the role of financial institutions, it brings out clearly the role of different stake holders such as government, industry, civil society and public. Some of the policies such as enforcement of laws to conserve the common resources, improving technical capacities for better monitoring and compliance and involvement of local people in the enforcement process are certainly going to improve the environmental management system in India. Further, NEP emphasizes industries to adopt standardized environmental management practices by acquiring ISO 14000. Overall, NEP has brought about clarity in many ways to control environmental degradation and it covers many areas which would force industries as well as the other stake holders such as banking sector to be more responsible for environmental management. Further, the emphasis of the NEP on capacity building in financial institutions for evaluation of proposal for switching existing production facilities in industries to clean technology is welcome step.

CHAPTER-8

Corporate Governance in India: Evolution and Issues

Dr. O. P. Mahendra

Head, Department of EAFM, Seth G.L.Bihani S.D.P.G.College, Sriganganagar

Sanjay Garg

Assistant Professor, Department of Management, Central University of Rajasthan, Kishangarh, Ajmer (Rajasthan), India
Email: sanjaygarg05@gmail.com, Mobile No. 092144-22278

Ms. Kirti Bansal

INTRODUCTION

Corporate governance comprises the long-term management and oversight of the company in accordance with the principles of responsibility and transparency. The corporate governance structure specifies the distribution of rights and responsibilities among different participants in the organization, such as the Board, managers, shareholders and other stakeholders, and spells out the rules and procedures for making decisions on corporate affairs. In the broadest sense, which is increasingly widespread today, corporate governance is concerned with holding the balance between economic and social goals and between individual and communal goals. The governance framework is there to encourage the efficient use of resources and equally to require accountability for the stewardship of those resources. The aim is to align as nearly as possible the interests of individuals, corporations and society.

CORPORATE GOVERNANCE IN INDIA

The beginning of corporate developments in India were marked by the managing agency system that contributed not only to the birth of dispersed equity ownership but also gave rise to the practice of management enjoying control rights disproportionate to their stock ownership. The turn towards socialism in the decades after independence marked by the 1951 Industries Development and Regulation Act as well as the 1956 Industrial Policy Resolution put in place a regime and culture of licensing, protection and red-tapism that instigated corruption and affected the growth of the corporate sector. The situation grew from bad to worse in the following decades with corruption, nepotism and inefficiency became the hallmarks of the Indian corporate sector..

In the absence of a developed stock market, the three all-India development finance institutions – the Industrial Finance Corporation of India (IFCI), the Industrial Development Bank of India(IDBI) and the Industrial Credit and Investment Corporation of India (ICICI) – together with the state financial corporations became the main providers of long-term credit to companies. Along with the government owned mutual fund, the Unit Trust of India, they also held large blocks of shares in the companies they lent to and invariably had representations in their boards. In this respect, the corporate governance system resembled the bank-based German model where these institutions could have played a big role in keeping their clients on the right track. Unfortunately, they were themselves evaluated on the quantity rather than quality of their lending and thus had little incentive for either proper credit appraisal or effective follow-up and monitoring. Their nominee directors routinely served as rubber-stamps of the management of the day. With their support, promoters of businesses in India could actually enjoy managerial control with very little equity investment of their own. Borrowers, therefore, routinely recouped their investment in a short-period and then had little incentive to either repay the loans or run the business. Frequently they bled the company with impunity, siphoning off funds with the DFI nominee directors mute spectators in their boards. This sordid but increasingly familiar process usually continued till the company's net worth was completely eroded. This stage would come after the company has defaulted on its loan obligations for a while, but this would be the stage where India's bankruptcy reorganization system driven by the 1985 Sick Industrial Companies Act (SICA) would consider it "sick" and refer it to the Board for Industrial and Financial Reconstruction (BIFR). As soon as a company is registered with the BIFR it wins immediate protection from the creditors' claims for at least four years. Between 1987 and 1992 BIFR took well over two years on an average to reach a decision, after which period the delay has roughly doubled. Very few companies have emerged successfully from the BIFR and even for those that needed to be liquidated, the legal process takes over 10 years on average, by which time the assets of the company are practically worthless. Protection of creditors' rights has, therefore, existed only on paper in India. Given this situation, it is hardly surprising that banks, flush with depositors' funds routinely decide to lend only to blue chip companies and park their funds in government securities. Financial disclosure norms in India have traditionally been superior to most Asian countries though fell short of those in the USA and other advanced countries. Non-compliance with disclosure norms and even the failure of auditor's reports to conform to the law attract nominal fines with hardly any punitive action.

ISSUES IN CORPORATE GOVERNANCE

The numerous shareholders who contribute to the capital of the company are the actual owners of business. They elect a Board of Directors to monitor the running of the company on their behalf. The Board, in turn, appoints a team of managers who actually handle the day-to-day functioning of the company and report periodically to the Board. Thus, mangers are the agents of shareholders and function with the objective of maximizing shareholders' wealth. Even if this power pattern held in reality, it would still be a challenge for the Board to effectively monitor management. The central issue is the nature of the contract between shareholder representatives and managers telling the latter what to do with the funds contributed by the former. The main challenge comes from the fact that such contracts are necessarily "incomplete". It is not possible for the Board to fully instruct management on the desired course of action under every possible business situation. The list of possible situations is infinitely long. Consequently, no contract can be written between representatives of shareholders and the management that specifies the right course of action in every situation, so that the management can be held for violation of such a contract in the event it does something else under the circumstances. Because of this "incomplete contracts" situation, some "residual powers" over the funds of the company must be vested with either the financiers or the management. Clearly the former does not have the expertise or the inclination to run the business in the situations unspecified in the contract, so these residual powers must go to management. The efficient limits to these powers constitute much of the subject of corporate governance. The reality is even more complicated and biased in favor of management. In real life, managers wield an enormous amount of power in joint-stock companies and the common shareholder has very little say in the way his or her money is used in the company. In companies with highly dispersed ownership, the manager (CEO or Managing Director) functions with negligible accountability. Most shareholders do not care to attend the General Meetings to elect or change the Board of Directors and often grant their "proxies" to the management. Even those that attend the meeting find it difficult to have a say in the selection of directors as only the management gets to propose a slate of directors for voting. On his part the CEO frequently packs the board with his friends and allies who rarely differ with him. Often the CEO himself is the Chairman of the Board of Directors as well. Consequently the supervisory role of the Board is often severely compromised and the management, who really has the keys to the business, can potentially use corporate resources to further their own self-interests rather than the interests of the shareholders.

The inefficacy of the Board of Directors in monitoring the activities of management is particularly marked in the Anglo-Saxon corporate structure where real monitoring is expected to come from financial markets. The underlying premise is that shareholders dissatisfied with a particular management would simply dispose of their shares in the company. As this would drive down the share price, the company would become a takeover target. If and when the acquisition actually happens, the acquiring company would get rid of the existing management. It is thus the fear of a takeover rather than shareholder action that is supposed to keep the management honest and on its toes. This mechanism, however, presupposes the existence of a deep and liquid stock market with considerable informational efficiency as well as a legal and financial system conducive to M&A activity. More often than not, these features do not exist in developing countries like India. An alternative corporate governance model is that provided by the bank-based economies like Germany where the main bank ("Hausbank" in Germany) lending to the company exerts considerable influence and carries out continuous project-level supervision of the management and the supervisory board has representatives of multiple stakeholders of the firm.

CONCLUSION

It can be said that the importance of corporate governance lies in its contribution both to business prosperity and to accountability. Public companies are now among the most accountable organisations in society. They can enhance their value by following corporate governance. There are several issues involved in to the implementation of corporate governance, but these can be sorted by implementing some of the successful models of corporate governance

REFERENCES

Farber, D. "Restoring trust after fraud: Does corporate governance matter?" working paper, Michigan State University, 2004.

Gompers, P., J. Ishii, and A. Metrick. "Corporate governance and equity prices." *Quarterly Journal of Economics* 118 (2003): 107-155.

Shleifer, A. and R. Vishny. "A survey of corporate governance." *Journal of Finance*, 52 (1997): 737-783.

Sundaramurthy, C., J. Mahoney, and J. Mahoney. "Board structure, anti-takeover provisions, and stockholder wealth." *Strategic Management Journal* 18 (1997): 231-245.

Yermack, D. "Higher market valuation of companies with a small board of directors." *Journal of Financial Economics* 40 (1996): 185-211

CHAPTER-9

Corporate Governance at ONGC (Oil and Natural Commission) Ltd. in India

Mrs. Renu Shekhawat

Lecturer in EAFM, Seth G.L Bihani S.D. P.G College Sri Ganga Nagar (Rajasthan)

Dr. S. S. Verma

Professor in Post Graduate Department of Business Administration, Seth G.L Bihani S.D. P.G College Sri Ganga Nagar (Rajasthan)

Sh. Laxman Singh Shekhawat

Centre Head, BIMIT, Sri Ganganagar

INTRODUCTION

A social institution including a public sector entity derives its legitimacy from its ability and desire to fulfil social needs. It is therefore, accountable to the society. No institution, however high and mighty it is, can ignore its responsibility towards society from which it derives its strength and sustenance. In the case of public sector the public stake is very high as it owned by the Govt. Therefore, the accountability of public sector to public is much higher. As the performance of Public sector is declining day-to-day. Faith of the nation and public call for a greater need for corporate governance .The only option to rebuild the Public faith to run the Public sector is to apply the Policy of corporate governance.

The term Corporate Governance is not easy to define the term governance relates to a process of decision making and implementing the decisions in the interest of all stake holder. It is the system through which the organization is guided and directed.

The objectives of corporate governance are focus transparency, participation, accountability efficiency and effectiveness and stake holder satisfaction.

It is a system of running a business organization on certain ethical principles. There cannot be a universally accepted definition of the term corporate governance. It can be broadly understood as a system of accountability and control for ethical and socially responsible organizational decision and use of resources to achieve the long term objectives of the organization to satisfy shareholders, employees, customers and suppliers and complying with the legal and regulatory requirements, apart from meeting environmental and local community needs Corporate governess arrangements are key determinants of an organist ion's relationship with the world and encompass the following aspects:

A. Power to given to management and control over management's use of such power

B. Management's accountability to stake holders

C. Factor influencing management decisions

LITERATURE REVIEW

Over a period of time, with fast developments in the world, the scope of the corporate governance has widened. It now encompasses the interest of not only the owners but also many other stake holders. Organization of Economic Co-operation and Development (OECD) defined Corporate Governance as the system by which business corporations are directed and controlled. It involves a set of relationships between a company's management, its board, its shareholders and other stakeholders and also specifies the rules and procedures for making decisions on

Corporate affairs. The main aim of corporate governance is to maintain a balance between economic and social goals and between individual and commercial goals.

The trend of developing corporate governance guidelines and codes of best practices begin in the early in the early 1990s in UK and Canada in response to problem in performance in some leading organizations, presumably due to lack of effective board oversight leading to pressure from institutional investor for change .The Cadbury report 1992 in UK become a pioneering reference code for stock markets. The BLUE RIBBON COMMITTEE set up in US in 1998 by New York sock exchange and National Association of Securities Dealer studied the effectiveness of audit committees and provided recommendations for improvements. In response to these recommendations New York Stock Exchange and National Association of Securities Dealer as well as other exchange revised their listing standards related to audit committees. After the publication of Cadbury Committee Report in 1992, the Indian authorities including corporate sector became pro-active to frame rules on corporate governance. In 1995 Confederation of Indian Industries (CII) set up a committee under the chairmanship of Kumar Mangalam Birla (popularly known as Kumar Mangalam Committee) with the aim of taking care of investor's interests. The committee made 25 recommendations, 19 of them mandatory. The listed companies with SEBI are obliged to comply with these on account of their contractual obligations arising out of the listing agreement with stock exchange.

FINDINGS

The corporate governance structure of ONGC has been chosen to be included; as ONGC has received many awards for best corporate governance practices

ONGC has been practicing corporate governance principle much before it become mandatory. The company believes that it is rewarding to be better managed and governed and to identify its activities with national interest .ONGC has implemented the provision of corporate governance as under:

1. Audit and ethics committee

:The committee is headed under the stewardship of Shri PK Choudhary independent non executive director w.e.f. 11 Sep 2006. Shri Choudhary has multifarious and enriched experience of more then 35 years in finance and banking. All member of the committee have requisite financial and management experience and have held or hold senior position in other reputed organizations Company Secretary acts as secretary to the committees.

2. Remunerations committee

ONGC being a Govt. company appointment and term and conditions of remuneration of Executive Directors are determined by the Govt. through the administrative ministry. The Ministry of Petroleum and Natural Gas. The part time Non-official directors receive sitting fee of Rs. 10,000 for each Board /committee meeting attended by them.

3. Shareholders/Investors Grievance committee

Above mentioned committee specifically looks in to redressing of shareholders and investors complain pertain to share transfer, non-receipt of annual report, dividend payments, issue of duplicate certificates of shares and other miscellaneous complaints. The committee also monitor

Implementations of company's .code of conduct for prevention of insider trading in ONGC Securities.

The Company Secretary acts as secretary to the committee.

Minutes of the meeting of the shareholder'/investor's Grievance committee are approved by the chairman of the committee and are noted and confirmed by the Board of the Next meeting.

4. Human Resource Management Committee

The term of reference include consideration of all issue/area concerning Human Resource Planning and Management .HR Polices and initiatives and Promotions from E6 to E7 and above level.

Minutes of the meeting of the HRM Committee are approved by the chairman of the committee and noted and confirmed by the Board of the ensuing Board Meeting.

5. Project appraisal committee

The Project appraisal committee examines and makes recommendations to the Board on appraised in-house, while the Proposals exceeding Rs. 250 Crore are first appraised by outside technical and financial consultant

Minutes of the meeting of the committee are approved by the chairman of the committee and are noted and confirmed by the Board of the Next meeting.

6. Share Transfer committee

Above mentioned committee has been empowered to approve the requests received for share transfer /Transmission, issue of duplicate share certificates, subdivision, consolidation change of status etc. These requests are processed through the registrar and share transfer agent, M/s Karvy Computer Share Private Ltd. generally once in a fortnight.

Minutes of the meeting of committee are circulated to the members of the committee and the Board is kept appraised.

7. Health, Safety and Environment committee

The terms of reference includes review of policy, processes and system on safety, Health, Environment and Ecology aspects.

8. Financial Management committee

The Mandates includes looks in to the matter pertaining to Budget, Delegation of powers commercial issues, Forex and Treasury Managements, investments, Risk management, Capital Structure, issue of Securities short and long term loans.

Minutes of the meeting of committee are circulated to the members of the committee and the Board is kept appraised.

9. Other Functional committee

Apart from the above Board also from time to time, constitute Functional Committees with specific terms of reference as it may deem fit .Meeting of such committees are held as and when need arise.

Minutes of the meeting of committee are circulated to the members of the committee and the Board is kept appraised.

Code of conduct for members of the Board and senior management

A code of conduct, evolved in line with the industry practices was adopted by the Board on the recommendations of audit and ethics committee and all members of the Board and senior management have compliance with the code of conduct.

ONGC Code on insider trading

In pursuance of SEBI (Prohibition of insider trading) Regulations 1992 (amended).

The Board has approved the "Code of Conduct for Prevention of Insider Trading". The objective of the code is to prevent purchase and /or sale of share of the company by an insider on the basis of unpublished.

All Director/Advisor/Officers are required to disclose related information periodically as define in the code, which is being forwarded in the stock exchanges.

Company Secretary has designated as the compliance officers.

CONCLUSIONS

Since the Oil and Natural Gas Commission is a PSU .The corporate governance structure of ONGC cannot be exactly the same as that of private sector enterprises, because the objective function of a ONGC may not necessarily be the 'maximization of firm value'. Moreover, the government cannot participate directly in the day-to-day management of the enterprise like a private promoter or the controlling group of shareholders, because political and bureaucratic interference affects the performance of an enterprise adversely. Therefore, the corporate governance structure of a ONGC should ensure effective control and monitoring by the government without political and bureaucratic interference.

CHAPTER-10

CORPORATE GOVERNANCE - A CHANGING SCENARIO

Dr. Sanjeev Garg
email-sanjeevgargkumar@yahoo.com

Anuj Garg

INTRODUCTION

Corporate Governance is about commitments to values, about ethical business conducts. It is a system of structuring, operating and controlling a company with a view to achieve long term strategic goals to satisfy shareholders, creditors, employees, customers and suppliers, and complying with the legal and regulatory requirements, apart from meeting environmental and local community needs. Parties involved in corporate governance include the regulatory body (e.g. the Chief Executive Officer, the board of directors, management, shareholders and Auditors). Other stackholder who take part include suppliers, employees, creditors, customers and the community at large.

PRINCIPLES

Key elements of good corporate governance principles include honesty, trust and integrity, openness, performance orientation, responsibility and accountability, mutual respect, and commitment to the organization. In particular, senior executives should conduct themselves honestly and ethically, especially concerning actual or apparent conflicts of interest, and disclosure in financial reports.

COMMONLY ACCEPTED PRINCIPLES OF CORPORATE GOVERNANCE INCLUDE

(a) Rights and equitable treatment of shareholders: Organizations should respect the rights of shareholders and help shareholders to exercise those rights. They can help shareholders exercise their rights by effectively communicating information that is understandable and accessible and encouraging shareholders to participate in general meetings.

(b) Interests of other stackholder: Organizations should recognize that they have legal and other obligations to all legitimate stakeholders.

(c) Role and responsibilities of the board: The board needs a range of skills and understanding to be able to deal with various business issues and have the ability to review and challenge management performance. It needs to be of sufficient size and have an appropriate level of commitment to fulfill its responsibilities and duties. There are issues about the appropriate mix of executive and non-executive directors.

(d) Integrity and ethical behaviour: Ethical and responsible decision making is not only important for public relations, but it is also a necessary element in risk management and avoiding lawsuits. Organizations should develop a code of conduct for their directors and executives that promotes ethical and responsible decision making.

(e) Disclosure and transparency: Organizations should clarify and make publicly known the roles and responsibilities of board and management to provide shareholders with a level of accountability.

ISSUES INVOLVING CORPORATE GOVERNANCE PRINCIPLES INCLUDE

(a) internal controls and internal auditors

(b) the independence of the entity's external auditors and the quality of their audits

(c) oversight and management of risk

(d) oversight of the preparation of the entity's financial statements

(e) review of the compensation arrangements for the chief executive officer and other senior executives

(f) the resources made available to directors in carrying out their duties

(g) the way in which individuals are nominated for positions on the board

(h) dividend policy

Nevertheless "corporate governance," despite some feeble attempts from various quarters, remains an ambiguous and often misunderstood phrase. For quite some time it was confined only to corporate management. That is not so. It is something much broader, for it must include a fair, efficient and transparent administration and strive to meet certain well defined, written objectives. Corporate governance must go well beyond law.

Corporate governance mechanisms and controls are designed to reduce the inefficiencies that arise from moral hazard and adverse selection. For example, to monitor managers' behaviour, an independent third party (the external auditor) attests the accuracy of information provided by management to investors. An ideal control system should regulate both motivation and ability.

Internal corporate governance controls monitor activities and then take corrective action to accomplish organisational goals. Examples include:

(a) Monitoring by the board of directors: The board of directors, with its legal authority to hire, fire and compensate top management, safeguards invested capital. Regular board meetings allow potential problems to be identified, discussed and avoided. Executive directors possess superior knowledge of the decision-making process and therefore evaluate top management on the basis of the quality of its decisions that lead to financial performance outcomes.

(b) Internal control procedures and internal auditors: Internal control procedures are policies implemented by an entity's board of directors, audit committee, management, and other personnel to provide reasonable assurance of the entity achieving its objectives related to reliable financial reporting, operating efficiency, and compliance with laws and regulations.

(c) Balance of power: The simplest balance of power is very common; require that the President be a different person from the Treasurer. This application of separation of power is further developed in companies where separate divisions check and balance each other's actions.

(d) Remuneration: Performance-based remuneration is designed to relate some proportion of salary to individual performance. It may be in the form of cash or non-cash payments such as shares and share options, superannuation or other benefits.

External corporate governance controls encompass the controls external stakeholders exercise over the organisation. Examples include:

- competition
- debt covenants
- demand for and assessment of performance information (especially financial statements)
- government regulations
- managerial labour market
- media pressure

SYSTEMIC PROBLEMS OF CORPORATE GOVERNANCE

Demand for information: In order to influence the directors, the shareholders must combine with others to form a voting group which can pose a real threat of carrying resolutions or appointing directors at a general meeting.

A barrier to shareholders using good information is the cost of processing it, especially to a small shareholder. The traditional answer to this problem is the efficient market hypothesis.

Financial accounts form a crucial link in enabling providers of finance to monitor directors. Imperfections in the financial reporting process will cause imperfections in the effectiveness of corporate governance. This should, ideally, be corrected by the working of the external auditing process.

RULES VERSUS PRINCIPLES

Rules are typically thought to be simpler to follow than principles, demarcating a clear line between acceptabie and unacceptable behaviour. Rules also reduce discretion on the part of individual managers or auditors.

Principles on the other hand is a form of self regulation. It allows the sector to determine what standards are acceptable or unacceptable. It also pre-empts over zealous legislation that might not be practical.

ACTION BEYOND OBLIGATION

Enlightened boards regard their mission as helping management lead the company. They are more likely to be supportive of the senior management team. Because enlightened directors strongly believe that it is their duty to involve themselves in an intellectual analysis of how the company should move forward into the future, most of the time, the enlightened board is aligned on the critically important issues facing the company.

At the same time, enlightened directors recognize that it is not their role to be involved in the day-to-day operations of the corporation. They lead by example. Overall, what most distinguishes enlightened directors from traditional and standard directors is the passionate obligation they feel to engage in the day-to-day challenges and strategizing of the company. Enlightened boards can be found in very large, complex companies, as well as smaller companies.

CORPORATE SOCIAL RESPONSIBILITY (CSR)

CSR policy functions as a built-in, self-regulating mechanism whereby business monitors and ensures its active compliance with the spirit of the law, ethical standards, and international norms. The goal of CSR is to embrace responsibility for the company's actions and encourage a positive impact through its activities on the environment, consumers, employees, communities, stakeholders and all other members of the public sphere.

Proponents argue that corporations make more long term profits by operating with a perspective, while critics argue that CSR distracts from the economic role of businesses. Others argue CSR is merely window-dressing, or an attempt to pre-empt the role of governments as a watchdog over powerful multinational corporations.

A more common approach of CSR is philanthropy. This includes monetary donations and aid given to local organizations and impoverished communities in developing countries.

The scale and nature of the benefits of CSR for an organization can vary depending on the nature of the enterprise, and are difficult to quantify, though there is a large body of literature exhorting business to adopt measures beyond financial ones

CONCLUSION

In the present day context in India the role of corporate governance can bring viable option to India leadership to lead India ahead. Corporate Governance as it defined in the introduction that is commitment to values, about the ethical business conduct. It is the responsibility of the board of directors or the CEO or the front runners of the organisations to assure their responsibility protect the interest of all parties in the efficient performance of the organisation. The organisation should take a long-term strategic view and share the responsibility in all for a better future. A business is most successful when it can meat the expectations of all its stackholders. Corporate governance through right leadership is very much important. There is dire need of transformation of governance if we want to excel India amongst the developed countries. Corporate work culture is required to be adopted . If all the organisations in India adopts corporate governance, it will bring better governance & it will be a milestone in creating better India.

CHAPTER-11

Social Responsibility and Business Ethics in Life Insurance Marketing

Ashraf Imam

PhD student –Department of Commerce-
Aligarh Muslim University-Aligarh, UP-India

INTRODUCTION

Perception with reference to ethical practices in the marketing of financial services especially life insurance has increased in recent years, despite an noticeable strengthening of the regulatory framework. In part the ethical problems associated with the promotion and distribution of life insurance products may be attributable to specific features of the market such as asymmetric information. From the customers' perspective, there is a range of unreliable substantiation concerning ethical problems in the marketing of life insurance products. Before we start doing to discuss about social and ethical aspects of life insurance marketing, let us discuss summary about life Insurance in India.

Life Insurance is the fastest growing sector in India since 2000 as Government allowed Private players and FDI up to 26%. Life Insurance in India was nationalized by incorporating Life Insurance Corporation (LIC) in 1956. All private life insurance companies at that time were taken over by LIC. In 1993 the Government of Republic of India appointed RN Malhotra Committee to lay down a road map for privatization of the life insurance sector. While the committee submitted its report in 1994, it took another six years before the enabling legislation was passed in the year 2000, legislation amending the Insurance Act of 1938 and legislating the Insurance Regulatory and Development Authority Act of 2000. The same year that the newly appointed insurance regulator - Insurance Regulatory and Development Authority IRDA —started issuing licenses to private life insurers.

Life insurance is a contract that pledges payment of an amount to the person assured (or his nominee) on the happening of the event insured against.

The contract is valid for payment of the insured amount during:

- The date of maturity, or
- Specified dates at periodic intervals, or
- Unfortunate death, if it occurs earlier.

Among other things, the contract also provides for the payment of premium periodically to the Corporation by the policyholder. Life insurance is universally acknowledged to be an institution, which eliminates 'risk', substituting certainty for uncertainty and comes to the timely aid of the family in the unfortunate event of death of the breadwinner.

By and large, life insurance is civilizations' partial solution to the problems caused by death. Life insurance, in short, is concerned with two hazards that stand across the life-path of every person:

- That of dying prematurely leaving a dependent family to fend for it.
- That of living till old age without visible means of support.

INDIAN LIFE INSURANCE INDUSTRY OVERVIEW

All life insurance companies in India have to comply with the strict regulations laid out by Insurance Regulatory and Development Authority of India (IRDA).

Life Insurance Corporation of India (LIC), the state owned behemoth, remains by far the largest player in the market. The private companies have come out with products called ULIPs (Unit Linked Investment Plans) which offer both life cover as well as scope for savings or investment options as the customer desires. These type of plans are subject to a minimum lock-in period of three years to prevent misuse of the significant tax benefits offered to such plans under the Income Tax Act. Comparison of such products with mutual funds would be erroneous.

SOCIAL RESPONSIBILITY IN LIFE INSURANCE MARKETING

Social responsibility marketing is about marketing with broader concerns of the society at large, like social, legal, ethical and environmental in the perspective of marketing activities. Companies operate in a society and so do their customers and hence they should never forget its contribution to the company. It requires that marketers carefully consider the role they are playing in terms of social welfare. Companies need to evaluate whether they are truly practicing ethical and socially responsible marketing. Several factors are driving the companies to practice higher level of corporate social responsibility, such as:

- Rising customer expectations,
- Changing employees expectations,
- Govt. Legislation and pressure,
- Investor interest in social criteria,
- Changing business procurement criteria.

Business success and continually satisfying the customers and other stakeholders are closely linked to adoption and implementation of high standard of business and marketing conduct. The most admired companies in the world adhere to a code of serving people's interests, not only there own. The following are the most important factors of socially responsible marketing:

1. Legal Behavior: Companies operate within the law of the land, and they must impart the employees with adequate knowledge of law and how to practice them. We have Govt. laws, Society laws, and the organizations must ensure the employees know and observe relevant law, and restrain themselves from practicing illegal, antisocial, corruptive, anticompetitive practices.
2. Ethical Behavior: Companies must evolve and adopt a properly written code of conduct based on the social and cultural ethics, decency, tradition and legal practices, and ensure that all concerned are responsible in observing these guidelines. Today customers are well

aware of the social, cultural, ecological & environmental affairs in their day-to-day lives.

3. Social Responsibility Behavior: As said above, the customers also want to know what the firm's contribution to the society is, or what the company's social conscience is while dealing with customers and the stakeholders.

4. Cause Related Marketing: Contribution to the society can be enormous, and hence companies choose a particular area of society for a particular cause. The examples are :

   - Health awareness - Heart Diseases, AIDS, Cancer, Diabetic, Obesity, Old age, etc.
   - Running children's home, old age home, rehabilitation centre, women's home, etc.
   - Infrastructure - rural housing, hospitals, preserving archaeological places, maintaining roads and parks, homes for endangered species;
   - Educational scholarship for the poor and needy, higher education facility, Institutes;
   - Treatment for destitute, food for the starving;
   - Information legal and technical help during the hour of need;
   - Volunteerism and Philanthropy.

Cause-related marketing is the concept where the specific cause is directly or indirectly linked to the particular revenue transaction. The company has at least one non-economic social objective and uses the revenue generated from the designated sales. This concept is also known as Corporate Societal Marketing (CSM). The CSM can include other activities like traditional and strategic philanthropy and volunteerism.

5. Social Marketing: Some marketing is conducted to directly address a social problem or cause. Social marketing is done mainly by NGOs, Non-Profit or Govt. organizations to further a cause, such as "No smoking", "Say NO to Drugs", etc.

BENEFITS OF SOCIALLY RESPONSIBLE

Some of the benefits of being socially responsible include (a) improvement in performance of company and brand image (b) Help in attracting and in retaining employees (c) Help in increased market share (d) Effective in lower operating costs and (e) easier to attract investors. A socially – responsible firm will care about customers, employees, suppliers, the local community, society, and the environment.

BUSINESS ETHICS IN LIFE INSURANCE MARKETING

Salespersons must be aware of ethical standards and acceptable behavior in marketing especially when we are talking about life insurance products. This awareness means that salespersons must recognize the viewpoints of three key elements: the company, the industry, and society. Since these three groups almost always have different needs and wants, ethical contradiction are likely to arise. Ethical contradiction in marketing arise in two contexts : First, when there is a difference between the needs of the three aforementioned groups (the company, the industry, and society) a conflict may arise. Second and ethical conflict may arise when one's personal values conflict with the organization. In either case, a conflict of interest is a possible outcome. Standards for ethical marketing guide business in efforts to do the right thing. Such standards have four functions: to help identify acceptable practices, foster internal control, avoid confusion, and facilitate a basis for discussion.

Ethics involves learning what is right or wrong, and then doing the right thing — but "the right thing" is not nearly as straightforward as conveyed in a great deal of business ethics literature. Several scholars emphasizes there's always a right thing to do based on moral principle, and others believe the right thing to do depend on the situation — ultimately it's up to the individual. Many philosophers consider ethics to be the "science of conduct." Values which guide how we ought to behave are considered moral values, e.g., values such as respect, honesty, fairness, responsibility, etc. Discussions around how these values are applied are sometimes called moral or ethical principles.

Business ethics has come to be considered a management discipline, especially since the birth of the social responsibility movement in the 1960s. In that decade, social awareness movements raised expectations of businesses to use their massive financial and social influence to address social problems such as poverty, crime, environmental protection, equal rights, public health and improving education. An increasing number of people asserted that because businesses were making a profit from using our country's resources, these businesses owed it to our country to work to improve society. Many researchers, business schools and managers have recognized this broader constituency, and in their planning and operations have replaced the word "stockholder" with "stakeholder," meaning to include employees, customers, suppliers and the wider community.

According to insurance stakeholders, the issue of compliance with ethics and best practices should govern market strategies and operations. Insurance operators need to devote more of their energies and resources to ensuring the emergence of a new order in terms of players' attitude to the issue of business ethics. Insurance, being a business that is based on trust, could only win the admiration and benefaction of the buying public when there is a widely acknowledged effort by operators to operate by the rules laid down by government bodies and the regulatory authorities. Once looked at carefully, insurance is a wonderful and much needed product. Insurance, at its core, is a pooling of community risks. It is a formalized way for people to come together and help each other. For example, when we pay life insurance premiums, we are putting our money together, not just to help ourselves but to help other families. When someone else dies, his family benefits because a payment can be made from this pool of premiums and the investment income that arises from it. When we die, our claim is paid to our family, from the same pool. People, in more informal ways, have done this for centuries. When someone dies, those remaining help the family. This may appear very basic, but insurance is much more powerful than just survivor benefits. Insurance, just like money, is not an evil unto itself. It is a channel that can be used in very good and helpful ways. Once we accept the proposition that insurance actually is a good business, the ethical concerns do not end. In fact, in many ways, they just begin. Every day in running an insurance business, ethical considerations arise.

In a business like Life Insurance where the customer entrusts the company with his/her financial savings, ethics has a direct relation to sales. "The greater the trust, the more the sales".

There are many ways to build trust through ethics, the most fundamental being the way the product is designed. It should offer complete clarity and transparency and the literature supporting the product should not over-promise the benefits or understate the risks.

For example : In ICICI Prudential Life Insurance Company Private Limited-INDIA, the use of the sales illustration, the inclusion of the policy proposal form, and the free look period they offer have served to win their customers' trust. By giving customers the option to track investments online and by publishing the performance of the funds against benchmark indices, they prove that they are an open and reliable organization.

Ethics is an attitude that needs to touch every aspect of the customer relationship. It entails having great admiration for the customer's needs, being open to suggestions and insights that might enhance his/her comfort levels, building in riders and flexibility options that address these needs, providing assistance and clarity in documentation and upgrades, and settling claims on time. Ethics means being fully accountable, not just to the company and to its customers, but to the industry they serve. The inspiration for ethics thus comes from the highest source from a need to impact the industry. On the flip side, a lack of ethics can have serious consequences. Legal action and costs of settlement, business losses, a reduction in ratings, and increased scrutiny are not half as damaging as the loss to image and reputation. It's a fact that good ethics makes good business sense. Of course, the mandate for good ethics always stems from the top. Which explains, why at ICICI Prudential Life Insurance, they have introduced a system of checks and balances that guards against concealment and why they follow norms of compliance and adhere to IRDA regulations so scrupulously that their books and processes are open to audit at all times. While top management can lay down a code of ethics and request adherence, its implementation depends on the individual. Ethics is that discipline, that momentum that challenges a company to rise above themselves and raise the bar each time they interact. It is the means by which they measure themselves, the strength by which they progress, and the light by which they shall be remembered. It is the way ahead - for each individual and for his industry.

CONCLUSION

Several forces are driving companies to practice a higher level of corporate social responsibility: rising customer expectations, changing employee expectations, government legislation and pressure, the inclusion of social criteria by investors, and changing business procurement practices. Companies need to evaluate whether they are truly practicing ethical and socially responsible marketing. Business success and continually satisfying the customer and other stakeholders are closely tied to adoption and implementation of high standards of business and marketing conduct. The most admired companies in the world abide by a code of serving people's interests, not only their own. Companies must adopt and disseminate a written code of ethics, build a company tradition of ethical behaviour, and hold its people fully responsible for observing ethical and legal guidelines and Individual marketers must practice a "social conscience" in their specific dealings with customers and various stakeholders. The ethical and spiritual path in insurance, and in life, is an individual one. At times, it can feel like a solitary path. Ethics is not reached by consensus but by conviction. The ethical path may not be popular but it does stand the test of time. Ethics is not a hard and fast set of rules but is based upon guiding principles. Ethics should guide our communities, yet they are deeply personal. What is good, right and true usually stands the test of time and may not always be immediately apparent. The ethical "stake in the ground" will always be scrutinized and criticized by someone.

The Nineteenth century American author Ralph Waldo Emerson had said, "This time like all times is a good one, if we but know what to do with it". Thus, the exciting time for marketing has arrived now. And also, in the relentless pursuit of marketing superiority and dominance, new concepts, new rules, new tools and practices are ever emerging. There are a number of benefits of successful twenty-first-century marketing. All we need are hard work, insight, right application of mind and tools, inspiration, perseverance and of course a willingness to achieve greater heights. The concept of corporate social responsibility has gained prominence from all avenues. Organizations must realize that government alone will not be able to get success in its endeavor to uplift the downtrodden of society. The present societal marketing concept of companies is constantly evolving and has given rise to a new concept- Corporate Social Responsibility. Many of the leading corporations across the world had realized the importance of being associated with socially relevant causes as a means of promoting their brands. It stems from the desire to do well and get self-satisfaction in return as well as societal obligation of business. The aim of this paper is to develop general idea and will educate members of the insurance and financial services industry, as well as the consuming public about the nature of ethics, social responsibility, and the application of high ethical standards. Unlike many other businesses, insurance is based on mutual trust between insurance producers and insurance clients. Trust, in turn, is based on the highest ethical standards. Through the proper training and awareness about the social responsibility and business ethics, customers will continue to gain trust and confidence in insurance professionals and in the insurance industry.

CHAPTER-12

CORPORATE GOVERNANCE IN MULTINATIONALS: THE INDIAN SCENARIO

Dr Sanjeev Bansal

Sr. Lecturer(ABST), SDPG College, Sriganganagar

Ms. Mandeep K Bhatia Goyal

Lecturer (QM/Finance), IIPS-Sriganganagar
mandeepkbhatiaster@gmail.com

Ms. Nafish

With the globalization came more opportunities and hence the role of Corporate Governance (CG) has become an essential part of the corporate disclosure practice of any successful organization. The most accepted corporate mantra today is that the better the CG practice of an organization the better the shareholder and stake holder value creation. Good corporate governance is imperative for promoting the global market at large. It is more about transparency, accountability and integrity of the company and its directors. A series of high profile corporate scandals in the past few years and augmented shareholder activism have reinforced the need for better governance. Regulators have responded to these scandals by either adopting or revising the legislation to restore the confidence of investors. One such regulation in the Securities and Exchange Board of India (SEBI) guidelines is Clause - 49, demanding the listed Indian companies to adopt and follow the corporate governance norms as it became necessary for every organization to ensure higher reputation and value creation.

This paper analyzes the Corporate Governance (CG) practices of some prominent private Indian multinationals, based on four parameters namely, "approach to Corporate Governance", "Governance structure and

Practices" and "Corporate Social Responsibility". Companies like ITC Ltd, Reliance Industries Ltd, Infosys Technologies Ltd, Tata group, HUL Ltd were chosen as they represent different ownership and control patterns, different period of origin among private sector companies. The paper concludes that though the CG practices are exemplary, there exists difference in the way the companies adopt the CG Practices, etc.

INTRODUCTION

Corporate Governance has become the buzzword for the corporate culture of India today. *Adrain Cadbury*[1], whose report has become the Bible of corporate governance, defines it as "system or process by which companies are directed and controlled". The bedrock of good corporate governance is to conduct the affairs of a company in such a way as to ensure fairness to the stakeholders in fulfilling the responsibility that requires quality of leadership, values, transparent management, vision and goals, respect for law and sense of social responsibility for which there are no rigid standards.

Though corporate governance in general focuses on all stakeholders, the researchers differ in their definitions with regard to those stakeholders, who get importance. While one set of researchers focus on shareholders, others give equal importance to all stake holders. Similarly countries also differ in the importance given to various stakeholders.

The Anglo-American countries give importance to the shareholders rather than stakeholders. However, the approach is different in continental Europe. In many European nations, shareholders exercise lesser control than the workers and in similarly in Germany the representatives of the union serve on supervisory boards. In Japan, shareholders virtually played no role except to provide capital. In India too, the institutional investors and other shareholders were passive investors and the companies were governed as family business. However the situation is changing fast with perceptible change in the profile of corporate ownership and improvement in corporate governance. With the advent of this worldwide change multinational companies in India also are becoming more conscious with their corporate governance policies. In this paper, the researchers have tried to describe the corporate governance practices of few Indian multinational companies. The companies chosen for the study are ITC Ltd., Infosys technologies Ltd, Reliance Industries Ltd., Tata Group and

HUL Ltd. These companies were chosen as they represent different categories among Indian Private Companies. ITC Ltd. is one of the very few Indian companies which does not have an identified promoter and is fully managed by professionals. Reliance Industries and Tata Group is at the other end of the spectrum, with one family in control of the management and controlling. Infosys Technologies falls between, as it has six promoters who do not belong to a single family and their stake is very less. Hence, a study on CG practices of these companies will throw light on the differences among the private companies with different management control and shareholding pattern.

APPROACH TO CORPORATE GOVERNANCE

ITC official believes and publicize 'commitment beyond the market'. It is also one of the companies that lead the way to put in place a formalized system of CG. ITC defines CG as a systematic process by which companies are directed and controlled in order to enhance their wealth generating capacity. ITC also believes that the growth process should ensure that these resources are utilized in a manner which meets the stakeholders' aspirations. According to ITC, CG must simultaneously empower the executive and management of the company while ensuring adequate checks. *The cornerstones of ITC's CG philosophy are trusteeship, Transparency, empowerment, accountability, control and ethical corporate practices.*

Reliance is the only private sector Fortune 500 Indian Company and whether it is a breakup of the empire, a new venture or its CG practices. Reliance believes that good governance practices stem from the culture and mindset of the organization. Reliance official policy says that the firm is committed to all its stakeholders – employees, customers, shareholders, investors, vendors and policy planners. At Reliance, every team member is encouraged to ensure that stakeholders' interests are primary. *Reliance has a well defined policy framework in this regard consisting of values and commitments, code of ethics, business policies, prohibition of insider trading, program of ethics and management.*

Infosys always seems to believe that the best CG attracts the best investors. Infosys is the first Indian company to get it listed on the NASDAQ and the first to benchmark its organizational practices to global standards. As CK Prabhad rightly points out the Infosys inclination towards ecosystem, wealth creation and CG has made an impact across Indian Industry in terms of raising confidence and aspiration levels. Infosys has undergone the CG Audit by ICRA and CRISIL. ICRA has rated Infosys CG practices at CGR 1 and CRISIL has assigned "CRISIL GVC Level 1". Infosys has also compiled with the Narayana Murthy Committee recommendations on CG. *Infosys' CG philosophy is based on satisfying the spirit of law and transparency to the highest degree, making a clear distinction between personal conveniences and corporate resources, proper disclosure of company's workings and having a firm belief that the management is the trustee of the shareholders capital and not the owner.*

HUL mentions that it has endeavored to continue to achieve the highest levels of governance and to benchmark itself with some of the best governed companies. *HUL provides their philosophy of corporate governance* in their website. It says that the company *believes that the principles of fairness, transparency and accountability are the cornerstones for good governance*

GOVERNANCE STRUCTURE AND PRACTICES

ITC has three-tier governance which includes strategic supervision by the BOD, Strategic Management by the Corporate Management Committee and Executive Management by the Divisional chief executives. Looking at the board composition one can find that ITC has a blend of Executive and Non-Executive Directors that include independent professionals. Executive Directors including the chairman do not generally exceed one third of the total strength of the board. One-third of the directors retire by rotation every year and are eligible for reelection. There does not seem to be any separate position of a managing Director in the company. The ITC's CG policy requires the board to meet at least six times a year. The intervening period between two board meetings is always the three months period in line with the clause 49 of the Listing Agreement.

Reliance's CG enforcement system is based on the following principles:

- Constitution of a BOD of appropriate composition, size and commitment to discharge its responsibilities and duties;

- Ensuring timely flow of information to the board and its committees to enable them to discharge their functions effectively;
- Independent verification and safeguarding the integrity of the company's financial reporting;
- A sound system of risk management and internal control;
- Timely and balanced disclosure of all material information about the internal affairs of the company to all the stakeholders;
- Transparency and accountability
- Compliance with law and regulations
- Fair and equitable treatment of all its stakeholders.

As, per CG practices of Reliance, the role of independent directors is to oversee the performance of the management, ensure accuracy of accounts, review the remuneration package for Executive and Non-Executive Directors, recommend the appointment of new members on the board and on the company's senior positions etc. *It is interesting to note that the positions of the Chairman and that of the CEO are vested in the same person in both ITC and Reliance.* The board at reliance meets at least six times a year and the agenda for the board meeting is very similar to that of ITC.

The CG practices of Infosys Technologies are well admired among the practitioners and researchers. The company has a well-defined board charter which defines the scope of the board. As for the board composition, nine out of 16 directors are independent Directors. Infosys seems to believe and practice that CG standard should go beyond the law. The annual report of the company also gives additional information like relationship with other directors, directorships held in other companies both in India and abroad, etc.

The board structure of HUL has a non-executive chairman on the board. It was not clear whether the chairman of HUL were promoter directors of the company, as no specific information was furnished in the corporate governance report. The Total No. of directors in HUL is 10.

Like the above companies HUL had also set up shareholder/grievance committee in line with the requirements of Clause 49 of the listing agreement, to look into the various complaints and queries of shareholders.

BOARD COMMITTEES

ITC currently has four Board Committees – Audit Committee, The Compensation Committee, the Investor Committee and Nominations Committee. The board committees in the case of Reliance comprises of the Audit Committee, Shareholders'/Investors' Grievance Committee, Remuneration Committee, CG and Stakeholders' Interface Committee, Finance Committee and Health, Safety and Environment Committee. Infosys board has six Committees. These are – Compensation Committee, The nomination Committee, the Investor Grievance Committee, the investment Committees and the Share Transfer Committee. Unlike ITC or Reliance, all the Committees, not just the Audit Committee, consist entirely of Independent Directors. HUL consist of Audit Committee, Investors Grievance committee, Remuneration Committee, Nomination Committee, Health Safety and Environment Committee, Ethics and Compliance Committee and Share Transfer Committee. It was observed that HUL had constituted other functional committees such as committee for approval disposal of surplus assets of the company, committee for allotment of shares under *ESOP*[2] and committee for buy back of shares, to raise the level of governance and also to meet the specific business needs.

CORPORATE SOCIAL RESPONSIBILITY PRACTICES

In 2005, ITC released its 'Sustainability Report' in accordance with internationally accepted global reporting initiative guidelines. ITC takes pride in the fact that it is a water positive company and aims to become a carbon positive company soon. ITC has made significant studies in natural resources management, sustainable livelihoods, community development, and social forestry and has been one of the major contributions to the Prime Minister's Relief Fund at the time of Tsunami.

RIL is committed to quality and has won prizes in this category. TQM has been introduced at all sites. State-of-the-art medical care facilities are provided to all the employees through occupational health centers located at various sites. RIL participates

[2]ESOP – EMPLOYEE STOCK OPTION PLAN

in national health programs like Pulse Polio, Revised National Tuberculosis Control Program, etc. RIL provides administrative and financial support for supplying drinking water to villages near its manufacturing sites.

Infosys emphasizes the value of each and every employee and is one of the first Indian companies to bring human capital on its balance sheet. Integrity, fairness and transparency across operations are the operating philosophy of Infosys. It believes in spreading education and has specific programs in this regard like Infosys Fellowship Program, Rural Reach Program, Catch them Young Program and Train the Trainer program. The Infosys foundation was set up at the initiative of this company which is devoted to the cause of the destitute, the rural poor, the mentally challenged etc.

CONCLUSION

To conclude, one may say that all the three companies are doing well both on the CG and the CSR fronts although Infosys seems to be doing much better than the other three. Though good but HUL need to strengthen its CG practices and have to be most practical on CSR fronts as compare to other three. Though these companies have set high standards for corporate governance which shall be revered, appreciated and followed by the generations to come, however the analysis indicates that with the increasing awareness in stakeholders and to meet the world wide standards the Indian multinationals still has a long way to go in order to achieve excellence in their corporate governance practices.

CHAPTER-13

Corporate Governance Practices – The New Strategic Imperative

HEMANT KUMAR SINGH

Post Graduate Department of Accounting & Finance
Seth G.L. Bihani S.D. P.G. College, Sri Ganganagar (Raj.)

J.P. SHARMA

Post Graduate Department of E.A.F.M.
Seth G.L. Bihani S.D. P.G. College, Sri Ganganagar (Raj.)

Dr. V. K. JANGIR

Govt. N. M. P. G. College, Hanumangarh

INTRODUCTION

Corporate governance is a key element in enhancing investor confidence, promoting competitiveness and ultimately improving economic growth. Corporate governance is the set of processes, customs, policies, laws, and institutions affecting the way a corporation is directed, administered or controlled. Corporate governance also includes the relationships among the many stakeholders involved and the goals for which the corporation is governed. It is a system of structuring, operating and controlling a company with a view to achieve long term strategic goals to satisfy shareholders, creditors, employees, customers and suppliers, and complying with the legal and regulatory requirements, apart from meeting environmental and local community needs.

According to Milton Friedam, "corporate governance is to conduct the business in accordance with owner's or shareholders desires, which generally will be to make as much money as possible" but this context is based on marked maximization that underpins shareholder capitalism. But this context was further expanded by J.Wolfensohn, president, World Bank, has said that "corporate governance is about promoting corporate fairness, transparency and accountability.

Even the Experts at Organization of Economic Co-Operation and Development (OECD) have defined "corporate governance" as the system by which business corporations are directed and controlled, it means according to them it is a structure which specifies the distribution of rights and responsibilities among different participants in the corporation.

But today the concept of corporate governance has taken a new dimension and it runs as follows, "Corporate governance is the application of best management practices, compliance of law in true letter and spirit and adherence to ethical standards for effective management and distribution of wealth and discharge of social responsibility for sustainable development of all stakeholders".

REVIEW OF LITERATURE

Issues of corporate governance have been hotly debated in the United States and Europe over the last decade or two. In India, these issues have come to the fore only in the last couple of years. Naturally, the debate in India has drawn heavily on the British and American literature on corporate governance. There has been a tendency to focus on the same issues and proffer the same solutions. For example, the corporate governance code proposed by the Confederation of Indian Industry (Bajaj, 1997) is modelled on the lines of the Cadbury Committee (Cadbury, 1992) in the United Kingdom. The corporate governance literature in the US and the UK focuses on the role of the Board as a bridge between the owners and the management (see for example; Cadbury, 1992; Salmon, 1993; Ward, 1997).

Gupta, Nair and Gogula (2003) analyzed the CG reporting practices of 30 selected Indian companies listed in BSE.The study found variations in the reporting practices of the companies, and in certain cases, omission of mandatory requirements as per Clause 49. Bhattacharyya and Rao (2005) examined whether adoption of Clause 49 predicts lower volatility and returns for large Indian firms.The authors find insignificant results for volatility and mixed results for returns. Collett and Hrasky (2005) analyzed the relationships between voluntary disclosure of CG information by the companies and their intention to raise capital in the financial market.

Barako et al., (2006) examined the extent of voluntary disclosure by the Kenyan companies over and above the mandatory requirements. The results revealed that "the audit committee was a significant factor associated with level of voluntary disclosure, while the proportion of non-executive directors on the board was negatively associated. Subramanian (2006), he identified the differences in disclosure pattern of financial information and governance attributes. The study finally concluded that "there were no differences in disclosure pattern of public/private sector companies, as far as financial transparency and information disclosure were concerned. K. C. Gupta (2006) traced out the differences in CG practices of few local companies of an automobile industry. The study did not observe significant deviations of actual governance practices from Clause 49.

WHY CORPORATE GOVERNANCE?

Investors primarily consider two variables before making investment decisions—the rate of return on invested capital and the risk associated with the investment. In recent years, the attractiveness of developing nations as a destination for foreign capital has increased, partly because of the high likelihood of obtaining robust returns and partly because of the decreasing attractiveness of developed nations. The lure of achieving a high rate of return, however, does not, by itself, guarantee foreign investment; the attendant risk weighs equally in an investor's decision-making calculus. Good corporate-governance practices reduce this risk by ensuring transparency, accountability, and enforceability in the marketplace.

The presence of a good corporate-governance framework ensures neither stability nor success, it is widely believed that corporate governance can raise efficiency and growth, especially for countries that rely heavily on stock markets to raise capital. In fact, some contend that the Asian financial crisis gave developing countries ... a lesson on the importance of a sound corporate governance system.

In an open market, investors choose from a variety of investment vehicles. The existence of a corporate-governance system is likely a part of this decision-making process. In such a scenario, firms that are more open and transparent, and thus well governed, are more likely to raise capital successfully because investors will have "the information and confidence necessary for them to lend funds directly" to such firms. Moreover, well-governed firms likely will obtain capital more cheaply than firms that have poor corporate-governance practices because investors will require a smaller risk premium for investing in well-governed firms.

Also, sound corporate-governance practices enable management to allocate resources more efficiently, which increases the likelihood that investors will obtain a higher rate of return on their investment. Finally, leading indices show that developing countries that have good governance structures consistently outperform developing countries with poor corporate-governance structures. Thus, in an efficient capital market, investors will invest in firms with better corporate-governance frameworks because of the lower risks and the likelihood of higher returns.

At a macro level, if firms in developing countries attract investment, they will stimulate growth in the local economy. If they cannot attract equity capital, they are doomed to remain on a small, inefficient scale, and they will be unable to stimulate growth in their host country.

Good corporate governance benefits developing countries in a number of ways. According to at least one scholar, good corporate-governance practices can decrease the likelihood of a domestic financial crisis and the severity if such a crisis does occur. Additionally, scholars have found strong evidence linking corporate governance to corporate efficiency and have shown that corporate governance creates more efficient corporate management. Finally, research shows that well-governed firms are valued significantly higher than firms with imperfect corporate-governance practices. The policy challenge that exists for governments in developing countries is to provide a hospitable environment for such funds; a sound corporate-governance framework can play a decisive role in creating this hospitable environment. Good corporate governance can reduce this wasteful behaviour and, thus, overcome the obstacles to productivity growth. Moreover, corporate governance can play a role in reducing corruption, and decreased corruption significantly enhances a country's developmental prospects. Ultimately, corporate governance is not just one of those imported western luxuries; it is a vital imperative.

CORPORATE GOVERNANCE IN INDIA

From the beginning of 1980s, situations have changed in India. There have been wide-ranging changes has taken place in both the laws and the regulations in the field of corporate law and the capital market. As a result of several scams in *Indiahttp://www.lawyersclubindia.com/articles/article_list_add.asp - _ftn5* a need has arisen to bring reforms, in response to that, reforms began in 1991 in India. The most important event in the field of investor protection in India was the establishment of Securities and Exchange Board of India (SEBI) in 1992.

In India, the Confederation of Indian Industry (CII) took the lead in framing a desirable code of corporate governance in April 1998. This was followed by the recommendation of the Kumar Mangalam Birla Committee on corporate governance appointed by the SEBI in the year 1997. The introduction of Clause 49 in Listing Agreements in the year 2000 by SEBI was a major turning point in the history of corporate governance in India.

In the Report of SEBI Committee (India) on Corporate Governance defines corporate governance as, the acceptance by management of the inalienable rights of shareholders as the true owners of the corporation and of their own role as trustees on behalf of the shareholders. The recommendations of the committee were enshrined in clause 49 of the Listing Agreement of every Indian Stock Exchange. Every Company which has opted to list its shares in the recognized Stock Exchanges should enter into a listing agreement and non-compliance of the terms and conditions of the agreement can lead to a stringent action by the Stock Exchanges like de-listing of shares.

CLAUSE 49 OF LISTING AGREEMENT

Clause 49 of the listing agreement to be entered into by the listed companies with the Stock Exchanges refers to certain conditions under the heading "Corporate Governance". The said clause 49 mandates various conditions to be complied with by the Companies under the head "Corporate Governance". Thus, it is specific to the Listed Public Companies though the word "Corporate Governance" is used in general and as a synonymous to "Good Governance". An important decision taken in this regard in India is that all listed companies should have 50% independent directors in their board.

The listing agreement to be complied with by all the listed companies, though lists out many conditions, clause 49 occupies significance. Clause 49 of the listing agreement emphasizes on executive directors, composition of directors, independent directors, disclosures by non-executive directors and their compensation, provisions as to committees like Audit Committee, Code of Conduct, some additional disclosures, CFO/CEO certification and a report on Corporate Governance etc. The logic behind the further conditions on the listed companies under clause 49 of the listing agreement is just a further effort to eliminate the loopholes and for the protection of investors/shareholders.

In 2002, the Naresh Chandra Committee on corporate audit and governance submitted its Report. Subsequently, in order to review the existing corporate governance code, SEBI constituted the Narayana Murthy Committee based on whose recommendations made in 2003, far-reaching changes were made in the Listing Agreement in 2004. The Ministry of Corporate Affairs also constituted an Expert Committee on Company Law under the chairmanship of Dr. J J Irani which released its Report in May 2005.

As per the revised clause 49 of the listing agreement based on the Narayana Murthy Committee , the companies are required to submit a quarterly report to the stock exchange within 15 days from the end of every quarter. The report should be signed by the compliance officer or CEO of the company. This revised clause is not applicable to mutual funds. The stock exchange should see whether the company has fulfilled all the provisions of the revised clause 49 like whether it has set up its Board and constituted committees such as, audit committee, investor grievance committee etc before seeking in principle approval for listing.

Along with that the Stock Exchanges shall also set up a separate monitoring cell with identified personnel to monitor the compliance with the provisions of the revised clause 49 on corporate governance. The cell, after receiving the quarterly compliance reports from the companies which are required to comply with the requirements of the revised clause 49, shall submit a consolidated compliance report to SEBI within 60 days from the end of each quarter. In the revised clause 49 it made mandatory that there should be a separate section on corporate governance in its annual report and its should obtain a certificate from either the auditors or practicing company secretaries regarding compliance of conditions of corporate governance. The certificate along with the directors report to be sent annually to all the shareholders of the company.

CONCLUSION AND SUGGESTIONS

In India, guidelines for corporate governance are provided in clause 49 of the listing agreement and also in various sections of the Companies Act. Industry experts hold view that once appointed, the performance and contributions of these directors should be monitored and evaluated objectively with peer reviews serving as a means of such evaluations. A stronger corporate governance framework is needed to prevent Satyam-like financial frauds. There is a need to strengthen regulators and company laws to improve corporate governance, by the corporate ministry. A new Companies Bill, which is pending in Parliament, would make regulation more stringent for auditors. The new bill seeks to revamp archaic laws to help India's growing corporate sector adopt international best practice, and make boards and senior management of companies more accountable.

What is to be kept in mind is that in India adequate safeguards are provided for in the form of various laws but the penalty stipulated for is comparatively meagre and thus the wrong doers have no fear of punishment. Only if the punishments to be imposed are made stringent and it acts as a deterrent can it be expected that such frauds can be controlled in future. More so, there is no expertise of the implementing authorities for detecting and curing the Economic Offences. There is a need to make a separate body to look into the affairs and implement the laws and other provisions to curtail such offences. There is also a lack of political will power to curb such offences, the politicians take a lenient view and leave the investigation and other vital steps into the hands of CBI which is not a body made to specifically deal with such white collar crimes. Unless there reason enough for the miscreants to be scared of penal provisions that send a shiver down their spine. Such offences will continue to happen and we will keep thinking of devising ways to tackle with them.

REFERENCES

Bajaj, R., Chairman, (1997) *Draft code on corporate governance*, Confederation of Indian Industry.

Balasubramaniam, N. (1997) "Towards Excellence in Board Performance", *The IIMB Management Review*, January-March, 67-84.

Barua, S. K. and Varma, J. R. (1993a), "FERA in Reverse Gear; MNCs Strike Gold", *Economic Times*, November 12, 1993.

Barua, S. K. and Varma, J. R. (1993b), "MNCs Must be Subjected to SEBI Acquisition Code", *Economic Times*, November 17, 1993.

Cadbury, A., Chairman, (1992), *Report on the Financial Aspects of Corporate Governance.*

King, M. E., Chairman, (1997), *Report on Insider Trading*

Pound J. (1993) in "The fight for good governance", *Harvard Business Review,* January-February, 76-83.

CHAPTER-14

Corporate Governance: Points to Ponder

Prof. S. K.Sharma

Professor in the Department of Business Administration, Bihani S. D. P. G. College, Sriganganagar (Rajasthan) India

Prof. S.K.Mangal

Professor in Department of Accountancy and Business Statistics, Govt. N.M.P. G. College, Hanumangarh (Rajasthan) India

Dr. R.P.Mathur

Professor in Department of Mathematics, Bihani S. D. P. G. College, Sriganganagar (Rajasthan) India

INTRODUCTION

It was believed that Indian companies were insulated from scams like Enron and Worldcom but Satyam has proved it wrong. The Satyam episode has brought 'corporate governance' at centre stage and has re-emphasised its importance like never before. Yet, it would not be untruthful to say that corporate governance has generally never been taken seriously by the India Inc. Had this not been the case, Satyam may have never happened. How did the regulatory framework fail?

Everything was left to the Auditors. Barring a few exceptions, Independent Directors and Audit Committees have been showcased for the sake of compliance; they are more loyal to the promoters and CEOs than to the shareholders. It seems that the scam of the magnitude of Satyam could have never been detected. We must be thankful for B. Ramalinga Raju's own final confession of wrong doing which left everyone red faced and without an alibi. But for his confession, wrong doing in Satyam could have continued undetected for many more years. It is a fear that there are many more 'Asatyams' lurking within India Inc. and all of those are flourishing on the sticky wicket of corporate governance.

CORPORATE GOVERNANCE DEFINED

Organisation for Economic Cooperation and Development (OECD) has defined Corporate Governance as under: "Corporate Governance is the system by which business corporations are directed and controlled. The corporate governance structure specifies the distribution of rights and responsibilities among different participants in the corporation, such as, the board, managers, shareholders and other stakeholders, and spells out the rules and procedures for making decisions on corporate affairs. By doing this, it also provides the structure through which the company's objectives are set and the means of attaining those objectives and monitoring performance".

In other words corporate governance is about commitment to values and ethical business conduct. It is about how an organisation is managed. This includes its corporate and other structure, its culture, policies and the manner in which it deals with various stakeholders.

BRIEF HISTORY OF CORPORATE GOVERNANCE

Corporate governance guidelines and best practices have evolved over a period of time. The Cadbury Report on the financial aspects of corporate governance, published in the United Kingdom in 1992 was a landmark in this regard. Cadbury Code made 19 recommendations addressing the structure, independence and responsibilities of boards, effective integral financial controls, and recommendation of the directors. The Sarbanes-Oxley Act, which was signed by the US President into law in July 2002 has brought sweeping changes in financial reporting. This is perceived to be the most significant change to federal securities law since 1930s. Besides directors and auditors, the act has also laid down new accountability standards for security analysis and legal counsels.

In Indian scenario, public sector companies began — and still do — as off shoots of a Ministry or a department. Hence, more often than not it bends to be run at least in the initial stages, more like a government department than a corporate entity with commercial objectives, and expected to generate a cash surplus. Since many state enterprises are incorporated with socio-economic objectives subservient to the political philosophy of the government, their commercial objective gets obfuscated. Needless to say, such entities even though corporate in form and commercial in orientation, often tend to turn into expenditure centres instead of profit centres. There are instances galore where public enterprises have completely eroded their capital base. According to the latest report of C&AG of India, as on 31 March 2008, 103 government companies and corporations (including 11 listed companies) had accumulated losses of Rs. 96,992.49 crore. Equity capital of 72 government companies (out of 103) had been completely eroded. The accumulated losses in these 72 companies were Rs. 94,428.27 crore against equity investment of Rs. 15,762.83 crore, making their combined net worth negative at Rs. 78,665.44 crore. At the state level, the position is even more alarming. Most of these had not prepared their financial statements for more than 10 years. Where accounts have been finalised (14 out of 28 states, 123companies) accumulated loss stands Rs. 23473.28 crore and negative net worth of Rs. 15484.28 crore. This scenario speaks volumes of the absence of Corporate Governance in these companies.

LEGAL FRAMEWORK OF CORPORATE GOVERNANCE IN INDIA

Clause 49 of Listing Agreement of SEBI lays down following guidelines for Corporate Governance:

I. Composition of Board of Directors

- The Board of directors of the company shall have an optimum combination of executive and non-executive directors with not less than 50 per cent of the board of directors comprising non-executive directors.
- Where the Chairman of the Board is a non-executive director, at least one-third of the board should comprise independent directors and in case he is an executive director, at least half of the board should comprise independent directors.

II. Audit Committee

- A qualified and independent audit committee shall be set up. Each such committee shall have minimum three directors as members. Two-thirds of the members of the audit committee shall be independent directors.
- All members of the audit committee shall be financially literate and at least one member shall have accounting or related financial management expertise,

III. CEO/CFO Certification

The CEO i.e. Managing Director and the CFO i.e. the Finance Director shall certify to the Board that:

(a) they have reviewed the financial statements and the cash flow statement for the year and that, to the best of their knowledge and belief,

(i) these statements do not contain any materially untrue statement or do not omit any material fact or contain statements that might be misleading,

(ii) these statements together present a true and fair view of the company's affairs and are in compliance with the existing accounting standards, applicable laws and regulations,

(b) there are, to the best of their knowledge and belief, no transactions entered into by the company during the year which are fraudulent, illegal or violative of the company's code conduct.

IV. Report on Corporate Governance

There shall be a separate section on corporate governance in the Annual Reports of the company, with a detailed compliance report on Corporate Governance.

ROLE OF BOARD OF DIRECTORS

The key to organisational health is a thoughtful and committed board of directors which sits at the heart of the enterprise. It is the responsibility of the board to keep a balance between the external and internal pressures on the organisations in order to ensure its survival. Board is expected to give a clear direction to the business and create the emotional climate in which its people can align and attune themselves to its directions. It is the boards' job to ensure that sufficient number of board members are pointing in the same direction, are committed to a common purpose, hold similar values and exhibit similar behaviour, so that the enterprise can function in unison to enable it to perform effectively and efficiently.

A corporation needs effective management to keep its day-to-day operation running, but also needs to ensure that the enterprise sustains itself over long-term to deal with the complex web of customers, suppliers, staff, local communities and the change of political, physical, economic, social, technological and trade environment that impacts its business. Effective stewardship on the part of Board of Directors is an imperative to negotiate an enterprise through this maze. If this is not recognised by the Board of Directors, incompetence and corruption can multiply. "The fish rots from the head," so goes a Chinese saying. Whether or not this saying is literally correct, it is indeed a powerful metaphor for the Board to consider. During my association with the public sector enterprises, I observed managing directors were changed very frequently.

SYMPTOMS OF CORPORATE COLLAPSE

Sir Bob Gratt. in his book "The Fish Rots from the Head" attributes following situations to corporate failure:

- One man rule
- Non-participating board
- Unbalanced top team
- Lack of management depth
- Weak finance function
- A combined chairman and chief executives' roles

It has been observed that many of these symptoms in companies owned by the State Governments where CMD and MD is often the same person and is all in all. His word is final.

CONCLUSIONS

The issues involving corporate governance, which are beyond the ambit of Clause 49 of Listing Agreements and not covered by section 292A of the Companies Act, either need to be seriously delivered and resolved before more damage is done to the public interest (exchequer) or before another "Satyam-like" phenomenon arises in India. This is an important issue for a large number of PSUs, where billions and billions of public funds are invested and yet are not covered under Clause 49 of listing agreements of the section 292(A) of the Companies the Act. Corporate governance should indeed be embedded in the corporate culture and procedures and not be seen as merely an element of compliance. After Satyam, investors' confidence has been badly shaken. The degree of firmness with which the government and the regulators uphold the standard of corporate governance would decide how the foreign investors react and what will be the level of investment in a country.

CHAPTER-15

CORPORATE GOVERNANCE IN INDIAN COMPANIES

Prof. S. S. Aggarwal

Head, Post Graduate Department of Accountancy and Business Statistics, Bihani S. D. P. G. College , Sriganganagar (Rajasthan) India
Email: ssasdpg@yahoo.in

Prof. D. P. Singh

Senior professor in the Department of Business Administration, Bihani S. D. P. G. College , Sriganganagar (Rajasthan) India

Prof. Gopal Sharma

Professor in Department of Accountancy and Business Statistics, Bihani S. D. P. G. College , Sriganganagar (Rajasthan) India

INTRODUCTION

Corporate Governance may be defined as "A set of systems, processes and principles which ensure that a company is governed in the best interest of all stakeholders." It ensures Commitment to values and ethical conduct of business; Transparency in business transactions; Statutory and legal compliance; adequate disclosures and Effective decision-making to achieve corporate objectives. In other words, Corporate Governance is about promoting corporate fairness, transparency and accountability. Good Corporate Governance is simply Good Business.

It is known fact that vital needs of success of any organization lingers on its ability to mobilize and utilize all kinds of resources to meet the objectives clearly set as part of the planning process. Managing well depends on internal and external factors, the latter include availability, cost effectiveness; technological advancement. Increasingly, revelations of deterioration in quality and transparency, have called for adoption of internationally accepted 'Best Practices'. The acceptance of the concept gave rise of 'Corporate Governance'. 'Corporate Governance' encompasses commitment to values and to ethical business conduct to maximize shareholder values on a sustainable basis, while ensuring fairness to all stakeholders including customers, employees, and investors, vendors, Government and society at large. Corporate Governance is the system by which companies are directed and managed. It influences how the objectives of the company are set and achieved, how risk is monitored and assessed and how performance is optimized. Sound Corporate Governance is therefore critical to enhance and retain investors' trust.

Corporate governance is about ethical conduct in business. Ethics is concerned with the code of values and principles that enables a person to choose between right and wrong, and therefore, select from alternative courses of action. Further, ethical dilemmas arise from conflicting interests of the parties involved. In this regard, managers make decisions based on a set of principles influenced by the values, context and culture of the organization. Ethical leadership is good for business as the organization is seen to conduct its business in line with the expectations of all stakeholders. What constitutes good Corporate Governance will evolve with the changing circumstances of a company and must be tailored to meet these circumstances. There is therefore no one single model of Corporate Governance.

REVIEW OF LITERATURE

Since its financial liberalization began in 1991, India has undergone significant corporate governance reform. By the time of Independence in 1947 India had functioning stock markets, an active manufacturing sector, a fairly developed corporate sector, and comparatively well developed, British-derived corporate governance. However, from 1947 through 1991, the Indian government pursued socialist policies. The state nationalized most banks, and became the principal provider of both debt and equity capital for private companies. The government agencies who provided capital to private companies were evaluated based on the amount of capital invested rather than return on investment. Competition, especially foreign competition, was suppressed. Private providers of debt and equity capital faced serious obstacles to exercising oversight over managers due to long delays in judicial proceedings and difficulty enforcing claims in bankruptcy. Public equity offerings could be made only at government-set prices. Indian corporate governance deteriorated, and Indian firms looking for outside capital had to rely primarily on government sources (Bhattacharyya &

Rao, (2005; World Bank, 2005). The Indian economy performed poorly. In 1991, the Indian government faced a fiscal crisis. It responded by enacting a series of reforms including reduction in state-provided financing, bank privatization, and general economic liberalization. The Securities and Exchange Board of India (SEBI) — India's securities market regulator – was formed in 1992. By the mid-1990s, the Indian economy was growing steadily, and Indian firms began to seek equity capital to finance expansion into the market spaces created by liberalization and the growth of outsourcing. The need for capital, amongst other things, led to corporate governance reform. The Confederation of Indian Industry (CII), an association of major Indian firms, issued a voluntary Corporate Governance Code in 1998, and then pressed the government to make the central elements of the code mandatory for public firms, which SEBI did the following year, by adopting a reform package known as Clause 49. The principal elements of Clause 49

- firms should have an audit committee with at least three non-executive members, all with experience in financial matters;
- the CEO and CFO should certify the firm's financial statements and the adequacy of its internal controls; and
- firms should provide disclosure similar to that required for firms cross-listed in Europe.

Firms that do not comply with Clause 49 can be delisted and face financial penalties. However, at the 2006 date of our survey, SEBI had not yet imposed sanctions on noncomplying firms. The first enforcement actions were in 2007. Legal reform has been ongoing, with SEBI amending Clause 49, the government amending the Companies Law, and a recent Irani Committee report (2005) recommending further changes.

NEED OF STUDY

Since the commencement of the liberalization process, India's economic scenario has begun to alter radically. Globalization has not only significantly heightened business risks, but has also compelled Indian companies to adopt international norms and good governance. Much has been heard, talked and said about the topic of corporate governance, but unfortunately the parameters To judge its practical implementation is still not very clear. It is a theme of apprehension for the Indian corporate that needs to initiate hard core action so as to evolve and devour corporate governance at a rapid speed for their survival and growth. Corporate governance is the enduring process that requires integrated efforts and in today's highly specialized times. It is indispensable to be the specialist to achieve excellence. The question arises that whether the compliance of good corporate governance has grown and espoused with the changing circumstances of the corporate life and customized to meet those circumstances. This whole exercise calls for professional capability, deliberation, devotion of time and focused awareness with unprejudiced approach. Vast differences nonetheless may have occurred in laying down the rules of practices and in their practical implementation because of too many legal provisions and their intertwined regulations while, the core objective of corporate governance practices requires upholding significance in creating value to the stakeholders as well as to the nation. Thus, the surfacing of a growing consensus in regard to the compliance of good corporate governance practices imbibed through appropriate reporting in Indian industries has been studied. This has been done to explore the vital dimensions of corporate governance reporting compliance for getting pledged into the ideology, with underlying effective analysis that sets to be a way of the life, and not more compliance with a set of rules.

HYPOTHESIS

We posit that institutional environments through state regulation have directly influenced corporate governance practices across the countries. Based on our theoretical model we empirically test how aspects of the country-specific institutional environment affects corporate governance. Our formal hypotheses as tested in the model linkages are as follows:

Ho1 : All companies in India follow all the recommendations of Clause 49.

Ho2 : There is no significant relation between the compliance of various companies of corporate governance reporting.

Ho3 : The compliance of governance structures results in good corporate governance.

Ho4 : The corporate governance reporting in the published annual reports of Indian . companies as per SEBI, is not satisfactory.

RESEARCH METHODOLOGY AND DATA SOURCES

This study relies on a survey we conducted in 2009 and 2010 of 40 Indian companies. We received 32 responses, for an overall response rate of 80%. The survey was conducted with support from S. D. (P.G.) College, Sri Ganganagar (Rajasthan), one of India's top business schools, which provided a cover letter urging companies to respond. We mailed a written survey to each firm, followed up with additional mailings and phone calls, and arranged site visits to each company. We promised confidentiality to all respondents, and thus do not name individual companies in this research. We surveyed companies with offices in one of India's largest cities – Mumbai, New Delhi, Noida and others. We approached essentially all companies offices in these cities. The response rates were higher.. Thus, it was important to ensure that the survey was completed by a knowledgeable person. Of the 32 respondents, 28 were the company secretary or chief legal officer, 4 were the senior official in the finance department.

LIMITATIONS OF STUDY

There are some limitations to this research. It used a small sample of directors, which may not have been representative of the population, and was not randomly chosen. The criteria were that the interviewee had to be a current non-executive director, irrespective of the type of organization or length of service. The researcher used her own contacts and those of colleagues to approach potential interviewees. The directors who responded did so because of their own interest in participating in the research. They were also asked for names of contacts who also may be interested. The problem with this method of selection is that 'similar types' of personalities may dominate the research.

CORPORATE GOVERNANCE IN INDIAN COMPANIES

Larsen and Turbo Ltd. – Totally committed to customer satisfaction and enhancing shareholders value for attaining global benchmarks.

Reliance Industries – To attain highest levels of transparency, accountability and equity in all facets of its operations and in all its interactions with the stakeholders to enhance overall shareholder's value.

Ranbaxy Laboratories Ltd. –To institutionalize a framework of CG as an enabling methodology to further strengthens managements and decision-making processes through a harmonious and transparent board.

TISCO Ltd – The objective has been to go well beyond the statutory requirements of the code of CG by instituting such systems and procedures as are in accordance with the latest global trend of making management completely transparent and sound.

The Aditya Birla Group India) – Their businesses are committed to the principles of CG and strive for constant improvement upon standards to wealth creation.

ITC Ltd – To safeguard its competitive standing in constantly realigning global market place , the sobering values of business ethics need to enlighten by fulfilment of CG principles.

IPCL Ltd – It strives to become the preferred buisness enterprise of all stakholders by attaching due importance to meeting the expectation of the shareholders through CG practices

SATYAM SCAM

Satyam is the fourth largest Indian It company and it has been known as the one of the best Indian IT companies to work with and it has risen past several companies to bag several projects. It's revenues were in the range of 10,000 crores a year and has a roster of about 650 clients all over the world who used to offshore their work to Satyam. 10000 crores will mean about 2 billion dollars or rather more based on the valuation of the rupee. This companies founder is Mr. Ramalinga Raju who in a letter to the Board of Directors said that he has for the past seven years overstated the accounts and that the total profit margin of the company is only 3% even though he has been fraudulently showing a profit margin of about 25%. That means he was showing a cash at hand I mean in the bank accounts to be 5000 crore about a billion dollars whereas the cash is only 640 crores or even less in the accounts. That letter caused a stir and the jobs of about 55000 employees is at stake as well as the the whole future of the company is at stake.

A COMPARISON WITH OTHER IT COMPANIES

Other IT companies especially those operating from Indian IT shores such as Wipro, Infosys and TCS have more revenues than Satyam but the fact is that each of them and even some companies smaller than Satyam have a profit margin of about 25% or so. Satyam is saying that the profit margin is only 3% which is very hard to believe and hence the big question is where is the money and the reason for overstating the profits and the cash in hand. The problem is why Satyam has such low profit margins which means that there are more employess than there is work and secondly if indeed the revenue is that much then why the profit margin is less and if it is same as other companies the where did the money go ?

CONCLUSION

The corporate governance practices of both public sector and private sector companies are almost similar. We found that the corporate governance practices exert great influence on the performance of the company. Companies which are having good governance practices will have good image among the investors and public as a whole. Though a lion's share of the focus in the Satyam episode was on the role of the independent directors, experts believe the role of auditors is now in spotlight.

We believe that it is the institutional investors who have the tools, bandwidth and clout to extract information and play an activist role (as had happened in Satyam's case) in ensuring that managements don't go off-track. If institutional investors act collectively, they can demand the required changes at companies they have invested in. While the corporate governance framework in the country is seen at par with other developed markets, the same has to be implemented in 'letter as well as spirit'.

Additionally, shareholders should ensure that the composition of Board of Directors is a balanced mix of independent directors and management appointees. This would help keep a check on the internal processes of the company. With shareholder activism on the rise, the proactive role of institutional investors will also make the company management more accountable. While things have improved substantially over the last five years, experts believe that more needs to be done, which will further improve disclosure levels and make managements accountable.

At the retail shareholder level, one could look at a company's past track record (including significant events that reflect management excesses), qualitative and quantitative disclosures (vis-a-vis peers) and consistency in delivering on promises. Experts believe that more rigorous vetting is needed when small and medium companies are considered for investment. Good public sector governance relies on keeping pace with best practice in private sector corporate governance. That is, of harnessing the *potential* that corporate governance principles and practices can offer. Importantly, however, it also requires an understanding of the tensions and gaps that arise in the transposition of corporate governance from the private to public sector, so that public sector corporate governance can be modified accordingly.

REFERENCES

Porter, M.E. (1985). Competitive Advantage: Creating and Sustaining Superior Performance. New York: The Free Press.

Porter, M.E., & Kramer, R. (2006). Strategy & Society: The Link Between Competitive Advantage and Corporate Social Responsibility. *Harvard Business Review*. Harvard Business School Publishing Corporation.

Schepers, D.H., & Sethi, P. (2003). Do Socially Responsible Funds Actually Deliver What They Premise? Business and Society Review, 108:1.

Tanimoto, K. (2004). CSR keiei. (Cyuokeizaisha, in Japanese). Toshiba.

CHAPTER-16

Corporate Governance in India in comparison with Anglo-American

Ravneet Singh Pahwa,

Cognizant Technology Solutions, New Jersey, USA

Amanpreet Kaur

Infosys Ltd.

Pawitpreet Singh

INTRODUCTION

BASELINE STUDY ON Corporate Social Responsibility (CSR) represents one of the most progressive developments in the private sector, urging private companies to evaluate their operations differently from what they are accustomed to and to stretch the borders of their responsibilities. Narrow shareholder value approach is no longer valid under current environmental and social challenges and a more open stakeholder model is paving the way into the business world as a tool for creating more innovative, competitive and sustainable business that benefits both business and society. Issues of corporate governance have been hotly debated in the United States and Europe over the last decade or two. In India, these issues have come to the fore only in the last couple of years. Naturally, the debate in India has drawn heavily on the British and American literature on corporate governance. There has been a tendency to focus on the same issues and proffer the same solutions. For example, the corporate governance code proposed by the Confederation of Indian Industry (Bajaj, 1997) is modelled on the lines of the Cadbury Committee (Cadbury, 1992) in the United Kingdom. This paper argues however that the crucial issues in Indian corporate governance are very different from those in the US or the UK.

INSIDE AND OUTSIDE DIRECTORS

A group of individuals that are elected as, or elected to act as, representatives of the stockholders to establish corporate management related policies and to make decisions on major company issues. Such issues include the hiring/firing of executives, dividend policies, options policies and executive compensation. Every public company must have a board of directors.

Outside Director- Any member of a company's board of directors who is not an employee or stakeholder in the company. Outside directors are advantageous because they have very little conflict of interest.

Inside Director- Any member of a company's board of directors who is either an employee or stakeholder in the company. Inside directors can either be management or major shareholders in the company.

In general, the chief executive officer (CEO) is thought of as the highest ranking officer in a company while the president is second in command. However, in corporate governance and structure, many permutations can take place, so the roles of both CEO and president may be different across various firms. For this reason it is important to have a general understanding of the corporate environment and how different positions ultimately fit into it.

First of all, the board of directors is elected by the shareholders of a company and is composed usually of both inside directors (senior officers of the company) and outside directors (individuals independent of the company). The board establishes corporate management policies and decides on "big picture" corporate issues. Because the board is in charge of executive functions, and as the CEO is responsible for integrating company policy into day-to-day operations, the CEO often (but not always) fills the role of chairman of the board.

ROLE OF THE BOARD

Among the many shortcomings of the Satyam episode has been the role of independent directors who were supposed to safeguard the interests of all stakeholders.

While the three committees (See: Corporate Governance Committees) have explicitly mentioned the role, independence, remuneration and responsibilities of independent directors, the same has not translated into becoming an adequate check on managerial excesses. Says Andrew Holland, CEO, equities, Ambit Capital, "Independent directors should also (in addition to the management) be held accountable for board decisions and audit-related compliance practices." While there have been suggestions for a selection committee to choose independent directors, mandatory training, performance assessments, limit on directorships and compulsory attendance of Board meetings, two key areas relating to CEO/Board chair segregation and number of independent directors could be the right steps forward.

CORPORATE GOVERNANCE SYSTEM

The Company uses the corporate auditor system. The Company's Board of Directors comprises several members, of whom some are outside directors. To facilitate prompt decisionmaking and execution in a rapidly changing management environment, we have introduced the executive officer system. Under this system, the supervisory functions of the Board of Directors are separate from the execution functions of the executive officers. The Board of Directors is able to focus on the formulation of management strategies and the supervision of business execution while the executive officers can focus on business execution. To ensure prompt reflection of the wishes of shareholders, the term of directors has been set at one year.

AUDITING SYSTEM

The Company monitors management through the corporate auditor system. The Board of Corporate Auditors comprises five members, including three outside corporate auditors. Each corporate auditor takes steps to audit the work of the directors, such as attending meetings of the Board of Directors and other important meetings, exchanging opinions with the Representative Directors, periodically receiving reports from directors and others regarding business execution, and actively exchanging information with the Auditing Office. Information is also actively exchanged with the independent auditors, and a close relationship with the independent auditors is maintained.

MINORITY SHAREHOLDERS

It can be believed that it is the institutional investors who have the tools, bandwidth and clout to extract information and play an activist role (as had happened in Satyam's case) in ensuring that managements don't go off-track. If institutional investors act collectively, they can demand the required changes at companies they have invested in. Says Anup Bagchi, executive director, ICICI Securities, "While independent directors can certainly play an important role in ensuring better risk management, demand for good governance by institutional shareholders is the best driver towards higher governance standards." Establishing minority shareholders' groups can also be a positive step. Individual shareholders through these groups can communicate with institutional shareholders for taking up their concerns with the company's management.

PROTECTION OF MINORITY SHAREHOLDERS

Company law provides that a company can be wound up if the Court is of the opinion that it is just and equitable to do so. This is, of course, the ultimate resort for a shareholder to enforce his ownership rights. Rather than let the value of his shareholding be frittered away by the enrichment of the dominant shareholder, he approaches the court to wind up the company and give him his share of the assets of the company. In most realistic situations, this is hardly a meaningful remedy as the break-up value of a company when it is wound up is far less than its value as a "going concern". It is well known that winding up and other bankruptcy procedures usually lead only to the enrichment of the lawyers and other intermediaries involved. Company law also provides for another remedy if the minority shareholders can show that the company's affairs are being conducted in a manner prejudicial to the interests of the company or its shareholders to such an extent as to make it just and equitable to wind it up. Instead of approaching the Court, they can approach the Company Law Board (now proposed to be renamed as the Company Law Tribunal). The Company Law Tribunal which is a quasi-judicial body can make suitable orders if it is satisfied that it is just and equitable to wind up the company on these grounds, but that such winding up would unfairly prejudice the members. In particular, the Tribunal may regulate the conduct of the company's affairs in future, order the buyout of the minority shareholders by the other shareholders or by the company itself, set aside or modify certain contracts entered into by the company, or appoint a receiver. The Tribunal could also provide for some directors of the company to be appointed by the Central Government, or by proportional representation. The Tribunal normally entertains such complaints only from a group of shareholders who are at least one hundred in number or constitute 10% of the shareholders by number or by value.

The powers given to the Company Law Tribunal are perhaps more effective remedies than the power of winding up which is vested in the Courts, though one may wonder whether these powers are too sweeping. However, their scope is limited to very extreme cases of misgovernance where it is just and equitable to wind up a company.

INFORMATION DISCLOSURE

As discussed above, the company law itself mandates certain standards of information disclosure both in prospectuses and in annual accounts. SEBI has added substantially to these requirements in an attempt to make these documents more meaningful. Some of these disclosures are important in the context of dealing with the dominant shareholder. One of the most valuable is the information on the performance of other companies in the same group, particularly those companies which have accessed the capital markets in the recent past. This information enables investors to make a judgement about the past conduct of the dominant shareholder and factor that into any future dealings with him.

RECOMMENDATIONS FOR FUTURE ACTIVITIES

Public authorities and all other stakeholders in their respective capacities and fields of responsibility should increase awareness on the meaning of CSR, its scope, the potential benefits that can be derived from the implementation of the key principles and how they can be translated into practice. Targeted campaigns are needed in order to reach the various stakeholder groups. Media and educational institutions can play a leading role in the overall awareness raising efforts. Efforts need to be made to develop awareness that the large companies, as entities with considerable influence on the other businesses, should adopt practices that would aim to popularize socially responsible behaviour among their business partners.

CONCLUSION

In this study, we investigate whether an increase in outside directors is likely to influence one, arguably primary, board decision - - the appointment of the company's CEO performance. The law makers in India, they believe, need to ascertain the merits of encouraging a principle-based approach (like in the case of the combined code in the UK) to compliance where the nature, size and complexities of a business govern compliance and disclosures - instead of a standard rules based approach for universal compliance (like in the US). Says Monish Chatrath, national markets leader, Grant Thornton: "Companies in India must have the flexibility to ascertain those aspects which are practical to comply with and others where they can provide suitable and logical explanations for non compliance. This will enable them demonstrate their true intend to comply, where practical, and make to transparent disclosures in other cases."

The Satyam scandal has, ironically, uncovered the second most populated country in the world, of having a problem with numbers in terms of finding the requisite number of directors who can exercise their independence while influencing decisions of the board. The challenge for India Inc, believe industry experts, is to come out of the mindset that only well known personalities can be nominated as independent directors.

CHAPTER-17

Corporate Governance in Family-Run Hospitals

Sheenam Aggarwal

BDS II year

Post Graduate Institute of Medical Science, Rohtak (Haryana)

INTRODUCTION

Various new developments are constantly taking place in the Healthcare industry and competition for international and domestic investment in this sector is also growing. Hence, organizations, healthcare administrators, and policy makers are increasingly challenged to reflect on the importance of good corporate governance and how they can implement it in the healthcare system.

In India, family-owned hospitals form a major component of the healthcare delivery mechanism and cannot be underestimated due to their impact on the overall healthcare delivery system and well-being of people. However, due to uncertainties of the present economic scenario, it is necessary to develop a governance system for family-run hospitals in order to provide tangible benefits to the patients, stakeholders, various healthcare providers, and businesses. It will help family-run hospitals to be competitive, more viable and effective organizations, and more growth-oriented sustainable corporations.

REVIEW OF LITERATURE

Attention to the governance in this sector, especially in the government owned and non-profit components, has not been commensurate with the enormity of the challenges faced. Rising costs, developments in science, technological change, political and economic change, and escalating service expectations together with increasing demands for greater patient safety (Kulmann, Allsop & Saks 2009), efficiency and effectiveness from hospitals and healthcare providers (Barnett, Perkins & Powell 2001), simultaneously with complex ethical issues and calls for sustainable hospitals and sustainable healthcare and waste management practices, have been added to the burden for healthcare boards (Hall 2008; Hamilton 2008; Townend & Vallini 2008). Moreover, inquiries into medical errors across the health systems of many countries (see Auditor-General Victoria 2008; Bevan 2010; Braithwaite & Travaglia 2008; Callaly, Arya & Minas 2005; Cowan 2007) have raised both clinical governance[1] and medical staff governance as yet further factors in modern hospital governance (see Petasnick 2007; Scholten & van der Grinten 2002). Good governance is a somewhat elusive and complex concept with social, political and economic dimensions (Eekloo, Delesie & Vleugels, 2007). It has been beset by differing theoretical perspectives and real difficulties in accessing the necessary research data, primarily due to the level of market sensitivity associated with observations of board processes and decisions (Payne, Benson & Finegold, 2009).

WHAT IS CORPORATE GOVERNANCE?

Corporate governance is about how companies or organizations are controlled. It is concerned with striking the balance between social and economic goals, and between individual and community goals. The corporate governance process is implemented to ensure that the management and business of the entities is conducted in line with highest standards of ethics and efficacy, assuming the best option to safeguard stakeholders' interest.

NEED FOR CORPORATE GOVERNANCE IN FAMILY-RUN HOSPITALS

Increasing expectations of patients, increasing competition from different healthcare players, changing perceptions of stakeholders, and development of new technologies have created an urgent need to implement corporate governance in family-run hospitals. Most family-run hospitals eventually close down or are taken over by Corporates. Many family-run hospitals are supposed to be managed by the fourth or fifth generation, who do not want to take the responsibility due to their own career plans in other fields. Corporate governance is required in family-run hospitals to bring transparency, focus on sound patient care, accountability, team and leadership building, cost control, latest technology implementation, and adoption of best practices. These can be achieved keeping in mind the expenses and investment guidelines of the organizations.

TRANSFORMATION STAGE – SHIFT FROM FAMILY-RUN TO CORPORATE STYLE OR CORPORATE HOSPITAL

Before understanding the dynamics and frame of corporate governance in family-run hospitals, the following key questions need to be asked.

OVERALL PERSPECTIVE OF THE HOSPITAL'S KEY DECISION-MAKERS

1. Has our Board understood its changing role in the context of corporate transformation?

2. How well is the organization positioned to go ahead with the right skills, competition, various committees, and decision-making team structure?

3. Are there changes to be made within the organization and in liaison with other healthcare providers to achieve more efficiencies and organizational growth?

4. What can the organization do to further support the payers, stakeholders, employees, and service providers within the community to ensure all are committing best practices?

5. What will the entire transformation mean to the community, employees, stakeholders, etc, and what will be the engagement process implemented for external and internal customers?

6. How confident is the organization? Are the clinicians performing the right procedures in line with evidence-based best practices (both existing and emerging)?

7. Is there a strong mechanism in place to ensure exchange of ideas, viewpoints, and have insightful discussions with the management, stakeholders, clinicians, employees, patients, etc?

8. Are the patients' needs and clinical outcomes top priority across the organization? Does the organization have a strong mechanism to track all quality indicators?

CONCEPTUAL FRAMEWORKS OF CORPORATE GOVERNANCE IN FAMILY-RUN HOSPITALS

To answer the above-mentioned questions, a conceptual delivery model is formed to implement good corporate governance in family-run hospitals. Family-run hospitals in India (small, mid-sized or large hospitals) are undergoing a major transformation and are in the process of adopting strong corporate governance models to stay ahead of the competition. Some of the challenges faced by hospitals in adopting corporate governance are:

Governance beyond basics: The Board has to ensure that all the skills and competencies needed to implement the corporate governance framework are in place. Understanding the crisis: Members of the Board have to prepare according to the current economic circumstances. The impact of investment has to be calculated in advance ensuring that the risk of failure is managed.

Risk management: In family-run hospitals, the responsibility of overall organization performance lies on the Board. Hence, good corporate governance helps estimate the risks involved due to effective oversight and internal control by the Board members. Quality, productivity and safety: The management's responsibility is to implement quality initiatives and processes to increase productivity and safety of the patients.

Efficiency: The top management has to focus on cost-saving exercises with emphasis laid on revenue cycle management. Priority areas like employees, service mix, clinicians, drugs, and consumables can be reworked to achieve the long-term vision and objective of the organization.

Transparency and trust: Transparency and trust are the two important pillars responsible for overall growth of any organization. The Board will have to work together to build a strong relationship with the corporate governance body, knowing that the effort in building both trust and transparency will be an important success factor.

Best clinical practices: A workforce model to support the adoption of best clinical practices performed in emerging and developed healthcare facilities should be implemented. The senior management of the hospital should track all the applicable clinical indicators for future references. There should be a clinical committee to govern the same, which would also be responsible for the clinical outcomes in the hospital. The committee would also ensure the implementation and execution of the best practices, concentrating on the very critical component of the delivery cycle, i.e. re-look the entire clinician engagement model. Support from clinicians, technical staff, and management will help to implement best practices in the hospital and to market the best clinical and corporate governance hospital.

Change management: This is one of the major components to develop leadership within the organization. These leaders are responsible for change in the processes and framework, which lead towards the betterment of the family-run hospital. There should be a commonly-shared vision within the clinical and management team to make the change management process swift in the hospital.

FAMILY-RUN HOSPITAL: "CORPORATE GOVERNANCE ONE-STOP SOLUTION"

Introduction of corporate governance in majority of the family-run hospitals will attract more patients due to improved clinical outcomes and services. It will attract more clinical talent due to the strong clinician engagement model, and more investment due to trust and transparency followed within the organization. It will attract non-clinical talents due to high brand image and retention power. It will also attract more suppliers willing to offer better prices due to transparent supply chain management.

THERE ARE MULTIPLE ASPECTS OF CORPORATE GOVERNANCE IN FAMILY-RUN HOSPITALS

It's all in the mindset: Before introduction and at the time of implementing corporate governance, all the stakeholders like shareholders, employees, clinicians, suppliers, etc., should be very well informed about the structure and should have a clear-cut sense of responsibility and accountability regarding each department.

Cost control models: The top management should implement cost saving models in various segments of the hospitals, like the introduction of a cost-effective supply chain management system, bulk purchases of drugs and consumables to get a better price. Strong control on pilferage level within the organization, formulation, pharmaceutical and therapeutic drug committee will help govern the type of medicines and consumables used and purchased by clinicians and the material department. Periodic stock audit will help the organization to save a lot of costs in terms of identifying slow and fast-moving materials within thc organization.

Information Technology: Driver for change: Introduction of the right information technology at various levels in the hospital will ensure transparency and smooth management of different departments in the hospital. There is an increase in the adoption of Information Technology such as hospital information systems and other clinical applications like Picture Archiving and Communication System (PACS), Radiology Information System, (RIS), Clinical Applications etc. which facilitates quick and precise disease diagnosis and fast data retrieval.

Better care with best profits: Along with good infrastructure, good clinicians and best technology, it is very important to have patient-oriented service delivery programs and the implementation of best practices in all the clinical as well as non-clinical areas of the hospital.. This will work as a parallel support in faster recovery of the patients. Also, reduction in average lcngth of stay with best clinical outcome, bundled with good service to the patient, will add up in the top-line of overall growth of the organization.

ADVANTAGES OF CORPORATE GOVERNANCE IN FAMILY-RUN HOSPITALS

Following are some of the key advantages of corporate governance:

Image builder: Corporate governance acts as an image builder for a hospital, as people associate this with better management, streamlined processes, and hassle-free treatment.

Credibility: Corporate governance runs on an open platform, i.e. the financial result of each year is publically posted. Hence, the trust level of investors and general masses is also with the facility.

Accountability: Corporate governance is based on the best practices in a particular business domain. It results in regular audits and quality initiatives, thereby reducing wastage of resources and resulting in better control and better profit margins.

Better Growth Prospects: Corporate governance is run by various stakeholders and the financial results are declared transparently. Therefore, if a business unit makes profit, there is an increase in the number of stakeholders inclined to invest their money in the projects. This increases the options for the organization to opt for organic or inorganic expansion.

CONCLUSION

In corporate governance, it is fundamental to keep the investors informed about decisions made by the Board. This makes the investors feel safe. Most hospitals find it difficult to arrange funds at the time of expansion, as they do not follow corporate governance until the eleventh hour, which leads to an increase in the cost of operation. In India, where healthcare is supposed to be one of the most important aspects of one's life, it is important to appreciate and realize that good governance is very important not only for the organization's sustainable growth, but also to maintain community trust. In the coming years, majority of family-run hospitals will adopt good corporate governance models to sustain themselves and for the growth of their stakeholders, patients, employees, clinicians, suppliers, and the community at large.

REFERENCES

John Carver on Board Leadership: Selected Writings From the Creator of the World's Most Provocative and Systematic Governance Model. San Francisco: Jossey-Bass, 2002.

Reinventing Your Board: A Step-By-Step Guide to Implementing Policy Governance. Co-authored with Miriam Carver. San Francisco: Jossey-Bass, 1997; 2nd edition, 2006.

A New Vision for Board Leadership: Governing the Community College. Co-authored with Miriam Carver. Washington: Association of Community College Trustees, 1994.

CHAPTER-18

CORPORATE GOVERNANCE IN INDIA

Naveen Kumar Makkar *[H.E.S.]*

Assist. Prof. in Commerce, Govt. College, Bhattu Kalan (Fatehabad)

Rakesh Jhamb *[R.E.S]*

Assist. Prof. in Commerce(A.B.St.), Govt.College, Nohar (Raj.)

Corporate Governance in India

INTRODUCTION

Corporate governance has been an important field of query within the finance discipline for decades. Researchers in finance have actively investigated the topic for at least a quarter century and the father of modern economics, Adam Smith, himself had recognized the problem over two centuries ago. There have been debates about whether the Anglo-Saxon market- model of corporate governance is better than the bank - based models of Germany and Japan.

Corporate governance has been a central issue in developing countries long before the recent spate of corporate scandals in advanced economies made headlines. Indeed corporate governance and economic development are intrinsically linked.

Poor corporate governance also hinders the creation and development of new firms. Good corporate governance also lowers of the cost of capital by reducing risk and creates higher firm valuation once again boosting real investments.

Effective corporate governance mechanisms ensure better resource allocation and management raising the return to capital. The return on assets (ROA) is about twice as high in the countries with the highest level of equity rights protection as in countries with the lowest protection.

Good corporate governance can significantly reduce the risk of nation-wide financial crises. There is a strong inverse relationship between the quality of corporate governance and currency depreciation.

CORPORATE GOVERNANCE IN INDIA – A BACKGROUND

The history of the development of Indian corporate laws has been marked by interesting contrasts. At independence, India inherited one of the world's poorest economies but one which had a factory sector accounting for a tenth of the national product. In terms of corporate laws and financial system, therefore, India emerged far better endowed than most other colonies. The Companies Act, 1956 as well as other laws governing the functioning of joint-stock companies and protecting the investors' rights built on this foundation.

The beginning of corporate developments in India were marked by the managing agency system that contributed to the birth of dispersed equity ownership but also gave rise to the practice of management enjoying control rights disproportionately greater than their stock ownership.

In the absence of a developed stock market, the three all-India development finance institutions (DFIs)– the Industrial Finance Corporation of India, the Industrial Development Bank of India and the Industrial Credit and Investment Corporation of India – together with the state financial corporations became the main providers of long- term credit to companies. Along with the government owned mutual fund, the Unit Trust of India, they also held large blocks of sha res in the companies they lent to and invariably had representations in their boards.

Issues of corporate governance have been hotly debated in the United States and Europe over the last decade or two. In India, these issues have come to the force only in the last couple of years. Naturally, the debate in India has drawn heavily on the British and American literature on corporate governance. There has been a tendency to focus on the same issues and proffer the same solutions. For example, the corporate governance code proposed by the Confederation of Indian Industry (Bajaj, 1997) is modelled on the lines of the Cadbury Committee (Cadbury, 1992) in the United Kingdom. This paper argues however that the crucial issues in Indian corporate governance are very different from those in the US or the UK. Consequently, the corporate governance problems in India require very different solutions at this stage of our corporate development.

CORPORATE GOVERNANCE IN INDIA: DISCIPLINING THE DOMINANT SHAREHOLDER

It is useful at this point to take a closer look at corporate governance abuses by dominant shareholders in India. The problem of the dominant shareholder arises in three large categories of Indian companies.

First are the public sector units (PSUs) where the government is the dominant (in fact, majority) shareholder and the general public holds a minority stake.

Second are the multi national companies (MNCs) where the foreign parent is the dominant (in most cases, majority) shareholder.

Third are the Indian business groups where the promoters (together with their friends and relatives) are the dominant shareholders with large minority stakes, government owned financial institutions hold a comparable stake, and the balance is held by the general public.

The governance problems posed by the dominant shareholders in these three categories of companies are slightly different.

MULTI NATIONAL CORPORATIONS (MNCS)

Government regulations have required most MNCs in India to operate through subsidiaries which are not 100% owned by the parent. In the 70s, the government enacted a law limiting foreign ownership in most industries to 40% while allowing 51% in a few high technology areas. This law was liberalized in the 90s and now 51% is permitted in most industries while 74% or even 100% ownership is allowed in some cases. These regulations have created severe corporate governance problems in several key areas as may be seen fro m the examples below.

1. In the 70s, MNCs were forced to issue shares to the Indian public to comply with the law. The controls that then existed on pricing of public issues meant that these issues were at substantial discounts to the market price. In the 90s when the law permitted higher foreign ownership, these MNCs raised the foreign stake by issuing shares at very deep discounts to the market price. This obviously meant a large loss to the minority shareholders.

2. Another corporate governance problem arises where the foreign parent has two subsidiaries in India in one of which it holds a higher stake (say 100%) while in the other it holds a smaller stake (say 51%). The manner in which the MNC structures its business in India between these two subsidiaries is riddled with problems as far as the minority shareholder is concerned. There have been allegations in some cases that the most profitable brands and businesses have been transferred from the long established 51% subsidiary to the newly formed 100% subsidiary at artificially low prices. This implies a large loss to the minority share holders of the 51% subsidiary who have after all contributed to in equal measure to the investments that were made in the past to build up these businesses to their current dominant position.

3. Yet another problem is the payment s that parent companies increasingly demand for all the services that they provide to their subsidiaries. One well-known example involves a company where the parent has recently started collecting royalties for the use of a brand. In this case, India is actually the principal market for this brand and the Indian company had assiduously cultivated the brand through decades of advertising paid for in part by the minority shareholders. Minority shareholders could only watch in dismay as the royalties knocked off a sizeable chunk of the earnings of the company.

INDIAN BUSINESS GROUPS

The situation in this category of companies is more complex than in the PSUs and the MNCs where there are clearly defined dominant shareholders. In the Indian business groups, the concept of dominant shareholders is more unstructured for two reasons.

First, the promoters' shareholding is spread across several friends and relatives as well as corporate entities. It is sometimes difficult to establish the total effective holding of this group.

Second, the aggregate holding of all these entities taken together is typically well below a majority stake. In many cases, the promoter may not even be the largest single shareholder. What makes the promoters the dominant shareholders is that a large chunk of the shares is held by state owned financial institutions which have historically played a passive role. So long as the financial institutions play a passive role, the promoters are effectively dominant shareholders and are able to get general body approval for all their actions. This allows the promoters to play all the games that dominant shareholders play in PSUs and MNCs –

- structuring of businesses and transfer of assets between group companies,
- preferential allotments of shares to the dominant shareholder,
- payments for "services" to closely held group companies and so on.

In short, we can say that "Promoters do what they want". They play games like politicians play in PSUs and Foreign investors play in MNCs. It is the standard joke among bankers in India that there are many financially sick companies but no financially sick promoters.

THE REGULATORY PROBLEM

Regulators face a number of difficulties in tackling the problem of corporate governance abuses by the dominant shareholders. In many cases, it is difficult to decide how far the regulator should go in interfering with the normal course of corporate functioning. Some of these problems are highlighted below.

- Shareholder Democracy
- The Problem of Micro-Management

CONCLUSION

The past few years have witnessed a silent revolution in Indian corporate governance where managements have woken up to the power of minority shareholders who vote with their wallets. In response to this power, the more progressive companies are voluntarily accepting tougher accounting standards and more stringent disclosure norms than are mandated by law. They are also adopting more healthy governance practices. It is evident that these tendencies would be strengthened by a variety of forces that are acting today and would become stronger in years to come:

- Deregulation: Economic reforms have not only increased growth prospects, but they have also made markets more competitive. This mea means that order to survive companies will need to invest continuously on a large scale.

- Disintermediation: Meanwhile, financial sect or reforms have made it imperative for firms to rely on capital markets to a greater degree for their needs of additional capital.

- Institutionalization: Simultaneously, the increasing institutionalization of the capital markets has tremendously enhanced the disciplining power of the market.

- Globalization: Globalization of our financial markets has exposed issuers, investors and intermediaries to the higher standards of disclosure and corporate governance that prevail in more developed capital markets.

- Tax reforms: Tax reforms coupled with deregulation and competition have tilted the balance away from black money transactions. This makes the worst forms of misgovernance less attractive than in the past.

- While these factors will make the capital markets more effective in disciplining the dominant shareholder, there are many things that the government and the regulators can do to enhance this ability:

- Disclosure of information is the pre-requisite for the minority shareholders or for the capital market to act against errant managements. The regulator can enhance the scope, frequency, quality and reliability of the information that is disclosed.

- Regulatory measures that promote an efficient market for corporate control would create an effective threat to some classes of dominant shareholders as discussed earlier.

- Reforms in bankruptcy and related laws would bring the disciplining power of the debtholders to bear upon recalcitrant managements.

- Large blocks of shares in corporate India are held by public sector financial institutions who have proved to be passive spectators. These shareholdings could be transferred to other investors who could exercise more effective discipline on the company managements. Alternatively, these institutions could be restructured and privatized to make them more vigilant guardians of the wealth that they control.

In short, the key to better corporate governance in India today lies in a more efficient and vibrant capital market. Over a period of time, it is possible that Indian corporate structures may approach the Anglo-American pattern of near complete separation of management and ownership. At that stage, India too would have to grapple with governance issues like empowerment of the board. Until then, these issues which dominate the Anglo –American literature on corporate governance are of peripheral relevance to India.

CHAPTER-19

ETHICAL AND SOCIAL ISSUES IN INSURANCE DISTRIBUTION CHANNEL MANAGEMENT

Ashraf Imam

Shahid Alam

Dr. Mohd Ashraf Ali

M N Zadeh

INTRODUCTION

Insurance policy sold in India mainly through insurance agents. India's growing markets require that products like life insurance must be sold. Many people in India still need to be introduced and closed on certain products. The products will not sell themselves without a person on the ground building a relationship backed by a trusted company. In India, penetration is very low making distribution channels is more important. India's insurance penetration (gross premium as a percentage of gross domestic products) was 2.53% in 2005, against a global average of 4.34% the same year. The distribution channels' importance also puts them in a position to influence customer choice. "Most people do not understand insurance; what they understand is what is conveyed by distributors," says Rahul Agarwal, director, Optima Risk Management Services Ltd, which carries out broking in both life and non-life products. In today's scenario, insurance companies must move from selling insurance to marketing an essential financial product. The distributors have to become trusted financial advisors for the clients and trusted business associates for the insurance companies.

Indian insurance market, there is two main challenge to insurers and intermediaries is

- Building faith about the company in the mind of the client
- Intermediaries being able to build personal credibility with the clients.

Traditionally individual agents have been the primary channels for insurance distribution in the Indian market; the public sector insurance companies have their branches in almost all parts of the country and have attracted local people to become their agents. The agents are from various segments in society and collectively cover the entire spectrum of society. A person who has lived in the locality for many years sells the products of the insurance company with a local branch nearby. This ensures the last mile touch point being closer to the customer. Of course, the profile of the people who acted as agents suggests they may not have been sufficiently knowledgeable about the different products offered, and may not have sold the best possible product to the client. Nonetheless, the customer trusted the agent and company. This arrangement worked adequately in the absence of competition. But in today's scenario agents continue as the prime channel for insurance distribution in India, as is the case in most markets, supported by call centers to a small extent. Almost all the new players follow this model primarily because the regulations for other channels are yet to be put in place. These days insurance marketplace is undergoing a transformation which may eventually lead to significant changes like how consumers will purchase insurance products. A variety of distribution channels are currently used in this market place and some insurers utilize a combination of distribution channels, and these include the internet-led channels, company-led channels, bank-led channels, and agent-led channels. As insurance industry is the most sought by common man for savings for his future, the success of the insurance company depends on the better customer service that is provided by them and largely due to the practices that are adopted by the company. So what are the insurance market best practices?

INSURANCE DISTRIBUTION CHANNEL

An insurance product is an intangible product evidenced by a written contract known as the 'policy'. Insurers market various insurance covers either directly or through various distribution channels-individual agents, corporate agents (including Bancassurance) and Brokers. The marketer in the distribution network is in direct interface with the prospect and the customer. Life insurance products are sold through individual agents and many of them have this as their only career occupation. General insurance products are sold through individual agents, corporate agents and brokers. The concept of a "channel" of distribution is an interesting one.

"Channel" means "a closed course or conduit through which anything flows," or "that through which anything passes." And distribution means Movement of goods and services from the source and now channel distribution means flow of goods and services right up to the final customer, consumer, or user and the movement of payment in the opposite direction, right up to the original producer or supplier.

Distribution channels such as agents are licensed by the IRDA. To get an agency licence, one has to have certain minimum qualifications; practical training in insurance subjects and passes an examination conducted by the Insurance Institute of India. IRDA regulations on licensing of agents/ brokers lay down the code of conduct for individual agents, corporate agents and brokers. Thus it is seen that the dos and don'ts for these intermediaries are given by IRDA at the point of sale as well as in the event of a claim. Service does not end with the customer receiving his document; it in fact only begins here. After sales service is as important or even more important – like when a refund has to be made or when a claim has to be made.

One of the issues that is of great concern affecting professionalism in insurance activities is resorting rebating by intermediaries. Rebating is prohibited as per Section 41 of the Insurance Act, 1938 and the public are advised not to deal with intermediaries offering rebate of any kind. Rebating means a share of commission receivable by the agent/broker is given to the prospect/client. This is done to attract the client in the purchase of insurance contract by offering cash. Competition among agents/ brokers is so cut-throat, some agents indulge in such unethical practices. Public are advised not to ask for any prohibited rebates in premium since commission payment to an agent is the only income for some to take care of their families. Similarly, agents are also advised not to indulge in such practices which could cause them loss of agency income.

Managing channels is one of the most important dimensions of businesses across the world for improving their value in the market. Customers are constantly on the lookout for convenience and service, when purchasing goods and buying policies in case of insurance company. Effective channel management helps companies decrease costs and reach potential customers profitably. Effective channel management involves proper recruitment of channel members. Recruiting channel members should be a continuous process. All channels in insurance distribution are based on the premise that anyone joining the channel and performing channel functions stands to benefit. Channel conflicts arise in channel systems when one or more channel members start perceiving the behavior and actions of another channel member as an impediment to goal attainment. There are many sources of channel conflicts. They can originate from competing roles, clash of domains and differing perceptions of reality. Marketing channel strategies and channel structures are also important sources of conflict. Channel conflicts can be of different types. They can be primarily divided into pre-contractual and post-contractual conflicts and conflicts based on channel levels. Based on the timing of conflicts, they are divided into conflicts that arise before channel members enter into agreements and those that arise after channel members enter into agreements. Channel level conflicts may be vertical, horizontal or multi-level. To ensure effective coordination and channel functioning, different conflict management techniques can be used. They are primarily segregated into structural and behavioral conflict resolution strategies. Some commonly used strategies include negotiation, persuasion, problem solving, co-optation, arbitration and mediation. Channel members can also resolve conflicts by exchange of personnel between channels and by association with different trade organizations. Creative and effective channel leadership result in channel members moving towards shared goals. If this ideal situation is achieved, distribution channels will be in a better position to satisfy the demands of target customers and maximize profits of individual channel members.

ETHICAL AND SOCIAL ISSUES IN DISTRIBUTION OF INSURANCE PRODUCTS

Ethics is the practice of behaving with honesty and integrity. In the insurance industry, ethical behavior is required of those who sell insurance policies, and insurance companies often come under scrutiny regarding ethical behavior. Insurance companies are not the only ones who could be guilty of unethical behavior. Policyholders who commit insurance fraud to obtain claim payments they are not entitled to are also engaging in unethical and possibly illegal behavior. Insurance is often a confusing topic to the customers. Ethical practices by insurance companies and agents help ensure that insurers serve the best interests of the customers. For instance, an agent should sell a customer coverage he does not need or cannot afford. Ethical and social concerns in distribution are considered as moral judgement and behaviour standards in distribution practice or moral code or system in marketing area especially placing of products to final customers. In other words, ethics in distribution is the research of the base and structure of rules of conduct, standards, and moral decisions relating to marketing decisions and practices. Marketing executives who take strategic decisions related to distribution channels often face with ethical conditions and their decisions is related to all sides of marketing mix. Marketing executives' ethical decision making process related to these decisions is affected by miscellaneous ways as philosophical, economical, sociological, psychological, and religious. Ethical issues in direct marketing are the subjects which are privacy, confidentiality and intrusion. Ethical problems which are faced while in channel distribution are reliability of channel member's means agents, banks, broker and corporate broker's etc. illegal activities like rebating, false claims, misguiding insurer and many more, privacy means customers personal information's, accuracy means transparency in products brochure and each and every details, and deceptive advertisements.

While it is impossible for all insurance professionals to reach consensus on every aspect of ethical ideology, those professional organizations have recognized the merit in providing a platform for continued ethics awareness and discussion. When discussing professional ethics, it is necessary to examine the core beliefs and underlying precepts that comprise our particular value system. What forms the basis for your values–is it religion, philosophy, family, tradition, society, mentor, etc? For the good of the society, we should not unquestioningly embrace just any value system. We consider at least three universal precepts that exist in nearly every civilized society and in most every religion: honesty, respect for other persons and respect for others' property.

CORE BELIEFS OF ETHICAL IDEOLOGY

The first tenet of the triad is honesty. Without honesty, there is no chance of a successful business relationship. While dishonesty is destructive in one's personal life, it usually is fatal in business. People are inclined to be more forgiving in personal relationships than they are in business relationships. One dishonest act can tarnish an entire career. Would you buy anything from someone you knew to be dishonest?

The second tenet of the triad is respect for other persons, meaning respect for a person's physical and emotional well-being. Disrespect could manifest itself by such actions as rudeness, harassment, slander, discrimination, abuse, assault and murder. Some transgressions of this tenet, as well as the other two, are so nefarious that there are laws against such behavior. While there may be no law against rudeness, would you continue to do business with someone who was rude to you?

The third tenet of the triad is respect for a person's property. Disrespect could manifest itself by such actions as neglect, carelessness, vandalism, theft and destruction. Property and casualty insurance producers are in the express business of preserving the assets of clients. Disrespect for a person's property is the antithesis of the noble mission of an insurance professional.

Business management these days become conscious for considering ethical and social issues and distribution channel management is no exception to this trend despite an apparent strengthening of the regulatory framework. Opinion of public can strongly influence the success of businesses in a democratic society, and this realization has made business organizations more sensitive to ethical issues in marketing especially when we talk about distribution channels. It is becoming increasingly main-stream to pay conscious attention to social and ethical issues in marketing. In fact, the trend is to consciously engage in activities that are seen as benefiting society and publicize these activities to gain a marketing advantage. In part the ethical problems associated with the promotion and distribution of insurance may be attributable to specific features of the market such as asymmetric information. From the customers' perspective, there is a range of unreliable evidence concerning ethical problems in the marketing of insurance services in general and life insurance products in particular. Everyone, at some time or the other, must surely have been sold a product that he or she did not need. Selling is a profession that has been widely criticized for the unethical dimensions associated with it. Ethics is the set of rules or standards that govern the conduct of a person or members of a profession. Ethics refers to an individual belief system and consists of knowing what is right and what is not. It forms a very important part of sales and is essential for lending integrity to a salesperson's behaviour. No discussion on ethics is complete without a reference being made to social responsibility. Social responsibility exemplifies ethical behavior and is defined as an individual's or institution's concern for the consequences of his/its actions as these might affect the interests of others in the society. Companies doing business with no regard to social responsibility run the risk of attracting the attention of environmental groups, earning negative publicity, and losing the goodwill of society. Therefore, companies try to instill a sense of ethics in their employees and conduct business in a socially responsible way. Indian companies are now more concerned with corporate social responsibility than ever before. Companies in the past were concerned more about making profits than anything else. In recent times, firms have realized the importance of ethical and social practices in their business and distribution channels. In order to fulfill their ethical and social responsibility, companies need to effectively communicate to the public about the company's ethical policies, set high ethical standards for themselves, and evaluate themselves on ethical performance from time to time through means of ethical audits.

In organizations, the management is largely responsible for the ethical or unethical behavior of its employees. A sales manager faces ethical issues that cover the ethical dilemmas of his sales people as well as the ethical aspects pertaining to his decisions regarding hiring and evaluating of salespersons, assigning territories, etc. The ethical issues facing a sales manager may be studied with regard to the sales manager's relationship with his subordinates, the company, customers, and competitors. On the other hand, the ethical issues facing a salesperson pertain to the salesperson's accountability to the top management, and his relationship with other salespeople and with customers.

CONCLUSION

As insurance industry is the most sought by common man for savings for his future, the success of the insurance company depends on the better customer service that is provided by them and largely due to the practices that are adopted by the company. So what are the insurance market best practices? A marketing revolution is taking place in the insurance business, the center of which is in the channels of distribution. Both the insured's and the insurers are feeding the revolution, with the agents being whipsawed. Insurers, insured's, and government are seeking ways to improve the rate of flow through the channels. The end sought by the revolution is improved efficiency leading toward lower costs to the insured, greater profits for the insurer, and more effective coverage of the market. Several forces are driving companies to practice a higher level of corporate social responsibility: rising customer expectations, changing employee expectations, government legislation and pressure, the inclusion of social criteria by investors, and changing business procurement practices. Companies need to evaluate whether they are truly practicing ethical and socially responsible marketing. Business success and continually satisfying the customer and other stakeholders are closely tied to adoption and implementation of high standards of business and marketing conduct. The most admired companies in the world abide by a code of serving people's interests, not only their own. At times, it can feel like a solitary path. Ethics is not reached by consensus but by conviction. The ethical path may not be popular but it does stand the test of time. Ethics is not a hard and fast set of rules but is based upon guiding principles. Ethics should guide our communities, yet they are deeply personal. Above all, ethics and the spiritual compass that underlies our individual ethical code, is not a destination, it is not even a journey, it is the journey. What is good, right and true usually stands the test of time and may not always be immediately apparent. The ethical "stake in the ground" will always be scrutinized and criticized by someone.

It will be very difficult for any country to keep continuous monitoring the companies not allowing them to cheat the other party. Only the business community should believe in business in an ethical way. All the other parties dealing with business community like Government, people, customers, banks, employees and others should also follow ethics when they deal with the company.

REFERENCES

1. Ex-Branch Manager-Reliance Life Insurance- Sikandrarao Branch -Aligarh Region and currently enrolled as PhD student–Department of Commerce-Aligarh Muslim University-Aligarh, UP-India. (imamashraf1@rediffmail.com)

2. Research Scholar-Department of Commerce, AMU Aligarh-India. (shahidalig1@gmail.com)

3. Associate Professor-Department of Commerce-Aligarh Muslim University-Aligarh, UP-India. (drashrafali1@gmail.com)

4. MS.C Dairy Economic (Final)-N.D.R.I-Karnal-India.(sofya_nasiry @yahoo.com)

CHAPTER-20

Corporate Governance in Indian Banking Sector

Dr Rana Zehra Masood

Faculty Member, Aligarh Muslim University, Aligarh

Dr Seema Mahlawat

Associate Professor, SBMIMSAR, Asthal Bohar, Rohtak

INTRODUCTION

Corporate Governance has become a "buzz word" these days mainly due to Globalization and is a key element in enhancing investor confidence, promoting competitiveness and ultimately improving economic growth. It is the set of processes, customs, policies, laws, and institutions affecting the way a corporation is directed, administered or controlled. Corporate Governance in the present day context encompasses the interests of not only the shareholders but also many stakeholders, which includes employees, customers, suppliers and the community and complying with the legal and regulatory requirements, apart from meeting environmental and local community needs. Due to the unique role of banks in national and local economies and financial systems, supervisors and Governments are also stakeholders.A good corporate governance mechanism improves the health of the corporate sector, thus enhancing national competitiveness.

CORPORATE GOVERNANCE IN INDIAN CONTEXT

In the Indian context, the need for corporate governance has been highlighted because of the scams occurring frequently since the emergence of the concept of liberalization from 1991 such as the Harshad Mehta Scam, Ketan Parikh Scam, UTI Scam, Vanishing Company Scam, Bhansali Scam and so on. In the Indian corporate scene, there is a need to induct global standards so that at least while the scope for scams may still exist, it can be at least reduced to the minimum.

From the beginning of 1980s, situations have changed in India. There have been wide-ranging changes has taken place in both the laws and the regulations in the field of corporate law and the capital market. As a result of several scams in India a need has arisen to bring reforms, in response to that, reforms began in 1991 in India. The most important event in the field of investor protection in India was the establishment of Securities and Exchange Board of India (SEBI) in 1992.

Corporate governance is a multi-faceted subject. An important theme of corporate governance deals with issues of accountability and fiduciary duty, essentially advocating the implementation of policies and mechanisms to ensure good behaviour and protect shareholders. Another key focus is the economic efficiency view, through which the corporate governance system should aim to optimize economic results, with a strong emphasis on shareholders welfare.

In India the concept of corporate governance is gaining importance because of two reasons.

- After liberalization, there has been institutionalization of financial markets, FIIs and FIs became dominant players in the stock markets. The market began to discriminate between wealth destroyers. Corporate governance is a critical by product of market discipline.

- Another factor is the increased role being played by the private sector. Companies are realizing that investors love to stay with those corporate that create values for their investors. This is only possible by adopting fair, honest and transparent corporate practices.

CORPORATE GOVERNANCE IN BANKS

Corporate Governance has become very important for banks to perform and remain in competition in this era of liberalization and globalization. Banks in a broad sense are institutions whose business is handling other people's money. A Joint stock bank also known as Commercial Bank which is nothing but a company whose business is banking. Protecting the interest of depositors becomes a matter of paramount interest to banks.

In banking parlance, the Corporate Governance refers to conducting the affairs of a banking organization in such a manner that gives a fair deal to all the stake holders i.e. shareholders, bank customers, regulatory authority, society at large, employees, etc.

The significance of corporate governance in banking sector weighs very much due to very nature of banking transactions. Banking is the crucial factor effecting economic development of an economy. It is the life-blood of a country. It is responsible for the flow of credit and for maintaining the financial balances of the economy. In India, since the nationalization process banks emerged as a tool of economic development along with social justice.

As per Basel committee Report 1999, Banks have to display the exemplary of corporate governance practices in their financial performance, transparency in the balance sheets and compliance with other norms laid down by section 49 of corporate governance rules. Most importantly, their annual report should disclose accounting ratios, relating to operating profit, return on assets, business per employee, NPAs, maturity profile of loans, advances, investments, borrowings and deposits. Similarly the audit reports of bank should highlight those disclosures which are in line with corporate governance rules. Hence, auditors should have the complete know how about all the features of the latest guidelines given by Reserve Bank of India (RBI) and ensure that the financial statements are made in a fraud free manner and should mirror the implementation of corporate governance. Apart from auditor's seriousness to bring those requirements appropriately in audit report, there should be adequate internal control systems in the operational activities of banks. It is very much essential for banks to devote adequate attention on internal control system so as to maximize their returns on each unit of capital inducted through an effective funds management strategy and mechanism. (Basel Committee Report, 1999)

An effective system of corporate governance in banks will impose appropriate standards of conduct on managers and control and monitoring procedures on banks in order to maximize opportunities for legitimate profits subject to the best interests of depositors and shareholders. Good corporate governance regulates the relationships between banks' stakeholders, their Boards and their management. It prevents the abuse of power and self-serving conduct, as well as imprudent and high risk behaviour by bank managers, and resolves conflicts of interests between managers and board members on the one hand and shareholders and depositors on the other. Indeed, the current state of the world economy is in some measure attributed to the fact that boards (and their risk management committees) have not properly discharged their duties in exercising oversight on managers engaging in high risk activities. The corporate governance of the financial sector, therefore, has important implications for the stability of the whole economy.

From the perspective of banking industry, corporate governance also includes in its ambit the manner in which their Board of Directors governs the business and affairs of individual institutions and their functional relationship with senior management. This is determined by how banks:

- set corporate objectives (including generating economic returns to owners);
- run the day-to-day operations of the business and;
- consider the interests of recognized stakeholders, i.e., employees, customers, suppliers, supervisors, governments and the community and
- line up corporate activities and behaviors with the expectation that banks will operate in a safe and sound manner, and in compliance with applicable laws and regulations; and of course protect the interests of depositors, which is supreme.

For ensuring good corporate governance, the importance of overseeing the various aspects of the corporate functioning needs to be properly understood, appreciated and implemented.

There are four important forms of oversight that should be included in the organizational structure of any bank in order to ensure the appropriate checks and balances:

(1) Oversight by the board of directors or supervisory board;

(2) Oversight by individuals not involved in the day-to-day running of the various business areas;

(3) Direct line supervision of different business areas; and

(4) Independent risk management and audit functions. In addition to these, it is important that the key personnel are fit and proper for their jobs.

NEED FOR CORPORATE GOVERNANCE IN BANKS

Banks in India are facing increasing competition, within and outside India, both in terms of markets for its products and for sources of fund. It has, therefore become necessary for banks to constantly reengineer, to provide the products and services to suit the ever-changing requirements, to accelerate the speed with which the transactions are completed and to constantly evaluate and provide training to the workforce update the knowledge and impress upon them the necessity to have a professional and competitive approach.

In order to meet the statutory need of having a sound Capital Adequacy requirements, banks are accessing the Capital Market at regular intervals. Hence the Banks need to stimulate the interest of investors at all times. Investors believe that a bank with good governance will provide them a safe place for investment and also give better returns. Good Corporate Governance is, therefore, an important factor in a competitive environment.

Investors, customers, employees and vendors have all become more discerning and are demanding greater transparency and fairness in all dealings. To attract and retain the commitment of investors, customers, employees, Banks should ensure that they match the global benchmarks in Corporate Governance practices.

CORPORATE GOVERNANCE IN PUBLIC SECTOR BANKS

A substantial chunk of Indian Banking sectors still remains under the control of public sector banks despite the strong wave of Globalization, Liberalization and privatization and entrance of private and foreign banks in the arena. The major shareholding of the public banks with the Government the reasons for such ownership may include solving the severe informational problems inherent in developing financial systems, aiding the development process or supporting the vested interests and tributional cartels.

Banks have been making pivotal contributions over the years to nation's economic growth and development. Government-owned (Public Sector) banks have played a major role in economic development. During the last few years, these institutions are slowly getting "corporative" and consequently corporate governance issues in banks assumes greater significance in the coming years. Considering the importance of banking sector the practice of corporate governance and how it helps banking industry in India in terms of bringing more transparency and overall growth of banking sector.

Basel Committee has underscored the need for the banks to establish the strategies and to become accountable for executing as well as implementing them. The existing legal institutional framework of public sector banks is not aligned with principles of good corporate governance. The bureaucratic hassles, red tapes and de motivated work culture add further fuel to the fire. So far banks have been burdened with "social responsibility" and compelled to tow the line of thinking dictated by the political party in power, healthy banking policies will not be able to become the top priority. Monopoly of PSB in banking business had protected them from competition and bank Managements have thereby became complacent.

Corporate Governance in PSBs is important, not only because PSBs happen to dominate the banking industry, but also because, they are unlikely to exit from banking business though they may get transformed. To the extent there is public ownership of PSBs, the multiple objectives of the Government as owner and the complex principal-agent relationships cannot be wished away. PSBs cannot be expected to blindly mimic private corporate banks in governance though general principles are equally valid. Complications arise when there is a widespread feeling of uncertainty of the ownership and public ownership is treated as a transitional phenomenon. The anticipation or threat of change in ownership has also some impact on governance, since expected change is not merely of owner but the very nature of owner. Mixed ownership where government has controlling interest is an institutional structure that poses issues of significant difference between one set of owners who look for commercial return and another who seeks something more and different, to justify ownership. Furthermore, the expectations, the reputation risks and the implied even if not exercised authority in respect of the part-ownership of government in the governance of such PSBs should be recognized. In brief, the issue of corporate governance in PSBs is important and also complex.

From the banking industry perspective, the attributes of corporate governance provide guidelines to the directors and the top level managers to govern the business of banks. These guidelines relate to how banks establish corporate aims, carry out their daily activities, and take into account the interest of stakeholders and making sure that the corporate activities are in tune with the public expectations that banks will function in an ethical and legal manner thereby protecting the interest of its depositors (Basel Committee, 1999). All these broad issues relating to governance apply to other companies also, but they assume more significance for banks because they deal with public deposits directly.

Banks' philosophy for Corporate Governance should lay emphasis on the cardinal values of 'fairness', 'transparency' and 'accountability', as enunciated by World Bank, for performance at all levels, thereby, enhancing the shareholders' value and protecting the interest of the stakeholders.

The Banks consider themselves as trustee of its shareholders and should acknowledge its responsibility towards them for creation and safeguarding shareholders' wealth. Banks should continue its pursuit of achieving these objectives through the adoption and monitoring of corporate strategies, prudent business plans, monitoring of major risks of the banks business and pursuing the policies and procedures to satisfy its legal and ethical responsibilities. Hence, banks should aim at enhancing the long-term shareholder value while protecting the 'interest of shareholders, customers and other in line with international best practices.

CORPORATE GOVERNANCE IN PRIVATE SECTOR BANKS

Private sector banks have entered niche areas, listed their scrip and being market driven they have been more transparent in their functioning. They have also been more tech savvy, growth oriented and have less of NPAs. Private sector banks has to conform with standard of good banking practices such as

- Ensuring a fair and transparent relationship between the customer and bank

- Instituting comprehensive risk management system and its adequate disclosure
- Proactively handling the customer complaints and evolving scheme of redressal for grievances.
- Building systems and processes to ensure compliance with the statutes concerning banking.

RECENT STEPS TAKEN BY BANKS IN INDIA FOR CORPORATE GOVERNANCE

(a) Induction of non executive members on the Boards

(b) Constitution of various Committees like Management Committee, Audit Committee, Investor's Grievances Committee, ALM Committee, etc.

(c) Gradual implementation of prudential norms as prescribed by RBI,

(d) Introduction of Citizens Charter in Banks

(e) Implementation of "Know Your Customer" concept,

The primary responsibility for good governance lies with the Board of Directors and the senior management of the Banks.

CONCLUSION

Globalization and liberalization is sweeping across the sectors of economy and banking industry is not an exception. In this era of revolutionary changes, banks shall confront various risks and managing these risks shall be the future challenges of banks. In competitive business environment, organizations that adopt good corporate governance and best practices will be able to survive and attain sustainable growth levels. Public Sector Banks need greater functional autonomy in a deregulated environment. Such autonomy, however, needs to be accompanied by greater accountability on the part of their boards to the stakeholders. A Corporate Governance Policy shall serve as an effective instrument for achieving this goal. The success of corporate governance rests on the awareness on the part of the banks of their own responsibilities. While law can control and regularize certain practices, the ultimate responsibility of being ethical and moral remains with the banks. It is this enlightenment that would bring banks closure to their goals. The following aspects require special mention while judging the standard of corporate governance in a banking institution:

(a) Constitution of the Board of directors:

(b) Transparency

(c) Policy formulation

(d) Internal controls

(e) Committees of the Board

By fixing prudential standards, the regulators can improve the corporate governance and RBI has already taken a no. of steps during the recent years to enhance the usefulness of good corporate governance. However, there is lot, which the banks themselves have to do, since adherence to prudential norms is the minimum level of compliance and banks have to achieve higher standards for good governance. The success of corporate governance lies in minimizing the regulatory norms and adoption of voluntary codes.

CHAPTER-21

Corporate Governance in Indian Companies

Prof. S. N. Vyas

Head, Post Graduate Deptt. of Business Administration (Commerce), Maharshi Dayanand P. G. College, Sri Ganganagar (Rajasthan) India

Dr. K. B. Sharma

Head, Post Graduate Deptt. of Accountancy and Business Statistics (Commerce), Maharshi Dayanand P. G. College, Sri Ganganagar (Rajasthan) India

Prof. J. S. Mujral

Lecturer, Post Graduate Deptt. of Accountancy and Business Statistics (Commerce), Maharshi Dayanand P. G. College, Sri Ganganagar (Rajasthan) India

INTRODUCTION

Corporate governance is the set of processes, customs, policies, laws and institutions affecting the way a corporation is directed, administered or controlled. Corporate governance also includes the relationships among the many stakeholders involved and the goals for which the corporation is governed. The principal stakeholders are the shareholders, management and the board of directors. Other stakeholders include employees, suppliers, customers, banks and other lenders, regulators, the environment and the community at large. Corporate governance is a multi-faceted subject. An important theme of corporate governance is to ensure the accountability of certain individuals in an organization through mechanisms that try to reduce or eliminate the principal-agent problem.

LITERATURE REVIEW

From the agency theory perspective, the objective of corporate governance is to ensure that managers resort to value maximizing strategies

(Shleifer & Vishny, 1997). Management ownership, market for corporate control, product market competition, shareholder activism, and trading activity are considered as various mechanisms through which shareholders exercise this control (Walsh & Seward, 1990; Shleifer & Vishny, 1997). There have also been attempts to link the "resource based view" and the "managerial rents theory" (Castanias & Helfat, 2001) with corporate governance, in the strategic management literature. This view maintains that corporate governance is a key managerial resource or human capital, and thus a potential source of competitive advantage to the firm. Most empirical studies in corporate governance focus on the linkage between corporate governance and firm performance.

The Securities and Exchange Board of India (SEBI) followed by setting up the Kumar Mangalam Birla Committee on Corporate Governance, whose recommendations in December 1999 formed the basis for Clause 49 of the Listing Agreement. SEBI revised Clause 49 in late 2004 on the recommendations of the Narayana Murthy Committee on Corporate Governance, with the revisions coming into effect on January 1, 2006.

METHODOLOGY

The project will use the latest lines of research that are being pursued in regard to both theoretical and empirical analysis of corporate governance. It will draw on new areas of research in the field of economics, finance, management, political economy and law. It will exploit the rich endowment that Europe possesses in the field of corporate governance reflecting its diverse institutional, legal and political structures. It will also draw on the varied historical evolution of corporate governance systems. It will therefore utilise these cross-sectional differences across countries and time, as well as between institutions and firms within countries.

The first line of research involves providing training in relevant theoretical tools. There have been considerable advances in the modelling of corporate governance arrangements drawing on principal-agent, imperfect information and incomplete contract models. These have broadened our knowledge of the relevance of corporate governance systems and the different instruments of corporate governance. However, there remains a great deal of theoretical modelling to be done. There are, firstly, econometric techniques that provide methods for testing and correcting for endogeneity. Secondly, there are differences across countries and across time in Europe that can be exploited to great advantage to evaluate the impact of exogenous influences on corporate performance.

THE IMPORTANCE OF CORPORATE GOVERNANCE

Sound corporate governance principles are the foundation upon which the trust of investors is built. These principles are critical to growing the reputation that we have established over decades as a company dedicated to excellence in both performance and integrity. Competent and qualified independent directors play an important role in the stewardship and strategy formulation of companies. Indian corporates that have appointed such directors to their Board have benefited immensely from their guidance and inputs. Transparency in business transactions; Statutory and legal compliance; adequate disclosures and Effective decision-making to achieve corporate objectives.In other words, Corporate Governance is about promoting corporate fairness, transparency and accountability. Good Corporate Governance is simply Good Business.

The current financial crisis across the world is a case of massive failure of corporate governance. "The essence of corporate governance is ensuring transparency in the operation of the business enterprises so that accountability for the decision taken is fixed." The current financial meltdown arose as a result of unregulated speculation on the issue of sequestering the risks leading to an unprecedented economic crisis comparable to the great depression of 1929-30,

THE CONTEXT TO THE ISSUE – SATYAM COMPUTER SERVICES

The latest imbroglio involving one of India's largest IT companies, Satyam Computer Services has virtually discredited the concept of corporate governance. Satyam, as it is widely reported sought to invest into another company involving a conflict of interest for its promoters. This in turn involved a change in the fundamental character of the company and utilization of virtually its entire cash balance. Satyam was also being accused by the World Bank for bribing its employees to get certain contracts awarded in the company's favour. While these are allegations at this point in time, it may be noted, that the company had approached suitable independent professionals to get the necessary clearances under the extant law of the land as well as appoint independent directors.

Ostensibly, the idea is to 'comply' with the code of corporate governance on paper. What is interesting to note here is that as negative reports about the company come out into the open, let us not forget that it won the prestigious Golden Peacock Global Award for excellence in Corporate Governance. The company was named the winner by the World Council for Corporate Governance as recently as in September 2008!

CORPORATE GOVERNANCE AT RELIANCE IS BASED ON THE FOLLOWING MAIN PRINCIPLES

- Constitution of a Board of Directors of appropriate composition, size, varied expertise and commitment to discharge its responsibilities and duties.
- Ensuring timely flow of information to the Board and its Committees to enable them to discharge their functions effectively.
- Independent verification and safeguarding integrity of the Company's financial reporting.
- A sound system of risk management and internal control.
- Timely and balanced disclosure of all material information concerning the Company to all stakeholders.
- Transparency and accountability.
- Compliance with all the applicable rules and regulations.
- Fair and equitable treatment of all its stakeholders including employees, customers, shareholders and investors.

CONCLUSION

Does product and labor market globalization cause convergence in corporate governance? Our case analysis suggests that the answer to this question is a constrained yes. A summary of our interpretation of the case follows.

Software firms', and especially Infosys', exposure to global product markets, first, and then to global talent markets, seems to have driven some adoption of shareholder-style corporate governance in India.

In contrast to the stance taken by the existing literature on the convergence of corporate governance, we do not find much of a role for capital markets as drivers of this process. If anything, Infosys and some other Indian software firms accessed global capital markets long after their exposure to global product and global talent markets had driven them to adopt good corporate governance practices. In ongoing work, we are hand-collecting large sample data to shed light on both a positive and a normative question. The positive question has to do with quantifying various barriers to the diffusion of U.S.-style corporate governance. The normative question has to do with the extent to which such practices should diffuse in the emerging market context of India.

CHAPTER-22

Corporate Governance and the Financial Crisis

Prof. D. K. Verma

Head, Post Graduate Deptt. of Economics Administration and Financial Management, Maharshi Dayanand P. G. College, Sri Ganganagar (Rajasthan) India

Dr. Rajesh Dhingra

Lecturer, Post Graduate Deptt. of Economics Administration and Financial Management, Maharshi Dayanand P. G. College, Sri Ganganagar (Rajasthan) India

Dr. Suresh Dhaka

Lecturer, Post Graduate Deptt. of Business Administration (Commerce), Maharshi Dayanand P. G. College, Sri Ganganagar (Rajasthan) India

INTRODUCTION

Corporate governance is the set of processes, customs, policies, laws and institutions affecting the way a corporation is directed, administered or controlled. Corporate governance also includes the relationships among the many stakeholders involved and the goals for which the corporation is governed. The principal stakeholders are the shareholders, management and the board of directors. Other stakeholders include employees, suppliers, customers, banks and other lenders, regulators, the environment and the community at large. Corporate governance is a multi-faceted subject. An important theme of corporate governance is to ensure the accountability of certain individuals in an organization through mechanisms that try to reduce or eliminate the principal-agent problem.

The financial crisis proves beyond a doubt that we are living in a global age. Starting as a problem in the US, it has spread through the world and left investors in seemingly unrelated markets and instruments nursing large losses. Corporate governance failings were not the only cause but they were significant, above all because boards failed to understand and manage risk and tolerated perverse incentives. Enhanced governance practices should therefore be integral to an overall solution aimed at restoring confidence to markets and protecting us from future crises. This statement draws on the ICGN's international experience of exercising

GOVERNANCE IN THE CONTEXT OF THE FINANCIAL CRISIS

Some commentators have criticised shareholders for failing to hold boards to account. It is true that shareholders sometimes encouraged companies, including investment banks, to ramp up short-term returns through leverage. They were not always as close as they could have been to companies they owned. Yet, a larger problem has been failure of regulators. They did not respond decisively when they realised that markets were mispricing risk. They allowed banks to operate with too little capital, with excessive leverage and too little attention to liquidity risk. They failed to pick up on poor risk management by boards and on poor lending practices in the mortgage market.

LITERATURE REVIEW

From the agency theory perspective, the objective of corporate governance is to ensure that managers resort to value maximizing strategies (Shleifer & Vishny, 1997). Management ownership, market for corporate control, product market competition, shareholder activism, and trading activity are considered as various mechanisms through which shareholders exercise this control (Walsh & Seward, 1990; Shleifer & Vishny, 1997). There have also been attempts to link the "resource based view" and the "managerial rents theory" (Castanias & Helfat, 2001) with corporate governance, in the strategic management literature. This view maintains that corporate governance is a key managerial resource or human capital, and thus a potential source of competitive advantage to the firm. Most empirical studies in corporate governance focus on the linkage between corporate governance and firm performance.

The Securities and Exchange Board of India (SEBI) followed by setting up the Kumar Mangalam Birla Committee on Corporate

Governance, whose recommendations in December 1999 formed the basis for Clause 49 of the Listing Agreement. SEBI revised Clause 49 in late 2004 on the recommendations of the Narayana Murthy Committee on Corporate Governance, with the revisions coming into effect on January 1, 2006.

THE IMPORTANCE OF CORPORATE GOVERNANCE

Sound corporate governance principles are the foundation upon which the trust of investors is built. These principles are critical to growing the reputation that we have established over decades as a company dedicated to excellence in both performance and integrity. Competent and qualified independent directors play an important role in the stewardship and strategy formulation of companies. Indian corporates that have appointed such directors to their Board have benefited immensely from their guidance and inputs. Transparency in business transactions; Statutory and legal compliance; adequate disclosures and Effective decision-making to achieve corporate objectives.In other words, Corporate Governance is about promoting corporate fairness, transparency and accountability. Good Corporate Governance is simply Good Business.

The current financial crisis across the world is a case of massive failure of corporate governance. "The essence of corporate governance is ensuring transparency in the operation of the business enterprises so that accountability for the decision taken is fixed." The current financial meltdown arose as a result of unregulated speculation on the issue of sequestering the risks leading to an unprecedented economic crisis comparable to the great depression of 1929-30.

CORPORATE GOVERNANCE AND FINANCIAL CRISIS

The following corporate governance issues emerging from the financial crisis need to be addressed globally and at the level of the MENA region:

(a) The regulatory and supervisory powers of central banks should be extended to investment banking and related non-bank financial intermediation.

(b) Risk management frameworks, processes, and implementation practices require reform in order to redress the shortcomings revealed by the turmoil.

(c) The role and form of regulation of credit rating agencies needs to be addressed.

(d) Executive remuneration and incentive structures need to be linked to long-term performance and risk profile of firms. More disclosure on executive remuneration schemes is required and companies should put their remuneration schemes to shareholder scrutiny and approval.

(e) Corporate governance practices need to be strengthened, in particular by increasing board competence and responsibility. Board members need to have up-to-date knowledge on financial issues and risk management to fulfill their functions and training should be required when necessary. Boards should conduct annual evaluations of their performance and report to shareholders.

(f) Governance and accountability of regulators are equally essential and the region should adopt and implement existing guidelines on good practices as promoted by the Bank for International Settlements and IOSCO.

(g) Islamic finance is a viable and credible complement to conventional financing and has been resilient to date to banking and financial crisis, as a result of equity sharing arrangements and its focus on ethical investment practices. Islamic finance institutions should continue improving their corporate governance by focusing specifically on the disclosure rights of Investment Account Holders, the role of Shari'a boards, their integration with the corporate governance structure of the Islamic Finance Institution. The development and implementation of a harmonized Corporate Governance Framework Regulation and market oversight should fully cover these institutions.

(h) Effective creditor rights and insolvency systems and the development of strong rescue and restructuring frameworks are important for the region. Based on the survey of existing frameworks and practices in the MENA, these should be modernized as a matter of priority to allow effective rescue and restructuring of viable enterprises facing temporary and potential distress. Countries in the region should avail themselves of international guidance, such as the World Bank Principles on Insolvency/ROSC Diagnostic programme and the UNCITRAL Legislative Guide on Insolvency for reforming domestic insolvency systems.

(i) Good corporate governance is important not only for listed companies, but also for State and Family-Owned enterprises. To successfully address potential issues of succession of family-owned enterprises and preservation and protection of wealth, their progressive integration into capital markets should be encouraged.

(j) Investments of Sovereign Wealth Funds (SWFs) taking a long-term perspective can contribute to financial stability. The "Santiago Principles" of the International Working Group (IWG) on SWFs coordinated by the International Monetary Fund provide a welcome contribution to improved transparency and sound management of these funds. They should be followed up by a continuous dialogue and review within the IWG. An open investment climate should be maintained by recipient countries in line with OECD guidance and instruments.

(k) Private equity has recently emerged as a popular alternative asset class in the region supporting regional economic development and small and medium-sized enterprises. Private equity managers should play a critical role in diffusing corporate governance principles and best practices across their portfolio companies in terms of board structures, administrative procedures, disclosure requirements and minority interest protection.

THE EFFECTS OF THE FINANCIAL CRISIS ON CORPORATE GOVERNANCE

The massive realignment that's occurring in the financial markets must be affecting the mechanisms of governance. Our assumptions about governance have to change accordingly, particularly if we're going to impose massive new regulation. Consider these two quotes from this morning:

What's really going on is another effect of the disappearance of dealer and arbitrageur capital. The dealers can't afford to make efficient markets, given their decapitalisation, downsizing, and outright disappearance. That means anomalies sit there for weeks and months, where they would have disappeared in minutes or seconds.

So far this year, 46 outside directors who are CEOs or chief financial officers left the boards of 42 companies in three struggling industries — financial services, retail and residential construction — concludes an analysis for The Wall Street Journal by Corporate Library in Portland, Maine. George Davis, co-head of the global board practice at recruiters Egon Zehnder International, said about a half-dozen CEOs he had been wooing for board seats withdrew their names after investment bank Lehman Brothers Holdings Inc. collapsed in September. Their own boards told them, "Keep your hand on the tiller," the recruiter remembers.

We should keep these effects in mind before we impose regulation that could exacerbate the strains – e.g., short-selling bans that further weaken market efficiency; and imposing additional pressures and monitoring burdens on outside directors.

CONCLUSION

Corporate governance has an important role to play in overcoming the present crisis, restoring confidence for the future and preventing regulatory overkill that would damage the entrepreneurialism needed to secure economic growth. The global authorities should work with market participants to develop enhanced governance practices that will underpin other actions being taken to address the current problems. Most importantly this involves securing and maintaining the rights of shareholders and developing the transparency needed for them to exercise these rights in a responsible, informed and considered way. Properly equipped, shareholders can play an important role in holding companies to account for the way the manage risk and incentivise board directors. However shareholders must also recognise that they should use their share-ownership rights responsibly in the interest of creating long-term value for their beneficiaries. If they do not act responsibly their rights will be at risk. the financial crisis has posed a significant challenge to the global economic system. It is a challenge from which no country is exempt. As policy makers seek to respond to this crisis, a number of difficult questions are being asked of corporate governance frameworks, and their degree of culpability in the crisis. It is important, therefore, that the right lessons are learnt. Recent progress in corporate governance reform around the world must not be reversed by the erroneous view that corporate governance systems as a whole have somehow "failed" during the current financial crisis. Corporate governance is a work in progress, but it is global financial regulation that is a more urgent topic for the attention of regulators and policy makers.

CHAPTER-23

Whistleblower Policy and Corporate Governance

Nikhil Varshney

Amartya Saha

2nd Year, B.A. LLB(Hons.)

Gujarat National Law University

Gandhinagar

INTRODUCTION

The term 'whistleblowing' is a relatively recent entry into the jargon of public and corporate affairs, although it might be apposite to add that the phenomenon itself has been a regular feature plaguing the *avant garde* of corruption and nepotism in the public space. It refers to a phenomenon by which insiders 'go public' with their claims of malpractices by, or within, organisations – which is usually after failing to remedy the matters from inside, and most often with their feet ensconced with great personal risk to their own career, future and personal being. [1] Since the incidence of whistle-blowing in India has witnessed a sharp rising curve, the phenomenon would be dubiously regarded as increasingly important. The question that begs to be answered is what would be responsible for such a sharp upswing? Whether it is due to new-found increased willingness to dissent from the actions of one's employer or because so many organisations engage in palpable, identifiable wrongdoing, the end result seems to be that the media gets in its kitty a sizeable corpus of whistleblowing reports, which it is compelled to routinely produce under pressure for the competitive struggle for readers.

In order to conclusively determine an optimal Whistleblower policy, one must look into all the various aspects of whistleblowing. These include the nature of wrongdoing, the reasons for whistleblowing, the methods employed therein, etc.

NATURE AND CONTEXT OF WRONGDOING

A critical issue is that before one sets about to debate on whether whistleblowing in a particular context is valid, it is critical that they agree on what constitutes wrongdoing. In order to have an integrated perspective, one must take into consideration the different approaches towards understanding whistleblowing from different disciplines. Auditors, in the first case would scrounge for "materiality," in other words whether the wrongdoing is sufficiently hefty and costly to warrant pursuit, while from the legal perspective[2], whistle-blowing is warranted if the whistle blower believes, in good faith, that the ingress has implications for public policy; that is to say, a part of the society is bound to be endangered in way or the other by the organization's actions. This is held as the dominant view, both in the U.S. and Great Britain.[3]

PROCLIVITY TO RESORT TO EXTERNAL CHANNELS

Empirical findings have indicated that basic process of whistle-blowing tends to be the same, irrespective of whether whistle-blowers prefer to use external channels in order to seek protection from retaliation probably reflecting their understanding that they usually lack powe relative to the wrongdoer of the organization.[4] This is not surprising, a since most whistle-blowers who use external channels have also use internal channels, presumably as a first step in reporting the wrongdoing Thus one could argue that internal and external whistle-blowing are relate phenomena.[5]

REASONABLE SUPPOSITION OF SUCCESS

Keenan and McLain[6] go so far as to argue that whistle-blowe ought to believe that the recipient of the information will take action th in all likelihood would terminate the wrongdoing. In other words, we argu that whistle-blowing should have some definite goal, in an attempt t terminate the current wrongdoing or prevent future wrongdoing of a simil type.

PERSONAL CHARACTERISTICS AS PREDICTORS

Empirical investigation of predictors of whistle-blowing suggest th both individual and situational variables play a part, but that situation variables explain more variance in whistle-blower's decisions to act than individual variables.[7]

If we are to list some of the personal variables pertaining to the whistle-blower, they are personality variables, moral behaviour (including values and Public Service Motivation or PSM), demographics, job situation. Although some results conflict, it appears that whistle-blowers are older or have more service, are better educated, and are more likely to be male than inactive observers (i.e., those observers of wrongdoing who do not report it). Whistle-blowers are also more likely than inactive observers to be highly paid, have high job performance, hold supervisory or professional status, and report that they have the role responsibility to report wrongdoing and the knowledge of channels for doing so. In some studies, whistle-blowers are more satisfied and committed than inactive observers and perceive the organization to be more just. To date, empirical evidence has shown that whistle-blowing is more likely in organizations that support whistle-blowing in various ways, but not including incentives for it, and where whistle-blowers report greater value congruence with top managers.

AUXILIARY THEORIES

Three competing perspectives have been proposed to explain why observers of wrongdoing take the step of actually reporting it:

(a) Whistle-blower's moral development

(b) Whistle-blower's loyalty, and

(c) Situational variables and their potential interaction effects with personal variables. Each is considered in turn.

While it is most expected that moral development or behaviour is the crunch point for whistle-blowers, Brewer and Selden argue for the looming influence that Public Service Motivation(PSM) can have among public servants that serve as the litmus test between those who report observed wrongdoing and those who do not. However, moral behaviour can be invigorated by the influence of the workspace culture and socialization of employees.[8]

A second argument would be that whistle-blowers are more or less disloyal than inactive observers. Arguments can fly in all directions, while some might argue that whistle-blowers are less loyal to the employing organization than to the public at large, as they are motivated by a sense of public good, rather than the self-interested ploy of stonewalling on behalf of their organization. Society also influences the perception of greater good in this case: for instance, whistle-blowers in sexual harassment cases receive more support than whistle-blowers in public safety because it is an open secret in the society that the former should be pursued and the norms against this sort of wrongdoing are clearer.[9] In as much as legal changes seem to support this stance, by offering monetary rewards, it is a symbolic sanction for the notion that whistle-blowing is the loyal and ethical behaviour to take, because it places citizen's duties above those of the employee's duties.

HOW TO REIN IN RETALIATION

The relevant part would be what organizations can do to support whistle-blowers and take actions at the right point of time. Encouraging people to bring out problems concerning the functioning and governance of the organization would be critical here and the HR is the primary candidate for the same, as it is a neutral department and is the primary vent for hearing and voicing out the concerns of the employees.

Mandate of the HR and the organization as a whole

- Setting up channels and other mechanisms that not only allow but also promote healthy, open communication are critical to setting up an employee friendly culture.
- Institutionalization- Training of and assigning accountability officers and bringing in such mechanisms such as special telephone numbers would undeniably embolden employees to bring out issues, in seamless anonymity.[10]
- Audit teams – external and internal
- Importance for ethics pronounced in recruitment and training
- Corporate ethics policy

Since most whistle blowers would consider it an overwhelming determinant of their actions in deciding whether to report the wrongdoing, setting up of a clear value system in the organization which is implied in recruitment, training, performance appraisal etc. would help and sustain an open, honest culture.

LEGAL PROVISIONS FOR WHISTLEBLOWING

CURRENT STATUS

Eight murders and twenty serious attacks on Right to Information activists across the country alone this year highlights the grim situation that whistleblowers in our country are in. The brazen murder recently of Amit Jethwa[11] is only one such example. There is the absence of strong legal protection to such whistleblowers, which leads them to vulnerability. Even in cases where there are statutory provisions for such whistleblowing, in all practicality such provisions are ineffective.

For instance, the case of petitioners regards tax evasions. The Income Tax Act[12] clearly wants people to blow the whistle on tax evasion and even provides for a policy of rewarding such whistleblowers. Yet we have seen in cases decided before the CIC how the IT department calumniates such people who lay a claim on the promised reward. They are treated like scum in the arguments placed before the CIC.

The RTI whose whole objective is to impart greater transparency to the system has little meaning if those who seek information under it cannot be protected. The same goes for whistle-blowers inside organisations where there is corruption. That's why legislation with some teeth is needed. In our country marred by endemic corruption, such laws are all the more required.

LAWS ELSEWHERE

The U.S. Whistleblowers Protect Act of 1989 (amended in 1994) protects public interest disclosures by federal employees. An Office of Special Counsel (OSC) was created to aid whistleblowers in the investigation of their disclosures and prevention of retaliatory action against them. It has had only modest success due to a series of hostile judicial rulings undercutting the protection afforded by the Act. More than 40 States have passed similar or even stronger legislation in respect of State employees.

The $591 million Enron fraud and the $3.8 billion WorldCom case spurred the U.S. administration to pass the Sarbanes-Oxley Act, 2002, which provided legal protection to whistleblowers in public companies. Under the Act, retaliation against a corporate whistleblower can invite a jail term of up to 10 years, and a fired employee can be reinstated and receive arrears of salary along with interest and damages. Section 806 of Sarbox, intended to protect employees of public companies from retaliation for reporting financial misdeeds, is administered by the Department of Labor's (DOL) Occupational Safety and Health Administration, which handles similar provisions for 13 other laws.

The UK Public Interest Disclosure Act (1999) and the US Whistleblower Protection Act (1989) provide similar legal protection in their jurisdictional spheres. The U.K.'s Public Interest Disclosure Act of 1998 is a unique piece of legislation providing protection to employees in the public, private and non-profit sectors, including those working outside the U.K. Under the law, employment tribunals have power to 'freeze' a dismissal and make unlimited compensation awards. South Africa has followed the U.K. example in providing protection to employees of all organisations through its Protected Disclosures Act of 2000.

A number of countries such as Australia, Canada, South Korea, Argentina, Russia, Slovakia, Mexico and Nigeria have enacted or are in the process of enacting whistleblowers protection legislation (but only to government employees).

STATUTORY PROVISIONS

In India, a strong whistleblower protection Bill is still needed. The Law Commission had drafted a Bill in its 179th report in this regard called the Public Interest Disclosure (Protection of Informers) Act, 2002. It was "a Bill to encourage disclosure of information relating to the conduct of any public servant involving the commission of any offence under the Prevention of Corruption Act, 1988 or any other law for the time being in force,abuse of official position or mal-administration, to protect the persons making such disclosures and for matters connected therewith or incidental thereto. A Bill to encourage disclosure of information relating to the conduct of any public servant involving the commission of any offence under the Prevention of Corruption Act, 1988 or any other law for the time being in force,abuse of official position or mal-administration, to protect the persons making such disclosures and for matters connected therewith or incidental thereto."[13]

Meanwhile, the Government of India instituted the Public Interest Disclosure and Protection of Informers Resolution (PIDPIR) in 2004. This PIDPIR applies only to the GOI and its instrumentalities. The CVC is the competent authority to receive complaints of this nature. This policy does not apply to officials of the State Governments. The Whistle Blowers (Protection in Public Interest Disclosures) Bill, 2006 was introduced by Mr. Vijay Darda (INC Maharashtra) sitting MP as a Private Member's Bill in the Rajya Sabha in 2006. All these can be considered precursor to the Bill recently introduced in the Lok Sabha.

What is to be noted is that the Private Sector has always remained untouched by any of the above developments, as all of them were aimed at public servants and the public sector.

For Corporate houses, SEBI- the Securities and Exchange Board of India, the market regulator, included guidelines for companies in an amendment to Clause 49 of the listing agreement in August 2003. Under the guidelines:

- An employee wanting to report a fraud or malpractice in his organization has direct access to his company's audit committee and can approach it without seeking the consent of his superiors
- The company will send a circular or other correspondence to all its employees informing them that they enjoy this right; it will also protect them from harassment such as termination of services or otherwise discriminate against them

REFERENCES

1. Adapted from "Theorizing Whistleblowing- Hyper reality and global culture", Nick Perry, Routledge, 1998

2. Brewer, G.A. & Selden, S.C. (1995). Whistleblowers in the federal civil service: New evidence of the public service ethic? Revised version of paper presented at the annual meeting of the American Political Science Association, Chicago, IL.

3. Dandekar, N. (1990). Contrasting consequences: Bringing charges of sexual harassment compared with other cases of whistleblowing. Journal of Business Ethics, 9:151-158.

4. Meindertsma, an expert in whistle blowing litigation suggest that it is important for organizations to formulate a zero-tolerance policy, capacity to respond quickly, grasp the legal implications and provide integrated training to managers and supervisors who might facilitate in drawing up an independent and neutral provision for reporting.

5. Amit Jethwa was an Indian environmentalist and social worker, active in the Gir Forest area near Junagadh, Gujarat. He had filed several court cases against illegal mining in the protected area, naming Bharatiya Janata Party member of parliament, Dinu Solanki as one of the respondents. On 20 July 2010 he was shot dead by two assailants on a motorbike.

6. Income Tax Act, 1961 (43 of 1961)

7. As provided in the Bill in the 179th Law Commission Report dated January 13, 2003.

8. Brewer, G.A. & Selden, S.C. (1995). Whistleblowers in the federal civil service: New evidence of the public service ethic? Revised version of paper presented at the annual meeting of the American Political Science Association, Chicago, IL.

9. Dandekar, N. (1990). Contrasting consequences: Bringing charges of sexual harassment compared with other cases of whistleblowing. Journal of Business Ethics, 9:151-158.

10. Meindertsma, an expert in whistle blowing litigation suggest that it is important for organizations to formulate a zero-tolerance policy, capacity to respond quickly, grasp the legal implications and provide integrated training to managers and supervisors who might facilitate in drawing up an independent and neutral provision for reporting.

11. Amit Jethwa was an Indian environmentalist and social worker, active in the Gir Forest area near Junagadh, Gujarat. He had filed several court cases against illegal mining in the protected area, naming Bharatiya Janata Party member of parliament, Dinu Solanki as one of the respondents. On 20 July 2010 he was shot dead by two assailants on a motorbike.

12. Income Tax Act, 1961 (43 of 1961)

13. As provided in the Bill in the 179th Law Commission Report dated January 13, 2003.

CHAPTER-24

Integrate E-governance in School Education

Dr Neelam Sharma, Lecturer Sociology

G.G.Sr. Sec. School, Goluwala Hanumangarh (Raj.)

INTRODUCTION

E-Governance is the public sector's use of information and communication technologies with the aim of improving information and service delivery, encouraging citizen participation in the decision-making process and making government more accountable, transparent and effective. Today, India is vibrant with innovative ideas in the field of usage of information technology and is keen to see that the fruits of this new technology brings happiness into their life, which can change the plight of millions, who are deprived of knowledge about the strength of science and technology reaching at their door step. Most Indian live in villages and are still living with the curse of poverty and helplessness. So far, to reach them is a Herculean task.

The planning for efficient administration of educational institutions, increasing global communication skill, to achieve the world class standard it is necessary to have improved collaboration and access to informations available in all the parts of the world are possible only by introducing IT in educational sector with e- governance as a security for maintaining standard. The organizational growth and development are possible only by exploiting the facility of IT sector. Implementing e-governance in educational system wll enable effective monitoring of academic standards, says, N.N. sachitanand , a technology writer,

Educational as a sector has remained relatively untouched by e-governance. This is the most distressing. keeping in views above facts, the study was concentrating an integration of e-governance in school education.

METHODOLOGY

The present study was carried out in the Hanumangarh District of Rajasthan. Out of 33 districts, Hanumangarh was choosen purposively, for the convience and easy approach to the place by the researcher. From the Hanumangarh District, Hanumangarh Town and Junction were selected as research areas. From these places highly educated employees i.e. 30 (School principals, lecturers and heads of educational institutions) respondents were selected purposively. The interview method was applied for seeking answers of queries.

RESULTS AND DISCUSSION

Technology is impacting education in revolutionary ways the momentum towards these changes is irreversible when students, parents, teachers, administrators and community care-givers able to communicate electronically about issues critical to education, the traditional process will under go a fundamental transformation, with decisions about a students learning being resolved in new and more effective ways.

In this regard two-third majority (70%) of the respondents were aware about e-governance and rest of them were not.

The use of information technology an increase the broad involvement of citizens in the process of governance at all levels by providing the possibility of on line discussion groups and by enhancing the rapid better service in terms of time, making governance more efficient and more effective stated by more tha n half of the respondents i.e. sixty percent.

Majority of the respondents (83%) favoured that transaction cost can be lowered and government services become more accessible.

During the 1990s the nation established the foundation for extensive use of technology in schools and classrooms . Access in school and libraries to computers and the web is now widespread, on its way to becoming universal. Ninty percent of the respondents were agreed regarding the use of technology in the classroom is more sporadic, and few teachers use technology to offer educational experiences previously unavailable

As we are standing at the door of virtually unlimited opportunity, using technology in school administration enable administrative tasks to be completed more quickly and efficiently and in turn enable school personnel to more actively participate in organization and use data to make more effective educational decisions responded by nearly fifty percent of the respondents.

SUGGESTIVE MEASURES

The holistic nature of public governance enhance governance. Good governance is generally characterized by participation, transparency, accountability and cut down avenues of corruption.

The present education system lacks means of continuous monitoring, meaningful evaluation of the teacher and the taught, constant feed back by concerned administrators, appropriate timely control and correction mechanism, If the quantity and quality of output from our education system have to be substantially improved, then there is no alternative to introducing e-governance in this sphere.

If the education experts system gets linked to other national e-governance systems, then the possibilities are endless.

To provide the opportunities for schools, teachers and students all across the nation, to express and share their creative and academic potential via the internet and creating such an environment by providing facilities for content development and collaboration.

CONCLUSION

Today the IT has become an integral part of life the people in the world. India is one of the world leader in the IT sector and, therefore, the talent in this field is abounds. It is time to applying the skill for the betterment of Indian education system as well. The implementation of e-governance education merely to increase the productivity and exercise greater creativity by reducing the amount of mundane and repetitive work.

CHAPTER-25

CREATING A BETTER INDIA THROUGH CORPORATE GOVERNANCE

Meenu Nagpal

B.Ed., S.D. Mahila B.Ed. College, SGNR.

Usha Nagpal

B,Ed., M.Com.

INTRODUCTION

Corporate governance plays essential role in all walk of life. As you know the common theme has been to harness the power of organization for an agreed purpose rather than letting it get diverted to some other purpose. The principal characteristics of effective corporate governance include transparency which is reflected in the disclosures made by the firm.

Review of Literature several major CSR initiatives have been launched in India since the mid-1990. Among these in the first voluntary code of corporate governance, Desirable Corporate Governance. A code, established in april 1998. This was in initiative by the confederation of indian Industry (CII India's largest industry and business association. A national foundation for corporate governance (NFCG) has been established by the ministry of corporate affairs. This is a partnership with the confederation of Indian Industry CII, the institute of company secretaries of india (ICSI) and the institute of charted accounts of India (ICAI). The purpose of the National foundation for corporate Governance is to promote better Corporate Governance Practices.

What is Corporate Governance

Corporate governance is about promoting corporate fairness, transparency and accountability.

According to confederation of Indian industry's code, "Corporate Governance refers to an economic legal and institutional environment that allows companies to diversity, grow, restructure and exit and do everything necessary to maximize long-term stake holder value."

On an overall basis Corporate Governance is an umbrella term encompassing various, issues arising from interaction among senior management share holder's boards of directors and other corporate stake holders.

HOW CORPORATE GOVERNANCE PLAYS ESSENTIAL ROLE IN ALL WALK OF LIFE?

To answer the above mentioned question.

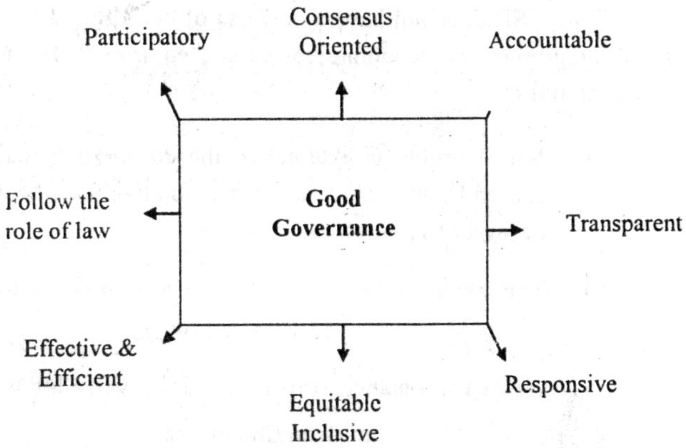

When a good governance embellish with the characteristics of Accountable, transparent, Responsible and follow the rules of law etc. and keep working from dawn to dusk than it spell a golden effect in the streams of share-holder for an employee, for a customer and a local Communities

(1) If we talk about for an employee it can mean fair images, no discrimination etc.

(2) For a shareholder it can mean making responsible and transparent decisions regarding the use of capital.

(3) For customers, it can mean delivery on time, etc.

(4) For local communities and authorities it can mean taking measures to protect the environment from pollution. Thus,

we can head on success from earth to sky, using good governance.

HOW CSR (CORPORATE SOCIAL RESPONSIBILITY) PLAYS VITAL ROLE IN CORPORATE GOVERNANCE.

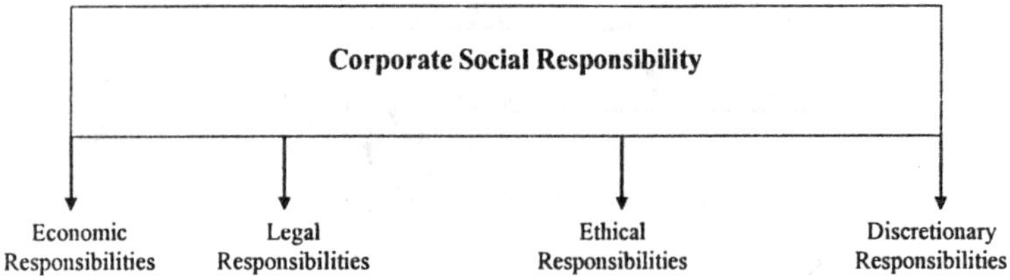

Corporate social responsibility is achieving commercial success in major that honour ethical values and respect people communities and the natural environmental.

While CSR does not have a universe of definition many see it as a way of integrating the economic social and environmental necessity of business activities.

(a) Social problems external to the corporation that were not caused by any direct business action like poverty, drug abuse, decay of the cities and so on.

(b) The external impart of regular economic activities (for example) pollution caused by production.

By Using Corporate Governance, How India has earned a big fortune.

(1) Kumar Mangalam Birla Committee.

(2) Mr. Naresh Cahnder, nine members committee.

(3) S.E.B.I.

Protection of investor interests is strong capital markets studies clear evidence that good governance is rewarded with a higher market valuation

HOW CSR INITIATIVES IN INDIA AND HOW WE CAN CREATE BETTER INDIA THROUGH CORPORATE GOVERNANCE

(1) Indian companies like **Tata & Birla** groups have regularly maintained since several decades a certain level of expenditure

for social and charitable causes some of the observation made by the sachar committee (1978) which was formed by Govt. of India.

(2) Some progressive companies in India like **SAIL, BHEL, Mint & ONGC etc.** (Public Sector)

(3) **TISCO, ITC, BATA** etc. in (Private Sector)

(4) Companies like **Infosys, Wipro, Hero Honda & Bharti Enterprises** have taken various initiative to promote and support the environment edution health, cultural harmony and welfare in the society.

(5) Now a days a **Bread winner** person can purchase a mobile of any company.

CONCLUSION

Responsibility is the commitment of Business to behave ethically and to contribute to sustainable economic development by working with all relevant stake holders to improve their lives in ways that are group for business. The social responsibility becomes an integral part of the wealth creation process which if managed properly should enhance the competitiveness of business and maximize the value of wealth creation to society.

REFERENCES

C.A.R. Devarajan, Law, Ethics and communication, The publication department on behalf of C.A. Noida – 20130,India

M.R. Aggarwal, Management Accounting, Gajender, Aggarwal Governance Publications, S-10 Major Tower, Nehru Bazar

John cover on board leadership selected writing from the creator of the world's most provocative and systematic governance model san francisco : Jossey of – Bass, 2002.

Newspaper – Rajasthan Patrika, Hindustan Times

Magazines – India Today.

CHAPTER-26

Corporate Governance Catering to The Needs of India

Jainender Bhati[1], Monika Vig[1] and Nevadita Sharma[1]

1. Lecturers, Post Graduate Department of Biotechnology, Seth G.L. Bihani S. D. P. G. College, Sriganganagar (Rajasthan) India

INTRODUCTION

Corporate governance is the set of processes, customs, policies, laws, and institutions affecting the way a corporation (or company) is directed, administered or controlled. Corporate governance also includes the relationships among the many stakeholders involved and the goals for which the corporation is governed. The principal stakeholders are the shareholders, the board of directors, executives, employees, customers, creditors, suppliers, and the community at large. Corporate governance is a multi-faceted subject. Because of its role in better management of a company, influence of corporate governance is widespread and no company has escaped from its effect. Now a days Biotechnology industries are also adopting this system. In our further text we have quoted the examples of a few well-known companies of biotechnology sector; the corporate governance strategy followed by them and the role it is playing in raising the economic standard of India. The companies following this concept require many participants. Parties involved in corporate governance include the regulatory body (e.g. the Chief Executive Officer, the board of directors, management, shareholders and Auditors). Other stakeholders who take part include suppliers, employees, creditors, customers and the community at large.

CORPORATE GOVERNANCE IN INDIA

The history of the development of indian corporate laws has been marked by interesting contrasts. At independence, India inherited one of the world's poorest economies but one which had a factory sector accounting for a tenth of the national product; four functioning stock markets with clearly defined rules governing listing, trading and settlements; a well-developed equity culture and a banking system replete with well-developed lending norms and recovery procedures. Unlike most OECD countries, the initiative in India was initially driven by an industry association, the Confederation of Indian Industry in December 1995. CII set up a task force to design a voluntary code of corporate governance. The final draft of this code was widely circulated in 1997. In April 1998, the code was released which was called *Desirable Corporate Governance: A Code.* Between 1998 and 2000, over 25 leading companies including Bajaj Auto, Nicholas Piramal and many others voluntarily followed the code.

WHY GO FOR CORPORATE GOVERNANCE?

Corporate governance has been a central issue in developing countries long before the recent spate of corporate scandals in advanced economies made headlines. Indeed corporate governance and economic development are intrinsically linked. Effective corporate governance systems promote the development of strong financial systems which, in turn, have an unmistakably positive effect on economic growth and poverty reduction. Besides dictating the economic prospects of developing countries, corporate governance plays an integral role in shaping them. It has an indispensable role in attracting foreign investment. Good corporate governance also lowers the cost of capital by reducing risk and creates higher firm valuation thus boosting real investments. Effective corporate governance mechanisms ensure better resource allocation and management raising the return to capital. It can significantly reduce the risk of nation-wide financial crisis. There is a strong inverse relationship between the quality of corporate governance and currency depreciation. The positive effect of corporate governance on different stakeholders ultimately is a strengthened economy, and hence good corporate governance is a tool for socio-economic development.

MANDATORY GUIDELINES AND DISCLOSURES

Constitution of Board of Directors and meetings- One-third of the company's board should consist of independent directors and 50% otherwise directors if the Chairman of the company is a non-executive where 'independent refers to those directors who, apart from receiving director's remuneration do not have any other material pecuniary relationship or transactions with the company, its promoters, management or subsidiaries, which in the view of the board may affect independence of judgment. Board meetings must be held quarterly with a maximum time gap of four months between two successive meetings.

Audit committee and Disclosures to shareholders- Audit committee is a prerequisite with a minimum of three members, all non-executive directors, the majority of whom are independent. Presence of Chairman, who must be an independent director, is must at annual shareholder's meeting to answer audit or finance related questions. At least one member of the committee should be an expert in finance/accounts. It should have minimum of three meetings per year including one before finalization of annual accounts. In addition to balance sheet, P&L and cash flow statement, shareholders must be well-versed with all information concerning the directors. They must have the details of grievances of shareholders, and how quickly these were addressed along with the date, time and venue of annual general meeting of shareholders. They should be informed about dates of book closure and dividend payment, details of shareholding pattern, etc.

CORPORATE GOVERNANCE IN BIOTECHNOLOGY

Corporate governance in biotechnology based industries is catering to the needs of India by providing a boost to the nation's progress and strengthening its economy. Biotechnology deals with any technological application that uses biological systems, living organisms, or derivatives thereof, to make or modify products or processes for specific use. It can be better explained by citing instances of renowned companies and the corporate governance plans they follow:

BIOCON

It is an Indian biotechnology company located in Bangalore which was founded in 1978 by Kiran Mazumdar-Shaw. Biocon has two subsidiaries, Syngene and Clinigene along with world-class research outsourcing capabilities, US FDA-compliant bio-manufacturing facilities and a self-financed Research and Development sector.

Few Board of Directors and revenue- Dr. Neville Bain (Chairman, Institute of Directors, UK; Board Member, Scottish & Newcastle Plc.,

Provexis Ltd), Prof. Charles L. Cooney (Professor, Chemical & Biochemical Engineering, MIT, USA; Director, Genzyme Inc), Dr.Bala S. Manian (Chairman and Founder, Reametrix Inc.; Co-founder, Quantum Dot Corporation and Surromed Corporation, USA), etc. The company's revenue went up from Rs.70 crore in 1998, to Rs.500 crore in 2004 when it went public.[8] In 2009-10, Biocon's net income increased 44% to Rs.24,048 million, crossing the half-billion-dollar mark and profits grew 215% to Rs.2,933 million. The pharmaceutical business exceeded Rs.200,871 million in revenue and the net Research and Development expenditure increased to Rs.917 million, growing 42% over 2008 and up 282% over 2005, while its research services business crossed Rs.2, 807 million.

JOHNSON AND JOHNSON

Johnson & Johnson is a global American pharmaceutical, medical devices and consumer packaged goods manufacturer founded in 1886. Johnson & Johnson consistently ranks at the top of Harris Interactive's National Corporate Reputation Survey, ranking as the world's most respected company by *Barron's Magazine*.

Few Board of Directors and revenue- Mary Sue Coleman (PhD President, University of Michigan), James G. Cullen (Retired President and Chief Operating Officer, Bell Atlantic Corporation), Ian E. L. Davis (Former Worldwide Managing Director of McKinsey & Company), William C. Weldon (Chairman, Board of Directors and CEO), etc. As per 2009 results, worldwide sales were $61.9 billion, a decrease of 2.9% from 2008. Operational results declined 0.3%, and the negative impact of currency was 2.6%. Adjusted earnings were $12.9 billion, and adjusted earnings per share increased 1.8%. Company also generated free cash flow of approximately $14.2 billion. During 2009, Johnson & Johnson delivered a total shareholder return of 11.3%.

NESTLE

It is one of the largest food and nutrition companies in the world, founded and headquartered in Vevey, Switzerland. Nestlé originated in a 1905 merger of the Anglo-Swiss Milk Company, which was established in 1866 by brothers George Page and Charles Page, and the Farine Lactée Henri Nestlé Company, which was founded in 1866 by Henri Nestlé.

Few Board of Directors and revenue- Peter Brabeck (Chairman of the Board of Directors, Nestlé S.A.), Paul Bulcke (CEO, Nestlé S.A.), Werner Bauer (Executive Vice President, Nestlé S.A., Chief Technology Officer, Head of Innovation, Technology, Research & Development), Friz van Dijk (Executive Vice President, Nestlé S.A. Asia, Oceania, Africa, Middle East), Luis Cantarell (Executive Vice President, Nestlé S.A. USA, Canada, Latin America, Caribbean), etc. According to a 2006 global survey of online consumers by the Reputation Institute, Nestlé has a reputation score of 70.4 on a scale of 1–100. In 2009, consolidated sales were CHF 107.6 billion and net profit was CHF 10.43 billion. Research and development investment was CHF 2.02 billion.[12] Sales by activity breakdown: 27% from drinks, 26% from dairy and food products, 18% from ready-prepared dishes and ready-cooked dishes, 12% from chocolate, 11% from pet products, 6% from pharmaceutical products and 2% from baby milks. Sales by geographic area breakdown: 32% from Europe, 31% from Americas (26% from US), 16% from Asia, 21% from rest of the world.

CONCLUSION

With the recent spate of corporate scandals and the subsequent interest in corporate governance, a plethora of corporate governance norms and standards have sprouted around the globe. In developing countries, over a hundred different codes and norms have been identified in recent surveys[13] and their number is steadily increasing. Indian listed companies have been legally mandated to follow fairly strict standards of corporate governance and disclosure which are far stronger than all Asian countries, and in general stronger than most OECD countries. The bigger challenge in India, however, lies in the proper implementation of rules at the ground level. It appears that outside agencies like analysts and stock markets have the most influence on the actions of managers in the leading companies. Nevertheless, with industry organizations and chambers of commerce themselves pushing for an improved corporate governance system, the future of corporate governance in India promises to be distinctly better than the past.

CHAPTER-27

Corporate Governance in Telecom Sector

Vijay Chhabra

Asst. Professor, D.A.V.College, Abohar

Gaurav Vij

Asst. Professor, D.A.V.College, Abohar

In the development of Corporate sector, business has become very Complicated, dynamic Because of Evaluation of company farm of organization, many business opportunities has arisen because of involvement of money of general public , government's responsibility has also increased. It is the prime responsibility of the government that public's money is utilized in the best way and public is provide full information of the company. As a result Government has made many rules and regulation, which company must follow and these regulation are amended time to time according to circumstances. Regulating the corporate sector with help of such regulations is called Corporate Governance.

In India, SEBI (Securities Exchange Board of India) is responsible for issuing code of Corporate Governance by way of Amending to Listing Agreements with Stock Exchanges. This made the Organisations follow regulations and listing rules bearing societal values in nature.

TELECOM SECTOR IN INDIA

Indian telecom industry is one of the fastest growing in the world. Economic reforms initiated in the 1990's, by inviting private services providers resulted in the growth of the industry. Number of Telecom subscribers in India reached 621.28 millions as on 31st march 2010. as per records of TRAI. Indian telecommunication sector, like many other industrial sectors, has gone many phases of growth and diversification and has reached the present position.

The government controlled all aspects of the telecom sectors through the ministry of Post and Telegraphic as monopoly till the mid 80s. Then telephones were looked upon as luxury rather than as an essential means of communication. In 1985, the department of telecommunication (DOT) was established under the ministry of communication and information technology. DOT is the concerned authority for all matters related to Telecom. This department is entrusted with the formulation of development polices, granting licenses for various telecom services, promoting standardization, research and development and allowing private investment in the sector. In 1997, telecom regulatory authority of India (TRAI), an independent regulatory body was established under the telecom regulatory authority of India act 1997.its functions are recommending , regulatory and tariff setting.

SWOT ANALYSIS OF TELECOM SECTOR

There are three types of service providers in Indian Telecom Sector

1. State Owned Companies (BSNL, MTNL)
2. Private Indian Owned Companies (Reliance Infocom, Tata Telecom)
3. Foreign Invested Companies (Idea, Vodafone, Bharti Telecom)

There is strong competition among the service providers and that has caused to bring down tariffs. We may focus on the present position of Indian Telecom Sectorby carrying out SWOT (Strength, Weakness, Opportunities, and Threats) Analysis

STRENGTHS

1. There exists well developed infrastructure for Telecom Industry
2. Call Cost is one of the cheapest in the world.
3. Services of this sector not confined to basic telephone but also extends to internet, broadband , cable.tv., SMS, IPTV, etc.

4. India has one of the fastest growing cellular markets in the world in terms of number of subscribers.

5. Telecom Regulatory Authority of India's performance is transparent.

6. Because of availability of advanced technology at low costs. The companies can also provide services at low cost.

WEAKNESSES

1. The Indian telecom sector has one of the highest levies and taxes imposed on it.

2. The service providers have to incure a huge initial fixed cost. Achieving break even point may prove to be difficult.

3. This sector requires players with huge financial resources in due to infrastructure requirement.

4. Problem of limited Spectrum availability.

5. Broadband Experience is very bad. Net charges in India are very high as compare to US. Slow internet speed frustrates the user.

6. Return on Capital Expenditure is very low because of low tariff and high taxes.

7. The Current Telecom Policy has lowered the entry through barriers, while making it difficult to exit due to three year look in period.

OPPORTUNITIES

1. The Indian Telecom Market is expected to grow massively by 2012.

2. Indian Telecom Industry is growing at a great pace. As a result, India is expected become the manufacturing hub for telephone equipment.

3. Excellent opportunities will be created to domestic and foreign investors in the manufacturing sector due huge demand of telephone equipments.

4. Due to rapid growth of telecom network, there are further opportunities to expand telecom infrastructure and research and development.

5. With the development of rural sector, the telecom sector is likely to see tremendous growth in India's rural and semi-urban areas in the years of overcome.

6. There is a wide scope of telecom service providers with a large untapped potential market due to the country's increasing population and its low teledensity.

7. arrival of 3G will provide a big market for Value Added Services like downloading songs, movies , games Live TV etc.

8. Infrastructure Equipment cost is down to a fraction of what prevailing just a few years ago. Telecom companies can think about Expansion plans.

THREATS

1. Increase in unhealthy competition from different new players. New players offers schemes at loss for attracting customers.

2. Due to rapid growth of cellular phone industry in India, landline providers are facing stiff competition.

3. The Price war is going to hunt all players in the industry.

4. There is a downfall in adjusted gross profit reveals the gloomy financial position of telecom industry.

CODE OF CORPORATE GOVERNANCE

SEBI (Securities Exchange Board of India) is responsible for issuing code of Corporate Governance by way of Amendments to Listing Agreements with Stock Exchanges. LPG policy of government attracts many foreign investors, specially in Telecom sectors. These foreign investors wish to assured that the companies they invest their money will be well managed and expect the law of the land to be open and transparent in functioning. SEBI issue clause 49 of its "Listing Agreement". These codes are as follow:-

1. Board of Directors

According to the guidelines of SEBI, Board of Directors must be a optimum mix of Executives and Non-Executive Directors. At least one third of the directors should be Independent Directors. Independence of a Director is determined on the basis that such Director does not have any material pecuniary relationship with company, its promoters or its management which may affect the independence of the judgment of a Director. The board members possess requisite skiils, experience and expertise required to take decisions, which are in the best interest of the company.

2. Audit Committee

According to Corporate Governance guidelines, an Audit Committee must be formed to audit the management of the company. At least one third of the members of the committee must be independent directors. The company secretary or his/her nominee act as the secretary of the committee. The committee shall meet atleast 4 times a year and time gap between two meetings shall not be more than 4 months. The main functions of the committee is to oversight of the Financial Reporting processes and disclosure that Financial Statements are true and accurate and provide sufficient information.

3. H R Committee

H R Committee must be constituted consisting of Non Executive Directors for the development of Human resources and ensuring that they are getting adequate remuneration. At least one third of the members of the committee must be independent directors. The company secretary or his/ her nominee acts as the secretary of the committee.

The key functions of the committee are attraction and retention strategy for employees, Employees Development Strategy, Compensation and Performance targets for the Chairman and Managing Director (CMD), Joint Managing Director (JMD) and Executive Directors.

4. ESOP, Compensation Committee

ESOP Compensation Committee must be constituted consisting of Non Executive Directors. At least one-third of the members of the committee must be independent directors. The company secretary or his/ her nominee acts as the secretary of the committee.

The key functions of the committee is formulating ESOP plans and deciding future grants. To formulate terms and conditions on present two Employee Stock Option Schemes. This committee is to ensure that employees are getting maximum benefits of ESOP and company is getting the loyalty of the employees.

INVESTOR GRIEVANCE COMMITTEE

Investor Grievance Committee of the Board is constituted in accordance the clause 49 of listing agreement, consisting Executive as well as Non-Executive Directors. The key functions of the committee are formulation of procedures in line with the statutory guidelines to ensure speedy disposal of various requests received from shareholders from time to time. Redressal of shareholders and investors complaints/ grievances e.g. transfer of shares, non receipt of balance sheet, non receipt of dividend etc. to approve, register, refuse to register, transfer/ transmission of shares and other securities. To authorize fixation of common seal of the company. To issue of duplicate share or security and other investor related grievance.

BETTER INDIA THROUGH CORPORATE GOVERNANCE

1. Companies responding positively with corporate Governance enjoy better Goodwill. Several studies in India and abroad have indicated that markets and investors take notice of well managed companies and respond positively with them. Its framework allow sufficient freedom to the board and management to take decisions towards the progress of their companies ant to innovate. Bharti Airtel is welcomed by investors because of freedom to management.

2. Corporate Governance also emphasis is developing and maintaining Human Resources. Compaines complies with corporate Governance has a better work force. In telecom sector, where technical staff is of great importance,corporate governance ensure of retaintion of skilled technical staff and also ensure of retaintion of skilled technical staff and also ensure its development.

3. The creditability offered by good corporate governance procedures also helps to maintain the confidence of investors ,both foreign and domestic, to attract more long term capital.

In telecom sector, where huge in vestment is required for infrastructure and development, compliance with corporate Governance become more important.

4. A corporation is a congregation of various stakeholders like customers, employees, investors, vendors,partners, government and society. Its growth requires the co-opretion of all the stakeholders. Hence it is imperative for a corporation to be fair and transparent to all its transections by following best governance practices.

5. Good governance system demonstrated by adoption of good corporate governance practices, built confidence amongst stakeholders as well as prospective stakeholders. Investors are willing to pay higher prices to corporates accepting norms of corporate governance. Specially in Telecom Sector where there is always a good market and need strong infrastructure, gaining the confidence of stakeholders is of atmost importance.

6. Effective Governance reduces perceived risks which reduces the cost of capital and enables the directors to take quick and better decisions, which ultimately improves the bottom line of the corporates. Investment of Bharti Airtel and BSNL are treated as Blue Chip Investment because of low perceived risks.

7. Adaptation of good corporate governance practices provide long term sustenance and strengthens Stakeholders' relationship.

CHAPTER-28

BIOTECHNOLOGY: A SCIENCE FOR CREATING BETTER INDIA

Charan Singh, Nidhi Mehrotra

Department of Biotechnology S.D. P.G. College Sri Ganganagar

INTRODUCTION

Any technique that use leaving organism or a part of living organism to make or modify products to improve plants, animals to process or to develop microorganisms for various uses and recent development in molecular biology and their commercial applications is known as Biotechnology it includes micro propagation formation of eco-friendly products, cell and tissue culture technique as well as recombinant DNA technology which has opened avenues for existing possibilities and a new era as research and development.

The 21st century will witness application of biotechnology for increasing and diversifying food production. The need for new and innovative research leading to increase in agricultural productivity has been fully recognised and the pace is steadily increasing worldwide, and, is especially important for the developing countries.

The term biotechnology came into prominence with the application of the knowledge and techniques of molecular biology. However, over the years, a wider definition of biotechnology as given by the office of the Technology Assessment of the US Congress is accepted. It defines biotechnology as any technique that uses living organisms or substances from those organisms to make or modify a product, to improve plants or animals or to develop micro-organisms for specific uses.

INFRASTRUCTURE AND PERFORMANCE

Biotechnology is one of the fastest growing sector in India and elsewhere. This emerging filed is going to take a leap forward in the next five years.

Biotech sector may earn upto rupee five million dollars having job opportunities for 15 lakh qualified biotechnologists in several fields such as agriculture, medicine environment, bioinformatics, industries, food processing units pharmaceuticals dairy and veterinary biodiversity conservation, neuroscience, marine, informatics, teaching training and entreprenship development in both government and private sectors. Modern science and technology along with research and discoveries are comfortable journeys from one revolution to the other, where the connectional technology blended with the new scientific discoveries and their fusion has been creating wonders Biotechnology undoubtedly holds great promise for the creating better future of India genetic engineering, genomics, Bio composting, Bio medical engineering, Biosensors and bioinformatics, etc.

Stupendous strides have been made in making the earthy a better place to live in, through human interference. Biotechnology innovations have been used as the means to relegate Precarious Predicaments. The firmament of biotechnology has broadened to envelope the entire earth lings in its fold. Advances in biotechnology have created a revolution in life sciences including genetics and profoundly changes its face worldwide. Applications of biotechnology in human and animal health, agriculture, biomass, green cover, environmental protection and non-conventional energy sources are of great significance. The future of mankind depends on developing the basic and applied biotechnology suited to the needs of humanity.

Biotechnology has provided a great opportunity for direct manipulation of gene structure, function and expression to serve the humanity and meet the growing demand of the millions. Several policy initiatives have been take to great excellent human resource base, build up the requisite infrastructure, identify & set up centers of excellence, support R&D & manufacturing activities to meet the demands of future and growing population.

All basic economic needs can be fulfilled by application of biotechnology as once imagined by the scientist, A wishful thing has transformed itself to a glaring reality. Globalization is leading to intense completion with consequent higher stress levels in work places, healthcare sector is one such with a large share of global investment. The development of new generation drugs, their targeting, recombinant vaccines and newer diagnostic tools are same of the possibilities. The development of vaccines for important diseases affecting livestock and diagnostic kits for farm animal health care are among several activities in this sector. All the antibiotics come under biotech banner. The chemicals we use are being replaced by biochemical or other alternative biotech products. It will provide new ways of influencing raw material processing. Most of future medicines will be of biotech origin. Handling humanly impossible gene sequence have now become possible, claming and designer babies may become usual features in future. In the filed of scribiotechnology, the DBT has initiated a program in the genetic enhancement of mulberry and non-mulberry silkworm races and the host (mulberry) plants. The program includes development of immune-diagnostics tools for detection of pathogens, bio control measures for major pests and diseases of silkworm and new races of silkworm considerable efforts have been put in to ensure food and nutritional security through biotechnology R&D, under food biotech initiatives, technologies for scale-up of low-cast nutrient food have been standardized.

CONCLUSION

There is great scope of starting biotechnology based business and industries in these fast changing time sustainable development at the globe is only possible with green scientific and technological breakthrough which can be brought by developing and adopting biotechnological tools and technique food and nutritional security, industrial development, waste management, health care, climate change management are major areas which have the potential of establishing useful and profitable enterprises. Biotechnologist have the potential to make the nation better and leader of the globe.

CHAPTER-29

Commercial Plant Tissue Culture for Creating Better India

Bhawna Nain, Priyanka Bedi, Dr. Anil Kumar Soni

Department of Biotechnology, S.D. P.G. College Sri Ganganagar

INTRODUCTION

World population is expected to touch the 8 billion mark by 2015 from 6.2 billion in, 2000, and this alarming projected increase has brought tremendous pressure on increasing, food production. At least three-fourth of the required increase ought to result from intensified ; cultural practices on the existing cultivable land. As the traditional methods of breeding, have almost reached a stagnation point in terms of productivity, they obviously need to be supplemented by biotechnological methods.

The term biotechnology came into prominence with the application of the knowledge and techniques of molecular biology. However, over the years, a wider definition of biotechnology as given by the office of the Technology Assessment of the US Congress is accepted. It defines biotechnology as any technique that uses living organisms or substances from those organisms to make or modify a product, to improve plants or animals or to develop micro-organisms for specific uses.

THE INDIAN SCENARIO

The most popular and widely commercialized application of plant biotechnology the world over is, perhaps, micropropagation. Global biotech business is estimated at around 150 billion US dollars. About 50-60% of this constitutes agribusiness. Annual demand of tissue-cultured products constitutes about 10% of the total, i.e., 15 million US dollars. The annual growth rate is estimated to be around 15%.

Advances made in commercialization of plant tissue culture and acceptance of tissue-cultured plantlets by commercial nursery trade globally led to the growth of this industry. However, the high cost of production in the developed countries of Europe and North America has acted as a deterrent to further expansion. Needless to say, India, among the developing nations, is positioned advantageously to exploit the market.

The Government of India has identified micropropagation of plants as an industrial activity under the I (D& R) Act of 1951 made effective in 1991 and several incentives are being offered (Govil & Gupta 1997)

Thus, liberalized industrial licensing policy, coupled with simplified procedures and incentives provided by the Government of India, would go a long way in helping Indian tissue culture industries to carry out profitable business in the global market and bring in foreign exchange. Being pollution-free and intensely labour-oriented, the micropropagation industry is particularly well suited for India as it will also solve our unemployment problems to some extent. It has unique advantage of offering entry to young entrepreneurs and can generate gainful employment for housewives. The industry adds to the aesthetic value and will give a boost to ancillary industries such as transportation, packing and airlines.

ROLE OF BIOTECHNOLOGY

The major role of biotechnology lies in the genetic improvement of cultivars for increasing productivity, improved quality and in enhancing their resistance to pests and diseases. Micropropagation using tissue culture methods provides unique opportunities to rapidly multiply the elite types as a superior alternative to vegetatively propagated plants. Micropropagation techniques have been commercialized globally, especially in nations with industrialized agriculture. It is reported that over 800 commercial companies are engaged in such activities all over the world and their number is increasing. Annual production is approximately 513 million plantlets. In India, approximately 76 companies have plans for selling tissue cultured plants and more than a thirty are already in the market with their products. Annual production is estimated at 25 million plantlets. Tissue culture planting materials of banana, strawberries, grapes, papaya, cardamom and ornamental flowers such as gerbera, carnation and orchids are available besides a number of foliage ornamentals.

Great strides have been promised for humankind through the intervention of biotechnology in horticulture. Biotechnological tools would ensure improvement in productivity, decrease our dependence on pesticides and other potentially harmful chemicals by genetically redesigning plants to offer resistance to natural and man-made enemies.

CONCLUSION

India is a country rich in natural resources and precious biodiversity. The diverse agroclimatic zones have the potential to produce a wide variety of agricultural and commercially valuable crops. We have a wide germplasm of rare ornamental and medicinal species. In general, India has many advantages over other countries to meaningfully use the latest biotechnological tools for micropropagatiori and improvement of our horticultural crops.

Managing biotechnology companies involves directing and controlling the interface between basic research and development, manufacturing and marketing. Several factors set biotechnology apart. It is technology driven and multidisciplinary in nature.

A concerted effort in R&D aimed at commercialization of the products and processes utilising the existing natural resources of the country would provide economic benefit not only to the resource poor communities, but would also help the nation to compete in the international market. Biotechnology needs to be harnessed to convert the biological wealth of the country into economic wealth resulting in sustainable development. This would be our aim as we move into the next millennium.

CHAPTER-30

Sports Management and Governance of Sports

Bhawani Singh Bera, Naseeb Singh and Mandeep Singh

Department of Physical Education

Seth G.L. Bihani S.D.P.G. College, Sri Ganganagar (Rajasthan)

**Department of Physical Education*
S.G.N. Khalsa P.G.College, Sri Ganganagar (Rajasthan) India

INTRODUCTION

Organizational governance is concerned with the exercise of power within organizations and provides the system by which the elements of organizations are controlled and directed. Governance is necessary for all groups, nation, states, corporate entities, societies, associations and sport organizations to function properly and effectively. An organizational governance system not only provides a framework in which the business of organizations are directed and controlled but also 'helps to provide a degree of confidence that is necessary for the proper functioning of a market economy' (Organization for Economic Cooperation and Development, 2004). Governance deals with issues of policy and direction for the enhancement of organizational performance rather than day-to-day operational management decision-making. The importance of governance and its implied influence on organizational performance was highlighted by Tricker (1984) when he noted, 'if management is about running business, governance is about seeing that it is run properly'. The Australian Sports Commission (ASC) deûnes governance as, 'the structures and processes used by an organization to develop its strategic goals and direction, monitor its performance against these goals and ensure that its board acts in the best interests of the members' (ASC, 2004).

Good organizational governance should ensure that the board and management seek to deliver outcomes for the beneût of the organization and its members and that the means used to attain these outcomes are effectively monitored. A 1997 report to the Australian Standing Committee on Recreation and Sport (SCORS) identiûed a major concern among the sporting community, which was the 'perceived lack of effectiveness at board and council level in national and state sporting organizations' (SCORS Working Party on Management Improvement, 1997). Major sport agencies in the UK, New Zealand and Canada have also identiûed improving governance of sport organizations as a strategic priority. Failures in the governance of national sport organizations such as the Australian Soccer Association and Athletics Australia in 2003 and 2004 respectively, together with reviews of professional sport governance such as those conducted by the Football Governance Research Centre at the University of London, continue to highlight the importance of developing and implementing sound governance practices in both amateur and professional sport organizations.

GOVERNANCE: A USEFUL TOOL

One of the aims of this resource guide is to flag up a range of uses of the governance concept drawn from the existing literature, which may contribute to the study of sport policy, sports management and related areas. These are governance as steering, governance as networks and good governance. These applications provide three different meanings of governance - governance as a strategy, as an analytical tool and as a normative device.

To elaborate, the notion of governance as steering is broadly about strategic direction. It recognizes that the responsibility of modern government is changing - increasingly involving 'steering' rather than 'rowing' so that the role of government is to facilitate and co-ordinate rather than direct and control. The emphasis on steering suggests dispersal rather than a concentration of power, with governments involving a greater number of policy actors and interests both inside and outside government.

The second conception - governance as networks - suggests partnership, cooperation and collaboration as an alternative to hierarchical authority. The network approach focuses on relations between organizations, thereby implying that policy emerges as a result of bargaining between organizations rather than as a result of authoritative decision-making by a single individual or institution. Its primary use then, is that of an analytical tool to explore the interaction between the organizations involved in the formation of policy.

The third application of governance is that of good governance, which refers to the ethical standards underpinning the relationships, methods and instruments of relationships between organizations. While there may be no best way of achieving good governance, the term is essentially normative, that is, founded on a number of common elements, such as accountability, transparency, stakeholder participation and a clear legal and ethical framework. Broken down, the chief questions raised by the three-pronged conception of governance are:

- Can the three uses of the concept of governance be defined and applied as analytical tools?
- To what extent can we talk about sport policy as being 'steered'?
- Is it possible to identify a policy community or network for sport and how does a governance network differ?
- How useful are the interrelated terms of good governance and corporate governance in understanding relations between sports governing bodies and primary and secondary stakeholders?

GOVERNANCE AND SPORT

Despite the burgeoning literature on governance, relatively little research has been undertaken which examines the term in relation to the organization, administration and management of sports organizations. The ways in which sport is governed and, in particular, failures of governance have, however, brought the issue into critical focus. Such interest has been fostered by misgivings about strategic directions and manifold complications involved in the decision-making process. An example of this is the confusion surrounding the proposals for the redevelopment of Wembley Stadium, the lack of infrastructure investment for Picketts Lock, and the failed bid for the 2006 FIFA World Cup Finals.

Rising interest in sports governance has also been cultivated by concerns about the management of amateur sport organizations in light of a significant shift from volunteer-run 'kitchen table operations' to organizations with professional managers attempting to function in a highly rational, bureaucratic manner. It has also been stimulated by appeals for greater organizational effectiveness and for more controls on potential abuse of executive power, and by demands for more effective stakeholder representation and far greater accountability of board members.

Within international sports federations (IFs) and national governing bodies of sport (NGBs) the notion of stake holding has raised a number of pertinent questions concerning how the interests of groups such as athletes, volunteers, and supporters are articulated. Closely related to this is the emergence of issue centered groups that contribute to a debate about the future governance of various sports. An example of this is the campaign led and orchestrated by Manchester United Supporters Trust (MUST) to secure a meaningful ownership stake in their football club in light of the takeover of Manchester United by the Glazer family. The latter also led to the formation of FC United of Manchester (FCUM) a semi-professional football club set up by supporters, disaffected by the Glazer takeover. The formation of MUST and FCUM can be located within a wider attempt by supporters to try and influence the running of the game - raising questions of regulation and control but also of participation and exclusion, of the organization and exercise of power in football. There are now over one hundred supporter trusts across England, Wales and Scotland, formed as democratic, transparent, representative bodies for fans at their clubs and whose aim is to ensure supporter

CHAPTER-31

Codes of Conduct as an Instrument of Corporate Governance – A Study of MNC's

Ashish Kumar Sharma, Ashok Singh Rathore and Anjali Sharma

INTRODUCTION

The 1990s saw a proliferation of corporate codes of conduct and an increased emphasis on Corporate Social Responsibility (CSR). The integration of international markets for goods and finance, the massive privatization of state assets and, in developing countries, the shift to trade liberalization and export promotion, all served to redefine the economic role of the government. The change in the role of the government and the increased reliance on market forces has not been unproblematic, however. Capitalism has always required the establishment of certain "rules of the game" in order to avoid being subject to over-regulation by the government. Yet both the ideological shifts of the 1980s, and the globalization of economic activity, meant that nation states have been less willing and less able, to perform many of these regulatory functions in recent years.

It is in this context that a new emphasis has been placed on self-regulation and the social responsibility of business. Corporate codes of conduct are a manifestation of this in the areas of labor and environmental standards, and of human rights. Instead of the social and environmental impacts of big business being seen as issues primarily for governments to deal with, they are now regarded as matters of corporate responsibility for which companies themselves, or their trade associations, should set standards.

DEVELOPMENT OF CODES OF CONDUCT

A code of conduct is in the nature of a 'private law' or a 'promise voluntarily made' whereby an institution makes a public commitment to certain standards of conduct. The nature of voluntariness and, by implication, the flexibility afforded to a corporation make it imperative that the codes pertain to issues that are important both to the Multinational Corporation (MNC) and to the individuals and groups that are affected by their operations.

The corporate codes of conduct developed in the 1990s and adopted by several MNCs were preceded by international codes of conduct in the 1970s. However, the efforts at international regulation of MNCs during the 1970s and 1980s did not meet with much success. The two major international codes to survive from the 1970s were those of Organization for Economic Cooperation and Development (OECD) and the International Labor Organization (ILO). Compliance to both these codes was voluntary.

The early 1990s witnessed the second wave of corporate codes. In 1992, Levi Strauss adopted its code, 'Business Partner Terms of Engagement'. A number of other clothing manufacturers and retailers in the United States followed suit. By the mid-1990s, the fashion for codes had spread to Europe. Again clothing manufacturers were among the first to adopt codes covering labour conditions. These included Otto Versand in Germany and the Pentland Group in the United Kingdom.

RATIONALE FOR ADOPTING CODES OF CONDUCT

Large corporations tend to be the target of Non-Governmental Organization (NGO) campaigners and have taken a lead in adopting codes of conduct. In some cases, they are large supermarket chains such as Sainsbury and Tesco, or retailers such as C&A in Europe and Wal-Mart and Sears in the United States. In others, they are sellers of branded products such as Levi Strauss in clothing and Nike and Reebok in sports footwear. They may have some domestic production but mostly rely on foreign contractors to manufacture their products. Other large companies, which adopted codes, are more directly involved in foreign production as in the case of oil or mining companies such as Shell, BP Amoco and Rio Tinto-Zinc.

These companies have a high public profile and tend to rely heavily on their corporate image. Hence they have been particularly vulnerable to negative publicity and NGO campaigns. It is quite common for a code to be adopted by such companies after the occurrence of some major event that has caused negative publicity for the company concerned. Shell, for example, incorporated human rights into its code of conduct as a result of the criticism of its Nigerian operations following the execution of Ken Saro-Wiwa.

In some cases, the adoption of ethical principles can increase the commitment of company staff. If a corporation relies heavily on attracting motivated personnel, such an approach can help raise productivity and improve overall performance. The British organization, Investors in People (IIP) claims that high productivity requires committed staff, which in return requires a company to earn that commitment. The Body Shop is often quoted as an example of a company that has used such a strategy successfully.

In developing countries, CSR is not generally seen as being very high on the business agenda. For many, the demand for codes of conduct has been externally driven. Therefore, firms in developing countries, which produce for developed country markets, have a somewhat ambivalent attitude toward codes of conduct. Since their customers need them to meet the required labour or environmental standards, they comply mainly to keep their markets. On the other hand, they are more likely to treat the adoption of codes as mere increases in costs. This leads to a situation in which the sub-contractors are more likely to favour relatively weak codes of conduct, which will meet the requirements of their customers without imposing undue costs.

TYPES OF CODES OF CONDUCT

Codes of conduct come in a variety of different forms, and this can be a cause of some confusion. While it is possible to classify codes in a number of ways, here five main types of codes are identified.

- Company Codes: These codes are adopted unilaterally by companies. They can relate to their own operations. For example, Disney's, "Code of Conduct for Manufacturers," or Mattel's, "Mattel Independent Monitoring Council for Global Manufacturing Principles (MIMCO)."

- Trade Association Codes: These codes are adopted by a group of firms in a particular industry. They also tend to be a unilateral measure adopted by the firms. They can be adopted by associations of firms based in developed countries, e.g., British Toy and Hobby Association code, or by developing country firms, e.g., Bangladesh Garments Manufacturers and Exporters Association (BGMEA) code.

- Multi-stakeholder Codes: These codes are based on negotiations between several stakeholders, including firms, NGOs and/or trade unions. Governments may also be involved in the development of such codes. E.g., The UK's Ethical Trade Initiative (ETI) Base Code.

- Model Codes: These codes are designed to provide a benchmark with respect to codes of conduct. Although they are not generally applied in practice, they serve as a model which companies or trade associations could follow. E.g., the International Confederation's Free Trade Union's (ICFTU's) Basic Code of Conduct covering Labour Practices.

- Inter-governmental Codes: These are negotiated at an international level and are agreed upon by national governments. They date back to the 1970s when both the OECD's Guidelines for Multinational Enterprises and the ILO's Tripartite Declaration of Principles Concerning Multinational Enterprises were adopted.

EVALUATION OF CORPORATE CODES OF CONDUCT

Although the increased adoption of corporate codes of conduct in the 1990s represents a significant new development, the question of what they really represent remains to be answered. There are a number of limitations to codes of conduct. While some of these are practical limitations which refer to the effectiveness of their implementation, others refer to the nature of corporate codes.

Many company codes tend to be general statements of business ethics with no specifics with regard to their implementation. As far as model codes are concerned, they are, by their very nature, intended as examples of best practice. Some codes have limited takers. The

International Federation of Football Associations Code of Labour Practices has not yet been adopted by any firm, and relatively few have so far been accredited with SA8000. Codes also tend to be taken up by industry leaders.

With respect to the scope of most corporate codes, many do not even cover the ILO core labour standards, especially those on freedom of association and collective bargaining. Apart from this, there is a tendency for codes to focus on particular issues regarded as highly damaging for companies to be associated with, such as the usage of child labour in some countries. This does not necessarily coincide with the concerns of other stakeholders, particularly those in the developing countries.

Some industry observers go to the extent of pointing out the potential dangers associated with the growth of codes of conduct. Codes may come to be seen as something more than they really are. The current state of corporate codes of conduct reveals that codes are presented as public statements of lofty corporate intent and purpose, but are short on specific content. CSR proponents confer on organizations which are not politically accountable, both businesses and NGOs, for powers and responsibilities that do not rightly belong to them.

Notwithstanding the limitations of codes, they can and have generated positive benefits for stakeholders. Gap Inc. agreed to continue to source from the Mandarin factory in El Salvador, following improvements in working conditions. Concrete improvements have also been reported in Nike's factories in Vietnam, including the reduction of hazardous chemicals and improvements in ventilation and safety conditions.

Another important advancement associated with codes of conduct is the acceptance by firms of responsibility for the activities of their suppliers as well as their own subsidiaries. This concept of extended responsibility makes it more difficult for firms to externalize costs, whether social or environmental, and then claim that they themselves are behaving ethically or in an environmentally friendly way.

CONCLUSION

Everybody is optimistic about the potential of codes of conduct to enable companies to fulfil a wide range of roles - economic, social, and environmental. The problem is not with the concept of voluntary codes, which is a highly desirable concept because it offers a flexible approach to resolving issues that have not been satisfactorily resolved through existing legal and other socio-political mechanisms, but lies largely with the MNCs' unwillingness to use this approach in a substantive and meaningful manner.

In conclusion, the economic and socio-political problems of the 21st century will be largely connected with the interdependent nature of the world and its people, a world in which individual goodwill is not possible without thought for the common good. It makes good business sense to relate moral principles with institutional behaviour, political power with economic influence, and environmental values with material rewards.

CHAPTER-32

Governance of Communicable Diseases to Create A Better India: Case Study – Aids

Arun Vats, Antaryami Kaushik and Seema Sharma

Post Graduate Department of Botany
Seth G. L. Bihani S.d. (Pg) College, Sriganganagar (Rajasthan)

INTRODUCTION

AIDS stands for Acquired Immune Deficiency Syndrome. HIV is the virus that causes AIDS.

H – Human: because this virus can only infect human beings.

I – Immuno-deficiency: because the effect of the virus is to create a deficiency, a failure to work properly, within the body's immune system.

V – Virus: because this organism is a virus, which means one of its characteristics is that it is incapable of reproducing by itself. It reproduces by taking over the machinery of the human cell.

A – Acquired: because its affects the body's immune system, the part of the body which usually works to fight off germs such as bacteria and viruses.

I – Immune: because it affects the body's immune system, the part of the body which usually works to fight off germs such as bacteria and viruses.

D – Deficiency: because it makes the immune system deficient (makes it not work properly)

S – Syndrome: because some with AIDS may experience a wide range of different diseases and opportunistic infections.

Having a sexually transmitted disease (STD) can increase a person's risk of becoming infected with HIV, whether or not that STD causes lesions or breaks in the skin. If the STD infection causes irritation of the skin, breaks or sores may make it easier for HIV to enter the body during sexual contact. Even an STD that causes no breaks or sores can stimulate an immune response in the genital area that can make HIV transmission more likely. (Source: Centers for Disease Control – CDC)

The most recent presentation on the origin of HIV was presented at the 6th Conference on Retroviruses and Opportunitistic Infections (Chicago, January: 1999). At that conference, research was presented that suggested that HIV had "Crossed over" into the human population from a particular species of Chimpanzee, probably through blood contact that occurred during hunting and field dressing of animals. The CDC states that the findings presented at this conference provide the strongest evidence to date that HIV – 1 originated in non-human primates. The research findings were featured in the February 4, 1999 issue of the journal, Nature.

SYMPTOMS OF HIV AND AIDS

Primary HIV infection is the first stage of HIV disease, when the virus first establishes itself in the body. Some researchers use the term acute HIV infection to describe the period of time between when a person is first infected with HIV and when antibodies against the virus are produced by the body (usually 6-12 weeks).

Some people newly infected with HIV will experience some "flu-like" symptoms. These symptoms, which usually last no more than a few days, might include fevers, chills, night sweats and rashes (not cold-like symptoms). Other people either do not experience "acute infection", or have symptoms so mild that they may not notice them.

Given the general character of the symptoms of acute infection, they can easily have causes other than HIV, such as a flu infection. For example, if you had some risk for HIV a few days ago and are now experiencing flu-like symptoms, it might be possible that HIV is responsible for the symptoms, but it is also possible that you have some other viral infection.

There are no common symptoms for individuals diagnosed with AIDS. When immune system damage is more severe, people may experience opportunistic infections (called opportunistic because they are caused by organisms which cannot induce disease in people with normal immune systems, but take the "opportunity" to flourish in people with HIV). Most of these more severe infections, diseases and symptoms fall under the Centers for Disease Control's definition of full-blown "AIDS". The median time to receive an AIDS diagnosis among those infected with HIV is 7-10 years.

HOW LONG AFTER A POSSIBLE EXPOSURE SHOULD I BE TESTED FOR HIV

The time if takes for a person who has been infected with HIV to seroconvert (test positive) for HIV antibodies is commonly called the "Window Period".

The California office of AIDS, published in 1998, says about the window period: "When a person is infected with the HIV virus, statistics show that 95-97% of all infected individuals develop antibodies within 12 weeks (3-months).

The National CDC has said that in some rare cases, it may take up to six months for one to seroconvert (test positive). At this point the results would be 99.9% accurate.

LITERATURE REVIEW

We know that the virus has existed in the United States, Haiti and Africa since at least 1977-78. In 1979. Rare types of pneumonia, cancer and other illnesses were being reported by doctors in Los Angeles and New York. The common thread was that these conditions were not usually found in person with healthy immune systems.

In 1982 the Centres for Disease Control and Prevention (CDC) officially named the condition AIDS (Acquired Immune Deficiency Syndrome). In 1984 the virus responsible for weakening the immune system was identified as HIV (Human Immunodeficiency Virus).

Worldwide: UNAIDS estimates that as of December 2000, there were an estimated 36.1 million people living with HIV/AIDS (34.7 million adults and 1.4 million children under 15). Since the epidemic began, an estimated 21.8 million people have died of AIDS (17.5 million adults and 4.3 million children under 15)

In the United States: According to the Centers for Disease Control and Prevention (CDC), there are between 800,000 and 900,000 people living with HIV. Through December 2010, a total of 884,864 cases of AIDS have been reported to the CDC; of this number, 58% have died.

CONTROLLING THROUGH CORPORATE GOVERNANCE

India stands at a critical junction of HIV pandemic. Controlling spread of HIV is critical. Ignoring this will lead millions of Indians in grip of this pandemic. Ever since HIV/AIDS was acknowledged as a problem, the strategies to address the issue have focused on prevention, treatment and research. This paper discusses the treatment aspect. With currently available antiretroviral agents, eradication of HIV infection is not likely. The aim of treatment is thus to prolong and improve the quality of life by maintaining maximal suppression of virus replication for as long as possible. Brazil has shown how to implement antiretroviral therapy programme. India has embarked upon an ambitious programmed to introduce antiretroviral therapy in six high prevalent states and the national capital. The paper discusses the technical, management and financing challenge in implementing this intervention.

The development of antiretroviral therapy has given a new hope for people living with acquired immuno deficiency syndrome. In the face of increased disease burden due to HIV the global and political commitment towards controlling the pandemic has received renewed thrust in recent times. The Government of India has initiated antiretroviral treatment as a part of national public health programme in the six high-prevalence states. The aim of the paper is to provide the programme planners and other stakeholders, information about the impact of initiating antiretroviral therapy programme in the country. The paper discusses the global commitment towards fighting the disease in the light of the development in affordability and accessibility of antiretroviral drugs therapy. The paper highlights the importance of infrastructure and logistic requirement for developing a comprehensive treatment programme for the affected population in India. Finally, the paper has drawn broad financial implications of the antiretroviral therapy under different treatment scenarios. The estimated financial requirement for treatment vary from Rs. 92 crore per annum if focusing on 400,000 HIV/AIDS cases to identify patients requiring ARV Therapy to 1008 crore per annum if all 4 million patients are screened for coverage. Against this NACO has allocated total of Rs. 113 crore for treatment part of the proposed intervention. Even under the most conservative estimate achieving the treatment target in India with the proposed programme budget will be a Challenging task.

CHAPTER-33

Creating A Better India Through Hydroponics in Corporate Governance

Dr. Ajay Kumar Sharma

Lecture Botany Department
Seth G. L. Bihani S.D. P.G. College, Sri Ganganagar

INTRODUCTION

Hydroponics (From the Greek words hydro, water and ponos, labor) is a method of growing plants using mineral nutrient solutions, in water, without soil. Terrestrial plants may be grown with their roots in the mineral nutrient solution only or in an inert medium, such as perlite, gravel, mineral wool, or coconut husk.

REVIEW OF LITERATURE

The earliest published work on growing terrestrial plants without soil was the 1627 book, Sylva Sylvarum by Sir Francis Bacon, printed a year after his death. Water culture became a popular research technique after that. In 1699, John Woodward published his water culture experiments with spearmint. He found that plants in less pure water sources grew better than plants in distilled water. By 1842 a list of nine elements believed to be essential to plant growth had been made out, and the discoveries of the German botanists, Julius von Sachs and Wilhelm Knop, in the years 1859-65, resulted in a development of the technique of soilless cultivation. Growth of terrestrial plants without soil in mineral nutrient solutions was called solution culture. It quickly became a standard research and teaching technique and is still widely used today. Solution culture is now considered a type of hydroponics where there is no inert medium.

In 1929, Professor William Frederick Gericke of the University of California at Berkeley began publicly promoting that solution culture be used for agricultural crop production. He first termed it aquaculture but later found that aquaculture was already applied to culture of aquatic organisms.

METHODOLOGY

The two main types of hydroponics are solution culture and medium culture. Solution culture does not use a solid medium for the roots, just the nutrient solution. The three main types of solution culture are static solution culture, continuous flow solution culture and aeroponics.

In static solution culture, plants are grown in containers of nutrient solution, such as glass Mason jars (typically in-home applications), plastic buckets, tubs or tanks. The solution is usually gently aerated but may be unaerated. If unaerated, the solution level is kept low enough that enough roots are above the solution so they get adequate oxygen. A hole is cut in the lid of the reservoir for each plant. There can be one to many plants per reservoir.

CONTINUOUS FLOW SOLUTION CULTURE

In continuous flow solution culture the nutrient solution constantly flows past the roots. It is much easier to automate than the static solution culture because sampling and adjustments to the temperature and nutrient concentrations can be made in a large storage tank that serves potentially thousands of plants.

AEROPONICS

Aeroponics is a system where roots are continuously or discontinuously kept in an environment saturated with fine drops (a mist or aerosol) of nutrient solution. The method requires no substrate and entails growing plants with their roots suspended in a deep air or growth chamber with the roots periodically wetted with a fine mist of atomized nutrients. Excellent aeration is the main advantage of aeroponics.

PASSIVE SUBIRRIGATION

Passive subirrigation, also known as passive hydroponics or semi-hydroponics, is a method where plants are grown in an inert porous medium that transports water and fertilizer to the roots by capillary action from a separate reservoir as necessary, reducing labour and providing a constant supply of water to the roots.

CULUTRE MEDIA

Diahydro

Expanded clay (Ex-clay)

Rock wool

Coir

Pumice

Vermiculite

Nutrient solutions

Plant nutrients used in hydroponics are dissolved in the water and are mostly in inorganic and ionic form. Primary among the dissolved cations (positively charged ions) are Ca2+ (calcium), Mg2+ (magnesium), and K+ (potassium); the major nutrient anions in nutrient solutions are (nitrate), (sulfate), and (dihydrogen phosphate).

COMMERCIAL ADVANTAGE

The largest commercial hydroponics facility in the world is Eurofresh Farms in Willcox, Arizona, which sold 200 million kilograms of tomatoes in 2008. Eurofresh has 318 acres under glass and represents about a third of the commercial hydroponic greenhouse area in the U.S. Eurofresh does not consider its tomatoes organic, but they are pesticide-free. They are grown in rockwool using the run to waste technique.

Some commercial installations use no pesticides or herbicides, preferring integrated pest management techniques. There is often a price premium willingly paid by consumers for produce which is labeled "organic". Some states in the USA require soil as an essential to obtain organic certification. There are also overlapping and somewhat contradictory rules established by the US Federal Government, so some food grown with hydroponics can be certified organic.

Hydroponics also saves water; it uses as little as 1/20 the amount as a regular farm to produce the same amount of food. The water table can be impacted by the water use and run-off of chemicals from farms, but hydroponics may minimize impact as well as having the advantage that water use and water returns are easier to measure. This can save the farmer money by allowing reduced water use and the ability to measure consequences to the land around a farm.

The environment in a hydroponics greenhouse is tightly controlled for maximum efficiency and this new mindset is called soil-less/controlled-environment agriculture (CEA). With this growers can make ultra-premium foods anywhere in the world, regardless of temperature and growing seasons. Growers monitor the temperature, humidity, and pH level constantly.

Hydroponics have been used to enhance vegetables to provide more nutritional value. A hydroponic farmer in Virginia has developed a calcium and potassium enriched head of lettuce, scheduled to be widely available in April 2007. Grocers in test markets have said that the lettuce sells "very well", and the farmers claim that their hydroponic lettuce uses 90% less water than traditional soil farming.

Some of the reasons why hydroponics is being adapted around the world for food production are the following:

- No soil is needed
- The water stays in the system and can be reused- thus, lower water costs
- It is possible to control the nutrition levels in their entirety- thus, lower nutrition costs
- No nutrition pollution is released into the environment because of the controlled system
- Stable and high yields

Pests and diseases are easier to get rid of than in soil because of the container's mobility

Today, hydroponics is an established branch of agronomy. Progress has been rapid, and results obtained in various countries have proved it to be thoroughly practical and to have very definite advantages over conventional methods of horticulture. The two chief merits of the soil-less cultivation of plants are, first, much higher crop yields, and second, hydroponics can be used in places where in-ground agriculture or gardening is not possible.

CHAPTER-34

Role of Clause 49 For Board Structure and Size in India Through Corporate Governance

Pawan Bhattar, Varun Maheshwari

Deptt. of Abst, S.D.P.G. College, Sriganganagar

INTRODUCTION

The changes to Clause 49 of the Listing Agreement by the Securities Exchange Board of India (SEBI) in 2005 (effective 1 January 2006) requiring a minimum number of non-executive directors brought mixed reactions. However, as noted by Thornton (2006), which in April 2006 surveyed a sample of listed firms about compliance with the new regulation, Indian firms generally embraced the changes and thought that it sent positive signals to investors about the quality of corporate governance of Indian business.

The Indian economy is one of the fastest growing economies in the world, and is having a significant impact on world economic growth through both its domestic and international business activities. Its stock market has had to mature quickly to cope with the ever increasing capital requirements necessary to fuel the spectacular private corporate growth.

The very largeness of India's potential as a market, and the relative large size of many of its successful private companies make India a huge driving force within the global economic landscape. With this, the changes in Indian regulation of corporate governance announce the intention to create a business landscape which embodies international governance standards.

CORPORATE GOVERNANCE AND BOARD STRUCTURE

The role of independent directors has been well documented with particular reference to agency theory. The inter-connectivity of contractual relationships and board structure is discussed in Lange, Ramsay and Woo (2000).While there is broad agreement about the importance of independent directors, there is less understanding of the size and composition of the board, and their value (refer John and Senbet, 1998; and Hermalin and Weisbach, 2003; for example). This is surprising as so many countries, including India, have introduced legislation and regulations which outline specific requirements for board structure. Much of this regulatory change followed the 2002 Sarbanes-Oxley Act in the US, which mandatorily restricted corporate board structure in an attempt to improve corporate governance. Other countries such as the UK and Australia have introduced compliance codes rather than mandatory requirements. India's 2006 regulations are mandatory requiring a certain proportion of independent directors on the board depending on the independence of the chair. While regulation sets the minimum proportion of independent directors, the proportion differs markedly and so the determinant of the proportion of outsiders, even if impacted by regulation, is not absolutely clear from the literature to date. Some evidence outside US has revealed mixed results and also results which differ from those found in US studies. For example, Guest (2008) examines the determinants of board size and structure in the UK. Guest notes that while there are some similarities between the US and the UK, there are some important differences which lead one to question whether board structure is determined by country specific as well as international governance trends, and whether we are seeing a trend of convergence of corporate governance models across the globe.

CORPORATE GOVERNANCE CLIMATE IN INDIA

India's economy has improved considerably in the last decade, fuelled in part by both its large and growing skilled labour force and global economic growth. The country's success is reflected in its ability to attract investment grade ratings from International rating agencies like Moody's and Fitch. Table 1 shows the growth in foreign institutional investment in India, an annual compound growth of over 22 percent. India's equity market has had a long history dating back to 1875 when Bombay Stock Exchange

(BSE) was established, creating an environment for dispersed corporate ownership. This foundation led to a culture where corporate control is attainable with far lesser equity ownership than the theoretical threshold of 51%. The modern corporate environment commenced in 1956, when almost a decade after independence from Britain, the Companies Act, 1956 laid down the legal corporate framework for the regulation of listed and unlisted companies in India. Similarly, the Securities Contracts (Regulation) Act (SCRA), 1956 gave government jurisdiction over all aspects of the securities regulation. The Indian economy and financial markets underwent radical reforms in the early 1990s, largely in response to the country's economic crisis in the late 1980s. India's weak integration with external economies and the relatively late onset of reforms are viewed as reasons why the Indian economy was relatively unaffected by the 1997 Asian financial crisis. The reforms caused extensive change to the Indian capital market and its corporate governance landscape. In 1992 the Securities and Exchange Board of India (SEBI) was established with a mandate to protect investors and improve transparency in the securities market, and led to securities regulation by this autonomous body. The incorporation of National Stock Exchange (NSE) in 1992 provided further impetus to capital market transparency, and provided significant competition for the BSE, introducing an electronic trading platform to overcome agency conflicts often associated with the broker-owned BSE. Increased transactions volumes resulted from healthy competition between the two exchanges, and led to improved technology to process both trading and settlements, making the securities market accessible to the geographically dispersed population, thereby fuelling increased participation by both institutional and retail investors. Since 2006, listed companies are required to submit quarterly compliance reports to the SEBI, similar to those required in the US by Sarbanes-Oxley.

THE DETERMINANTS OF THE SIZE AND COMPOSITION OF INDIAN BOARDS

Method

In this paper, we analyse the determinants of the size and composition of Indian boards using a series of multivariate regressions, and focus on the decisions taken by Indian companies about the size and structure of their boards, especially in the light of the 2006 changes to Clause 49. The approach taken follows many similar papers testing other markets, and summarised in Guest (2008).

As reported above, in the main, previous studies test the competing hypotheses relating to the two roles taken by directors – that of monitoring the CEO, and that of advising the board and CEO, and the potential trade-off benefits that result from these two roles and the interaction of the insiders and outsiders on a board. Such studies focus on determinants which arise from the two roles of boards. In addition, we see from previous literature, firm size and complexity may also impact the board structure and size. In this paper we attempt to test similar determinants in the Indian market.

In addition, we test the alternative theory of board structure (Hermalin and Weisbach, 1998) that the greater the CEO power, the smaller the board and proportion of outsiders, to determine if previous results are country specific.

Time period analysed

Compliance with the amended Clause 49 was required at 1 January 2006. As such, we are interested to see if there was any lagged impact of the variables tested on the particular size and composition of the board chosen by the companies. As such, we used data on board size and proportion of independent directors as at 16 June 2008, as the proxy for board size and composition. We argue that any change to the board following Clause 49 would have taken place either immediately before the compliance due date, or in the years immediately following. We note, however, that seven of the 50 Nifty companies either did not comply or did not report their composition in the BSE online database, and so were excluded from analysis when examining the determinants of board composition. The decisions taken about board size, however, were most likely to be made in 2005 immediately prior to the compliance date, or immediately after in 2006 or even 2007. Hence, we run three multivariate regressions to test the determinants of board composition and three multivariate regressions to test the determinants of the proportion of independent directors, based on data from 2005, 2006 and 2007. The data collected for each of the three years was financial year end data – i.e. as at 31 March each year.

Variable Proxies

We measure size and complexity by market valuation and debt to equity ratio respectively. A further test of complexity is whether the firm is in the finance industry or not. We argue that as the finance industry of emerging countries tends to be a leader in engagement with the global economy, it is also a reasonable proxy for complexity, and in this study we use a dummy variable for finance versus non-finance industry status. Similar to most previous studies, monitoring costs are peroxide by Tobin's Q ratio (market to book ratio); R&D expenditure and share price volatility. The private benefits accruing to insiders from monitoring is tested with the proxy of free cash flow, and to test the power of the CEO, we use the proxy of ROA – both also consistent with the proxies used in many previous studies, as reported in Guest (2008). To test the impact of the Indian ownership structure, and in particular the ownership of the original entrepreneur, we use the proportion of ownership by the original Indian entrepreneur..

CONCLUSION

The empirical analysis of the determinants of board size and composition of Indian companies has revealed some interesting results. While there is strong evidence to suggest that there are country specific factors influencing the size of the board, there is little evidence at all of the determinants of board composition. The opposite signage for entrepreneurial holdings for both board size (+ive) and composition (-ive) is in itself curious. One explanation could be that while the entrepreneur and related control of Indian firms is comfortable with larger boards, consistent with improved corporate governance, the presence of insiders may threaten the private benefits gained from their control position. Moreover, the performance of the models analyzing board composition were poor, and this possibly indicates that this particular aspect of Clause 49 is compliance driven and not determined by any of the firm or director factors analyzed. In addition, the results reveal that there is no consistency with the studies of the more developed countries, and in particular the US. This lends further support to Guest's (2008) suggestion that country specific forces could be at play. Finally, the support of the institutional shareholders in India for good corporate governance standards is supported by this research. This is one of the first studies of the emerging corporate governance structures in India. It has raised more questions than it has answered, and provides a good foundation for future research of Indian boards and board structures, and their impact on corporate performance and corporate governance outcomes.

CHAPTER-35

Create A Better India Through Corporate Governance

Sushil Singhal

(Lecturer, Deptt. of Comp. Sc.)
Seth G.L. Bihani S.D. (PG) College, Sri Ganganagar (Raj.) – INDIA

INTRODUCTION

Corporate governance refers to the structures and processes for the direction and control of companies. Corporate governance concerns the relationships among the management, Board of Directors, controlling shareholders, minority shareholders and other stakeholders. Good corporate governance contributes to sustainable economic development by enhancing the performance of companies and increasing their access to outside capital.

Corporate governance is the set of processes, customs, policies, laws, and institutions affecting the way a corporation or company is directed, administered or controlled. Corporate governance also includes the relationships among the many stakeholders involved and the goals for which the corporation is governed. The principal stakeholders are the shareholders, the board of directors, employees, customers, creditors, suppliers, and the community at large.

Corporate governance is a multi-faceted subject. An important theme of corporate governance is to ensure the accountability of certain individuals in an organization through mechanisms that try to reduce or eliminate the principal-agent problem. Corporate governance deals with the rights and responsibilities of a company's management, its board, shareholders and various stakeholders.

Corporate governance deals with laws, procedures, practices and implicit rules that determine the ability of the company to make managerial decisions.

India has followed the UK model for corporate governance. It is true that Audit Committees, Managing Committees and Remuneration Committees.

WHY CORPORATE GOVERNANCE

Investors primarily consider two variables before making investment decisions-the rate of return on invested capital and the risk associated with the investment. Good corporate-governance practices reduce this risk by ensuring transparency, accountability, and enforceability in the marketplace. While strong corporate-governance systems help ensure a country's long-term success, weak systems often lead to serious problems. While the presence of a good corporate-governance framework ensures neither stability nor success, It is widely believed that corporate governance can "raise efficiency and growth," especially for countries that rely heavily on stock markets to raise capital.

Improving access to capital. Attention to corporate governance issues in up-and-coming markets among policymakers and academics has focused on the role governance can play in improving access for emerging market companies.

Improving performance. Equally important and, irrespective of the need to access capital, good corporate governance brings better performance for shareholders. Improved governance structures and processes help ensure quality decision-making, encourage effective succession planning for senior management and enhance the long-term prosperity of companies.

IMPACT OF CORPORATE GOVERNANCE

The positive effect of corporate governance on different stakeholders ultimately is a strengthened economy, and hence good corporate governance is a tool for socio-economic development.

NEED, IMPORTANCE AND OBJECTIVES OF CORPORATE GOVERNANCE

In order to overcome the under noted serious concerns within the business community, there is a need to introduce a system of corporate governance that will ensure the transparency, integrity and accountability of Management including non-executivedirectors.

- Concentration of greater financial power and authority in a lesser number of individuals.
- Violations of foreign exchange rules and regulations.
- Large-scale diversion of funds to associate companies and risky ventures.
- Unfocussed business decisions leading to losses.
- Preferential allotment of shares to promoters at low prices,
- Exploited the weaknesses in the Accounting Standards to inflate profits and understate liabilities.
- Frequent changes in Board structures.
- Spinning off profitable business operations to subsidiary companies.
- Charging of royalty for use of brand name by the parent company by leading companies.

Good corporate governance practices also enable Management to allocate resources more efficiently, which increases the likelihood that investors will obtain a higher rate of return on their investment.

Good corporate governance practices ensure

- Adequate disclosures and effective decision making to achieve corporate objectives;
- Transparency in business transactions;
- Statutory and legal compliances;
- Protection of shareholder interests;
- Commitment to values and ethical conduct of business.
- Long-term survival of the companies.

Good corporate governance is very important because of its role in attracting foreign investment. The extent of foreign investment, in turn, shapes the prospects for economic growth for many developing countries.

Corporate governance can play a role in reducing corruption, and decreased corruption significantly enhances a country's development prospects. The aim of "Good Corporate Governance" is to ensure commitment of the board in managing the company in a transparent manner for maximizing long- term value of the company for its shareholders and all other partners.

PRINCIPLES

Key elements of good corporate governance principles include honesty, trust and integrity, openness, performance orientation, responsibility and accountability, mutual respect, and commitment to the organization.

Commonly accepted principles of corporate governance include

- **Rights and equitable treatment of shareholders**: Organizations should respect the rights of shareholders and help shareholders to exercise those rights. They can help shareholders exercise their rights by effectively communicating information that is understandable and accessible and encouraging shareholders to participate in general meetings.

- **Interests of other stakeholders**: Organizations should recognize that they have legal and other obligations to all legitimate stakeholders.

- **Role and responsibilities of the board**: The board needs a range of skills and understanding to be able to deal with various business issues and have the ability to review and challenge management performance..

- **Integrity and ethical behaviour**: Ethical and responsible decision making is not only important for public relations, but it is also a necessary element in risk management and avoiding lawsuits. Organizations should develop a code of conduct for their directors and executives that promotes ethical and responsible decision-making.

- **Disclosure and transparency**: Organizations should clarify and make publicly known the roles and responsibilities of board and management to provide shareholders with a level of accountability. They should also implement procedures to independently verify and safeguard the integrity of the company's financial reporting.

CODES AND GUIDELINES

Corporate governance principles and codes have been developed in different countries and issued from stock exchanges, corporations, institutional investors, or associations (institutes) of directors and managers with the support of governments and international organizations. As a rule, compliance with these governance recommendations is not mandated by law, although the codes linked to stock exchange listing requirements may have a coercive effect.

CONCLUSION

Good corporate governance may not be the engine of economic growth, but it is essential for the proper functioning of the engine. The investors both National and International would be loyal to invest in the Indian companies if they follow all the standards of corporate governance practices.

Good corporate governance practices in India will be shaped by our administrative and regulatory authorities like SEBI, MCA, etc. by implementing transparent and effective corporate governance laws.

CHAPTER-36

CSR: A Perspective of True Transparency

Sumanta Dutta

Lecturer, Department of Business Administration, Dinabandhu Andrews Institute of Technology & Management, Garia, Kolkata.

&

Visiting Faculty

West Bengal State University, Barasat, Kolkata,

Department of Commerce and Management

West Bengal

INTRODUCTION

CSR in reality is the alignment of business operations with social values. It takes into account the interests of stakeholders in the company's business policies and actions. It focuses on the social, environmental, and financial success of a company – the so-called "triple bottom line" – with the aim to achieve social development while achieving business success. More importantly, CSR is the point of convergence of various initiatives aimed at ensuring socio-economic development of the community as a whole in a credible and sustainable manner.

Fortunately, with the popularity of CSR, more and more companies now perform in non-financial arenas such as human rights, business ethics, environmental policies, community development corporate governance, and workplace issues.Now, social and environmental performances are considered side by side with financial performance. From local economic development concerns to international human rights policies, companies are being held accountable for their actions and their impacts. Companies are also more transparent in disclosing and communicating their policies and practices as these impact employees, communities, and the environment as per global reporting norms. The belief among the companies is that every aspect of a corporation's CSR should be linked to corporate strategy by connecting it as tightly as possible to the company's unique capabilities and competitive context.

CSR has moved from being a public relations tool or a feel-good factor to a key parameter to keep companies open and transparent. It now no longer stands in isolation but has become a part of good Corporate Governance policies. The reality today is that companies are taking the issues of 'reputational risk' very seriously and it is no longer considered as an option. Most CSR models are based on the principle that goodwill earned from the stakeholders leads to benefits to the corporation. This in turn enables the corporation to further enhance stakeholder value.

The oft-quoted concept of triple bottom line reporting of CSR suggests that there are three separate and distinct bottom lines – each of equivalent standing. It is believed that in the context of sustainable development, it's impossible to consider the economic dimension in isolation from the social or the environmental, and vice versa. To be a truly sustainable organization, in the broadest definition of the terms, and organization must perform well across all three dimensions. Corporate social responsibility is also seen as basically a new business strategy to reduce investment risks and maximize profits by taking all the key stake-holders into confidence. The proponents of this perspective often include corporate social responsibility in their advertising and marketing initiatives.

There is also the eco-social perspective of corporate social responsibility. The proponents of this perspective are the new generation of corporations and the new-economy entrepreneurs who created a tremendous amount of wealth in a relatively short span of time. They recognize the fact that social and environmental stability and sustainability are two important prerequisites for the sustainability of the market in the long run. They also recognize the fact that increasing poverty can lead to social and political instability. Such socio-political instability can, in turn, be detrimental to business, which operates from a variety of socio-political and cultural back grounds. Seen from the eco-social perspective, corporate social responsibility is both a value and a strategy to ensuring the sustainability of business. It is a value because it stresses the fact that business and markets are essentially aimed at the well-being of society. It is a strategy because it helps reduce social tensions and facilitate markets.

REVIEW OF LITERATURE ON CSR TRANSPARENCY

Amitav Joseph (2009) viewed CSR in the acknowledgement of the debt that the Corporation owes to the community within the periphery in which it operates. He also pointed out that the emerging prospective perspective of CSR focuses on stakeholders rather than on Maximisation of profit of shareholders. Hence, it is considered as the password to overcome the competition but to ensure sustainable growth.

Imran Ali (2010) et al. considered CSR a prominent matter for corporation's sustainable growth than wealth creation. They highlighted on the issue that corporations presently realized the multifaceted benefits of CSR are paying great attention to incorporate it in all spheres of business strategies. They analyzed the impact of CSR actions in developing employee organizational commitment and corporate performance. An exploratory research was done on the basis of 500 employees with a response rate of 63% provide an insight that there exist a significant positive relationship between CSR and employee organizational commitment CSR & organizational performance.

Study conducted by **Dr. Moushumi Dutta (2010)** provides an insight that CSR allows business organizations to develop responsible attitude towards society and the environment and contribute to economic development of the nation. The study was undertaken in respect of selected pharmaceutical companies with special reference to India. The investigation disclose that a strengthen CSR evaluation is essential to make corporate initiative more effective.

Mare Vilanova et. al. (2008) explores the interrelationship between CSR & competitiveness. The three possible conclusion that can are drawn from this is that, it explore a clear connection between CSR and competitiveness in creating and maintaining image and reputation of the corporation. Second view is that despite the nature of CSR policies, internally acceptance of CSR by companies provoke some unexpected transformations in company's business values and processes and lastly CSR provide companies 'a license to operate' to become competitive one.

Gupta & Sharma (2007) viewed CSR not on a cost centre but considered it as an effective management tool with multidimensional benefits. To them CSR will play a major role in managing a sustainable business. They provide strong emphasis on four inter-locking priorities named

- From Philanthropy to social investment
- Sustaining critical Natural Capital
- Ensuring transparency
- Linking CSR and financial performance

Mrityunjay Athreya (2009) in this introductory article signifies the role of CSR in maintaining inclusive growth. He considered three actions and their interrelationship in order to maintain sustained inclusive growth. These are Government Social responsibility **(GSR),** corporate social responsibility **(CSR)** and personal social responsibility **(PSR).** He also focuses on the strategic need to incorporate the disclosure of CSR activities by corporate to make system more transparent and sustainable.

Mintzberg et. al. (2002) belief that 'Greed has been raised to some sort of higher calling, corporation have been urged to ignore broader social responsibilities in favour of narrow stakeholder value.'

Carroll (1919) developed a stakeholder based framework that delineates & ranks four forms of CSR named economic, legal, Ethical and philanthropic responsibilities that can be used by the corporate for better understanding of how corporates fulfill its various responsibilities.

Miles & Covin(2000) proposed that firm should adopt environmental management either for compliance purpose or strategically leveraging CSR as a means to create & renew competitive advantage.

Van Marrewijk's (2003) provided a comprehensive Framework regarding adoption of CSR philosophy by the firm.He identified the following driven forces that includes (i) Compliance driven (ii) Profit driven (iii) Driven by caring (iv) Synergistic and (v) Holistic.He opined that adoption of such a new orientation towards CSR, transform corporate culture to a more innovative, quality focused corporation.

UdayaSankar Krishna (2008) studied the impact of firms size on firms CSR initiative. It examines the different economic motivations of firms with varying combinations of visibility, resource access and scale of operation. The study revealed that the small & very large firms are likely to participate more in CSR initiatives, whereas mid sized firms will have the least participation.

CSR: TOWARDS A NEW WAY CORPORATE TRANSPARENCY

A CSR can be viewed as an organized "Balance Sheet" which deliberately prevents chaotic thinking in the pursuit of improved stakeholder relationships as well as the Triple Bottom Line. It calls for companies to be held accountable for their social and environmental records as well as for their financial performance. Corporate sustainability reporting beyond traditional measures of financial performance is that it integrates the traditional financial information along with non-financial information, which can help firm in enhance economic value addition, besides putting it on a firm financial footing.

Such corporate performance, which is considered to be three major pillars, knows as Triple Bottom Line Reporting (TBLR) which provides greatest challenges in building reputation in the community. Companies, business and society are more connected and interactive today than ever before. Corporations are more aware of their role towards the society. They are expected to be responsible bodies with a sense of duty towards common resources and the environment and there is a growing realization that they, as an integral part of this society themselves, can contribute to its development. Corporate Social Responsibility or CSR constitutes the foundation of the tripartite relationships among companies, society and the nation. corporate Social Responsibility (CSR) is expected to be integral to business today. It has also become the password to not only overcome competition but to ensure sustainable growth. It has been supported by the shareholders and stakeholders, by and large encompassing the whole community. CSR in reality is the alignment of business operations with social values. It takes into account the interests of stakeholders in the company's business policies and actions. It focuses on the social, environmental, and financial success of a company – the so-called "triple bottom line" – with the aim to achieve social development while achieving business success.

Table: 36.1 : Comparative study between Financial Reporting and Triple Bottom Line Reporting

Point of Difference	Financial Reporting	Triple Bottom Line Reporting
User of the Reporting	External Investors and creditors	Diversified Stakeholders both internal and external
Process	Mature and standardized	Evolving
Option	Mandatory	Mostly voluntary
Data content	Easily understood; common metric; monetary unit	Technical;inconsistent,variable metrics
Format	Established and standardized	Evolving; numerous guidelines available
Measurement Basis	Financial Bottom line	Triple Bottom Line, Financial prosperity, environmental quality and social equity
Regulation	Public governance	Private governance
Verification	Required; audits and auditing standard prevalent	Not required; many possible approaches; Attestation,assurance,management statement and /or Stakeholder review and feedback
Support	Accounting Bodies and Associations	No dominant group-global NGOs,Industry Trade groups, Assurance providers and Companies

Source: K.Chatterjee, 2005

CONCLUSIONS

CSR is generally understood to be the way a company achieves a balance or integration of economic, environmental and social imperatives while at the same time addressing shareholder and stakeholder expectations. It is about meeting the current needs and ensuring the future generation's needs are not compromised upon. Good CSR goes a step further, increased belongingness in employees, enhanced skills and better motivation brings better productivity, lower rate of attrition, fair practices in supply chain will add to transparency in the organization, public image, efficiency and effectiveness. Responsibility towards the environment and community will improve the conditions around work space in many dimensions.

CHAPTER-37

Corporate Governance and Its Dimension

Suman Bhatia

Vipin Sharma

INTRODUCTION

Corporate Governance is a method used by corporations for streamlining the various participants in an organization having conflicting interests.

Corporate Governance can be said to deal with the entire network of formal and informal relationships both between the company's management and its shareholders and between the management and other key stockholders including employees, customers supplies, creditors, local communities and society in general. SEBI committee defines " Corporate Governance is the acceptance by management of the inalienable rights of shareholders as the true owners of the corporation and of their own role as trustees on behalf of the shareholders. It is about commitment to values, ethical business conduct and about corporate funds in the management of the company". Corporate Governance deals with the right and responsibilities of a company's management its board, shareholders and various stake holders.

The directive principle of the Indian Constitution and the Gandhian Principle of trusteeship is reflected in this definition.

This is the revolutionary key to socio economic development.

Elements of Corporate Governance

Various key aspects and elements are interlocked to ensure the existence of good Corporate Governance in any company.

1. Regulatory boards – the back bone of the whole system.
2. Boards of director and CEO one of the manor elements that play a great role in finalizing company's strategy, policies and ensure the accountability of the organization.
3. Management
4. Share holders
5. Auditors
6. Others – Suppliers, employees, creditors, customers community at large.

LEGAL ENVIORNMENT

For the execution of responsible Corporate Governance in India corporations are governed by some regulatory institutions and authorities and common laws i.e. **Ministry of Company affairs, RBI, IRDA, SEBI Act 1992, SEBI (Disclosure and Investor Protection), guidelines 2000.**

Company Law 1956 – formation of company and rules for internal management rights of shareholders, steps to ensure the protection of the shareholders.

DEPOSITORIES ACT 1996

MRTP Act, 1969 – code of conduct to be followed by so that a healthy environment can be provided to the companies as well as the society.

Company Secretaries Act 1980 – A key to good Corporate Governance effective operations and compliance of rules and regulation and administration in a company.

Foreign contribution (Regulation) Act 1976

SUGGESTION & DIMENSIONS OF CORPORATE GOVERNANCE

PROTECTION TO SHAREHOLDERS

Provision are there to provide the shareholders with right and equitable treatment to share holders by various laws i.e. provisions of general meeting, their voting right, right to get information etc. Shareholder should ensure that the composition of Board of Directors is a balance mix of independent directors and management appointees. This would help keep a check on the internal process of the company, with shareholder activism on the rise, the proactive role of institutional investors will also make the company management more accountable. The share holders should be made aware of all these rules & laws by running corporate education drive.

TRANSPARENCY AND ACCOUNTABILITY

Board of Director should implement procedures and rules in a transparent and responsible manner. All material matters should be disclosed timely and in proper ways so that all investors and interested parties can access the information clearly and on time. Concealment of facts and fraud provide reasons for great disturbance in stock market and affects badly so they must be kept accountable for their conducts and duties.

CORPORATE GOVERNANCE AND SOCIAL RESPONSIBILITIES

Corporate Governance in the context of Social responsibility can be called corporate conscience, corporate societal performance or sustainable responsible business. The term "Corporate Social Responsibility" makes the corporate feel themselves responsible for their actions and encourage a positive impact through its activities on the environment, customers, employees, communities, stake holders and all other members of public sphere.

In changing scenario it has become essential for corporate to ensure themselves for compliance with the spirit of law ethical standards and international norms.

SOCIAL ACCOUNTING, AUDITING AND REPORTING

- Social auditing is a concept of communication of social and environmental effects of Corporate Governance economic actions to particular interest groups within society and to society at large.

- It makes the company accountable for its social performance and development of society.

For instances – Companies now produce externally audited annual reports that cover sustainable development and CSR issues. It also counts the following points :

1. Human Resource – Recruitment, training, relations, respect to Labour standard and Labour welfare
2. Risk Management
3. Branch differentiation
4. Social welfare

WHY

Corporate Governance plays a great role in attracting foreign investment

1. Investors usually consider two aspect before making any investment (a) rate of return on invested capital (b) risk associated with investment. Developing country India has become a hub for investment of foreign capital in the world with the help of good corporate governance practices.
2. Good Corporate Governance practice increase transparency accountability, enforceability in the market place.
3. It ensures country's long term success on financial platform as well on social responsibilities platform.
4. It boosts investor confidence, doesn't matter they are Indian or foreign.
5. Also strengthen the investors from sudden crisis.
6. Sound Corporate Governance is a back bone of those countries which strongly rely on stock market to raise foreign capital. As India is the emerging nation in this sector.
7. Emergence of Institutional Investors (Pension funds, MF, hedge funds, exchange traded funds, other investors groups, insurance companies, banks, brokers and other financial institutions) has brought professional diligence in investment sector. As a big number of individuals invest their money

indirectly through these Institutional Investors we can say, the majority of investment is described as "Institutional Investors". It also plays a great role in enrichment of corporate governance.

CONCLUSION

The fast pace Indian economy is getting more market oriented, in recent years. The going ahead of the Govt. of India towards liberalization and globalization of the economy has boosted the financial scenario more positively. The size of Indian corporate is becoming much bigger and accordingly. The expectation of various stake holders are also increasing which can be quenched only by the good Corporate Governance.Although Corporate Governance Framework in the country is seen at par with other developed markets the same has to be implemented in **"Letter as well as spirit".**

CHAPTER-38

EVOLUTION AND IMPACT OF CORPORATE GOVERNANCE IN INDIA

Prof. G. L. Sundaria

Professor in the Department of Business Management,
Bihani S. D. P. G. College , Sriganganagar (Rajasthan) India

Prof. S. Khan

Professor in Department of Mathematics,
Bihani S. D. P. G. College , Sriganganagar (Rajasthan) India

Sh. Sumit Kumawat, MBA

INTRODUCTION

The subject of corporate governance leapt to global business limelight from relative obscurity after a string of collapses of high profile companies. Enron, the Houston, Texas based energy giant, and WorldCom, the telecom behemoth, shocked the business world with both the scale and age of their unethical and illegal operations. Worse, they seemed to indicate only the tip of a dangerous iceberg. While corporate practices in the US companies came under attack, it appeared that the problem was far more widespread. Large and trusted companies from Parmalat in Italy to the multinational newspaper group Hollinger Inc., revealed significant and deep-rooted problems in their corporate governance. Even the prestigious New York Stock Exchange had to remove its director, Dick Grasso, amidst public outcry over excessive compensation. It was clear that something was amiss in the area of corporate governance all over the world.

Corporate governance has, of course, been an important field of query within the finance discipline for decades. Researchers in finance have actively investigated the topic for at least a quarter century and the father of modern economics, Adam Smith, himself had recognized the problem over two centuries ago. There have been debates about whether the Anglo-Saxon market- model of corporate governance is better than the bankbased models of Germany and Japan. However, the differences in the quality of corporate governance in these developed countries fade in comparison to the chasm that exists between corporate governance standards and practices in these countries as a group and those in the developing world..

WHAT IS CORPORATE GOVERNANCE

Corporate governance is a term that refers broadly to the rules, processes, or laws by which businesses are operated, regulated, and controlled. The term can refer to internal factors defined by the officers, stockholders or constitution of a corporation, as well as to external forces such as consumer groups, clients, and government regulations.

A well-defined and enforced corporate governance provides a structure that, at least in theory, works for the benefit of everyone concerned by ensuring that the enterprise adheres to accepted ethical standards and best practices as well as to formal laws. To that end, organizations have been formed at the regional, national, and global levels.

In recent years, corporate governance has received increased attention because of high- profile scandals involving abuse of corporate power and, in some cases, alleged criminal activity by corporate officers. An integral part of an effective corporate governance regime includes provisions for civil or criminal prosecution of individuals who conduct unethical or illegal acts in the name of the enterprise.

IMPACT OF CORPORATE GOVERNANCE

The positive effect of corporate governance on different stakeholders ultimately is a strengthened economy and hence good corporate governance is a tool for socio-economic development. 'Marc Lane's book on best corporate governance practices, "Representing Corporate Officers and Directors" was first published in 1987. He revisited his treatise on corporate governance in 2005. The new version is updated annually with the most recent supplement for the year 2010. With the goal of promoting positive social change, Lane provides companies and their directors, officers, auditors and shareholders with insights for the compliance of new legislation, rules and responsibilities in response to the avalanche of corporate accounting scandals.

CORPORATE GOVERNANCE IN INDIA – A BACKGROUND

The history of the development of Indian corporate laws has been marked by interesting contrasts. At independence, India inherited one of the world's poorest economies but one which had a factory sector accounting for a tenth of the national product; four functioning stock markets (predating the Tokyo Stock Exchange) with clearly defined rules governing listing, trading and settlements; a well-developed equity culture if only among the urban rich; and a banking system replete with well-developed lending norms and recovery procedures. In terms of corporate laws and financial system, therefore, India emerged far better endowed than most other colonies. The 1956 Companies Act as well as other laws governing the functioning of joint-stock companies and protecting the investors' rights built on this foundation.

The beginning of corporate developments in India were marked by the managing agency system that contributed to the birth of dispersed equity ownership but also gave rise to the practice of management enjoying control rights disproportionately greater than their stock ownership. The turn towards socialism in the decades after independence marked by the 1951 Industries (Development and Regulation) Act as well as the 1956 Industrial Policy Resolution put in place a regime and culture of licensing, protection and widespread red-tape that bred corruption and stilted the growth of the corporate sector. The situation grew from bad to worse in the following decades and corruption, nepotism and inefficiency became the hallmarks of the Indian corporate sector. Exorbitant tax rates encouraged creative accounting practices and complicated emolument structures to beat the system.

CHANGES SINCE LIBERALIZATION

The years since liberalization have witnessed wide-ranging changes in both laws and regulations driving corporate governance as well as general consciousness about it. Perhaps the single most important development in the field of corporate governance and investor protection in India has been the establishment of the Securities and Exchange Board of India (SEBI) in 1992 and its gradual empowerment since then. Established primarily to regulate and monitor stock trading, it has played a crucial role in establishing the basic minimum ground rules of corporate conduct in the country. Concerns about corporate governance in India were, however, largely triggered by a spate of crises in the early 90's – the Harshad Mehta stock market scam of 1992 followed by incidents of companies allotting preferential shares to their promoters at deeply discounted prices as well as those of companies simply disappearing with investors' money.

One of the first among such endeavors was the CII Code for Desirable Corporate Governance developed by a committee chaired by Rahul Bajaj. The committee was formed in 1996 and submitted its code in April 1998. Later SEBI constituted two committees to look into the issue of corporate governance – the first chaired by Kumar Mangalam Birla that submitted its report in early 2000 and the second by Narayana Murthy three years later. Table 1 provides a comparative view of the recommendations of these important efforts at improving corporate governance in India. The SEBI committee recommendations have had the maximum impact on changing the corporate governance situation in India. The Advisory Group on Corporate Governance of RBI's Standing Committee on International Financial Standards and Codes also submitted its own recommendations in 2001.

CONCLUSIONS

With the recent spate of corporate scandals and the subsequent interest in corporate governance, a plethora of corporate governance norms and standards have sprouted around the globe. The Sarbanes-Oxley legislation in the USA, the Cadbury Committee recommendations for European companies and the OECD principles of corporate governance are perhaps the best known among these. But developing countries have not fallen behind either. Well over a hundred different codes and norms have been identified in recent surveys and their number is steadily increasing. India has been no exception to the rule. Several committees and groups have looked into this issue that undoubtedly deserves all the attention it can get.

Development of norms and guidelines are an important first step in a serious effort to improve corporate governance. The bigger challenge in India, however, lies in the proper implementation of those rules at the ground level. More and more it appears that outside agencies like analysts and stock markets (particularly foreign markets for companies making GDR issues) have the most influence on the actions of managers in the leading companies of the country. But their influence is restricted to the few top (albeit largest) companies. More needs to be done to ensure adequate corporate governance in the *average* Indian company.

Even the most prudent norms can be hoodwinked in a system plagued with widespread corruption. Nevertheless, with industry organizations and chambers of commerce themselves pushing for an improved corporate governance system, the future of corporate governance in India promises to be distinctly better than the past.

CHAPTER-39

Operationalization of: Business Ethics, Social Responsibility and Environmental Sustainability

S.S.Bhushanam

BE, PG-DIIT, MBA, M.Phil Presently research student, pursuing PhD
Sree Residency, Vasavya Nagar, Vijayawad

UNDERSTANDING ETHICS

Ethics is the study and practice of: How to live a good life; How to build good families and communities. A good society is one that treats individuals fairly and protects their rights. This requires: efficient, non-corrupt government and business. A clean, non-toxic environment relationships, families, and communities require: loyalty, honor, friendship, humility, and self-sacrifice a clean and non-toxic environment.

Ethics are a set of moral principles or values that governs the conduct of an individual or a group. What is lawful conduct is not always ethical conduct. The law may permit something that would be ethically wrong.

MULTI DIMENTIONAL ETHICS

Businesses organized in a country are subject to its laws. They are also subject to the laws of other countries in which they operate. Business persons owe a duty to act ethically in the conduct of their affairs. This is Multi-Dimensional Ethics, and is the only path to long-term sustainable wealth creation.

A Multi-Dimensional Ethic will: Protect individuals and encourage individual development, promote strong families and friendships, Build a politically and economically strong country (region, globe), be fair and just, protect the environment, and create wealth.

SOCIAL RESPONSIBILITY

The Social Responsibility of Business: Business does not operate in a vacuum. Decisions made by business have far-reaching effects on society. In the past, many business decisions were made solely on a cost-benefit analysis, "bottom line" impact. Such decisions may cause negative externalities for others. Corporations are considered to owe some degree of *social responsibility* for their actions. Corporations that conduct **social audits** will be more apt to prevent unethical and illegal conduct by managers, employees, and agents

Businesses owe a social responsibility and not to harm society: Businesses are organized subject to the law of its country. They are also subject to the laws of other countries in which they operate. Business persons owe a duty to act ethically in the conduct of their affairs. A moral theory that dictates: - people must choose the action or follow the rule, provides the greatest good to society. A moral theory that says people owe moral duties that are based on *universal rules*. This theory would have people behave according to the *categorical imperative*: ***"Do unto others as you would have them do unto you."***

Universal rules are based on two important principles: Consistency – all cases are treated alike with no exceptions. Reversibility – the actor must abide by the rule he or she uses to judge the morality of someone else's conduct.

People must choose to act and follow Social Justice Theory. Social Justice Theory is a moral theory that says each person is presumed to have entered into a social contract, with all others in society, to obey moral rules that are necessary for people to live in peace and harmony.

Corporate Social Responsibility: Corporate Social Responsibility is manifested in organizing the following functions:

- Social audit, - Philanthropy, - Cause-Related Marketing, - Recycling Program - Humanitarian aid. – Charities, - Education, - Medical Research, - Worthy Causes,- Responsibility to Society and the Environment, - Natural Resources and Pollution, - Environmental Activism.

Activism consists of intentional action to bring about social, political, economic, or environmental change.

THEORIES OF SOCIAL RESPONSIBILITY

Theories of social responsibility include the following organizational strategies and actions.

- To maximize profits for stockholders. -To avoid causing harm and to compensate for harm caused. - To consider the interests of all stakeholders, including stockholders, employees, customers, suppliers, creditors, and local community. - To do good and solve social problems

THE CORPORATE SOCIAL AUDIT

Corporate audits should be extended to include the **moral health** of the corporation. Corporations that conduct social audits will be more apt to prevent unethical and illegal conduct by managers, employees, and agents. The audit would examine how well: Employees have adhered to the company's code of ethics; and The Corporation has met its duty of social responsibility. Such audits would focus on the corporation's efforts to: Promote employment opportunities for members of protected classes Worker safety Environmental protection Consumer protection

United Nations Code of Conduct for Transnational Corporations: Respect for National Sovereignty; Adherence to Socio-Cultural Objectives and Values; Respect for Human Rights and Fundamental Freedoms; Abstention from Corrupt Practices

RELATION BETWEEN ETHICS AND CORPORATE SOCIAL RESPONSIBILITY

Corporate social responsibility (CSR) and ethics are interwoven and inter dependent. The understanding is defined by the processes involved. **Processes and Relationships**: Corporate social responsibility (CSR) is the process by which businesses negotiate their role in society. In the business world, ethics is the study of morally appropriate behaviors and decisions, examining what "should be done". Although the two are linked in most firms, CSR activities are no guarantee of ethical behaviour.

Sometimes CSR are grounded by opposing objectives (Maximize profits to balance profits with Social Responsibility) and so, activities range widely. Do what it takes to make a profit; avoid the law; fly below social radar. In such situations, a balance has to created by a fight with CSR initiatives

- Comply with legal requirements - Do more than legally required, e.g., philanthropy - Articulate social (CSR) objectives - Integrate social objectives and business goals -Lead the industry on social objectives

Philanthropy: - give money or time or in kind to charity. - Integrative philanthropy—select beneficiaries aligned with company interests. Philanthropy will not enhance corporate reputation if a company: - fails to live up to its philanthropic image or - if consumers perceive philanthropy to be manipulative.

Integrate CSR Globally: Incorporate values to make it part of an articulated belief system. Act worldwide on those values in respect of: - Cause-related markets. - Cause-based cross sector partnerships.

Cultural context in Business Ethics Development: The cultural context influences organizational ethics. Top managers also influence ethics. The combined influence of culture and top management influence organizational ethics and ethical behaviours.

INTERNATIONAL ETHICS CODE - PRINCIPLES FOR INTERNATIONAL BUSINESS

The Caux Round Table promulgated an international ethics code called the **Principles for International Business.**

1. The Responsibilities of Business beyond Shareholders toward Shareholders 2. The Economic and Social Impact of Business: Toward Innovation, Justice, and World Community 3. Business Behavior: Beyond the Letter of Law toward a Spirit of Trust 4. Respect for Rules 5. Support for Multilateral Trade 6. Respect for the Environment 7. Avoidance of Illicit Operations

ETHICS IS GOOD BUSINESS

Ethics are no more in religious texts; they are a part of business law. Not only are ethics respected in business, they are a part of the law. Morality and ethics: Morality and ethics have their roots in religion. When did ethics begin? In most cultures, ethics are connected with divine origins

Babylonian civilization received laws of Hammurabi from sun god. God gave 10 commandments to Moses. In Greek civilization, Plato says that god Zeus gave morality to help mankind. Manusmriti Samhita incorporates earliest code of social and legal ethics in India.

Ethics and society: In fact both religion and ethics serve a common need: society. Societies are built on the plank of co-existence and mutuality. All societies need mutual support, forbearance and care. Two important pillars of all societies are: Reciprocity, kinship.

Ethics as per Indian view: The Vedas talked about 4 basic goals of existence: Prosperity, Satisfaction of desires, Moral duty, Salvation. - Upanishads distinguished between law and ethics – ethics come from inner desire -Jain philosophy was based on the ideal principle of non-violence - Buddha dwelt on compassion and brotherhood

APPROACHES FOR OPERATIONALIZATION

Following approaches are suggested towards implementation of sustainable initiatives for institutionalizing successful ethical practices and responsibilities.

(a) **Emergence of a Global Business Ethics**: The basis is the growing sense that responsibility for righting social wrongs belongs to all organizations and realizing that growing businesses need for integrative mechanisms such as ethics. Ethics reduce operating uncertainties. Voluntary guidelines avoid government impositions. Ethical conduct is needed in an increasingly interdependent world—everyone in the same game; Companies wish to avoid problems and/or be good public citizens

Ways for companies to integrate ethics are to institutionalize the following disciplines: - Top management commitment in word and deed; - Establishment of company codes of ethics; - Supply chain codes; - Develop, monitor, enforce ethical behavior; - Seek external assistance; External Assistance with Ethics will include the following: Industry or professional codes; Certification programs, e.g., ISO 9000; Adopt/follow global codes; Caux Round Table Principles

(b) **Challenges to a Global Ethic**: - Global rules emerge from negotiations and will reflect values of the strong; - Global rules may be viewed as an end rather than a beginning; - Rules can depress innovation and creativity; - Rules are static but globalization is dynamic.

(c) **Social responsibility/environmental sustainability:** Social and environmental responsibility (SER) is to be woven into the fabric of business. A vibrant successful business Values and ethics SER Programs have to be designed and implemented.

(d) **Document Code of Business Ethics**: A document that provides behavioral guidelines that cover daily activities and decisions within the organization.

(e) **Ethics Culture**: Ethics training should include: A message from the CEO; Development and discussion of codes of ethics; Procedures for discussing and reporting unethical behaviour.

(f) **Business Ethics for decision making**: Principles of conduct within organizations have to guide decision making and behavior at all levels. To align ethical and strategic decision making in the following ways: - Incorporate ethical considerations into long-term planning - Incorporate ethical considerations into performance appraisals - Encourage whistle-blowing - Monitor department and corporate performance regarding ethical issues.

(g) **Social Responsibility**: Actions an organization takes beyond what is legally required to protect or enhance the well-being of living things.

HUMAN ANGLE

Factors Influencing Ethical Behaviour: The desired behaviours of organizations and individuals have to be given due consideration in developing related strategies and their spread. What is ethical behaviour: Competing fairly and honestly; communicating truthfully; not harming others. The important factors to be considered are: cultural differences;

knowledge; corporate behavior; reporting systems. In the design, ethical situations to be taken care are ethical dilemma and ethical lapse.

Mother Teresa is an inspiration for Social Responsibility. "Be faithful in small things because it is in them that your strength lies". - Mother Teresa. Lessons from Mother Teresa: - Commitment to a cause. - Crises of faith - Persevering through criticism

BUSINESS ANGLE

(A). Business Efforts to Reduce Pollution: Environmental Issues; Environmental Staff; Performance Expectations; Performance Rewards; Long-Term Cost; Product Development; Supplier Expectations; Training and Awareness. **(B). Responsibility toward Consumers**: Product Safety; Accurate Information; Freedom of Choice; Right to Be Heard. **(C). Responsibility toward Investors**: Fair Profit Distribution; Social Responsibility; Ethical Behavior. **(D). Responsibility toward Employees**: Equal Employment Opportunity; Affirmative Action; Occupational Health and Safety; Disabilities Act.

SOCIETY ANGLE

Some of the important factors to be consistently and cautiously guarded are: - Global Ethics and Social Responsibility. - Bribery; Environmental Abuse. - Unscrupulous Business Practices

ENVIRONMENAL ANGLE

Sustainable development involves the simultaneous improvement of the economy, the environment, and the well-being of people. It is suggested to adhere to the global Green Standards: ISO 14000 for achieving sustainable development.

Standards are Important for Environmental Management Systems: The management system includes setting goals and priorities, assignment of responsibility for accomplishing them, measuring and reporting on results, and external verification of claims. ISO 14000 defines a voluntary environmental management system. Used in conjunction with appropriate goals, and with management commitment, the standards will help improve corporate performance.

They will provide an objective basis for verifying a company's claims about its performance. This is particularly important in relation to international trade, where at present almost anyone can make assertions about environmental performance—and there are only limited means to address genuineness and sincerity.

Consumers, governments, and companies up and down the supply chain are all seeking ways to reduce their environmental impact and increase their long-run sustainability. For companies, the key goals are to become more efficient—to get more output per unit of input— while earning profits and maintaining the trust of their stakeholders. Implementation of a management system based approach will help companies focus attention on environmental issues, and bring them into the main stream of corporate decision-making.

ISO 14000 is designed to provide customers with a reasonable assurance that the performance claims of a company are accurate. In fact, the standards will help integrate the environmental management systems of companies that trade with each other in all corners of the world.

Interest of Business: ISO 14000 can fill two requirements in an organization. The first is the internal need for a system that will help the organization address all of the legal, commercial and other challenges related to the environment that face it today. The second is the need to be able to assure those outside of the company that the company is meeting its stated environmental policies.

Internal Benefits: Reduce incidents and liability, Efficiency, Performance, Improved corporate culture. External benefits: Third party assurance and recognition, Market access, Regulatory relief, Public image and community relations

Interest of Environmentalists: ISO 14000 provides a useful tool with which to hold companies accountable. When a company does establish a positive environmental policy, the ISO 14000 system can be used to check that it is actually accomplishing its goals, and reporting appropriately on them.

Furthermore, companies can be encouraged to insist that all of their suppliers meet the environmental policy goals.

SUSTAINABLE DEVELOPMENT

Relevance to Sustainable Development: Sustainable development involves the simultaneous improvement of the economy, the environment, and the well-being of people.

The definition comes from the World Commission on Environment and Development: **Sustainable development is development that meets the needs of the present without compromising the ability of future generations to meet their own needs.**

The goals of economic and social development must be defined in terms of sustainability in all countries—developed or developing, market-oriented or centrally planned. Interpretations will vary, but must share certain general features and must flow from a consensus on the basic concept of sustainable development and on a broad strategic framework for achieving it.

In the corporate context: For the business enterprise, sustainable development means adopting business strategies and activities that meet the needs of the enterprise and its stakeholders today while protecting, sustaining and enhancing the human and natural resources that will be needed in the future.

Surroundings in which an organization operates, including air, water, land, natural resources, flora, fauna, humans, and their interrelation. Surroundings in this context extend from within an organization to the global system. The standards are Proactive Building Blocks for Achieving Sustainable Development.

SUMMARY OF THE APPROACHES FOR OPERATIONALIZATION

Culture of Integrity - Leadership and Structure - Auditing, Monitoring, and Assessment: Benchmarking, Maximizing the Benefit, Ethics and Compliance Training

- **Reputation and Corporate Responsibility:** Corporate compliance of ethics programs have to be linked up with corporate responsibility. That increases the reputation.

CONCLUSION

What is ethical behaviour? Competing Fairly and Honestly; Communicating Truthfully; Not Harming Others. Social responsibility and business ethics are often regarding as the same concepts. However, the social responsibility movement is but one aspect of the overall discipline of business ethics. The social responsibility movement arose particularly with increased public consciousness about the role of business in helping to cultivate and maintain highly ethical practices in society and particularly in the natural environment. A unified approach to business ethics is required to build and maintain an effective compliance and ethics program: The broad steps include the following: - Spread importance of compliance and ethics across the organization. - Identifying the essential elements of a compliance program - Develop organizational steps for an effective program implementation - Detailing and tailoring the compliance program towards a successful monitoring mechanism. - Prepare compliance materials, renewable training plans and institutionalization of business ethics. At the end it is all about compliance.

CHAPTER-40

The Importance of Corporate Governance in Hedging Against Global Financial Crisis in the Future India

Dr. Rita Yi Man Li

Department of Economics and Finance,
Hong Kong Shue Yan University, Hong Kong

INTRODUCTION

Financial crisis which happens recently in United States shows the side effect of globalization and global trade. While crisis in the past happens in one place does not always affect the other countries, it may not hold true in the future. It also reminds us the importance of corporate governance in our financial market. India, as a developing country, is vulnerable in financial crisis in the sense that foreign direct investment plays important role in economic development. In the following section, it reviews the history of financial crisis, corporate governance and its importance in India.

FINANCIAL CRISIS

History evidences that one of the crisis which happens periodically (Table 40.1) and affects lots of us around the globe is financial crisis. Financial crisis happened locally can bring negative impact to other parts of the World. Although crisis happens locally is uncommon to affect countries miles away centuries ago, globalization, international trade and World Wide Web shorten the distance between countries. Stulz (2005) proposes that cross border flow GDP increases in the past 2 decades (Figure 40.1). It provides vivid explanation on why problem of credit crunch in one local market may affect countries nearby so quickly.

Table 40.1 : Financial Crisis

Year	Financial Crisis
1907	US bank panic spreads to France and Italy after stock market collapse.
1921	Commodity prices crash.
1923	Hyperinflation in Germany starts monetary crisis.
1929	"The Great Depression" begins after equity crash.
1931	Financial crises experienced by the UK, Japan, Germany, and Austria.
1933	Gold standard given up by the US, starting panic in the banking system.
1966	US credit crisis creates deflation and huge economic slump.
1973	World financial crisis begins after OPEC quadruples the price of oil.
1982	Global credit crunch prevents many developing countries from paying their debt
1987	Bond and equity market crashes.
1989	Japanese bubble.
1989	Junk bond crisis.
1992	French Maastricht Treaty sparks crisis in European Monetary System
1994	Major bond market correction.
1995	Mexican financial crisis caused by the peso's peg to the dollar during excessive inflation.
1997	Asian financial crisis creates exchange rate and banking crisis, created from stock market and real estate speculation, along with many Asian currencies pegged to the US dollar.
1998	Russia defaults on payment obligations during major financial crisis.
2000	Dot-com bubble pops, creating a massive fall in equity markets from over-speculation in tech stocks.
2001	Another junk bond crisis.
2001	September 11 attacks create risk by hindering various critical communication hubs necessary for payment on the financial markets.
2001	Economic crisis in Argentina, resulting in the government defaulting on payment obligations.
2002	Bond market crisis in Brazil.
2007	US real estate crisis causes the collapse of massive international banks and financial institutions. Equity markets take a dive.

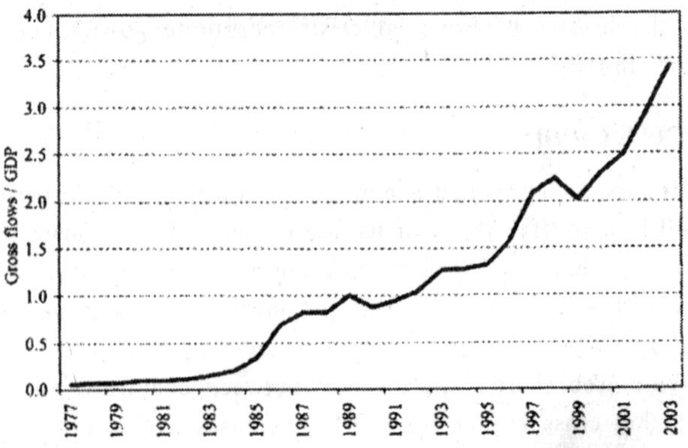

Figure 40.1 Gross cross-border flows to GDP (Stulz, 2005).

DECOUPLING THEORY IS REFUTED IN EMERGING ECONOMIES

The decoupling theory held that even if advanced economies suffers from an economic downturn, emerging economies remain unscathed because of their improved policy framework, relatively healthy banking sector, substantial foreign exchange reserves and robust corporate balance sheets. Nevertheless, empirical evidence from recent financial crisis refutes the 'decoupling theory' — emerging economies have been hit by the crisis too. In present rapidly globalizing world, the 'decoupling theory' is no longer persuasive. Empirical evidence from the last few months which includes capital flow reversals, sharp widening of spreads on sovereign and corporate debt and abrupt currency depreciations invalidated the 'decoupling theory' stands totally. It further reinforces the notion that no country can be an island in present globalized world. Growth prospects of emerging economies have been undermined by the cascading financial crisis with considerable variation across countries (Subbarao, 2009). In case of recent financial crisis, India's financial markets, equity markets, money markets, forex markets and credit markets are under pressure from a number of directions. First, as a result of the global liquidity squeeze, Indian firms and banks' overseas source of finance dry up, forcing them to shift their credit demand to the domestic banking sector (Subbarao, 2009). Besides, similar to many other BRICS (Brazil, Russia, India, China, South Africa) members, foreign direct investment (FDI) plays an important role in India's economic development. There is also evidence of FDI's growing importance. It has been increased from 42.7 million in 2003 to 415.54 in 2010 (Mingpao, 2010).

PRIVATE FIRMS AND COMPANIES DEVELOPMENT IN INDIA

There is a long history in India's mercantile tradition. The British came to India and opened up the East India Company. It grew up quickly with an increase in strength and power, controlled business activities in India. In 1875, the Bombay Stock Exchage was formed. The stock market coverage increases at a fast rate. In 1974, there were over 800 firms became listed companies. In spite of this, many companies and firms in India are owned and run by family members in early India times. The growth of family owned firms grew nearly in the same pace as those in other countries. One vivid explanation suggest that in developing economies where private property rights are not well-defined or/and not enforced effectively by the government, concentrated ownership offers significant advantages to these companies in terms of risk minimization (Gollakota and Gupta, 2006).

Another characteristic of India firms is the disconnection between equity ownership and actual control. It roots in the pre-independence period. As nationalized financial institutions control substantial amounts of equity, they are able to appoint their own directors to their family businesses. Nevertheless, because the financial institutions are not accountable for the profitability of the investments they make, there is no motivation for them to exercise a level of control which would have been commensurate with their equity interests. Control is usually left to the family members who run the businesses and hold relatively little equity as compared with those hold by public financial institutions (Gollakota and Gupta, 2006).

CORPORATE GOVERNANCE AND FINANCIAL CRISIS

'Corporate governance' is defined as a set of formal and informal institutions' constraints on behavior. It determinies a firm's stakeholder capacities on cash flows control and decisions-making in a firm. 'financial globalization provides... incentives for corporate insiders to protect the rights of their minority investors... through better corporate governance (Markus, 2008). Economists and legal scholars often refers corporate governance to the defense of shareholders' interests. Classical economists which include Adam Smith, Berle and Means concern separation of control and ownership, i.e. the agency relationship between the "principal" (investors are viewed as outsiders) and "agent" (manager and entrepreneur are regarded as insider) (Tirole, 2001).

Corporate governance is the one of the most important legal tools in predicting investor protection. It is also a factor which encourages the financial markets' development. When investors are well-protected, they are willing to pay more for securities, it also attract more entrepreneurs to issue securities in turn. Shareholders and creditors' protection under corporate governance includes not only the rights written into the regulations and laws but also the enforcement effectiveness of both. Countries which protect shareholders usually have a higher rate of IPO (initial public offering) activities, larger numbers of listed securities per capita, more valuable stock markets than those unprotected countries (Porta et al., 2000). Previous studies have also shown there is an ingenious connection between financial crisis and investor protection. Governance variables which include law enforcement quality and investor protection indices are powerful predictors of market declines extent during the crisis (Porta et al., 2000).

CORPORATE GOVERNANCE DEVELOPMENT IN INDIA

As India was once a British colony, India corporate law (includes corporate governance) ties to British corporate law (Afsharipour, 2009). Table 40.2 shows the history of corporate governance development in India and Table 40.3 illustrates the content and coverage of corporate governance under Clause 49.

Table 40.2 History of corporate governance development in India (Afsharipour, 2009)

Date	Corporate governance development in India
2001	31st March, Clause 49firstly come into effect for all the companiesin BSE.
31 March 2002	Compliance requirements were extended to cover all the listed companies with a net worth of Rs 25 crore (about US$ 5.5 million) paid-up capital of Rs 10 crore (about US$2.2 million).
31 March 2003	Companies with a paid-up capital of Rs. 3 crore had to comply with Clause 49.
26 Augusr 2003	SEDI amended Clause 49 according to the recommendations from Murthy Committee.
31 March 2004	The revised Clause 49 came into effect, mandatorily required all the previously listed and newly listed companies to comply with the new Clause. Nevertheless, this deadline was pushed to 1 January later on.

Table 40.3 Requirements in clause 49 concerning corporate governance (Afsharipour, 2009)

Item	Details
Board of director s' Independence requirement	• Requirement: if the chairman is an executive director, there should be 50% independent directors; in case the chairman is a non-executive director, there should be 33% independent directors.
Board of director requirements and limitations	• Code of Conduct (Ethics) is required. • Director may be present at most 10 committees and acts as chair of at most 5 meetings. • Members should meet 4 times a year (at most 3 months between meetings).
Audit committee's Role and powers	• Members should meet 4 times per year (the gap in between these meetings should not be more than 4 months). • They are responsible to oversee a company's financial reporting process and financial information disclosure quality, review statutory and internal editors and internal audit as well as whistleblower program.

Audit committee Composition	• It should be consisted of at least 3 directors and two-third of them must be independent. • All of them must be financially literate. • At least one of the committee members must process an accounting or finance management experience. • Chairman of Audit committee must be independent director. He should attend Annual General Meeting to answer shareholders' enquiries.
Disclosure	• In case of appointment and re-appointment of a director, shareholders have to provide (1) a brief resume of the director, (2) expertise in specific functional area, (3) companies that he holds directorship • Information includes presentation by analysts should be put in companies' websites. • Others include compliance history, corporate governance reports, annual report which includes detail description on management, industry structure and developments, financial performance, threats and opportunities, risk management, proceeds from offerings, compensation of director.
Certifications	• Company secretary and auditor certifies compliance with corporate governance. • CEO and CFO: effectiveness of financial control, financial statement, legal transactions and any changes in the abovementioned items.
Other recommendations in Clause 49	• Provision of board members' training. • Evaluate non-executive board members' performance. • Independent directors lose their status as independent if they have served in the company for 9 years.

CONCLUSION

As one of the members in BRICKS, India's economy is growing fast. Corporate governance is gaining its importance in her economic development. While previous financial crisis in the outside World may not affect India, it may not be true in the future. As there are getting more and more foreign direct investment activities in India, economic downturn in other parts of the globe may also badly affect India. Corporate governance not only lays down the foundation for India's economic development, it also provides a good legal regulation which can reduce the agency problem due to separation of owning and ruling firms. To better hedge against the side effect of future global crisis, it is expected that there will be some new requirements in Clause 49. Fine tuning of legal rules can also improve India's investment environment.

CHAPTER-41

Creating A Better India Through Higher Education Under Corporate Governance

(WITH SPECIAL REFERENCE TO THE PRIVATE COLLEGES IN RAJASTHAN)

Dr. Rajesh Kumar Sharma
Mr. Narendra Kumar Bansal
Dr. Mamta Verma

INTRODUCTION

Higher education is the backbone of a nation. The more highly educated the citizens of a nation are, the more progressive the nation is. India has long been enjoying the status of a developing nation. No doubt, there are numerous of its being developing, but the lack of higher education is one of them. However, the last decade made a revolution in the field of education, and particularly, in the field of higher education. The credit for bringing the most of the students closer to the various branches and courses relating to higher education goes to the corporates that have created an incredibly healthy environment for higher education. It will not be an exaggeration to say that the private sector of higher education has been hacked by the corporates. The result is that there are several engineering, medical and management colleges all over India. It is true that the purpose of the corporates is to make more and more money through them, but it cannot be denied that they are also pursuing the young men and women with distinct potential in them to create a better India that can acclaim itself to be one of the best nations in the field of higher education.As in the other parts of India, in Rajasthan too, there is an incredible revolution in the field of higher education.As a policy matter of the State Government gives every year a permission to open new degree, B.Ed., management and technical colleges. The purpose of opening private universities and colleges is to enable every individual to join higher education with no difficulty, and thus, to become a part of the process of globalization of higher education. Rajasthan is one of the most leading states of India. Quite rich in its cultural heritage and rigid traditions, it has often deprived its people of getting education, and especially higher education which had always been a privilege to the elites. However, with the wave of the concept of globalization of higher education, Rajasthan is now going to change its rigidity, and is now liberal enough to allow its people to join this process and to build up their career in the various fields through higher education. In fact, the role of the private colleges and universities in making the people of Rajasthan highly educated is so immense. At present there is every imaginable opportunity of getting higher education to the promising students in Rajasthan. In addition to the traditional educational courses, there are several technical, managerial and medical courses which are magnetically drawing the boys and the girls of Rajasthan to join them. More over, these courses are accessible to most of the students. If they fail to join them due to financial problem, the banks make it posssible by lending education loans.Many of the students are getting higher education by borrowing such loans.Indeed, the process of globalization higher education has incredibly changed the destiny of Rajasthan, the state which has always been blamed for its educational backwardness.

MEANING & OBJECTIVES OF HIGHER EDUCATION

Higher education is the study beyond the level of secondary education. Institutions of higher education include not only colleges and universities but also professional schools in such fields as law, theology, medicine, business, music, and art. They also include teacher-training schools, community colleges, and institutes of technology. At the end of a prescribed course of study, a degree, diploma, or certificate is awarded. To start with the definition of the term-Higher Education- In fact, There is no simple definition of higher education. The international definition of tertiary (post school) education divides it into two parts. Type A (Higher Education) and Type B (Further Education). A higher education qualification at degree level takes a minimum of three years to complete, more typically four. It will have a theoretical underpinning, it will be at a level which would qualify someone to work in a professional field and it will usually be taught in an environment which also includes advanced research activity. Shortly, Higher education mainly and generally means university level education. It offers a number of qualifications ranging from Higher National Diplomas and Foundation Degrees to Honors Degrees and as further step, Postgraduate programmes such as Masters Degrees and Doctorates. These are recognized throughout the world as representing specialist expertise supported by a wide range of skills that employers find very useful. Further education is generally includes those post graduate studies in where one can gain one's Master and Doctorate degrees.These degrees mark the highest one can earn, though they are divided into two levels.

MAIN PLAYERS IN THE HIGHER EDUCATION IN INDIA

India, like the other countries of the world provides its scholars the facility of higher education. There is a wide network of higher education which has several players or agencies to make the higher education accessible to every one.

University Grants Commission (UGC) is responsible for coordination, determination and maintenance of standards, release of grants.

Professional Councils are responsible for recognition of courses, promotion of professional institutions and providing grants to undergraduate programmes and various awards. The statutory professional councils are:All India Council for Technical Education (AICTE),Distance Education Council (DEC) Indian Council for Agriculture Research (ICAR), Bar Council of India (BCI), National Council for Teacher Education (NCTE) Rehabilitation Council of India (RCI) Medical Council of India (MCI), Pharmacy Council of India (PCI) Indian NursingCouncil (INC) Dentist Council of India (DCI) Central Council of Homeopathy (CCH)Central Council of Indian Medicine (CCIM).

Central Government is responsible for major policy relating to higher education in the country. It provides grants to the UGC and establishes central universities in the country. The Central Government is also responsible for declaration of Educational Institutions as 'Deemed to be University' on the recommendation of the UGC.

Presently there are twenty five Central Universities in the country. In pursuance of the Mizoram Accord, another Central University in the State of Mizoram is planned. There are 99 Institutions which have been declared as Deemed to be Universities by the Govt. of India as per Section of the UGC Act, 1956.

State Governments are responsible for establishment of State Universities and colleges, and provide plan grants for their development and non-plan grants for their maintenance. The coordination and cooperation between the Union and the States is brought about in the field of education through the Central Advisory Board of Education (CABE).Special Constitutional responsibility of the Central Government: Education is on the 'Concurrent list' subject to Entry 66 in the Union List of the Constitution. This gives exclusive Legislative Power to the Central Govt. for co-ordination and determination of standards in Institutions of higher education or research and scientific and technical institutions.

Thus, in India, various players are playing their role in bringing the student closer to higher education and helping them take benefit of the available courses of higher education. Indeed, in the present age, there may be seen a revolution in the field of higher education as everyone seems to be determined to get higher education even if his financial condition does not allow him to take admission in colleges and universities. It is probably so because now the people are aware of the fact that their problems may be over only through education.

HIGHER EDUCATION IN INDIA

Higher education has occupied a dominant position in independent India since it was perceived as a promoter of economic growth, technological development and also as an instrument of equal opportunity and upward social mobility. Various commissions and committees have deliberated on its criticality to the social and economic development of the country. The establishment of special institutions of national importance, of the Indian Institutes of Technology and Management — all of them make contributions to the increasing significance and excellence of higher education in India's development Higher ecucation in India has evolved in distinct and divergent streams with each stream monitored by an apex body, indirectly controlled by the Ministry of Human Resource Development. The 415 universities/institutions, are mostly funded by the state governments. However, there are 25 important universities called Central universities, which are maintained by the Union Government and because of relatively large funding, they have an edge over the others. The engineering education and business schools are monitored and accredited by the All India Council for Technical Education (AICTE) while medical education is monitored and accredited by the Medical Council of India (MCI). Like-wise, agriculture education and research is monitored by the Indian Council for Agriculture Research. Apart from these, National Council for Teacher Education (NCTE) controls all the teacher training institutions in the country. The country has some ace engineering, management and medical education institutions which are directly funded by the Ministry of Human Resource Development of the Union Government. Admission to all professional education colleges is done through all-India common admission tests of which the IIT-JEE, AIEEE, CAT and CPMT are the most popular ones. Most of the institutions reserve a small percentage of seats for foreign students.The total scenario of education has been fully decorated by higher education system. Higher education plays the most significant role in the society as well as in the life of the individual.

GLOBALIZATION OF HIGHER EDUCATION THROUGH PRIVATIZATION IN INDIA

Globalization is apparent in every field, and it reveals that now the whole world is globally united and has come at the one and same platform. Globalization is a generic term and it can be defined in a number of different ways depending on the context. The definition - description - given by Knight and de Wit (1997) appears to be the best operational one for any discussion pertaining to higher education in this context. According to them, Globalization "is the flow of technology, economy, knowledge, people, values, ideas...across the borders. Globalization affects each country in a different way due to a nation's individual history, traditions, culture and priorities." To cope with the 'Globalization', the higher education system has to re-orient its structure and function besides enlarging the scope of its provisions to meet the challenges of Globalization. This re-orientation process is termed as Internationalization. Internationalization of Higher Education is one of the ways a country responds to the demands of globalization. As part of the general thrust for increasing the size of enrollment in higher education, spurred by the need for additional resources, the countries in the region have already undertaken the initiatives to privatize the higher education. In India, establishment of new institutions by the governments (federal and State) with full grants was stopped as far back as in early 80s. All the new growth in terms of institutions, enrollment and diversification of higher education is through the private initiative. India, having the second largest network of higher education institutions in the world, with more than 265 universities and 11200 colleges, expanding its higher education system only through private resources during the past 15-20 years. From 1994-95 to 1991-99 alone, more than 2100 colleges have been established through privatization strategy.

HISTORICAL & CULTURAL BACKGROUND OF RAJASTHAN

Rajasthan is a wonderful land of praiseworthy history and culture. It is a land where the awe-inspiring legends of heroism and romance still resonate from its equally amazing architectures. Rajasthan is a land where historical monuments still stand to tell the tale of the bygone era. The magical land of Rajasthan exhibits splendor and royalty in every walk of life. The name Rajasthan is self- explanatory as it reflects the meaning 'Land of Rajas'; located in the north-west of India. It is surrounded by enduring Aravallis ranges on one hand and the distinctive Thar Desert on the other. The state of Rajasthan was formed in 1956 but its reference is found both in Ramayana and Mahabharata.Forts and Palaces Tour of Rajasthan include a visit to heritage hotels, which were once the Havelis of the kings and rich merchants. They stand as symbol of rich culture grandeur even today. It mystifies the audiences who specifically visit the land to see in reality what they have read in books about king and their subjects, and lifestyle in the imposing and monumental forts and palaces.The warrior class Rajput of the 6th and 7th century can easily be compared with European Knights. The legends of their valour are as old as 12th century; and they share their lineage with Kshatriyas, the combatant class that came to power in Vedic times. The arid zone of Great Indian Desert throbs with life when the multi-hued spruced population comes together to celebrate life in the form of fairs harvest celebration or religious occasions marked for deity. This culture dates back to antiquity; it is for this reason the architecture, arts and crafts, songs, dress-code, palaces and forts are facsimiles of tradition of the land.The Rajasthan Tours of forts and palaces showcases a rich historical background and includes cities like Bikaner, Jaisalmer, Udaipur with romantic Lake Palace, Bundi, and Jaipur- the capital of Rajasthan in its itinerary. A good India tour operator will also include interesting excursions for you as you tour the royal citadels in the desert state, depending on your interests and passions.Jaipur prides its City Palace comprising of Chandra Mahal, Shri Govind Dev Temple and City Palace Museum; the fusion of Mughal and Rajasthani architecture is very evident here. 5-storeyed structure of pink sandstone, Hawa Mahal or the Palace of Winds was built in 1799. Its symmetrical balconies were specifically designed for ladies viewing in privacy and the building garners a high souvenir value.Jaisalmer a bastion city in the heart of the desert state is enriched with yellow sandstone rhythmic architectural monuments. Jaisalmer Fort is the oldest one you will see in the state. Jodhpur or the blue city is fortified with 10 km stretch of stone wall on a sandstone hill. Inside, rests the well protected Mehrangarh fort, which never fails to mesmerize tourists. Udaipur, the jewel of the state, was under the Sisodia rule for 1200 years. Its City Palace highlights include an interior decor of mirror work and ivory inter-spaced inlay work that cannot be described in words.

SUGGESTIONS

- In order to bring all the scholars closer to the process of globalization of higher education, more and more colleges should be opened every year by the corporates so that more and more students of India may join this process.
- Only qualified teachers must be appointed so that they can impart the education in a proper and systematic way, and for it the corporates should be ready to pay such handsome salaries to the teachers as can provide them satisfaction and as can help them meet their economic needs.
- Every year there must be the orientation programmes and refresher programmes for the teachers.
- Communication gap should be made over through the classes of personality development.
- There must be the unified syllabus for the courses for the sake of higher education.
- In order to ensure the placement of the students more and more multinational companies should be invited to recruit the students.

- For the weak students remedial classes should be arranged.
- Seminars and conferences should be arranged regularly and systematically in order to provide opportunities to the students to explore the things and to be familiar with the latest trends.
- Eduacational awareness campaigns should be arranged from time-to-time in order to make the students of Rajasthan familiar with the educational courses.
- Rajasthan is a poor state of India where poverty can be seen among the people, therefore, there must be a proper arrangement of fee-concession and scholarship.

CHAPTER-42

CREATING A BETTER INDIA THROUGH CORPORATE GOVERNANCE

Priyanka Garg

(lecturer in deptt. of ABST and B.B.A.)

Ashok Kumar Sharma

Mrs. Rita Mudai

(lecturer in deptt. of Bus.Adm.)

INTRODUCTION

Corporate governance is a system of structuring, operating and controlling a company with a view to achieve long term strategic goals to satisfy shareholders, creditors, employees, customers and suppliers. It is a system by which business corporations are directed and controlled.

Laws regulating joint stock company's and the securities industry establish the legal framework interaction between different stakeholders. They provide the general framework for the governance structure of all joint stock company's in a given jurisdiction. This framework is further refined by; (1) each joint stock company's charter; and (2) additional external regulations. Regulations specific to each joint stock company are defined in the charter, it establishes the basic governing rules for each individual joint stock company and may define certain issues that are left to the discretion of each joint stock company. External regulations include rules of requirements established by self-regulatory organizations such as stock exchanges, chambers of commerce and industry or associations of listed companies. Both types of refinements are significant because they further define duties, responsibilites and relationships which are not prescribed by law.

The term "corporate governance" refers to the "governance" or administration of "corporations." It concerns a specific type of business entity, namely corporations. More specifically, it mostly concerns publicly-owned corporations whose shares are traded on a stock exchange or over the counter. It does not refer to the administration of other types of companies.

REVIEW OF LITERATURE

Regulations, laws on the books, or voluntary codes, enforcement is key to creating an effective business environment and good corporate governance, at least in developing countries and transition economies. A framework is presented to help explain enforcement, the impact on corporate governance when rules are not enforced, and what can be done to improve corporate governance in weak enforcement environments. The limited empirical evidence suggests that private enforcement tools are often more effective than public tools. However, some public enforcement is necessary, and private enforcement mechanisms often require public laws to function. Private initiatives are often also taken under the threat of legislation or regulation, although in some countries bottom-up, private-led initiatives preceded and even shaped public laws. Concentrated ownership aligns incentives and encourages monitoring, but it weakens other corporate governance mechanisms and can impose significant costs. Various steps can be taken to reduce these costs and reinforce other corporate governance mechanisms. But political economy constraints, resulting from the intermingling of business and politics, often prevent improvements in the enforcement environment and the adoption and implementation of public laws.

WHAT IS CORPORATE GOVERNANCE?

Corporate governance is about how companies or organizations are controlled. It is concerned with striking the balance between social and economic goals, and between individual and community goals. The corporate governance process is implemented to ensure that the management and business of the entities is conducted in line with highest standards of ethics and efficacy, assuming the best option to safeguard stakeholders' interest.

NEED FOR CORPORATE GOVERNANCE CREATING A BETTER INDIA

Corporate governance in India has undergone a paradigm shift by gradually becoming more conscience-driven due to interests of customers, employees, vendors and regulators, say experts.

The ever-changing dynamics of corporate governance was discussed and debated Monday in a seminar - "Visionary Corporate Governance Practices" - organized by the Confederation of Indian Industry (CII) here.

"Realizing the need for good governance, corporate governance has gradually evolved into a conscience approach from the traditional compliance one. There has been recognition of the need to balance interests of not just shareholders but different stakeholders who are equally important for the health of a company," said K.V. Kamath, managing director and chief executive of ICICI Bank Ltd.

ADVANTAGES OF CORPORATE GOVERNANCE CREATING A BETTER INDIA

Following are some of the key advantages of corporate governance:

Management

Good corporate governance allows even outsiders to assess the company on how well it is being governed. The core of corporate governance is its transparency and disclosure principles. An advantage with corporate governance is that the benefits are measurable. Good corporate governance ensures higher market valuation. Corporate governance initiatives should ensure that the board of control and management take the necessary steps that are in the best interest of the business of the company.

Transparency

Corporate governance encourages more transparency of the business, thereby attaining the trust of its stakeholders. This transparency is brought forward by improving access to capital and financial markets. Raising capital also becomes easier because of the support the company earns from its stakeholders. Asset diversification through mergers and acquisitions is made easier with a company that follows good corporate governance. Corporate governance practices encourage a system of internal control, which in turn leads to better profit margins. Thus, for a company, corporate governance initiatives make it possible to attract equity investors. The corporate value of the company is increased by adopting good corporate governance practices. If two companies have comparable financial records, institutional investors prefer to invest in the one that has shown a proven record as a well-governed company.

Benefits to Shareholders

Good corporate governance initiatives can assist the board of control and the management to act on objectives that are in the best interest of both the company and the shareholders. The shareholders also have greater security on the investments they have made because of the transparency and access to investment details. The shareholders are better informed on all important decisions of management, such as the sale of assets and amendments to articles.

Benefits to the National Economy

If a country has a reputation for its strong governance practices, this leads to greater confidence in the investors, which in turn leads to a good flow in capital. The reporting and accounting standards adopted by the country are also an important factor to bring in investments. Thus, good corporate governance practices can be beneficial for any country's national economy

CONCLUSION

Corporate governance philosophies differ around the world. However, with a few relatively minor exceptions, there exists a broad consensus on the elements of good corporate governance. It is widely understood that the most effective aspects of good corporate governance include:

- a strong board of directors, independent of management and with sufficient expertise to oversee corporate management on behalf of the company's shareholders;
- management compensation oversight, such as a compensation committee comprised of independent directors, to prevent opportunistic behaviour by management and help link management compensation to corporate performance;
- strong corporation laws and regulations designed to protect the rights of shareholders;
- extensive public disclosure requirements, including both financial and non-financial reporting designed to give shareholders and potential investors an accurate, timely and

thorough picture of the company's performance and liabilities; and

- a robust independent audit function, with sufficiently thorough procedures to confirm the accuracy of a public company's financial disclosure statements and overseen by a board committee comprised of independent directors, or by some other mechanism independent of management.

Furthermore, these aspects of good corporate governance must be made credible by strong government and private-sector enforcement mechanisms. Government regulators and law enforcement agencies must have the resources and legal authority to conduct thorough investigations of potential wrongdoing and self-dealing by corporate management. And regulators and law enforcement agencies must aggressively investigate and prosecute managerial and corporate wrongdoing on a constant, ongoing basis, not just when a major scandal arises. Likewise, corporate compliance officers must have the powers they need to ensure that all corporate employees (including senior management) comply with the law and abide by the company's internal corporate governance requirements. Other corporate governance 'gatekeepers' – such as lawyers and outside auditors – must be bound by a strong code of ethics and abide by the laws and professional requirements which apply to their profession. Without such aggressive overlapping enforcement mechanisms, even the best corporate governance standards can be undermined.

Despite the consensus, there remain differences in the degree of implementation, and until all markets converge their requirements on the highest quality corporate governance standards, investors will express different degrees of confidence in different markets, and markets and issuers demonstrating the highest standards will continue to attract investors on the most favourable terms. In short, the best public companies will continue to view strong corporate governance as an investment well worth making.

CHAPTER-43

CORPORATE SOCIAL RESPONSIBILITY AND CORPORATE GOVERNANCE

Lucky Goyal, MBA Sam. III

Khalsa Management Institute. Sri Ganganagar

Rovil Lalgarhia, CA (Final)

Ms. Monika Malpani CA (Final)

Harsh Singal, CA

INTRODUCTION

.CSR may affect the agency relationship between shareholder and manager, and how the shareholder may use it to his own benefit. Corporate Social Responsibility (CSR) has become an inescapable priority for business leaders across the globe. Governments, activists and the media have become adept at holding companies to account for the social consequences of their actions and there is a large and growing community of international, regional and national organizations working on sustainable development issues, both in the public and private sectors. It is no surprise then that firms are grappling on strategic, tactical and operational levels to identify ways to meet society's demands, this in combination with achieving company performance targets. This paper first sets a definition of CSR as an extended model of corporate governance and then accounts for a voluntary approach to CSR, meant as voluntary compliance with CSR strategic management standards, in terms of an economic theory of self-regulation based on the concepts of social contract, reputation and reciprocal conformism. Various forms of self-regulatory practices which are applied on a discretionary basis are explored in this paper, arguing that while incomplete contracts and imperfect knowledge debar form resorting to reputation effects in order to support discretional self-regulation, on the contrary an explicit standard for CSR strategic management, both publicly shared by stakeholders and firms through social dialogue - make it possible to put again at work the reputation mechanism inducing endogenous incentives of compliance with a voluntary standard; the result being that stakeholders are encouraged to 'trust' in the firm's practices and commitment to CSR.

MAIN AIMS OF THE STUDY

The research was carried out among all relevant stakeholders in the country: local and foreign businesses, business and professional associations, trade unions, local and national governments, non-governmental organizations, media and academia. The main aims of this baseline study were to:

- Identify the actors who promote CSR at country level.
- Assess the level of engagement in CSR of actors promoting CSR at country level through mapping their recent past and present CSR promotion activities.
- Assess the level of dialogue between different actors promoting CSR.
- Identify the level of foreign and domestic business engagement in CSR implementation at country level and collect examples of good practices.
- Identify capacity gaps/constraints of CSR promoters and business entities in engaging in CSR activities.
- Formulate recommendations and suggest specific activities based on the findings of the survey.

SOCIALLY RESPONSIBLE INVESTING – THE GROWING SOCIAL EXPECTATIONS OF SHAREHOLDERS

The topics of socially responsible investing (SRI) and sustainability investing (SI), have been gaining ground as investors seek to incorporate concepts such as sustainability and responsible corporate behaviour into their assessments of a company's long-term value. Yet socially responsible investing has always been an awkward science. Early approaches screened out "sin sectors" such as tobacco. Subsequent evolutions tilted toward rewarding good performers, largely in the oil and gas extraction industries (such as Shell and BP), oil and natural gas furnishing about three-fifths of our energy needs, fueling our homes, workplaces, factories, transportation systems and constituting the raw materials for plastics, chemicals, medicines and synthetic fibers. However, assessment of a firm's social responsibility level was carried out on the basis of often-vague criteria. Hence, these early approaches tended to force an unacceptable tradeoff between social criteria and investment returns. The scandal of Enron caused the concern about the state of corporate governance. Ironically, Sustainability investing is the explicit recognition that social, economic, environmental, and ethical factors directly affect business strategy, for example, how companies attract and retain employees, how they manage the risks and create opportunities from climate change, a company's culture, corporate governance standards, stakeholder-engagement strategies, philanthropy, reputation, and brand management. SRI brings together all of the approaches which consist in integrating non-financial criteria (social, environmental and societal) in decisions involving funds and portfolio management. Three types of socially responsible investment are commonly identified:

1. Exclusion funds: they exclude certain sectors of activity (gambling, weapons, tobacco, etc.) for moral or religious reasons.

2. Funds with a high shareholder commitment: managers exercise their shareholder's right (voting rights at AGMs, proposal of resolutions) to "force" the company to adopt a socially responsible policy. They also maintain regular dialogue with company management boards.

3. "Best in class" funds: the investment process is not based on ex ante exclusion of certain sectors of activity. Best in class is the philosophy of the Dow Jones Sustainability Indexes and the KLD Broad Market Social Index – these indexes replicate the underlying benchmarks but select only the best performers on environmental, social, and governance parameters.

However, these SRI approaches are somewhat generalized (one size fits all) and questionnaires do not allow for true insight into the decision-making process. A lack of an evaluation system of SRI funds is also problematic. Schepers and Sethi (2003) indicated in their paper that there are so many differences among SRI funds, for example, criteria of screening, methods of screening and the purpose of SRI funds that inconsistency occurs through the inability to make valid comparisons, resulting in mismatching problems between investor's expectations and the SRI fund. In addition, sustainability research analysis is complicated by the fact that it requires you to think long-term and to think about the first- and second-order effects of an issue, which is not in keeping with the traditionally opportunistic and short-termist approach to investment in stocks. Global companies are expected to meet global standards of corporate accountability, responsibility, and sustainability. Yet those standards are complex and contradictory, and despite best efforts to create order amidst this chaos, they continue to increase. Non-profit making organizations such as.

THE RELATIONSHIP BETWEEN SRI AND CSR

Does the SRI market really encourage a firm to take CSR to the core of its business strategy and can we identify a correlation here? On the basis of existing research, this is considered to be problematic according to some empirical studies, which have concluded that there is no significant correlation between SRI and CSR activities. However, when considering the correlation between SRI and CSR, one would expect that the on the disclosure of firms relating to their CSR. The effect of screening of SRI funds, leading to the investment decision, is also likely to be an influencing factor encouraging firms to report on their CSR activities. Indeed, it is also possible for a firm engaged in CSR activities to be rejected by SRI funds, which due to the objective nature of the assessment, may encourage the firm to revise its activities in line with the expectations of the SRI funds. This in turn may stimulate competing firms to improve their behavior and could produce a good social outcome as a whole.

OUTSOURCING OF CSR – THE EXTENDED CSR ENTERPRISE

According to the Indian business publication, 'Business Respect' (2008), Indian companies find themselves under growing pressure to account for their sustainability impacts as they seek to access global markets and to attract foreign investment. The Institute of Chartered Accountants of India (ICAI) has reported to the press (Business Respect newsletter, 2008) that it is working on a new set of rules on CSR disclosure, inspired by the Global Reporting Initiative guidelines on reporting. The ICAI has formed a committee to develop its framework in standardizing approaches to sustainability reporting. This initiative is not surprising considering the increase in business being outsourced to India from European countries. When outsourcing work to countries such as Vietnam, China or India, organizations have to consider a number of matters that have long ceased to be an issue when outsourcing work to well-established European vendors on- or near-shore. Striking a balance between the various interests involved in outsourcing ICT work or business processes via BPO is of key importance to firms.

DO SOCIALITY AND ENVIRONMENTAL CONSCIOUSNESS REALLY LEAD TO IMPROVED COMPANY PERFORMANCE?

It is also difficult to answer. Toyota has demonstrated that a product that is designed by environmental perspective succeeded and found a new market in Japan and this in turn led to competitive advantage. Attempts need to be made to answer such questions as; how could work be practiced more economically and how can we use material without waste? Such questions must not only be answered on operational level, but also taken to a strategic level – to enable the necessary changes in business practices – top down. One thing that is for sure - the pressure on business to play a role in social issues will continue to grow. Over the past ten years, those institutions that have grown in power and influence have been those that can operate effectively within a global sphere of operations. These are effectively the corporates and the NGOs. Those institutions that are predominantly tied to the nation state have been finding themselves increasingly frustrated at their lack of ability to shape and manage events. These include national governments, police, judiciary and others. There is a growing interest, therefore, in businesses taking a lead in addressing those issues in which they have an interest where national government have failed to come up with a solution. The focus Unilever has on supporting a sustainable fisheries approach is one example. Using the power of their supply chain, such companies are placed to have a real influence. Frequently, though, CSR efforts are counterproductive, for two reasons. Firstly, they pit business against society, when in reality the two are interdependent. Secondly, they pressure companies to regard corporate social responsibility in generic ways instead of in the way most appropriate to their individual strategies. The prevailing approaches to CSR are considered by Porter and Kramer to be so disconnected from trategy as to obscure many great opportunities for companies to benefit ociety.

:ONCLUSION

This paper only scratches the surface of several important issues. :learly further research is needed based on more empirical data and a case pproach to further knowledge in this field. We learn that corporate social esponsibility encompasses a wide spectrum of issues ranging from usiness ethics, corporate governance and socially responsible investing, o environmental sustainability and community investment. CSR envisages he ideal whereby enterprises integrate social and environmental concerns n their business operations and their interaction with their stakeholders sually on a voluntary 'trusted' basis. It is about the behaviour of usinesses over and above what is ordinarily required by regulatory bodies nd legal requirements, not least because it is voluntarily practised, but ecause businesses deem it to be in their long-term interest to do so. In xamining if CSR activities lead to competitive advantage, it is important ɔ address the CSR standardization discussion in which such tools as TBL nd CSR reporting provide a snapshot of an organization's achievements nd reinforce the realization of the importance to our planet of the three ets of perspectives; (1) sociality, (2) environmental and (3) economical.

CHAPTER-44

Creating A Better India Through Corporate Governance

Himanshu Jindal

B. Com Final Year

Kinshuk Mittal

B. Com Final Year

CORPORATE GOVERNANCE

Corporate Governance may be defined as a set of systems, processes and principles which ensure that a company is governed in the best interest of all stakeholders. It is the system by which companies are directed and controlled. It is about promoting corporate fairness, transparency and accountability. In other words, 'good corporate governance' is simply 'good business'.

CONCEPTUAL FRAMEWORK

"What is the spirit behind the term corporate governance"

Corporate governance is the acceptance by management of the inalienable rights of shareholders as the true owners of the corporation and of their own role as trustees on behalf of the shareholders. It deals with conducting the affairs of a company such that there is fairness to all stakeholders. In this regard, the management needs to prevent asymmetry of benefits between various sections of shareholders, especially between the owner-managers and the rest of the shareholders.

It is about commitment to values, about ethical business conduct and about making a distinction between personal and corporate funds in the management of a company. Ethical dilemmas arise from conflicting interests of the parties involved. In this regard, managers make decisions based on a set of principles influenced by the values, context and culture of the organization. It harmonizes the need for a company to strike a balance at all times between the need to enhance shareholders' wealth whilst not in any way being detrimental to the interests of the other stakeholders in the company. Further, its objective is to generate an environment of trust and confidence amongst those having competing and conflicting interests.

It assumes a **3-tier responsibility** i.e.

- **Political Responsibilities**: abiding by legitimate law; respect for the system of rights and the principles of constitutional state.
- **Social Responsibilities**: the corporate ethical responsibilities, towards the social framework of which the co. itself is an integral part.
- **Economic Responsibilities**: 'maximizing shareholders value' by depicting business ethics and enhancing corporate awareness of the environmental and societal interest of the communities, within which they operate.

The three key constituents of corporate governance are

- **the Board of Directors,**
- **the Shareholders and**
- **the Management**
- The pivotal role in any system of corporate governance is performed by THE BOARD OF DIRECTORS. It is accountable to the stakeholders and directs and controls the management. It stewards the company, sets its strategic aim and financial goals and oversees their implementation, puts in place adequate internal controls and periodically reports the activities and progress of the company in the company in a transparent manner to all the stakeholders.

- THE SHAREHOLDERS role is to appoint the directors and the auditors and to hold the board accountable for the proper governance of the company by requiring the board to provide them periodically with the requisite information in a transparent fashion, of the activities and progress of the company.

- The responsibility of THE MANAGEMENT is to undertake the management of the company in terms of the direction provided by the board, to ensure the operation of internal controls and to provide information to the board on a timely basis and in a transparent manner to enable the board to monitor the accountability of management to it.

What is good corporate governance?

"Corporate Governance is concerned with holding the balance between economic and social goals and between individual and communal goals. The corporate governance framework is there to encourage the efficient use of resources and equally to require accountability for the stewardship of those resources. The aim is to align as nearly as possible the interests of individuals, corporations and society."

Sir Adrian Cadbury

in 'Global Corporate Governance Forum', World Bank, 2000

Good corporate governance is characterized by a firm commitment and adoption of ethical practices by an organization across its entire value chain and in all of its dealings with a wide group of stakeholders encompassing employees, customers, vendors, regulators and shareholders (including the minority shareholders), in both good and bad times. To achieve this, certain checks and practices need to be whole heartedly embraced.

The underlying principles of corporate governance revolve around three basic inter-related segments.These are:

- Integrity and Fairness
- Transparency and Disclosures
- Accountability and Responsibility

Some considerations in this respect are outlined below:

- Codes of conduct and whistle blower policies are important, but more important are how they are communicated and practiced. It is vital for board members and senior management to lead by example.
- The concept of having independent directors is a good one in theory but more important is the process underlying selection of independent directors – is this process rigorous, transparent and objective and is it aligned to the company's needs?
- It is important to focus on not just earnings but on the sustainability of business models. Focus on not just "How much" but on "HOW", "AT WHAT COST" and "AT WHOSE EXPENSE".
- Rating agencies need to develop criteria that focus on substance rather than the form of governance.

ENFORCING AND IMPROVING CORPORATE GOVERNANCE

PRINCIPLE-BASED APPROACH

Improved corporate governance does not solely rest on control through increased regulations. What is required is a principle-based approach developed on strong fundamentals, preventing moral fragility that is enforced through pragmatic levels of regulations.

It is essential that a company have the ability to self-regulate. Many companies have outlined numerous standards and restrictions, yet staffs are not strictly required to adhere to any except those that pose legal issues. Allowing this attitude to develop or persist in an organization is a sign of poor and weak governance

Relating to the Non-executive Directors the recommendations are

- Non-executive Directors should bring an independent judgment to bear on issues of strategy, performance, resources, including key appointments, and standards of conduct.

- The majority should be independent of the management and free from any business or other relationship, which could materially interfere with the exercise of their independent judgment, apart from their fees and shareholding. Their fees should reflect the time, which they commit to the company.
- Non-executive Directors should be appointed for specified terms and reappointment should not be automatic.

QUALITY PERSONNEL

Making sure that positions are filled with people who live up to the requirements of those positions is one of the best tips for effective corporate governance. This means that organizations with a board of directors need to make sure that those individuals are serving the best interests of stakeholders. People who are in high ranking positions need to demonstrate high level of honesty and ethical behavior in their dealings.

CLEAR DISTINCTION OF AUTHORITY AND RESPONSIBILITY

Some companies operate to the other extreme. They are stricken with procedures and micromanagement and cross management, which makes it appear as though the organization has excellent corporate governance. In reality, what tends to happen in these situations is that the company becomes ineffective because people who are trying to perform their duties meet constant obstacles and other people are too occupied with overseeing duties that are not theirs. Effective corporate governance allows everyone adequate opportunity to perform and keeps everyone within the boundaries of their positions by making clear distinction of authority & responsibility of every employee.

PERFORMANCE LINKED REMUNERATION

Managers need to manage and specialists need to display their expertise. Effective corporate governance requires that people stop showing up to work just for a paycheck and that they be held responsible for their duties. Many companies are filled with people who have excellent salaries and benefits, yet their performance is substandard. This can negatively impact a company in several ways, including financially and by encouraging low employee morale.

Thus a comprehensive system should be designed and implemented by the companies linking the remuneration of personnel's directly with their performance, specially for the top level executives.

TRANSPARENCY AT ALL LEVELS

When people are allowed to operate under the cover of the ignorance of the masses, an organization can become unruly and riddled with problems that are difficult to correct. This is often seen when scandals are revealed and it is found that instead of a single illicit master plan, numerous people have simply become rogue.

Thus, companies require to maintain utmost level of transparency in their dealings. Every stakeholder should have complete access to information affecting their interests directly or indirectly.

QUALITY OF AUDIT COMMITTEES

Audit committees have high level of independence to identify any types of weakness in internal control of the company. They can act as a check on the activities of board of directors. Thus the level of auditing should be enhanced and made available at all levels of management. These committees should have an effective oversight of internal and external auditors, better understanding of risk, strategy and business models and direct oversight of whistle blower incidents

CONCLUSION: FUTURE PROSPECTS

The issues of governance, accountability and transparency in the affairs of the company, as well as about the rights of shareholders and role of Board of Directors have never been so prominent as it is today. India has become one of the fastest emerging nations to have aligned itself with the international trends in Corporate Governance. As a result, Indian companies have increasingly been able to access to newer and larger markets around the world; as well as able to acquire more businesses. But, as the global environment changing continuously, there is a greater need of adopting and sustaining good corporate governance practices for value creation and building corporations of the future.

CHAPTER-45

Multinationals and Corporate Social Responsibility: A Stand on Contemporary International Framework

Gaurav Govinda & Mansi Malik

National Law University, Delhi

INTRODUCTION

Corporate social responsibility (CSR) is certainly not a new concept. It has a long history, with attention having grown since the mid-1950s in particular. However, there is no clear consensus as to what it exactly means, as aptly phrased in 1973 already: To some it conveys the idea of legal responsibility or liability; to others, it means socially responsible behaviour in an ethical sense; the meaning transmitted is that of 'responsible for' in a causal mode; many simply equate it with a charitable contribution; some take it to mean socially conscious; many of those who embrace it most fervently see it as a mere synonym for 'legitimacy', in the context of 'belonging' or being proper or valid; a few see it as a sort of fiduciary duty imposing higher standards of behaviour on the businessmen than on citizens at large. Over the years, the notion has evolved, with the range of definitions narrowing down somewhat.

Due to Globalization its definition has been somewhat elusive. In the sphere of culture, it has something to do with the idea that our human ways of understanding the world around us are becoming more similar. Yet the importance of local context persists. This dynamic between the global and the local has an impact on expectations of corporate social responsibility (CSR). As a result, global MNEs often fail to respond effectively to issues of importance in their host countries. Well-known examples include protests and consumer boycotts experienced by Nestlé in selling baby formula in Africa and by Nike as a result child labour abuse in outsourcing in Asia. It is common practice for global MNEs to use strategies in which local market units have limited functions with small staffs and then find themselves unable to monitor and respond successfully to local CSR issues.

DIMENSIONS OF CORPORATE SOCIAL RESPONSIBILITY

The CSR debate has largely revolved around the conduct of multinational corporations (MNEs) and other large private companies which, due to their size, have the ability to significantly influence domestic and international policy and the communities in which they operate. While there has been a long debate about the concept of CSR, from the current literature we can distil a distinction between those who consider it to encompass activities to advance a social cause that are beyond compliance and those who view it not so much as voluntary activities beyond the law but rather, more broadly, as managing a firm in such a way that it can be "economically profitable, law abiding, ethical and socially supportive".

The first approach hinges upon delineating legal obligations, with CSR beginning where the law ends. While this seems a clear-cut definition, problems emerge when one considers that most firms operate in a large number of different contexts with widely varying legal rules and norms, something which also applies to levels of implementation and enforcement. It is also the case that firms are often fined, or that they do not fully conform to legal requirements without being punished for that, so even meeting the law is not standard for all. This implies that the 'beyond compliance' criterion may not reflect the realities of international business very well. Instead, it seems better to approach CSR from the perspective of the issues, whether regulated or not, and pressures, from whatever origin, that firms are confronted with, as long as these do not directly and only stem from the more traditional drive for profit and financial performance. Examples include green issues such as climate change, pollution and resource depletion, ethical problems, and social dimensions of firms' activities – inside and outside the firm, often in connection with communities and workers. They relate to broader societal repercussions and expectations from regulators and other stakeholders, which MNEs face in their activities across borders in particular, and that they choose to deal with, in a reactive, or pro-active/pre-emptive manner, and address in their strategies, governance structures and organisational processes one way or the other. Such a perspective means that CSR is very much embedded in several wider debates, including the question for whom and for what the firm exists, how different responsibilities can or should be managed and by whom, and what room there is for managerial discretion given the existence of different norms.

THE ROLE OF STAKEHOLDERS

One of the subjects of debate across the various literatures involves the relationship between firms and their stakeholders/shareholders. The question is an answer; For whom does the firm exist? Interestingly, this has also become the case to some extent in the field of corporate governance, which traditionally focused mostly on an agency-based, shareholder-centred notion, looking at questions such as "How do the suppliers of finance get managers to return some of the profits to them? How do they make sure that managers do not steal the capital they supply or invest it in bad projects? How do suppliers of finance control managers?"

In more recent years, however, attention has shifted to the relationship between companies and a broader set of stakeholders and concomitant concerns. Monks and Minow, for example, provide a list of constituents in which they include directors, managers, employees, shareholders, customers, creditors, suppliers, community members and the government. Furthermore, Claessens distinguishes three sets of relationships for companies, based on exchange relationships in connection with supply of resources: with shareholders and creditors; with financial markets and institutions; and with employees; to which he adds that under such a broad definition, "*corporate governance would also encompass the issue of corporate social responsibility, including such aspects as the dealings of the firm with respect to culture and the environment*". This exemplifies a certain convergence that has taken place in the direction of the older stakeholder approach, which was originally introduced to explain why business has responsibilities that go beyond the maximisation of profits to include the interests of non-stockholding agents. Indeed, if a company would focus solely on such narrow objectives, the expectations of other stakeholders would be neglected, and in turn their support could be compromised in the long term.

Freeman's definition of stakeholders as "any group or individual who can affect or is affected by the achievement of the organization's objectives" is most widely accepted. Advocates of the stakeholder perspective consider as a starting point that "all persons or groups with legitimate interests participating in an enterprise do so to obtain benefits and that there is no prima facie priority of one set of interests and benefits over another". From such a perspective, a company emerges as a nexus of relationships between a variety of actors with interests that are not always congruent. The stakeholder approach emphasises that actors have different motivations to engage in relationships with a company, and expect different benefits from their collaboration. This means that dealing with stakeholders poses complexities for business in view of conflicting interests, but also that companies can shape relations. In fact, they can, partly enabled by information asymmetries between managers and stakeholders, employ strategies to reduce the concentration of stakeholder power and/or increase the concentration of management power, thus also enabling stakeholder 'mismanagement'.

CSR, SOCIETAL WELFARE AND REGULATION

Related to 'for whom' is the question 'for what', as, depending on the interest(s) of main stakeholders, the dominant focus of the firm will come to the fore, and thus also the extent to which, for example, the profit motive is balanced against other objectives. In the context of CSR, the issue is often raised whether this is a win-win or a win-lose proposition. The former is often referred to as 'doing well' (by firms) and 'doing good' (for society) at the same time, while the latter is clearly expressed in the definition of CSR as "sacrificing profits in the social interest". However, there is no evidence that companies systematically do this, which points at a more generic lack of proof for either of the options, summarised as "*some* firms will generate long-term profits from *some* socially responsible activities *some* of the time".

Devinney has specified this a bit more by outlining four "necessary but not sufficient conditions" for companies to engage in CSR, which relate to demand (higher in total and/or in value due to higher prices paid), lower costs (higher efficiency), higher value and/or longer life span of assets, and lower risks. However, he also outlined that, even if these are met, this does not mean that society as a whole is automatically better off. In other words, CSR is not necessarily societally optimal, as companies' interests may well be different, with (part of) their skills, competences and inherent peculiarities being geared to other goals. Arguments as to why CSR can be an effective social policy instrument, with companies/markets as efficient mechanisms for realising societal goals. Interestingly, in a recent paper, Karnani dismissed "doing well by doing good" as "the grand illusion". He distinguishes a "zone of opportunity", in which markets work efficiently and private profits and public interest go hand in hand (with a private and social optimum, and CSR being seen as of no use there), and a "zone of trade-off", characterised by market failures and a conflict between private profits and public interests (and where government should intervene, with CSR being ineffective). In his view, the inconclusive evidence regarding win-win/win-lose can be explained from this as well: if the sample of firms is mostly located in the zone of opportunity, then a positive relationship between economic and social performance will be found, while it is negative if the firms studied are in the zone of trade-off; and if spread over the two zones, results are mixed. Complex societal problems, such as environmental degradation and poverty, reside in the zone of trade-off, and cannot be solved by markets alone, but they need government intervention to address externalities and/or abuse of asymmetric information and market power.

MORAL FREE SPACE AND INTERNATIONAL NORMS

Some authors have emphasised the importance of international moral norms for business, arguing that they should be in place and that this is already the case (to some extent). This is because societies can only exist and interact properly if there is agreement on at least some norms. And there are many of them indeed, as exemplified by a range of international treaties, UN declarations and conventions that have been adopted worldwide. Quite a number of them relate to business, as international production and trade also depends on acceptance of common rules and responsibilities across borders. They introduced the notion of "market morality, the set of ethical norms that the vast majority of MNEs would attempt to practice, because, other things being equal, adopting such more practices are either necessary for economic survival or confer advantages that enhance the MNE's prospects for success".

INTERNATIONAL MEASURES

RECENT TRENDS AND NEXT STEPS

The past few years has seen renewed attention to divergent norms in the international context due to the growing importance of emerging economies in general, and China in particular. This has been accompanied by the argument that the first two sources mentioned above intergovernmental and MNE-driven norms originate more from 'Western' countries (or developed countries more generally, as Japan is often included), and may neither be applicable nor appropriate for Chinese companies. The example of China is interesting and highly relevant because it is perhaps the most far-reaching illustration of a divergent approach from a large and very powerful emerging economy. It represents a difference to be taken into account, because developed countries have so far been most influential in the debate on international norms and standards, even though a country such as China ratified many international agreements, including those on human rights. However, a shifting economic and demographic balance to emerging economies, particularly in Asia, is likely to bring other changes as well. This will not only affect international negotiations (as shown, for example, in the case of climate change) but also norms relevant to MNEs, in terms of market morality and in certain home/host countries.

For research and managerial purposes, it might be worthwhile to distinguish home/host countries into different types: i.e. developed, emerging and least developed countries, as CSR conditions, stakeholder pressure and norms in the latter two categories in particular differ from those in the first one. In the case of US and European MNEs, home-country constituents exert most pressure and they have learned to adopt stakeholder-mandated CSR standards. In their activities abroad, these MNEs have often been confronted with host-country social, ethnic, religious, community and/or sustainability conflicts, often bundled in some way in protests against foreign investors, with MNEs' home-country constituents exerting pressure to accommodate these concerns properly and adhere to similar norms abroad. While this could offer opportunities as well, given that learning and experience might be used in 10 other settings if opportunities arise, in many cases it is vulnerability.

OECD GUIDELINES FOR MULTINATIONAL ENTERPRISES

The OECD Guidelines for Multinational Enterprises (the Guidelines), first adopted in 1976, are the longest standing initiative for the promotion of high corporate standards. The Guidelines contain voluntary principles and standards for responsible business conduct in areas such as human rights, supply chain management, disclosure of information, anti corruption, taxation, labour relations, environment, competition, and consumer welfare. The Guidelines aim to promote the positive contributions of MNEs to economic, environmental and social progress. The Guidelines express the shared values of 39 countries consisting of the 3032 OECD members and 933 non member countries. The adhering countries are the source of almost 90 per cent of the world's foreign direct investment and are home to most major MNEs. While observance of the Guidelines is voluntary for companies, adhering governments make a formal commitment to promote their observance among MNEs. The most concrete expression of this commitment is the National Contact Point (NCP), often a government office, which is responsible for encouraging observance of the Guidelines and for ensuring that the Guidelines are well-known and understood by the national business community and by other interested parties. Critics consider the NCP mechanism weak and ineffective. Accordingly, it has been suggested that the Guidelines and in particular the NCPs be strengthened. The Guidelines are part of a broader package of instruments, most of which address government responsibility and promote open and transparent policy frameworks for international investment.

ILO TRIPARTITE DECLARATION

The ILO, founded in 1919, is a specialised agency of the United Nations focusing on labour issues and has 178 member states to date. The ILO Tripartite Declaration (Declaration) also seeks to encourage the positive contribution of MNEs to economic and social progress and states, inter alia, that: MNEs should obey national laws, respect international standards, honour voluntary commitments and harmonise their operations with the social aims of countries in which they operate; governments should implement suitable measures to deal with the employment impact of MNE's and in developing countries, MNE's should provide the best possible wages, conditions of work (including health and safety) and benefits to adequately satisfy basic needs within the framework of government policies. Whilst the principles expressed in the Declaration are addressed to governments, employers and workers' organisations in both home and host countries, the principles are voluntary.

CONCLUSION

Regardless of one's views on these matters, however, it is the case that combining all these approaches further complicates the situation for international business. Traditionally, MNEs have been confronted already with a range of different legal obligations (international, regional, national, local) with frequently diverging degrees of implementation and enforcement, and the whole spectrum of soft, voluntary commitments adds further complexity. For their societal license to operate, consideration of both legal and social norms is necessary, but especially the latter can vary considerably across countries, and sometimes even for types of MNEs [e.g. domestic or foreign, large or small, more or less visible, sector(s) of activity] and issues. A multitude of stakeholders is involved, with often diverse perceptions, and degrees of power, legitimacy and urgency. MNEs in particular face difficult choices as to which norms are being used to establish what ethical and socially supportive behaviour is, and which ones should then be followed, and when and where.

CHAPTER-46

Combat Against Aids For Confident

Dr. Chandra Shekhar Ghanta

Assistant Professor,
Department of Mass Communication,
Telangana University, Dichpally, Pin No. 503 322
Nizamabad, Andhra Pradesh, India

INTRODUCTION

India is one of the largest and most populated countries in the world, with over one billion inhabitants. Of this number, it's estimated that around 2.4 million people are currently living with Human Immunodeficiency Virus (HIV). HIV is a lent virus (a member of the retrovirus family) that causes *Acquired Immune Deficiency Syndrome* (AIDS). HIV emerged later in India than it did in many other countries. Infection rates soared throughout the 1990s, and today the epidemic affects *all* sectors of Indian society, not just the groups-such as sex workers and truck drivers-with which it was originally associated. In a country where poverty, illiteracy and poor health are rife, the spread of HIV presents a daunting challenge. Despite being home to the world's third-largest population suffering from HIV/AIDS, the AIDS prevalence rate in India is lower than in many other countries.

Despite being home to the world's third-largest population suffering from HIV/AIDS, the AIDS prevalence rate in India is lower than in many other countries. In 2009, India's AIDS prevalence rate stood at approximately 0.30%—the 89th highest in the world. The spread of HIV in India is primarily restricted to the southern and north-eastern regions of the country and India has also been praised for its extensive anti-AIDS campaign. The US$2.5 billion National AIDS Control Plan III was set up by India in 2007 and received support from UNAIDS[7] The main factors which have contributed to India's large HIV-infected population are extensive labor migration and low literacy levels in certain rural areas resulting in lack of awareness and gender disparity

THE FIRST CASE

At the beginning of 1986, despite over 20,000 reported AIDS cases worldwide, India had no reported cases of HIV or AIDS. There was recognition, though, that this would not be the case for long, and concerns were raised about how India would cope once HIV and AIDS cases started to emerge. One report, published in a medical journal in January 1986, stated, "Unlike developed countries, India lacks the scientific laboratories, research facilities, equipment, and medical personnel to deal with an AIDS epidemic. In addition, factors such as cultural taboos against discussion of sexual practices, poor coordination between local health authorities and their communities, widespread poverty and malnutrition, and a lack of capacity to test and store blood would severely hinder the ability of the Government to control AIDS if the disease did become widespread."

In 1986, the first known case of HIV was diagnosed by Dr. Suniti Solmon amongst female sex workers in Chennai. Later that year, sex workers began showing signs of this deadly disease. At that time, foreigners in India were traveling in and out of the country. It is thought that these foreigners were the ones responsible for the first infections. By 1987, about 135 more cases came into light. Among these 14 had already progressed to AIDS. Prevelance in high-risk groups reached above 5% by 1990. As per UNDP's 2010 report, India had 2.39 million (23.95 lakh) people living with HIV at the end of 2009, up from 2.27 million (22.7 lakh) in 2008. Adult prevalence also rose from 0.29% in 2008 to 0.31% in 2009.

PROGRAMMES INITIATION

In 1987, a National AIDS Control Programme was launched to co-ordinate national responses. Its activities covered surveillance, blood screening, and health education. By the end of 1987, out of 52,907 who had been tested, around 135 people were found to be HIV positive and 14 had AIDS. Most of these initial cases had occurred through heterosexual sex, but at the end of the 1980s, a rapid spread of HIV was observed among injecting drug users (IDUs) in Manipur, Mizoram and Nagaland - three north-eastern states of India bordering Myanmar (Burma).

In 2006 UNAIDS estimated that there were 5.6 million people living with HIV in India, which indicated that there were more people with HIV in India than in any other country in the world. In 2007, following the first survey of HIV among the general population, UNAIDS and NACO agreed on a new estimate – between 2 million and 3.1 million people living with HIV. In 2008 the figure was estimated to be 2.31 million. In 2009, it was estimated that 2.4 million people were living with HIV in India, which equates to a prevalence of 0.3%. While this may seem low, because India's population is so large, it is third in the world in terms of greatest number of people living with HIV. With a population of around a billion, a mere 0.1% increase in HIV prevalence would increase the estimated number of people living with HIV by over half a million.

ROLE OF UNDP AND NACO

UNDP works with the National AIDS Control Organisation (NACO) to respond to HIV and AIDS in India and reduce its impact. UNDP supports the national efforts by offering knowledge, resources and technical expertise to effectively implement the National AIDS Control Programme. For the next five years, UNDP will be working to ensure that HIV becomes part of India's development response across districts vulnerable to HIV in nine states across India. In partnership with NACO and other UN agencies, UNDP is also designing a national programme to make migration safer. Since it is the agency mandated to work on human rights and gender, UNDP will work with sexual minorities, such as men having sex with men, to address their most urgent needs and to reduce stigma and discrimination against people living with HIV.

UNDP has helped the National AIDS Control Organisation to develop national policies for gender and HIV and for greater involvement of people living with HIV. Almost 15.6 million people across India were provided with information, training and services to improve their capacities to deal with HIV. 9,000 people living with HIV as well as trafficking survivors received livelihood training to expand their employment opportunities and skills. UNDP has also conducted pioneering research on the social dimensions of HIV. The first large-scale study of the socio-economic impact of HIV on households drew national and international attention from the media and policy makers.

ROLE OF NOGS

Non Governmental Organizations in India is dedicatedly working to giving helping hand to the HIV affected children in India. Children are the worst affected by the problems that HIV brings with it. They suffer severe stigma and neglect and are very often abandoned. Orphaned children are denied even necessities like food and nutrition by their extended families. If they are themselves HIV positive, the situation becomes worse and their very existence is threatened.

If the parents ailing with HIV, the children are likely to be withdrawn from, school to care for them or to go out and earn. Most of the examples are there in various states in India. It is the duties of the nation care for children those who are suffering with this kind of illness especially since it is a signatory to several international conventions and declarations on children and HIV/AIDS. The Government of India acceded to the UN Convention on the Rights of the Child (CRC) including protection against HIV/AIDS in 1992. Further, at the UN General Assembly Special Session on HIV/AIDS in 2001, India pledged to protect children affected by the epidemic. In June, 2006, the UN General Assembly adopted the Political Declaration on HIV/AIDS, which reiterated government commitment to "addressing as a priority the vulnerabilities faced by children affected by and living with HIV; providing support and rehabilitation to these children and their families, women and the elderly, particularly in their role as caregivers; promoting child-oriented HIV/AIDS policies and programmes and increased protection for children orphaned and affected by HIV/AIDS; ...and building, where needed, and supporting the social security systems that protect them."

WORLD BANK FUNDING

The World Bank underwrites India's national AIDS program with a $191 million loan. In the loan agreement, the bank and the government of India both pledged to respect the human rights of "marginalized groups at high risk" of HIV transmission, but there is no sign that any resource is being spent to monitor human-rights abuses suffered by these groups and by AIDS outreach workers who aim to assist them.

The investment made to combat the epidemic by both the Indian government and donor institutions in India will go down the drain if the police continue abusing AIDS outreach workers and those they serve. The Barcelona AIDS conference should send a wake-up call to the Indian government and its donors, reminding them that the fight against AIDS must also be a fight to protect human rights.

POLICY FRAMEWORK

Following on from this declaration, in July, 2007, the Ministry of Women and Child Development and National AIDS Control Organization released the *Policy Framework for Children and AIDS*. This policy acknowledges the need to realise the basic rights for all children as under the UN CRC for children affected by HIV/AIDS and has a goal of reaching 80% of the children most in need by 2010. 2 years after the policy framework was released, it exists largely on paper, and children continue to be deprived of most of their rights. Most of the states accepted this success. But it is completely restricted to the testing and access to treatment only. Still there is a gap in other areas like education, nutrition, etc.

This situation means that it is mainly non-governmental organisations and HIV-positive network groups that are working to reduce the effect of HIV/AIDS on children in India. They provide nutrition supplements, referrals to testing and treatment facilities, treatment for opportunistic infections, education support, and linkages with existing government child welfare schemes for children who need them. To fulfill these requirements the Ministry of Women and Child Development is in a strategic position to ensure access to basic services for affected children in collaboration with other concerned departments, especially through its two flagship programmes Integrated Child Development Scheme and Integrated Child Protection Scheme.

ROLE OF THE MEDIA

To counter the growing AIDS epidemic in India, BBC World Service Trust- the NGO arm of the BBC World Service, in partnership with Prasar Bharati and the National AIDS Control Organization has launched a broadcast campaign in 2002. The BBC had given great importance to Doordarshan to join hands to combat against the evil. The DD has got opportunity to share the same values of public service broadcasting and there can be no more vital public service work than mounting a campaign like this to head off the threat of AIDS to our country's social and economic development.

With this partnership, the DD-BBC World Services broadcasted various programmes in the regional DD stations. Dramas, reality shows called Haath Se Haath Milaa, a weekly radio phone-in show - Chat Chowk, aimed at 15 to 35 years old across the country, followed by the Social advertising spots that will run three times daily on both TV and Radio for the duration of the campaign. For the two-year project the Department for International Development - the British Government's aid ministry, as a part of their much larger commitment to combating AIDS in India. Rs. 26 crore allocated for this programme. This multi-media collaboration brings to the centre-stage, the public health strategy of prevention of AIDS through protection and safe sex.

The NACO-Prasar Bharati-BBC World Service Trust partnership will raise AIDS awareness in the low prevalence states of Uttar Pradesh, Uttaranchal, Delhi, Haryana and Rajasthan and other states. By promoting behaviour change in these states, the objective is to contain the epidemic before it takes hold.

In return for programming, production funds, training and workshops, Prasar Bharati has contributed producer time, in-house technical facilities and generous airtime to the project. It's a win-win situation for both broadcasting organisations and, more importantly, for the cause of combating AIDS. This initiative is novel and brings different leading players to contribute to the society.

CONCLUSION

We all know that information is power, and awareness empowers one to protect from HIV/AIDS. The tsunami of HIV/AIDS in India cannot be halted only by traditional efforts like informing people with brochures and advertisements. It is high time to utilize tremendous creative and communicating power of mainstream media for AIDS awareness and training to school students and their parents/ teachers. The use of educational media offers immense possibilities to create awareness and transmitting crucial information about HIV/AIDS issues to school students. The researcher has a belief that adoption of proposed strategies in India will be helpful to achieve one of the most crucial MDGs by UN "halting the spread of HIV/AIDS".

CHAPTER-47

Impact of Information Technology on Corporate Governance

Arathi Chitla

Associate professor, Dept. of Computer Science and Engineering Telangana University, Dichpally-503322, Nizamabad, Andhra Pradesh.

INTRODUCTION

Corporate governance is defined as the system by which business entities are monitored, managed and controlled. Corporate governance practices have become an essential prerequisite for the ability to acquire and retain financial resources necessary for restructuring long-term investment and sustainable growth. At one end of the spectrum the shareholders are the owners of business entity as they are risk takers. At the other end the managers or the executive director of the company who are in control of its day-to-day affairs. The concept of corporate governance may therefore be defined as "a system by which corporations are governed and controlled with a view to increasing shareholder value and meeting the expectations of the other stakeholders". It is the responsibility of entire board of directors for smooth running of the company; corporate disclosure and governance requirements though relatively low in some countries, are also changing.

Awareness of the developments of accounting standards, securities regulation, globalization of financial markets, world wide effect of corporate strategic alliance has led to some alternative view of governance process. A good structure of corporate governance is that encourages balanced relationship among shareholders, executive directors and the board of directors. The governance mechanism is shaped by its political, economic and social history and its legal frame work.

IT AND CORPORATE GOVERNANCE

Corporate governance is the set of processes, customs, policies, laws, management practices and institutions affecting the way an entity is controlled and managed. It incorporates all the relationships among the many stakeholders involved and aims to organize them to meet the goals of the organization in the most effective and efficient manner possible. An effective corporate governance strategy allows an organization to manage all aspects of its business in order to meet its objectives.

Information technology governance, however, is a subset discipline of Corporate Governance. Although it is sometimes mistaken as a field of study on its own, IT Governance is actually a part of the overall Corporate Governance Strategy of an organization.

In the Globalization era, the introduction of the computer and advent of the Internet has changed the way we live in the modern world. This spans across every aspect of human life. Modern innovations have led to the description of the age in which we live as "the Information age". In terms of corporate governance, the financial implications of these losses could be great on corporate entities when quantified in monetary terms and this has led several companies to invest in finding better ways of improving on Information systems. IT Governance is a subset discipline of Corporate Governance focused on Information Technology (IT) systems and their performance and risk management. As firms strive to generate value from information technology, managers are increasingly aware that IT-related decisions and behaviors must be aligned with organizational performance goals. But many individuals throughout organizations make daily decisions influencing the value received from IT.

WHY IT GOVERNANCE NEEDED

The IT governance is the process by which firms align IT actions with their performance goals and assign accountability for those actions and their outcomes. To be effective, IT governance must be actively designed, not the result of isolated mechanisms (e.g. steering committee, office of IT architecture, service level agreements) implemented at different times to address the challenge of the moment. The rising interest in IT governance is partly due to compliance initiatives, for instance Sarbanes-Oxley in the USA and Basel II in Europe, but more so because of the need for greater accountability for decision-making around the use of IT in the best interest of all stakeholders.

A characteristic theme of IT governance discussions is that the IT capability is directly related to the investment choices taken by top management that have long-term consequences for various stakeholders. The traditional involvement of board-level executives in IT issues was to defer all key decisions to the company's IT professionals. IT governance implies a system in which all stakeholders, including the board, executive management, customers, and staff have clear accountability for their respective responsibilities in the decision making processes affecting IT. This prevents IT or business leaders from independently making decisions about IT without retaining responsibility for their actions and the impact they have on supporting the achievement of strategic objectives.

AN IMPORTANT ETHICAL ISSUE

As consumer movements grow stronger and stakeholders become more knowledgeable and aware of company operations, it has become necessary for corporations to come to grips with ethical issues in order to continue surviving in business. Consumers and stakeholders are becoming increasingly aware of the adverse effects of unethical business practices like low quality products and services, financial embezzlement, disregard for environmental issues and unhealthy working conditions among others. Most companies have realized the importance of upholding virtues like transparency and integrity. It has therefore become necessary to formulate and implement appropriate corporate governance mechanisms.

Corporate governance refers to a system by which a company is properly managed by adopting internationally recognized 'best practices' of management. It involves the company's commitment values and ethics in order to achieve its objectives, manage risks, and improve performance. Corporate governance ensures that the company's shareholders, customers, the staff, and investors are all treated fairly in accordance to a code of business ethics. Corporate governance is indeed critical in enhancing and retaining clients' and investors' trust.

THE MANAGEMENT OF IT

The link between the managers responsible for managing an IT function and the board of their organization, according to the literature, is two-fold. Firstly, the actions of IT management are guided by a stable, formal, agreed business strategy and corporate objectives . The development of business strategy and the oversight of its implementation, as earlier noted, are board responsibilities.

Secondly, IT carries risks. Given the centrality of IT to the operation of most companies and the companies' heavy capital investments in IT, the risk of, for example, failure, underperformance or overspend on IT needs to be understood and managed at board level. The 2003 Chaos report of IT project failure shows that, based on data from 13,522 cases, only 34% of IT projects were considered successful. 15% of projects were complete failures and the balance of 51% was what is referred to as challenged. Challenged means a project overran on time and/or cost . Data from the projects surveyed showed that 52% of the specified features and functions of an IT project appear in the final released version. The risks that can arise with IT include both operational risk and strategic risk. Whereas the management of operational risk is assisted by a number of frameworks such as the risk processes, strategic risks that have potentially long latency periods and are difficult to detect.

As consumer movements grow stronger and stakeholders become more knowledgeable and aware of company operations, it has become necessary for corporations to come to grips with ethical issues in order to continue surviving in business. Consumers and stakeholders are becoming increasingly aware of the adverse effects of unethical business practices like low quality products and services, financial embezzlement, disregard for environmental issues and unhealthy working conditions among others. Most companies have realized the importance of upholding virtues like transparency and integrity. It has therefore become necessary to formulate and implement appropriate corporate governance mechanisms.

Corporate governance refers to a system by which a company is properly managed by adopting internationally recognized 'best practices' of management. It involves the company's commitment values and ethics in order to achieve its objectives, manage risks, and improve performance. Corporate governance ensures that the company's shareholders, customers, the staff, and investors are all treated fairly in accordance to a code of business ethics. Corporate governance is indeed critical in enhancing and retaining clients' and investors' trust.

THE BEST PRACTICE

Despite efforts of the software industry to identify and adopt best practices in the development of IT projects, there is still a high rate of failure and missed objectives. Most IT projects do not meet the organization's objectives – See summary of survey carried out by the Standish Group.

A key best practice is implementing an organizational structure, including an effective governance framework, with well-defined roles and responsibilities for IT stakeholders including IS auditors. Such a framework ensures that IT investments are aligned and delivered in accordance with corporate objectives and strategies; without this framework, IT projects are more susceptible to failure. But many organizations fail to consider the importance of IT governance. They take on IT projects without fully understanding what the organization's requirements are for the project and how this project links to the organization's objectives.

To be successful an organization should consider all of the following factors, which lead to best practices: high-level framework, independent assurance, performance management reporting, resource management, risk management, strategic alignment, and value delivery:

- High - level framework – including defining leadership, processes, roles and responsibilities, information requirements, and organizational structures – ensures the IT investment is aligned with the overall strategies of the organization, maximizing the application of available IT opportunities.

- Independent assurance, in the form of internal or external audits (or reviews), can provide timely feedback about compliance of IT with the organization's policies, standards, procedures, and overall objectives. These audits must be performed in an unbiased and objective manner, so that managers are provided with a fair assessment of the IT project being audited.

- Resource management, through regular assessments, ensures that IT has sufficient, competent, and efficient resources to meet the organization's demands.

- Risk management embedded in the responsibilities of the organization, ensures that the organization and IT regularly assess and report IT-related risks and organizational impact. Exposures of any problems are followed up, with special attention paid to any potential negative effects on the overall objectives of the organization.

- Strategic alignment – a shared understanding between the organization's management and the IT department, enables the board and senior management to understand strategic IT issues. IT strategy demonstrates the organization's technology insights and capabilities and ensures that the IT investment is aligned with the overall strategies of the organization, maximizing the use of available IT opportunities.

- Value delivery demonstrates the benefits that can be achieved from each IT investment. Such investment should always provide value to the organization and be driven by the needs of the investing entity.

- Performance management reporting, including accurate, timely, and relevant portfolio, programme, and IT project reports to senior management, provides a thorough review of the progress being made towards the identified objectives of the IT project. Through this review, the organization can assess IT performance in terms of which deliverables have been obtained, and what shortfalls need to be addressed. Performance metrics is a good way to get some of the data needed for performance.

CONCLUSION

When managerial self-dealings are excessive and left unchecked, they often have serious negative effects on corporate values and the proper functions of capital markets. Around the world there is growing consensus that it is vitally important to strengthen corporate governance to protect the rights of shareholders, curb managerial excesses, and restore confidence in capital markets.

Effective IT governance demands an actively designed governance to facilitate desirable behaviors consistent with objectives. Often firms have mature business governance processes to use as a starting point in designing IT governance. When the objectives of IT governance are clear, firms can design IT governance by outlining governance arrangements and then specifying the mechanisms that will implement the intended arrangements. Firms that have not been effective in using IT strategically should expect to invest in organizational learning. Early in the learning cycle, those decision making mechanisms may involve large numbers of managers.

Effective IT governance doesn't happen accidentally. Firms must establish their needs for synergy and autonomy recognize the limitations of organizational structure and thoughtfully design IT governance arrangements and specific mechanisms that encourage desirable behaviours. Governance requirements may change as firms change their view of the need for autonomy or synergy, as they alter the relationships between business units, or as they learn about IT and its role through existing governance mechanisms. Viewing a firm's IT governance on one page can help with designing, communicating and refining how IT creates business value. A firm's score on the IT governance performance self assessment is a good indicator for the urgency of action.

CHAPTER-48

Corporate Governance of Urban Co-operative Banks in India: An Overview

Mr. Anupam Mitra, AICWA,

Assistant Professor, R.P.M College, University of Calcutta, India.

INTRODUCTION

A social institution including a corporate entity derives its legitimacy from its ability and desire to fulfill social needs. It is, therefore, accountable to the society. No institution, however high and mighty it is, can ignore its responsibility towards society from which it derives its strength and sustenance. In the case of bank the public stake is very high as the maximum amount of deposit belongs to them in comparison to the owners of the bank; the public stake is very high as the maximum amount of deposits belongs to them in comparison to the owners of the bank. Therefore, the accountability of banks to public is much higher. The number and the magnitude of scams in the banking industry during the last few years and crisis in co-operative banks have rocked the nation and faith of the depositors which calls for a greater need for corporate governance. The only way which can rebuild public faith to run the financial institutions is to adopt good governance.

Corporate Governance is a very broad concept. As "Governance" is not "Government", Corporate Governance is not just Corporate Management. It is something much broader to include a fair, efficient and transparent administration to meet certain well- defined objectives.

It is the system by which businesses are directed and controlled by the management in the best interest of the stakeholders and others ensuring greater transparency and better and timely financial reporting. It is a system of running a business organization on certain ethical principles. There cannot be a universally accepted definition of the term corporate governance. It can be broadly understood as a system of structuring, operating and controlling a company with a view to achieve long-term strategic goals to satisfy shareholders, employees, customers and suppliers and complying with the legal and regulatory requirements, apart from meeting environmental and local community needs. Its main emphasis is on accountable business leadership, which is a vital element of corporate democracy. Corporate Governance strives to develop a system of checks and balances major key players namely Board of Directors, Management, Auditors and last but not least shareholders.

LITERATURE REVIEW

Over a period of time, wiın fast developments in the world, the scope of the corporate governance has widened. It now encompasses the interest of not only the owners but also many other stake-holders. Organization of Economic Co-operation and Development (OECD) defined Corporate Governance as the system by which business corporations are directed and controlled. It involves a set of relationships between a company's management, its board, its shareholders and other stakeholders and also specifies the rules and procedures for making decisions on corporate affairs. The main aim of corporate governance is to maintain a balance between economic and social goals and between individual and commercial goals.

The emergence of modern corporate governance is traced back to the Watergate Scandal in USA. The Watergate Scandal of the United States, making illegal contributions to the politicians and corrupt Government officials by the corporations was the eye-opener of the U.S.Legislative Authorities and led U.S Government to enact the Foreign and Corrupt Practice Act, 1977. It contained specific provisions regarding the establishment, maintenance and review of a system of internal controls. Thereafter, a number of other measures were initiated for internal financial controls, the most important of which was Tread way Commission after the collapse of savings and loans in USA. The committee submitted its report in 1987 and stressed the need for a proper control environment, independent audit committees and an objective internal audit function. On the other hand the collapse of many industrial houses in U.K during 1980's led the Government to think that the existing self-regulation and legislations were not enough to take care of such events. As a consequence, the London Stock Exchange appointed the Cadbury Committee in 1991 under the chairmanship of Sir Abiran Cadbury to draft a code of practices on internal controls. The stated objective of the committee was to help raise standards of corporate governance and the level of confidence in financial reporting and auditing.

METHODOLOGY

The recommendations of the aforesaid committees envisages that it is imperative to introduce corporate governance in the member driven co-operative also (more specifically co-operative banks) without sacrificing its co-operative identity, principles and values. To introduce the corporate governance in urban co-operative banks, one should not forget that there is a basic difference between corporate and the co-operatives. Corporate are Investor Oriented Firms (IOF) and basically are association of capitals. The co-operatives are member oriented and the members are owners, users and investors, whereas shareholders in IOF are not users of the enterprise as such. Co-operatives is an autonomous association of persons united voluntarily to meet their common economic, social and cultural needs and aspirations though a jointly owned and democratically controlled enterprise. One of the salient functions of co-operatives is its involvement in banking industries. These banks are constituted on co-operative principles of voluntary association, self help and mutual aid, one share one vote and non-discrimination and equality of members. A co-operative bank may be regarded as a mutual society formed, composed of and governed by a group of persons for encouraging regular savings and granting small loans on easy terms of interest and repayment.

The urban co-operative banks are constituted, with the objective of promoting sustainable banking practices among the lower and middle income strata of the urban population. Urban co-operative banks are the best vehicles for taking banking to the doorsteps of common men, unbanked people in urban and semi urban areas in particular. These banks are mostly located in towns and cities and cater to the credit requirement of the urban clientele. Tha main functions of these banks are to promote thrift by attracting deposits from members and non-members and to advance loans to the members. The urban co-operative banks are organized under dual control of Reserve Bank of India and the respective State Governments through Registrar of Co-operative Societies (RCS). UCBs with multi state presence are also regulated by the Central Government and registered under the Multi-State Co-operative Societies Act.

Table 48.1: Non Performing Assets of UCBs (Rs in crore)

As on 31st march	Gross NPA	Net NPA	Provisioning	Coverage Ratio
2009	12,862	5,161	7,701	59.9
2010	12,727	4,724	803	62.9

The serious scams in a number of UCBs also have brought a high degree of discomfort among the stakeholders of UCBs. As many as 214 UCBs were under liquidation as at end of March 2005. It is a fact that the functioning of the urban co-operative banks has come up for adverse criticism in recent years due to the collapse of a few urban co-operative banks in different states of the country like Maharashtra, Gujrat, Karnataka and Andhra Pradesh. The unethical practices adopted by some of the delinquent banks have caused serious concern. At present there are 84 UCBs, which are working under direction of Reserve Bank of India.

In the banking sector, some major developments has taken place in the form of introduction of prudential banking norms (in respect of Income Recognition, Assets classification, Provisioning and Capital Adequacy Standard as prescribed by Bank for International Settlement i.e. (BIS) and intensification of competition. Unfortunately, the co-operatives remained largely impervious of such changes. The operational efficiency of urban co-operative banks is unsatisfactory and characterized by low profitability, ever growing non-performing assets (NPA) and relatively low capital base. Their situation gradually worsened due to heavy overdue and non-collection of loans advances by them. Probably the crucial challenge encountered by the banking sector, specially the UCBs, is the availability of quality assets. In case banks are unable to generate income due to NPAs, it will put the banks into liquidity crunch. The problems of increasing NPAs are adversely affecting the profitability, liquidity and solvency position of the UCBs. Major concern suffering this sector include high levels of loan delinquency, erosion of capital base, paucity of funds for fresh deployment, ineffective credit planning, lack of of professionalism in conduct and management, deficiency in application of computerized system, poor management information system and inadequate internal controls governance structure. The large scale sickness in the UCBs has shaken the public confidence in co-operative banks.

Table 48.2: Financial Performance of Urban Co-operative Banks (as on 31st march)

(Rs in crore)

Item	All UCBs	
	2008-09	2009-10
Total Income	**18,409**	**20,029**
i. Interest Income	16,631	18,458
ii. Non Interest Income	1,778	1,571
Total Expenditure	**14,947**	**16,912**
i. Interest Expenditure	10,685	12,239
ii. Non Interest Expenditure	4,262	4,673
Profit		
i. Amount of Operating Profit	3,461	3,116
ii. Provisions, Contingencies, Taxes	1,899	1,632
iii. Amount of Net Profit	1,562	1,484

Thus Corporate Governance has great relevance in the present environment. Co-operative banks are supposed to run on ethical values to conduct their business and their success rest on the honesty and integrity of board members. The recent failure of a large number of UCBs has threatened the very survival of these banks. Most of the co-operative banks are reluctant to adopt strategies for good corporate governance though the concept was introduced to different companies and banks under clause 49 listing agreement of SEBI

FINDINGS

The major policy initiatives in the UCB sector during the recent years include implementation of the Vision Document 2005, initiatives for financial restructuring and asset liability management. The major policy initiatives in the UCB sector during the year 2009-10 are as under:

(i) New Bank Licenses—Consequent upon consolidation and improvement in the financial health of the banking sector, it was announced in the Annual Policy Statement in April 2010 that a Committee would be set up comprising all stakeholders for studying the advisability of granting new licenses to UCBs. Accordingly, an expert committee under the Chairmanship of Shri Y. H. Malegam has been set up. The committee, inter alia, will be reviewing the performance o UCBs over the last decade; review the need for organizatio of new UCBs and the extant regulatory policy on setting u of new UCBs; lay down entry point norms for new UCBs examine whether the licensing could be restricted only t financially sound and well managed cooperative credi societies through conversion route; and to mak recommendations relating to legal and regulatory structure t facilitate growth of sound UCBs.

(ii) Area of Operation—In order to provide avenues for organi growth to sound and well functioning uni-State Tier-II UCB it was decided to consider requests for expansion of area c operation to the entire state of registration for UCB conforming to the financial position of a Grade I bank. Whi considering such requests, RBI will give due consideration the system of internal control prevailing in the bank ar supervisory comfort.

(iii) Opening of off-site ATMs—In the Annual Policy Stateme of 2010-11, it was announced that well managed UCI would be allowed to set up off-site ATMs without seekir approval through Annual Business Plan. While consideri such requests, the Reserve Bank would give due considerati to the financial health of the bank in terms of the eligibili criteria laid down.

(iv) Maintenance of CSGL Accounts—The Reserve bank allow UCBs with a net worth of '200 crore and above, and havi CRAR of 10 per cent and above, to open and maintain CS(Accounts.

(v) Credit Information Companies—As UCBs fall under t category of credit institutions as defined in sub-section (f) Section 2 of the Credit Information Companies (Regulatic Act, 2005, they were advised to become members of at le one credit information company registered under the Act.

(vi) Capital for Market Risk—The Basel Committee on Bank Supervision (BCBS) had issued an amendment to the Cap Accord in 1996 to incorporate market risks. As an ini step towards prescribing capital requirement for market risks, UCBs were advised to assign an additional risk weight of 2.5 per cent on almost the entire investment portfolio. These additional risk weights are clubbed wtih the risk weights prescribed for credit risk in respect of investment portfolio of UCBs. UCBs were also advised to assign a risk weight of 100 per cent on the open position limits on foreign exchange and gold, and to build up Investment Fluctuation Reserve up to a minimum of 5 per cent of the investment held in Held for Trading and Available for Sale categories in the investment portfolio.

(vii) Non-SLR Investments—Investment by UCBs in unlisted non-SLR securities (subject to the minimum prescribed rating) should not exceed 10 per cent of total non-SLR investments at any time. Since there is a time lag between issuance and listing of securities, investment in non-SLR securities which are proposed to be listed but not listed at the time of subscription are exempted from the 10 per cent limit. Considering that long term bonds issued by companies engaged in infrastructure projects are generally held for a long period and not traded, UCBs investment in non-SLR bonds issued by such companies and having a residual maturity of seven years are allowed to be kept in HTM category.

The issues which are to be addressed for implementing the corporate governance in the field of co-operative banks are summarized in the following way:

- Composition of Board- As per Clause 49 listing agreement of SEBI, the Board of Directors of a company should consist at least 50% non-executive directors. But in case of co-operative banks there is no such scope (other than Multi-State Co-operative Societies), because members of the board are elected by the General Body. So the Act to be amended for co-option of professional directors in the Board, which is the urgent necessity of these days.

- Disclosure of Personal Identity- Every Board members are required to disclose their identity to the Board in the prescribed proforma, which ensures transparency.

- Code of Conduct- All Board members and senior management personnel should affirm compliance with the code on an annual basis. The members of the Board should give an undertaking that he has gone through the guidelines regarding the role and responsibility of a Director and has to perform that.

- Formation of different committees- The Board should constitute different committees, such as Audit committee, Supervision committee, Grievance committee, Fund Management committee, Risk Management committee, Loan committee, etc.

- Transparency in the Financial Statement and CEO Certificate- The Balance Sheet should be the true financial picture of the Bank disclosing different operational and accounting ratios relating to profit, return on assets, business per employee, capital adequacy ratio, true picture of nonperforming assets, maturity profile of loans, advances, investments, borrowings, deposits, etc. The Chief Executive should certify all reports and schedules, which is to be placed in the Board and in the AGM.

- Implementation of Internal Control System- the UCBs should adopt Internal Check and Control System, which is an in –built Safeguard against fraud, embezzlement, manipulation, etc.

CONCLUSION

In the post-liberalization period the urban co-operative banks, particularly those in larger towns, are facing tougher competition from commercial banks. Even public sector banks have shrugged off their traditional lethargy and have become very aggressive. One of the vital problems, which vitiate co-operative movement, is the interference of the politicians in the organization. Politically insulted environment prevailing in the urban co-operative banks at the management level is a hindrance of this sector. One of the most disturbing features of the movement is that it is increasingly passing on to the hands of the politicians and vested interests. Unless banking system, more specifically urban co-operative banks are freed from political interference, the efforts to introduce transparency and accountability, a pre-requisite of good governance, may not bring desired results. To exercise proper control on their operation in order to safeguard depositors and other stakeholder's interest, good Corporate Governance is a mind set, a question of value system, a way of keeping one above one's personal interest assigning priority to the co-operative interest and the way in which those with power, use that power. It is the reflection of quality of management. Now it is becoming the today's oath to implement standard practices on "Good Corporate Governance" for urban co-operative banks to improve their administration, business and control system and as a result this will ensure them a competitive edge in the changed scenario under open market economy.

CHAPTER-49

Corporate Governance in India – Evolution and Challenges

V.Anitha

Ph.D Research Scholar, Department of Commerce, Bharathiar University, Coimbatore-641046,

INTRODUCTION

The subject of corporate governance leapt to global business limelight from relative obscurity after a string of collapses of high profile companies. Enron, the Houston, Texas based energy giant, and WorldCom, the telecom behemoth, shocked the business world with both the scale and age of their unethical and illegal operations. Worse, they seemed to indicate only the tip of a dangerous iceberg. While corporate practices in the US companies came under attack, it appeared that the problem was far more widespread. Large and trusted companies from Parmalat in Italy to the multinational newspaper group Hollinger Inc., revealed significant and deep-rooted problems in their corporate governance. Even the prestigious New York Stock Exchange had to remove its director, Dick Grasso, amidst public outcry over excessive compensation. It was clear that something was amiss in the area of corporate governance all over the world.

Corporate governance has, of course, been an important field of query within the finance discipline for decades. Corporate governance has, of course, been an important field of query within the finance discipline for decades. There have been debates about whether the Anglo-Saxon market- model of corporate governance is better than the bank based models of Germany and Japan. However, the differences in the quality of corporate governance in these developed countries fade in comparison to the chasm that exists between corporate governance standards and practices in these countries as a group and those in the developing world.

Corporate governance has been a central issue in developing countries long before the recent spate of corporate scandals in advanced economies made headlines. Indeed corporate governance and economic development are intrinsically linked. Effective corporate governance systems promote the development of strong financial systems –irrespective of whether they are largely bank-based or market-based – which, in turn, have an unmistakably positive effect on economic growth and poverty reduction.

There are several channels through which the causality works. Effective corporate governance enhances access to external financing by firms, leading to greater investment, as well as higher growth and employment. The proportion of private credit to GDP in countries in the highest quartile of creditor right enactment and enforcement is more than double that in the countries in the lowest quartile. As for equity financing, the ratio of stock market capitalization to GDP in the countries in the highest quartile of shareholder right enactment and enforcement is about *four* times as large as that for countries in the lowest quartile. Poor corporate governance also hinders the creation and development of new firms.

CENTRAL ISSUES IN CORPORATE GOVERNANCE

The basic power structure of the joint-stock company form of business, in principle, is as follows. The numerous shareholders who contribute to the capital of the company are the actual owners of business. They elect a Board of Directors to monitor the running of the company on their behalf. The Board, in turn, appoints a team of managers who actually handle the day-to-day functioning of the company and report periodically to the Board. Thus mangers are the agents of shareholders and function with the objective of maximizing shareholders' wealth.

Even if this power pattern held in reality, it would still be a challenge for the Board to effectively monitor management. The central issue is the nature of the contract between shareholder representatives and managers telling the latter what to do with the funds contributed by the former. The main challenge comes from the fact that such contracts are necessarily "incomplete". It is not possible for the Board to fully instruct management on the desired course of action under every possible business situation. The list of possible situations is infinitely long. Consequently, no contract can be written between representatives of shareholders and the management that specifies the right course of action in every situation, so that the management can be held for violation of Shleifer and Vishny (1997) such a contract in the event it does something else under the circumstances. Because of this "incomplete contracts" situation, some "residual powers" over the funds of the company must be vested with either the financiers or the management. Clearly the former does not have the expertise or the inclination to run the business in the situations unspecified in the contract, so these residual powers must go to management. The efficient limits to these powers constitute much of the subject of corporate governance.

LEGAL ENVIRONMENT, OWNERSHIP PATTERNS AND CORPORATE GOVERNANCE

The legal system of a country plays a crucial role in creating an effective corporate governance mechanism in a country and protecting the rights of investors and creditors. The legal environment encompasses two important aspects – the protection offered in the laws (*de jure* protection) and to what extent the laws are enforced in real life (*de facto* protection). Both these aspects play important roles in determining the nature of corporate governance in the country in question.

Thus, English-origin legal systems provide the best protection to shareholder rights. India, for instance has a shareholder rights index of 5, highest in the sample examined – equal to that of the USA,UK, Canada, Hong Kong, Pakistan and South Africa (all English-origin- law countries) and better than all the other 42 countries in the study including countries like France, Germany, Japan and Switzerland.

CORPORATE GOVERNANCE IN INDIA – A BACKGROUND

The history of the development of Indian corporate laws has been marked by interesting contrasts. At independence, India inherited one of the world's poorest economies but one which had a factory sector accounting for a tenth of the national product; four functioning stock markets (predating the Tokyo Stock Exchange) with clearly defined rules governing listing, trading and settlements; a well-developed equity culture if only among the urban rich; and a banking system replete with well-developed lending norms and recovery procedures.24 In terms of corporate laws and financial system, therefore, India emerged far better endowed than most other colonies. The 1956 Companies Act as well as other laws governing the functioning of joint-stock companies and protecting the investors' rights built on this foundation. This section draws heavily from the history of Indian corporate governance in Goswami (2002).

The beginning of corporate developments in India were marked by the managing agency system that contributed to the birth of dispersed equity ownership but also gave rise to the practice of management enjoying control rights disproportionately greater than their stock ownership. The turn towards socialism in the decades after independence marked by the 1951 Industries (Development and Regulation) Act as well as the 1956. Industrial Policy Resolution put in place a regime and culture of licensing, protection and widespread red-tape that bred corruption and stilted the growth of the corporate sector.

CHANGES SINCE LIBERALIZATION

The years since liberalization have witnessed wide-ranging changes in both Laws and regulations driving corporate governance as well as general consciousness about it. Perhaps the single most important development in the field of corporate governance and investor protection in India has been the establishment of the Securities and Exchange Board of India (SEBI) in 1992 and its gradual empowerment since then. Concerns about corporate governance in India were, however, largely triggered by a spate of crises in the early 90's – the Harshad Mehta stock market scam of 1992 followed by incidents of companies allotting preferential shares to their promoters at deeply discounted prices as well as those of companies simply disappearing with investors' money.

CORPORATE GOVERNANCE OF BANKS

Nowhere is proper corporate governance more crucial than for banks and financial institutions. Given the pivotal role that banks play in the financial and economic system of a developing country, bank failure owing to unethical or incompetent management action poses a threat not just to the shareholders but to the depositing public and the economy at large. Two main features set banks apart from other business – the level of opaqueness in their functioning and the relatively greater role of government and regulatory agencies in their activities.

The opaqueness in banking creates considerable information asymmetries between the "insiders" – management – and "outsiders" owners and creditors. The very nature of the business makes it extremely easy and tempting for management to alter the risk profile of banks as well as siphon off funds. It is, therefore, much more difficult for the owners to effectively monitor the functioning of bank management. Existence of explicit or implicit deposit insurance also reduces the interest of depositors in monitoring bank management activities.

It is partly for these reasons that prudential norms of banking and close monitoring by the central bank of commercial bank activities are essential for smooth functioning of the banking sector. Government control or monitoring of banks, on the other hand, brings in its wake, the possibility of corruption and diversion of credit of political purposes which may, in the long run, jeopardize the financial health of the bank as well as the economy itself.

This market orientation of governance disciplining in banking has been accompanied by a stronger disclosure norms and stress on periodic RBI surveillance. From 1994, the Board for Financial Supervision (BFS) inspects and monitors banks using the "CAMELS" (Capital adequacy, Asset quality, Management, Earnings, Liquidity and Systems and controls) approach. Audit committees in banks have been stipulated since 1995.

Greater independence of public sector banks has also been a key feature of the reforms. Nominee directors – from government as well as RBIs – are being gradually phased off with a stress on Boards being more often elected than "appointed from above". There is increasing emphasis on greater professional representation on bank boards with the expectation that the boards will have the authority and competence to properly manage the banks within the broad prudential norms set by RBI. Rules like none lending to companies who have one or more of a bank's directors on their boards are being softened or removed altogether, thus allowing for "related party" transactions for banks. The need for professional advice in the election of executive directors is increasingly realized.

CONCLUSIONS

With the recent spate of corporate scandals and the subsequent interest in corporate governance, a plethora of corporate governance norms and standards have sprouted around the globe. The Sarbanes-Oxley legislation in the USA, the Cadbury Committee recommendations for European companies and the OECD principles of corporate governance are perhaps the best known among these. But developing countries have not fallen behind either.

Development of norms and guidelines are an important first step in a serious effort to improve corporate governance. The bigger challenge in India, however, lies in the proper implementation of those rules at the ground level. More and more it appears that outside agencies like analysts and stock markets (particularly foreign markets for companies making GDR issues) have the most influence on the actions of managers in the leading companies of the country. But their influence is restricted to the few top (albeit largest) companies. More needs to be done to ensure adequate corporate governance in the average Indian company.

CHAPTER-50

Impact of Corporate Governance and Its Practices in Indian Economy: Past and Present

Aanchal Singh[1]

Anubhuti Dungdung[2]

INTRODUCTION

Former World Bank President James Wolfensohn "has equated the importance of the governance of corporations to that of the governance of countries". Corporate governance is a field in economics that investigates how to secure/motivate efficient management of corporations by the use of incentive mechanisms, such as contracts, organizational designs and legislation. This is often limited to the question of improving financial performance, for example, how the corporate owners can secure/motivate that the corporate managers will deliver a competitive rate of return."

Corporate governance in a developing-country setting takes on additional importance. Good corporate governance is vital because of its role in attracting foreign investment. The extent of foreign investment, in turn, shapes the prospects for economic growth for many developing countries. This Note presents an in-depth inquiry into corporate governance in one such developing country, India. While India's corporate-governance framework is advanced for a developing country, it still can be significantly improved.

---

1. Third year student of Under graduate program of Hidayatullah National Law University, Raipur.

2. Third year student of Undergraduate program of Hidayatullah National Law University, Raipur.

Corporate governance is a very poorly defined concept; it covers so many different economic issues. It is difficult to give a first class definition in one sentence. Corporate governance has succeeded in attracting a great deal of interests of the public because of its obvious importance for the economic health of corporations and society in general. As a result, different people have come up with different definitions that basically mirror their special interest in the field. It is difficult to see that this 'disorder' will be any different in the future so the best way to define the concept is perhaps to list a few of the different definitions rather than just mentioning one definition.

HISTORY OF CORPORATE GOVERNANCE IN INDIA

A. Pre-Liberalization

When India attained independence from British rule in 1947, the country was poor, with an average per-capita annual income under thirty dollars. However, it still possessed sophisticated laws regarding "listing, trading, and settlements." It even had four fully operational stock exchanges. Subsequent laws, such as the 1956 Companies Act, further solidified the rights of investors.

In the decades following India's independence from Great Britain, the country turned away from its capitalist past and embraced socialism. The 1951 Industries Act was a step in this direction, requiring "that all industrial units obtain licenses from the central government." The 1956 Industrial Policy Resolution "stipulated that the public sector would dominate the economy." To put this plan into effect, the Indian government created enormous state-owned enterprises, and India steadily moved toward a culture of "corruption, nepotism and inefficiency." As the government took over floundering private enterprises and rejuvenated them, it essentially "converts private bankruptcy to high-cost public debt." One scholar referred to India's economic history as "the institutionalization of inefficiency."

Scholars believe that "takeover threats act as [a] disciplining mechanism to poorly performing companies" because as the stock price of poorly governed firms decreases (because disgruntled investors discard stock), the firms become susceptible to hostile-takeover attempts. Thus, "the fear of a takeover ... is supposed to keep the management honest." However, until recently, hostile takeovers were almost entirely non-existent in India, and therefore, the poorly governed Indian firms had little to worry about in terms of following corporate laws once they had raised capital through their initial public offering. Thus, corporate governance in India was in a dismal condition by the early 1990s.

B. Post-Liberalization

In 1999, in a defining moment in India's corporate-governance history, the Indian Parliament created the Securities and Exchange Board of India ("SEBI") to "protect the interests of investors in securities and to promote the development of, and to regulate[,] the securities market." In the years leading up to 2000, as Indian enterprises turned to the stock market for capital, it became important to ensure good corporate governance industry-wide. Additionally, a plethora of scams rocked the Indian business scene, and corporate governance emerged as a solution to the problem of unscrupulous corporate behaviour.

In 1998, the Confederation of Indian Industry ("CII"), "India's premier business association," unveiled India's first code of corporate governance. However, since the Code's adoption was voluntary, few firms embraced it. Soon after, SEBI appointed the Birla Committee to fashion a code of corporate governance. In 2000, SEBI accepted the recommendations of the Birla Committee and introduced Clause 49 into the Listing Agreement of Stock Exchanges. Clause 49 outlines requirements vis-a-vis corporate governance in exchange-traded companies. In 2003, SEBI instituted the Murthy Committee to scrutinize India's corporate-governance framework further and to make additional recommendations to enhance its effectiveness. SEBI has since incorporated the recommendations of the Murthy Committee, and the latest revisions to Clause 49 became law on January 1, 2006.

PROGRESS IN INDIAN SCENARIO

In India, the initiative on corporate governance was not a result of a major corporate scandal such as Enron, World Com, etc. It started as a self-regulatory move from the industry, rather than the rule of law.

The earliest developments in India began in 1991. After the report of the Cadbury Committee was released in the UK, Industry groups held seminars and conferences to discuss the Cadbury report and its relevance to India. The Confederation of Indian Industries (CII) was the first to introduce a code on corporate governance in April 1998. Some companies complied with this code in their annual reports of 1998-1999; it was voluntary in nature.

Over the years, the Government of India and the SEBI have constituted several committees to make recommendations. The recommendations of three landmark committee reports are milestones in the journey towards better governance.

The *Kumar Mangalam Birla Committee*, constituted by SEBI, was instrumental in the addition of a new Clause 49 to the listing agreement with the stock exchanges. This was a landmark in the history of corporate governance in India. These recommendations, aimed at improving the standards of corporate governance, are divided into 19 mandatory and six non mandatory recommendations.

The committee's major contribution was in recommending the constitution of the Board of Directors (specifying the minimum number of independent directors and board procedures), the audit Committee (including the mandatory requirement of an audit committee) and Disclosures (mandatory management discussion and analysis section in annual reports and other disclosures). For the first time in the history of corporate India, specific corporate governance processes and disclosures were mandated under the listing agreement with the stock exchanges.

This was followed by the *Naresh Chandra Committee* (Department of Company Affairs, Government of India) on Corporate Audit and Governance in 2002. The committee recommended best practices regarding the statutory relationship between auditors and companies, and set the highest standards for the role of audit committees. For example, Clause 49 has incorporated the recommendation of the Birla Committee that the audit committee should have three nonexecutive directors as members, with at least two independent directors, and that the chairman of the committee should be an independent director.

But the Naresh Chandra report had set the benchmark higher. It recommended that all members of the audit committee should be independent directors, thereby closing the loophole that could make it possible for a promoter-director without an executive role in the company to become a member of the audit committee.

Progressive companies like Infosys follow the benchmark spelt out by the Chandra report and all the members of its audit committee are independent directors.[11]

The *N.R. Narayana Murthy Committee* raised the bar by placing greater emphasis on internal controls and risk management systems in companies. Several of its recommendations concerning related party transactions and qualifications of audit committee members were accepted by SEBI and made mandatory under Clause 49. Interestingly, the committee made an important non mandatory recommendation that companies must be encouraged to move towards a regime of unqualified financial statements (in many cases auditors taint financial statements with their disapproval/objection to some of the accounting practices). This has not yet been accepted.

THE ROAD AHEAD: MOVING BEYOND SATYAM SCAM

In my view, however, all is not bleak. The Satyam episode has forced a rethink of the accounting and audit policies that Indian companies now follow. Many solutions have come up to plug the loopholes which were exposed by the Satyam scandal and if implemented, some of the solutions could be highly effective. With respect to accounting and audit, knee-jerk reactions like taking confirmations from banks with respect to amount of funds have already begun. Most of the big auditors have started to implement the aforesaid. However, these are procedural changes and not policy ones. It's the latter which can hope to accomplish anything. One very viable solution put forward by the IASC Foundation is a call for all major Indian companies to move towards full convergence with the International Financial Reporting Standards (IFRS). With this we expect a lot from the Indian government as to progress in the society as well as business era.

CONCLUSION

With the recent spate of corporate scandals and the subsequent interest in corporate governance, a plethora of corporate governance norms and standards have sprouted around the globe. The Sarbanes-Oxley legislation in the USA, the Cadbury Committee recommendations for European companies and the OECD principles of corporate governance are perhaps the best known among these. But developing countries have not fallen behind either. Well over a hundred different codes and norms have been identified in recent surveys and their number is steadily increasing. India has been no exception to the rule. Several committees and groups have looked into this issue that undoubtedly deserves all the attention it can get.

In the last few years the thinking on the topic in India has gradually crystallized into the development of norms for listed companies. The problem for private companies, that form a vast majority of Indian corporate entities, remains largely unaddressed. The agency problem is likely to be less marked there as ownership and control are generally not separated. Minority shareholder exploitation, however, can very well be an important issue in many cases.

REFERENCES

1. www.encycogov.com Mathiesen [2002].

2. Yeh, Y.H., T.S. Lee, and T. Woidtke (2001), Family Control and Corporate governance: Evidence from Taiwan, International Review of Finance, 2, 21-48.

3. Claessens, S. and J.P.H. Fan, 2003. Corporate Governance in Asia: A Survey, Working Paper, University of Amsterdam.

4. Johnson, S., P. Boone, A. Breach, and E. Friedman 2000. Corporate Governance in the Asian Financial Crisis, Journal of Financial Economics, 141-186.

5. Gregory, Holly J., 2001, International Comparison of Corporate Governance: Guidelines and Codes of Best Practice in Developed Markets, Weil, Gotshal & Manges LLP.

6. Das, A. and S. Ghosh, 2004. Corporate Governance in Banking System: An Empirical Investigation, Economic and Political Weekly, March 20, 2004, pp. 1263-1266.

7. Gibson, M.S. (forthcoming), Is Corporate Governance In effective in Emerging Markets? Journal of Financial and Quantitative Analysis.

8. Gregory, Holly J., 2000, International Comparison of Corporate Governance: Guidelines and Codes of Best Practice in Developing and Emerging Markets, Weil, Gotshal & Manges LLP.

9. Yeh, Y.H., T.S. Lee, and T. Woidtke (2001), Family Control and Corporate governance: Evidence from Taiwan, International Review of Finance, 2, 21-48.

10. Goswami, Omkar, 2002, "Corporate Governance in India," Taking Action against Corruption in Asia and the Pacific (Manila: Asian Development Bank), Chapter 9.

11. La Porta, R., F. Lopez-De-Silanes, and A. Shleifer 1999. Corporate ownership around the world, Journal of Finance, 54, 471-518.

CHAPTER-51

Creating A Better India Through Corporate Governance

Amit Kumar Swami

Seth G. L. Bihani S.D.P.G. College
Amit.swami@Yahoo.co.in

The corporate governance literature in the US and the UK focuses on the role of the Board as a bridge between the owners and the management (see for example; Cadbury, 1992; Salmon, 1993; Ward, 1997). In an environment in which ownership and management have become widely separated, the owners are unable to exercise effective control over the management or the Board. The management becomes self perpetuating and the composition of the Board itself is largely influenced by the likes and dislikes of the Chief Executive Officer (CEO). Corporate governance reforms in the US and UK have focused on making the Board independent of the CEO. Many companies have set up a Nominations Committee of the Board to enable the Board to recruit independent and talented members. There is now increased recognition of the role that the Board could play in providing a strategic vision to the company. The Compensation Committee of the Board has been strengthened to exercise greater control over CEO compensation following widespread complaints that top management pay is disproportionate to performance. There is also a great deal of discussion in the literature on the role of the Board in firing non performing management and in managing the CEO succession. Perhaps the most powerful and well-established of the Board committees is the Audit Committee. Apart from acting as a deterrent against financial improprieties and frauds, the Audit Committee also enables the Board to keep a pulse on the financial health of the company.

PUBLIC SECTOR UNITS (PSUS)

The governance structures of PSUs date back to the days when they were typically wholly owned by the government and were merely an extended arm of the state. These structures allowed the administrative departments in the concerned ministry to exercise virtually complete control over the functioning of these enterprises. It is now evident that these structures are incompatible with the efficient and successful operation of the PSUs in an increasingly competitive and deregulated economy. These issues are discussed extensively elsewhere in this volume (Vittal, 1997), and I shall not go into them again here.

It is interesting however to observe how totally irrelevant the Board really is in the governance of the PSUs today. The Board has no role to play in any of the areas where US and UK reformers have sought to strengthen the Board. The Board has very little say in the selection of the CEO or in the composition of the Board. The government as the majority shareholder takes these decisions through the concerned ministry with the help of the Public Enterprises Selection Board. The Board cannot fire the CEO nor can it vary his compensation package. As far as audit is concerned, again the dominant role is that of the Comptroller and Auditor General (CAG). There is very little that an Audit Committee could add to what the CAG does.

MULTI NATIONAL CORPORATIONS (MNCS)

Government regulations have required most MNCs in India to operate through subsidiaries which are not 100% owned by the parent. In the 70s, the government enacted a law limiting foreign ownership in most industries to 40% while allowing 51% in a few high technology areas. This law was liberalized in the 90s and now 51% is permitted in most industries while 74% or even 100% ownership is allowed in some cases. These regulations have created severe corporate governance problems in several key areas as may be seen from the examples below.

In the 70s, MNCs were forced to issue shares to the Indian public to comply with the law. The controls that then existed on pricing of public issues meant that these issues were at substantial discounts to the market price. In the 90s when the law permitted higher foreign ownership, these MNCs raised the foreign stake by issuing shares at very deep discounts to the market price. This obviously meant a large loss to the minority shareholders. One particular case where shares were issued to the parent at less than one-tenth the market price was analyzed in detail by Barua and Varma (1993a and 1993b). They calculated that the net gain to the foreign parent after compensating for the loss that it suffered in the 70s (together with interest thereon at market rates of interest) amounted to over $200 million. This and other similar share issues by MNCs were made with the explicit consent of the shareholders in general meeting. The parent companies with their dominant shareholding were able to get the resolutions passed with impressive majorities. In fact when the government introduced regulations to prevent such preferential issues, the MNCs protested against what they called an assault on "shareholder democracy".

Another corporate governance problem arises where the foreign parent has two subsidiaries in India in one of which it holds a higher stake (say 100%) while in the other it holds a smaller stake (say 51%). The manner in which the MNC structures its business in India between these two subsidiaries is riddled with problems as far as the minority shareholder is concerned.

PROTECTION OF MINORITY SHAREHOLDERS

Company law provides that a company can be wound up if the Court is of the opinion that it is just and equitable to do so. This is, of course, the ultimate resort for a shareholder to enforce his ownership rights. Rather than let the value of his shareholding be frittered away by the enrichment of the dominant shareholder, he approaches the court to wind up the company and give him his share of the assets of the company. In most realistic situations, this is hardly a meaningful remedy as the break-up value of a company when it is wound up is far less than its value as a "going concern". It is well known that winding up and other bankruptcy procedures usually lead only to the enrichment of the lawyers and other intermediaries involved.

Company law also provides for another remedy if the minority shareholders can show that the company's affairs are being conducted in a manner prejudicial to the interests of the company or its shareholders to such an extent as to make it just and equitable to wind it up. Instead of approaching the Court, they can approach the Company Law Board (now proposed to be renamed as the Company Law Tribunal). The Company Law Tribunal which is a quasi-judicial body can make suitable orders if it is satisfied that it is just and equitable to wind up the company on these grounds, but that such winding up would unfairly prejudice the members. In particular, the Tribunal may regulate the conduct of the company's affairs in future, order the buyout of the minority shareholders by the other shareholders or by the company itself, set aside or modify certain contracts entered into by the company, or appoint a receiver. The Tribunal could also provide for some directors of the company to be appointed by the Central Government, or by proportional representation. The Tribunal normally entertains such complaints only from a group of shareholders who are at least one hundred in number or constitute 10% of the shareholders by number or by value.

INFORMATION DISCLOSURE AND AUDIT

Company law provides for regular accounting information to be supplied to the shareholders along with a report by the auditors. It also requires that when shareholder approval is sought for various decisions the company must provide all material facts relating to these resolutions including the interest of directors and their relatives in the matter Disclosure does not by itself provide the means to block the dominant shareholders, but it is a prerequisite for the minority shareholders to be able to exercise any of the other means available to them. Disclosure is also a vital element in the ability of the capital market to exercise its discipline on the issuers of capital.

REGULATORY RESPONSE: SECURITIES LAW

Historically, most matters relating to the rights of shareholders wer governed by the company law. Over the last few decades, in man countries, the responsibility for protection of investors has shifted to th securities law and the securities regulators at least in case of large liste companies. In India, the Securities and Exchange Board of India (SEBI was set up as a statutory authority in 1992, and has taken a number c initiatives in the area of investor protection.

INFORMATION DISCLOSURE

As discussed above, the company law itself mandates certai standards of information disclosure both in prospectuses and in annu accounts. SEBI has added substantially to these requirements in an attemp to make these documents more meaningful. Some of these disclosures a important in the context of dealing with the dominant shareholder. One of the most valuable is the information on the performance of other companies in the same group, particularly those companies which have accessed the capital markets in the recent past. This information enables investors to make a judgement about the past conduct of the dominant shareholder and factor that into any future dealings with him.

INSIDER TRADING

Securities regulators around the world have framed various regulations to deal with the problem of insider trading. The existence of regulations does not necessarily mean that they are enforced. In South Africa, for example, a recent report on insider trading pointed out that in the quarter century that the insider trading law has been in existence in that country, there has not been a single prosecution (King, 1997). The situation is not very much better in many other countries. However, in the United States and the United Kingdom there have been a large number of well publicized and successful actions against insider trading.

Most instances of insider trading have nothing to do with the dominant shareholder. Many of them involve small trades by junior employees who come to know of price sensitive information. In a few instances, insider trading may be indulged in by directors and other senior employees. In the context of this paper, however, the interesting cases are large scale trades by the dominant shareholder. Market gossip has long speculated on the prevalence of such trades in the build up to large mergers especially between group companies. Some promoters have merged small companies in which they have a large stake into a larger more widely held company at a swap ratio which is highly unfavorable to the widely held company. These allegations have been difficult to prove in most instances as the promoters can act through numerous friends, relatives and other fronts. When SEBI recently initiated action for insider against a large multinational in a somewhat different situation, the action proved to be highly controversial and the ultimate resolution of this case remains uncertain.

TAKE-OVER'S

Instead of directly exploiting all the privileges that his controlling block gives him, the dominant shareholder can choose to sell his entire holding to somebody else. In a well functioning market for corporate control, he can expect to get a premium over the market price equal to the present value of all the privileges that the dominant shareholder can enjoy in future. The take-over regulations in India require that a slice of this cake be shared with other shareholders. The acquirer of a controlling block of shares must make an open offer to the public for at least 20% of the issued share capital of the target company at a price not below what he paid of the controlling block. Of course, if more than 20% of the shareholders want to sell at that price, the acquirer is bound to accept only 20% on a pro-rata basis.

CONCLUSION

This paper has argued that structural characteristics of the Indian corporate sector make the corporate governance problems in India very different from that in say the US or the UK. The governance issue in the US or the UK is essentially that of disciplining the management who have ceased to be effectively accountable to the owners. The solution has been to improve the functioning of vital organs of the company like the board of directors. The problem in the Indian corporate sector (be it the public sector, the multinationals or the Indian private sector) is that of disciplining the dominant shareholder and protecting the minority shareholders. A board which is accountable to the owners would only be one which is accountable to the dominant shareholder; it would not make the governance problem any easier to solve. Clearly, the problem of corporate governance abuses by the dominant shareholder can be solved only by forces outside the company itself. This paper has discussed the role of two such forces – the regulator (the company law administration as well as the securities regulator) and the capital market.

Corporate governance abuses perpetrated by a dominant shareholder pose a difficult regulatory dilemma in that regulatory intervention would often imply a micro-management of routine business decisions. The regulator is forced to confine himself to broad proscriptions which leave little room for discretionary action. Many corporate governance problems are ill suited to this style of regulation.

CHAPTER-52

Endangered Ethics : Business Ethics and Role of Directors

Alekhya Reddy. T

B.A. LL.B. (Hons.)
Hidayatulla Natioal Law University, Raipur.

31, Sai Enclave, Rd.No-12, Banjara Hills, Hyderabad, A.P-500034

Pranathi Singamaneni

B.Sc. LL.B. (Hons.), Gujrat Natioal Law University,Gandhinagar
Tirupati, Chittoor Dist, A.P -517501

CORPORATE GOVERNANCE

Corporate governance is the set of processes, customs, policies, laws, and institutions affecting the way a corporation (or company) is directed, administered or controlled. Corporate governance also includes the relationships among the many stakeholders involved and the goals for which the corporation is governed. The principal stakeholders are the shareholders, the board of directors, employees, customers, creditors, suppliers, and the community at large.[1]

Corporate governance is a multi-faceted subject.[2] An important theme of corporate governance is to ensure the accountability of certain individuals in an organization through mechanisms that try to reduce or eliminate the principal-agent problem. A related but separate thread of discussions focuses on the impact of a corporate governance system in economic efficiency, with a strong emphasis on shareholders' welfare. There are yet other aspects to the corporate governance subject, such as the stakeholder view and the corporate governance models around the world.[3]

BUSINESS ETHICS AND CORPORATE GOVERNANCE

Business Ethics and Corporate Governance have become topics of worldwide importance in present times. These issues have become top concerns at international business community and financial institutions. In recent years we have media filled shocking stories of corporate misconduct and wrong doing by individual business people. It is difficult to imagine areas of study that have greater importance to business, managerial leaders and society at large.

Business ethics relates to the behavior and obligations of business professionals. Here the focus is on people, how individuals should conduct themselves in fulfilling the ethical requirements of business. Business ethics requires managers to be honest with stakeholder's interest, society, environment and themselves. It is vitally important for any business, for progress of society and efficient economy. It is ethics alone, not government laws and regulations, which can protect the society. Business ethics and profits go together in the long-run, for sustenance of organizations. If a company wants to survive and grow, it has to discharge its obligations to the society. So corporates have to pave the way for stronger ethical foundations.

MYTH ABOUT CORPORATE GOVERNANCE

Corporate Governance can be interpreted as placing power and authority in the hands of stakeholders of corporate entity. This definition brings stakeholders of the corporate entity. This definition brings stakeholders to the forefront but is still too general to properly understand the term.[4]Across a broad spectrum of countries like Australia, Canada, UK and the US to developing countries like Brazil, Malaysia, Korea, Kyrgyz, corporate governance codes 'recognize and emphasize that the duty of the board is to maximize shareholders value.[5]

CAN GOODNESS BE REGULATED

Running a company with high ethical values is simply good business. Ethics is one area of governance where the direction is undoubtedly from top to bottom. Ethical behavior means protecting the long-term interests of shareholders rather than playing up to market sensibilities in the medium term.[6] Corporate governance is measured by how well the integrity and ethics of people at the top is institutionalized throughout the company. Whether ethical corporate behavior can be legislated is debatable. Take the case of Enron. For years together it had the finest system of internal control and audit oversight. Everything appeared perfect but it wasn't. Ethical behavior cannot be legislated it can only be conducted, especially if it is in the corporate sector.

ROLE OF DIRECTORS

'Director' as the term signifies is a person who directs. With reference to a company, 'director' means "a member of the managing board of commercial company"[7] Section 2(13)[8] of the Companies Act, 1956 defines that 'director' includes any person occupying the position of a director whatever he is called.[9] Section 253[10] declares that only an individual can be appointed as a director. According to Section 2(30)[11] of the Act an officer includes any director, manager or secretary or any person in accordance with whose directions or instructions the Board of directors or any one or more of the directors is accustomed to act.[12] Thus, director is an individual lawfully appointed to the Board of Directors of a company which is duly constituted to direct, control and supervise the activities and affairs of a company. Any person functioning as a director without being lawfully appointed cannot be treated as a director.[13]

The board of directors has a pivotal position in the structure of corporate governance. A company in law is equal to a natural person and has a legal entity of its own. Though a company is itself a 'person', it is an artificial legal person created by law, and can, therefore, of necessity, act only through the agency of natural persons. It is on account of the peculiar character of a company that the need for directors arises. The directors are not only agents of a company but they are also its trustees. The board of directors is called 'the directing mind and will of the company'

The Indian Company Law contemplates unitary board system and the division of the board into two categories of directors, executive and non-executive. The spirit of the company law clearly is that the board should function as a unitary body and act collectively so that the collective wisdom of the directors is pooled for the benefit of the company. The company law requires that except where individual directors have been entrusted with specific powers by the board, the powers are to be exercised by the directors collectively.

Meetings of directors provide a means to discuss the business and take formal decisions. The law therefore, specifically enjoins that the board must formally meet once a quarter. It also provides for the matters which the board should formally decide at its meetings by resolutions. That apart, the meetings provide a forum for deliberating on matters affecting the business and affairs of the company. It also constitutes the board as the supreme governing organ of a company.[14]

DISCIPLINARIAN OR COUNSELOR

Boards ought to be decision-makers for the corporate-at least in a strategic manner. Where boards routinely take decisions about who the CEO is going to be, what business the company will engage in, major funding avenues and such, it is really playing a strategic role which will set the pace for the company's functioning.

RISE OF CORPORATE FRAUDS

Ineffective control systems and diminishing ethical values are contributing to a growing prevalence of fraud in India.[15]

The report examined into corporate India found that 75 percent of those questioned believe that fraud cases had increased over the last two years. The report attributes this perception to the existence of mistrust within companies, individuals striving to achieve personal gains, pressure to meet earnings targets, and lack of control mechanisms.[16]

The survey's respondents were made up of chairman/managing directors, chief financial officers, heads of internal audit and compliance, fraud risk managers, and other senior personnel at close to 1,000 leading organizations operating in a wide range of industries throughout India.

Among these industry leaders, a discouraging 81 percent believe that financial statement fraud is a major issue facing the country. Regarding the motive, 63 percent indicate a desire to meet or exceed market expectations as a leading cause, while 61 percent feel performance-based remuneration it the underlying instigator. An absence of appropriate repercussions could also be a driver, as indicated by the 62 percent of respondents who believe strict disciplinary actions are not enforced for those who commit financial statement fraud.[17]

An astounding 87 percent of individuals surveyed have said that their firms have lost more than Rs.1 million to fraud, up from 47 percent in the company's 2008 survey. The perception of the Indian business environment, where 38 percent believe bribery is an integral part of company transactions, is also cause for concern.

ENRON

The Enron scandal, revealed in October 2001, eventually led to the bankruptcy of the Enron Corporation,[18] and the dissolution of Arthur Andersen, which was one of the five largest audit and accountancy partnerships in the world. In addition to being the largest bankruptcy reorganization in American history at that time, Enron undoubtedly is the biggest audit failure.[19]

Kenneth Lay founded Enron[20] in 1985.[21] By 1992, Enron was the largest merchant of natural gas in North America.[22] The creation of the online trading model, EnronOnline, in 1999 enabled the company to further develop and extend its abilities to negotiate and manage its trading business.[23] By December 31, 2000, Enron's stock was priced at $83.13 and its market capitalization exceeded $60 billion[24]. In addition, Enron was rated the most innovative large company in America in *Fortune*'s Most Admired Companies survey[25]Enron's nontransparent financial statements did not clearly detail its operations and finances with shareholders and analysts.[26] In addition, its complex business model stretched the limits of accounting, requiring that the company use accounting limitations to manage earnings and modify the balance sheet to portray a favorable depiction of its performance.[27] The combination of these issues later led to the bankruptcy of the company, and the majority of them were perpetuated by the indirect knowledge or direct actions of Lay, Jeffrey Skilling, Andrew Fastow, and other executives.[28] Which further led to the downfall of the company.

SATYAM SCAM

Satyam scam is not something that will shatter the peace and tranquility of Indian public beyond repair. The robbery may be big in terms of western standards but for us its just another brick in the wall- the wall of resilience and apathy.[29]

The Satyam Computer Services scandal was publicly announced.[30] 'Satyam Computer Services' founder-chairman Ramalinga Raju and his aides forged board resolutions and got loans/advances of Rs 1,220crore in an unauthorized manner in the name of Satyam Computers from banks but this is not reflected in the accounting books.[31] Raju has claimed that no one else in the company was privy to the fudging of accounts.[32] A total of 1,065 properties whose documented value was Rs 350 crore [33] has been identified which include around 6,000 acres, 40,000 square yards of housing plots and 90,000 square feet of built-up area.[34] In June 2001, Raju had nearly 23% shares.[35]

The Satyam scam, or rather, the promoter Chairman's decision to acquire the controlling stake in the Maytas, companies controlled by his family members is the last thing India Inc needed in the year of inflation, global meltdown and bomb blasts. India's image as a preferred investment destination, with best practices and transparent systems was badly dented, provoking a fresh debate on standards of corporate governance in India.[36] The brazenness of the promoter's statement and justifications of diversification in infrastructure, as opposed to Satyam's core business, had few takers. As did the management comment that there was no violation of any law or regulation, that no shareholders' approval was required as the promoters' holding in Satyam was less than10%.[37]

ROLE OF DIRECTORS

The Companies Act in India has stringent corporate governance requirements of board members. Yet Raju was able to steer the fabricated accounts through his board members for 6-years! This has bewildered the corporate sector and regulators. At times, the company was holding excessive cash, as per the books. This should have invited questions by board members.[38]

In particular, Independent Directors, who are appointed by shareholders at the behest of the board, are selected on the basis of their reputation, knowledge, and wisdom. They are the first defense of minority shareholders. Generally they bring specialized expertise. Independent directors have to meet standards set by stock exchanges too.[39] The Indian Government specifically delineates the role of independent directors in safeguarding the interests of the organization and the shareholders.[40] An independent director would normally assume that audited accounts have been rigorously examined. This is more so when an internationally credible firm- like Pricewaterhouse Coopers- has audited the numbers.[41] But, they need to still ask the right questions and probe. Sitting on numerous boards compresses the time an independent director has to reflect on what is happening inside the belly of a company.

ROLE OF AUDITORS

There is intense debate about the role of PricewaterhouseCoopers[42], the external auditors of the company in clearing the accounts of Satyam. PricewaterhouseCoopers (or PwC) is one of the world's largest professional services firms and the largest of the Big Four auditing firms.[43] In January 2009 PwC was criticized, along with the promoters of Satyam, an Indian IT firm listed on the NYSE, in a $1.5 billion fraud.[44] Auditors are supposed to have checked, verified cash balances, bank statements, assets with relevant confirmations. Satyam was a large company, not a street store; PricewaterhouseCoopers is a globally reputed firm. The auditors cannot hide under the standard clause 'auditors can be watchdogs and not blood-hounds' especially when cash and bank balances have been overstated.[45]

CONCLUSION

The extent of damage that India is doing by not acting in accordance with accepted norms cannot be fathomed. The global investor is gauging India and its ability to contain such individual acts of looting and daylight robbery. After all to make it a one off case there should be elaborate exhibition of swift and exemplary punitive action coupled with financial resuscitation programme for the company .It's time to show the world our sense of purpose to deliver justice and restore the stolen booty to its rightful owner-Satyam. Considering we are unable to deliver properly on this issue, then rest assured there will be many more Satyams that we have to deal with. Indian economy is at a threshold of either leapfrogging ten years ahead or retracing ten years backwards, after the global economic slow-down cycle gets completed. It is time we took charge of the situation and start amending things before it gets late. Afterall, better late than never.

REFERENCES

1. Available at http://en.wikipedia.*org/wiki/Corporate_governance*.

2. *Id*.

3. A V Vedpurswar, Leadership and Corporate Governance (ICFAI Printer, 2002).

4. Kshama V Kaushik and Kaushik Dutta, Corporate Governance: From Myth to Reality 19(Lexix Nexis 2005).

5. See Hooly J Gregory, 'Globalisation of Corporate Governance II' www.boardmember.com/network/index.pl?section=1032&article_id=10086&show =article.

6. K Shama, *supra* note 17, at 31.

7. Concise Oxford Dictionary.

8. *Section 2(13)* "director" includes any person occupying the position of director, by whatever name called;

9. Iyer, *Supra* note 9, at 3.

10. *Section 253. only Individuals to be Directors*- No body corporate, association or firm shall be appointed director of a **1**[***]company, and only an individual shall be so appointed.

11. *SECTION 2(30)*- "OFFICER" includes any director, manager or secretary, or any person in accordance with whose directions or instructions the Board of directors or any one or more of the directors is or are accustomed to act;]

12. Iyer, *supra* note 9, at 3.

13. Dean v. Hiesler, (1942) 2 All ER 340(KB).

14. *Section 129* COMPANIES ACT, 1956- 'Subject to the provisions of this act, the board of directors of a company shall be entitled to exercise all such powers and to do all such acts and things, as the company is authorized to exercise and do.'

15. *India Fraud Survey Report 2010* recent survey by professional service firm KPMG.

6. *Id.*

7. Available at *http://www.2point6billion.com/news/2010/04/07/ corporate-fraud-an-emerging- issue-in-india-5017.html*

8. An American *energy* company based in *Houston, Texas.*

9. Bratton, William W. "Enron and the Dark Side of Shareholder Value" (*Tulane Law Review*, New Orleans, May 2002) p.61.

0. It was the merger of *Houston Natural Gas* and *InterNorth*, two *natural gas pipeline* companies.

1. Healy, Paul M.; Krishna G. Palepu (Spring 2003). *"The Fall of Enron"* (PDF).. *Journal of Economic Perspectives***17** (2): 3. *http://www-personal.umich.edu/~kathrynd/JEP.FallofEnron.pdf.*

2. The gas trading business became the second largest contributor to Enron's net income, with *earnings before interest and taxes* of $122 million.

3. Healy, *supra* note 61.

4. 70 times *earnings* and six times *book value*, an indication of the stock market's high expectations about its future prospects.

5. *Key Witnesses in the Enron Trial". The Wall Street Journal. Associated Presshttp://online.wsj.com/article/SB113838648001558434.html?mod=googlewsj.*

. Bratton, *supra* note 59.

. Mack, Toni (2002-10-14). *"The Other Enron Story". Forbes. http://www.forbes.com/forbes/2002/1014/062_print.html.*

. McLean, Bethany; Peter Elkind. *The Smartest Guys in the Room.* pp. 132–133.

. Available at *ttp://www.satyamscam.info/satyam-scam-time-to-face-facts/*

. On 7 January 2009 Chairman Ramalinga Raju confessed that Satyam's accounts had been falsified. Later the chairman resigned after notifying board members and the Securities and Exchange Board of India.

31. Available at http://ibnlive.in.com/news/satyam-scam-over-rs-14000-crore-says-cbi/105885-7.html.

32. However BSE figures show a number of senior people in the company including Raju and CFO Vadlamani were reportedly selling Satyam's shares over the last 22 quarters.

33. Available at *http://sify.com/finance/cbi-files-supplementary-chargesheet-in-satyam-scam-news—news-jlzbOHaggha.html.*

34. Available at *http://ibnlive.in.com/news/the-inside-story-of-how-satyam-scam-unfolded/83158-7.html*

35. The agency, however, was contemplating to file separate charge sheets pertaining to the diversion of funds and the fraud perpetrated by the accused with regard to filing of income tax returns of Satyam. The additional charge sheet said Raju and the other accused had acquired assets worth Rs 350 crore. The huge assets acquired by the accused with the fraud amounts had been identified.

36. Satyam was quick to call off the acquisition, given the shareholders' opposition and has announced a reversal on the lines that the Maytas sellers will buy back the shares. A board meeting for this purpose is slated for later this week. But the deal cancellation modalities are yet to be worked out. There are rumours of Raju's stake being sold out.

37. Available at http://ipsnews.net/news.asp?idnews=45347.

38. http://www.rediff.com/money/2009/jan/14satyam-scam-prompts-clause-49-review.htm

39. Available at *http://news4u.co.in/?p=44538.*

40. Available at http://www.ibscdc.org/Case_ Studies/Corporate%20Governance/GOV0034.html.

41. Available at http://ibnlive.in.com/news/satyam-scam-over-rs-14000-crore-says-cbi/105885-7.html.

42. Raghavendra Verma, Keith Nuthall (2009-04-08). *"PwC partners charged over Satyam"*. Accountancy Age. *http://www.accountancyage.com/accountancyage/news/2240046/styam-partners-charged.*

43. It was formed in 1998 from a merger between Price Waterhouse and Coopers & Lybrand, both formed in London.

44. PwC's U.S. arm "was the reviewer for the U.S. filings for Satyam." Consequently, lawsuits have been filed in the U.S. with PwC as a defendant. Two partners of PricewaterhouseCoopers, Srinivas Talluri and Subramani Gopalakrishnan, have been charged by India's *Central Bureau of Investigation* in connection with the *Satyam* scandal. Since the scandal broke out, Subramani Gopalakrishnan retired from the firm after reaching mandatory retirement age; while Talluri remains on suspension from the firm. PwC has written a letter to the board of directors of Satyam that its audit may be rendered "inaccurate and unreliable" due to the disclosures made by Satyam's (ex)chairman.

45. Available at http://www.contentwriter.in/articles/others/satyam1.htm.

CHAPTER-53

SOCIAL RESPONSIBILITY AND BUSINESS ETHICS

Vipin Sharma

Asst Professor, Aravali College of Engg. &Mgt, Jasana, Faridabad

INTRODUCTION

Managers and theorists have discussed for many years about an organization's responsibility to society. Social responsibility focuses on what an organization does that affects the society in which it exists. More recently, managers and theorists have broadened their concerns to include basic ethical questions regarding relationship among employees. We find ethics broadly and simply as the study of how our decisions affect other people. It is also the study of people's rights and duties, the moral rules that people apply in making decisions, and the nature of the relationship among people. Perhaps, the first thing that becomes apparent in comparing the ethics standards and the social responsibility principles is that "ethics" are embedded in the social responsibility principles.

When we look of things today, the dominance of business ethics could be coming to an end though. Social responsibility has become increasingly more used - especially in the last decade which has seen an exponential growth in their incidence. Saying that, we'll see if the most recent financial scandals see another resurgence of business ethics post 2008 as the last data points on the graphs might seem to suggest. In fact people often tend to use SR when they're talking about the good thing companies are doing, and business ethics (or a lack of them) when talking about the bad things they do.

BRIEF REVIEW OF LITERATURE

Social responsibility and business ethics are often regarding as the same concepts. However, the social responsibility movement is but one aspect of the overall discipline of business ethics. The social responsibility movement arose particularly during the 1960s with increased public consciousness about the role of business in helping to cultivate and maintain highly ethical practices in society and particularly in the natural environment. Any entity, whether it is a state, government, corporation, organization or individual has a responsibility to society, foster a commitment and passion to improve the world.

SOCIAL RESPONSIBILITY AND BUSINESS ETHICS

'Social Responsibility' and 'Business ethics' and are two terms that are often used interchangeably, but at the same time represent somewhat different lenses on business practice. These concepts are fundamentally about the quality of our relationship over time. It has been observed that many vital decisions involve tricky problems where organizational interests affect the interest of others. Recent scandals- Commonwealth games, 2G spectrum, Adarsh Society, Citybank scam, corruption between business and government (recent involvement of IAS officers and CVC chief Mr Thomas), the possibilities and consequences of new technologies arising due to liberalization, privatization and globalization (LPG) and the increasing interplay of different culture are some of the examples and issues that have brought questions about the social responsibility and ethics of business to the leading role.

DYNAMIC CONCEPT OF SOCIAL RESPONSIBILITY

The world had always favoured small firms and criticizes large organizations. But in the last decade of last century, news headlines shocked the country with exposes of corrupt practices, touching off wave of government regulation. The depression of the 1930s, 1960s and 1970s resulting sudden rise in awareness of civil rights leading to consumer movements held organizations responsible for a growing list of social problems. Along with LPG factor and mergers and internal expansion, the attitude towards large business organizations grew rapidly around the end of last century. Our country has well established government embedded in rich culture and provided a counterbalance to large firms. This culture has made the relationship of the two sectors around issues of regulation quite often an adversarial and costly process. Government regulations provide some ground for managers, but they do not answer very basic questions and therefore we need to take a closer look at different views of business social responsibility and responsiveness that have developed in the last century.

PRINCIPLES OF SOCIAL RESPONSIBILITY

Today's dynamic business scenario has made mandatory to set some fundamental Principles of Social Responsibility as the mission to promote excellence in social responsibility through the development of principles and the sharing of tools, information and best practices that will assist in the implementation and continuous improvement organizations and professionals. Some successful managers feel that this is a key contributor in the development and implementation of social responsibility standards for an organization and can impact the all areas at all levels. It identifies the following reasons for the development of the principles: Increase management's awareness and provide tools to management professionals for the development of a proactive management social responsibility program. It creates a set of principles applicable across social, sector, organization (public, private and nonprofit) and country boundaries. It provides "one more say" to the significance of social responsibility in its many forms and applications. It complements existing standards or be used as a starting point from which to develop a set of standards unique to the needs of the organization. In most of the organizations' Principles of Social Responsibility frames certain programs of measurable corporate policies and procedures to benefit the workplace and, by extension, the individual, the organization, and the community. The social responsibility principles mainly cover: Community- consumers, fair price and good quality, etc., financial responsibility, Diversity, Human rights, Environment Safety.

PRINCIPLE OF COMMUNITY

The principle of Community provides support and adds value to communities and employees working in an organization and also encourages its own members to add value in their communities. Many organizations donate to community programs and have developed written policies encouraging employees to volunteer in community service. The principle, however, demands going beyond the boundaries of an organization and encouraging other organizations to add value in their communities.

PRINCIPLE OF CHARITY

It required the more fortunate members of society to assist its less fortunate members, including the unemployed, the handicapped, the sick, and the elderly. Community needs outgrew the wealth of even the most generous wealthy individuals, and business was expected to contribute its resources to charities aiding the unfortunate.

PRINCIPLE OF HUMAN RIGHTS

The principle of Human Rights inculcates a good habit of treating people with dignity and respect. It also support and respect the protection of international human rights within the organization's sphere of influence. It encourage the organization and its employees to avoid complicity in human or employment rights abuses while there may be no argument regarding the compatibility between ethical standards and social responsibility principles regarding supporting and respecting human rights and treating people with dignity and respect. This further prepares fertile ground for debate.

STEWARD PRINCIPLE

It is derived from the Bible that requires businesses and wealthy individuals to view themselves as stewards, or caretakers, holding their property in trust for the benefit of whole society. This type of donation can only be authenticated to recognized groups and there must be no deviation from the norm. One problem with the concept of social responsibility had to do with the specific of its implementation. The notion of social responsibility permits business firms to choose their firm's social obligations as per their own conviction but not related to the personal value. Friedman suggested that "There is one and only one social responsibility of business: to use its resources and energy in activities designed to increase its profits so long as it stays within the rules of the game...[and] engages in open and free competition without deception and fraud."

BUSINESS ETHICS

It is not prudent to avoid ethical issues in business any more than we can avoid them in other areas of lives. Most of the ethical questions in business fall into one or more of four categories- societal, stakeholder, internal policy and personal. The concept of ethics comes from the Greek word, "Ethos" that means both an individual's character and a community's culture. Generally it is believed that business ethics involves adhering to legal, professional, regulatory and company standards, keeping promises and commitments and abiding by general principles like truth, fairness, honesty and respect. The Institute of Global Ethics defines ethics as 'obedience to the unenforceable'.

This is a well known fact that Ethics is a complex area where no universal set of ethical principles exists and what is right and what is wrong often depends on circumstances. Due to global competition and rapidly developing technology change has become inevitable. The increasing realization of this has led to a change in thinking about the effective approaches to getting firms and their employees to behave ethically. Initial approaches were heavily based on "compliance', the creation of rules and systems that people and company had to follow. But rules are hard to draft and can quickly become obsolete while systems can tie people up in bureaucracy and hamper business efficiency. This has led to the evolution of the belief that although some level of compliance will always be necessary, it is more important to instill ethical "values" into the corporate body and the employees that inhibit it. To do this successfully, businesses must have a vision about why they exist and that ought to be shared by everyone connected with the organization. They must have also shared beliefs about acceptable standards of behavior.

It may be called an American subject in the sense that most recent work on the subject has been carried out in United States. The ethics movement has grown most strongly in United States because the risk of being penalized by the courts for unethical behavior is greatest there. Business values and business ethics have a worldwide dimension that must be looked after in an appropriate manner. Many people remain unconvinced by the business ethics movement. Business ethics matters because there is plenty of evidence that unethical behavior can cost a company its reputation and hard cash and reduce its stock price. Moreover companies that are perceived as ethical are more likely to build trust among their employees, customers, shareholders and the wider community and this surely is good for business.

In conclusion, Social Responsibility and Business Ethics are very important for modern businesses to possess to function productively and profitably. In a world that has been rocked by multiple corporate scandals and environmental disasters consistently, it is essential that companies put forth the effort to regain and maintain the trust of their customers and the public in general. Hopefully the efforts of eminent professional and reputed organizations will help to regain some of the footing that has been lost over the years. With a little effort and responsibility, perhaps the organizations of today can leave the world in a better shape for our children and the generations to come.

CHAPTER-54

Corporate Governance & Ethical Standards

K.Vimaladevi

Ph.D(F.T) Scholar, 196,6th street, Ganapathy Pudur, Coimbatore-641 006, Tamil Nadu

INTRODUCTION

It is widely accentuated that globally business is adopting and following the Classic Concept of Corporate Governance. It has come to be recognized that to be a successful Business entity, every company needs to attract and protect all stakeholders, be it shareholders, Creditors, society, employees, internal customers, external customers, suppliers and the environment in and around the company. Global capital investors feel comfortable in an environment where the fundamentals of Corporate Governance are best protected and practiced. Business stands to benefit by adopting systems that bolster Stake holder's trust through transparency, accountability and fairness. With increasing interdependence and free trade among countries and citizens across the globe, good Corporate Governance is of inevitable for companies seeking to distinguish and position themselves differently in the global environment. Practicing ethical business practices simply refers to adopting and practicing good Corporate Governance. The attitude to practice good business practices could be well evidenced basically by the mission and vision of an organization. Knowing the importance of adhering to the best business practices to reap the fruit of success, some of the ethical practices need to be practiced and being followed by the well-known Business and some of the unethical business practices necessarily to be avoided to become successful are discussed in this paper.

CORPORATE GOVERNANCE

From the academic viewpoint, Corporate Governance is seen as one that addresses "the agency problems that result from the separation of ownership and control". As per this view, Corporate Governance would focus on: The internal structure and rules of the board of Directors; the creation of independent audit committees; rules for disclosure of information to shareholders and creditors; and, control of the management. For example, Infosys Technologies which was conferred the National Award for Excellence in Corporate Governance by the government of India in 2000 has got a value based mission and vision. Its mission is "to achieve our objectives in an environment of fairness, honesty and courtesy towards our clients, employees, vendors and society at large". Its vision is "to be a globally respected corporation that provides best-of-breed business solutions, leveraging technology, delivered by best in-class people". Moreover Infosys has set standards in every business activity best campus, best working environment, best employer, most transparent dealings, highest quality standards as well as the highest ethical standards, never seeking any deviant benefits from the government. It would be interesting but to know the message that Infosys gives out to any discerning observer is its motto: Powered by intellect and Driven by Values.

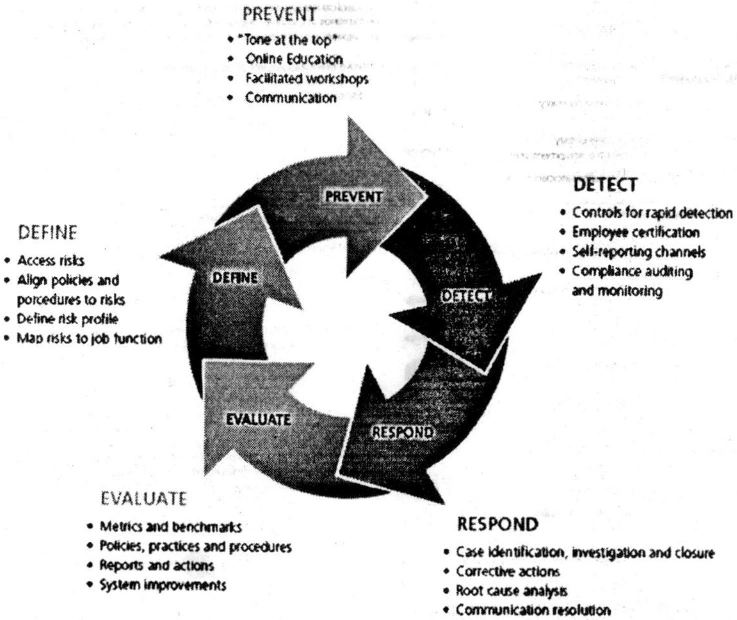

Figure 54.1: Ethical Model for Good Corporate Governance

SUSTAINABLE PERFORMANCE

We manage our sustainability performance across seven areas of accountability. Work is underway to hone our performance indicators and agree targets across the business. This table is a work in progress; it reflects that we are on a progressive journey to embed sustainability management, measurement and reporting across the organization.

Table 54.1 : Performance table

AREAS OF ACCOUNTABILITY	KEY INDICATORS	PERFORMANCE	OPPORTUNITIES
Business profitability & longevity	Revenue	↑	Maintain market leadership; renew focus on continuous improvement; conduct further long term planning to identify future market strategies.
	Profitability	↑	
	Market share	↑	
Corporate governance & compliance	Business compliance training	→	Integrate sustainability more explicitly into governance, planning and performance management frameworks; improve risk management and align with stakeholder analyses and materiality processes.
	Compliance with business ethics policy	→	
	Whistle blower disclosures	→	
Satisfying customers	Customer survey results	↑	Improve measurement of customer satisfaction and take a systemic approach to resolution of customer issues; address environmental performance of Customer Service and Logistics operations; leverage our capacity to improve customer environmental performance.
	Equipment reliability	→	
Providing a responsible solution	Energy efficiency of equipment	↑	Improve measurement of equipment and parts return; maintain pressure on paper suppliers to disclose compliance with our policy.
	% Resource recovery	→	
	% Environmentally responsible equipment sold	→	
	Product safety incidents	→	
Engaging employees	Attrition	→	Develop organisational capabilities in line with business objectives; engage employees in the business and sustainability more broadly; improve OH&S systems.
	Learning and development	→	
	Volunteering opportunities	→	
Influencing sustainability outcomes	Industry/Government	→	Continue efforts to develop a comprehensive sustainable supply chain program; engage dealers in sustainability.
	Engaging dealers	●	
	Screening suppliers	⇢	
Minimising environmental impact	Extended producer Responsibility	↑	Improve internal procedures, data collection and divisional accountability; develop and communicate carbon position more clearly; improve waste measurement; develop water targets and reduction programs.
	Resource efficiency - energy/water/waste/paper	↑	
	Carbon management	⇢	

↑ performance improved
→ performance tracking steady
⇢ performance requires improvement
● performance not managed

Source :http://www.fujixerox.com.au

Table 54.2 : Showing the factors of Legal & Ethical

Factors	Legal	Ethical
Ethos	Regards ethics as a set of limits and something that has to be done	Defines ethics as a set of principles to guide choices
Objectives	Geared toward preventing unlawful conduct	Geared toward achieving responsible conduct
Method	Emphasizes rules and uses increased monitoring and penalties to enforce these rules	Treats ethics as infused in business practice (leadership, core systems, decision-making processes, etc)
Behavioral	Assumptions Rooted in deterrence theory (how to prevent people from doing bad things by manipulating the costs of misconduct)	Rooted in individual and communal values (both material and spiritual)

NECESSITIES FOR BUSINESSES TO ACT ETHICALLY

There are number of reasons given below that justify why businesses should act ethically:

- To protect its own image,
- To protect the interests of the business community in which the organization is also a member,
- To keep the business involved for the commitment to the society to act ethically. "If there is no involvement, there is no commitment". – Dr. Steven Covey
- To meet the stakeholders' expectations. For example, for the Consumers – quality products at low cost; for the Investors – ensuring fair and profitable return on the investment,
- To build trust with key stakeholder groups,
- To protect the Organization from abuse of the unethical employees and competitors,
- To create an environment in which workers can act in ways consistent with the organizational values,

- To ensure the growth and future of the organization.
- To act as an agent of social change (being as a Good Business role model).

Additionally, an organization has to be ethical in its behaviour because it has to exist in the competitive world. A number of reasons could be found for being ethical in behavior, few of them are;

- Values give management credibility with its employees. Only perceived moral rectitude and social concern bring employee respect,
- Values help in better decision making,
- Hard decisions, which have been studied from both, ethical and economic perspectives, are more difficult to make, but they will stand up against all odds.

Ethics within organizations is a must, as only then, that can be conveyed through the activities they perform. Intangible is the nucleus to any substance in the tangible field. It triggers the collision between a substance both to create and act upon the Quality identified to the substance. Intangible has two planets revolving – 1. Ethical Responsibility and 2. Fiscal Responsibility. Ethical Responsibility is a standalone planet and it is the domain of the People. The other one is Fiscal Responsibility that has four Moons: i. Technology, ii. Managerial Force, iii. Operational Force and iv. Finance. The last one has a moon revolving it which is Balance Sheet.

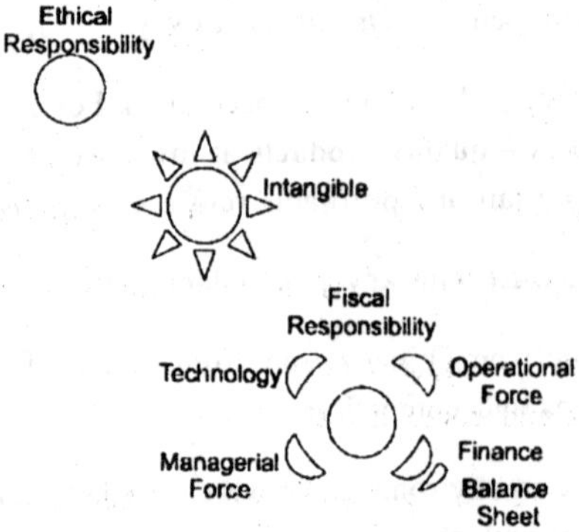

Figure 54.2: Intangible Elements of Responsibilities

Intangible is the most powerful antiparticle that makes a substance as well makes it work. A substance when yoked with another retains its independence but performs its duty. That duty is defined as Responsibility by each of the four moons of the planet Fiscal Responsibility. In Corporate functioning when a goal is set the goal must have a responsibility assigned to each of the five – note five – entities of Intangible. Otherwise is not worth setting a goal. Anything outside the gamut of Ethical Responsibility is Fiscal. Ethical Responsibility is the owner and Fiscal the Trustee. In every step of reaching towards accomplishment of a goal Ethical Responsibility's Quality statement must be complied with. These are the threshold values. 'Free enterprise is an expression of freedom, whereas Ethical Responsibility is an expression of liberty, that threshold values emanate to bridge Ethical and Fiscal Responsibility.' A BP or Lehman Bros or various instruments floated without defining the Ethical Responsibility would most likely end up in disaster.

As a matter of curiosity one can see within a moon of a moon of the planet Fiscal Responsibility holding the intangible asset trying to contain the most powerful force Intangible in it. Intangible Asset, an oxymoron, is a major reason for the Financial Crisis 2009. By controlling one goal, infinite succession of finite purposes is accomplished. That makes the Governance very easy.

MEASURING GOVERNANCE

Infinite numbers of blocks set upon one over the other have identical process of creation and action. Each is independent, has independent quality but has identical way of transforming from nothingness to a substance and having formed a substance the Action Process. Each is related to its own Quality but each layer added in both the processes in typically the same manner. The layer that gets added is the result of intangible triggering the collision.

The responsibility is assigned to each group of 5 entities – including Ethical Responsibility – in both the processes of the substance. When one layer does not get added the process comes to a stop, like remaining only as good intentions during creative process or resulting in wasteful spending or broken promises during action process.IBCM has built up a robust measuring device in identifying each of six layers, from layer 0 to layer 5 when it transforms into a substance and six layers from 0 to 5 in the

Action process when the task set is accomplished. It enables the construction for each Corporate for example the substance Business Ethics under Fiscal responsibility. It is a very powerful statement of Governance for a Corporate entity far far superior to a Balance Sheet.

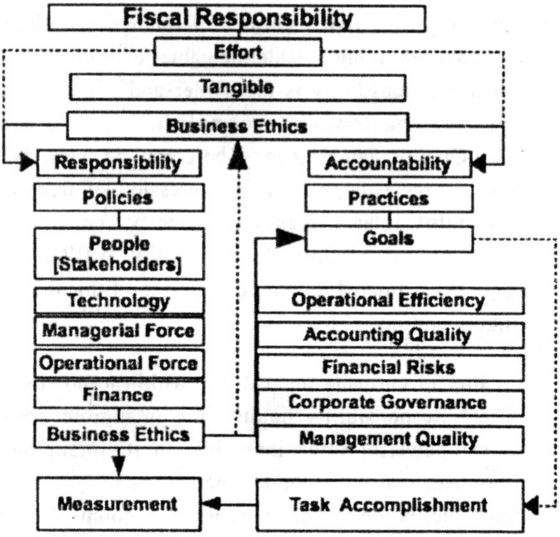

Figure 54.3: Responsibility flow Diagram

INDEX OF INACTIVITY

To start with Corporate can prepare an Index of Inactivity or in other words the status of each substance at a given stage. Since one substance is yoked with another and independent for each process area will show the status by each resource area the extent of action yet to be taken to accomplish the task set. During creative process it will show the status as it is and yet to be reached to become a substance. Corporate can look at the Intangible Asset area. AN IPR or a patented Process has gone through the six stages to become a substance. The ones yet in the process can be identified as to what the status as on today. If it has added the layer 3 there are 2 more pending to be completed to become a substance. The balance layers to be added are the index of inactivity.

CONCLUSION

Businesses can't function in a vacuum rather they need to function in the society. When the organization considers about the welfare of the akeholders in every possible manner without compromising its mission nd vision, the society takes care of the organization. It would be right to ıy that there are three sisters of corporation namely "Business ethics, orporate Governance and Business Social Responsibility". Though the oncept of Corporate Governance may sound a novelty in the Indian usiness context and may be linked to the era of liberalization, it should ot be ignored that the ancient Indian texts are the true originators of good orporate Governance as one important statement from ***'Rugveda' says: A businessman should benefit from business like a honey- bee which ıckles honey from the flower without affecting its charm and beauty."***

Ethics should be initiated from the top management to the bottom f the hierarchy. Before a company can expect to be viewed as ethical in e business community, ethical behavior within its own walls to and by nployees is a must, and top management dictates the mood. Ethical haviour by the leaders of the organization will inevitably set the right ne for the rest of the Company and the values of the company will also main consistent.

Analysis of Corporate Governance Mechanism in India- at par with Global Standards

Vikas Chaddha

Asst. Professor, RKG Group of institution, Ghaziabad, U.P

INTRODUCTION

Corporate governance is perhaps the toughest part of corpor handling. It requires an ideal control system which can regulate b motivation and ability. At one end of the spectrum are the shareholders owners of the business entity since they provide the ultimate risk capi At the other end are the "managers" or the "executive directors" of company who are in control of its day-to-day affairs. As the elec representatives of the shareholders it is the collective responsibility of board of directors to direct operations of the company in a manner tha best suited to the interests of the company. As the owners of business, shareholders are expected to monitor and evaluate operations of company as well as the performance of the entire board of directors an particular the effectiveness of the full time or executive directors.

The crisis highlights the need to develop more effective approac to corporate governance and risk management, as well as the importanc social responsibility in the financial sector; the role that corpo governance can and should play is in restoring trust (Internatio Corporate Governance Network, 2008).

UNETHICAL BUSINESS PRACTICES -SECURITY MARKET SCA AND SATYAM SCAM

The need for corporate governance was first realised in the cou with "Big Bull", Harshad Mehta's securities scam came in to light in 19 large number of banks have involved in the scam resulting in the stock arket distress for the first time in India. This was followed by a sudden owth of cases in 1993 when translational companies started consolidating eir ownership by issuing equity allotments to their respective controlling oups at steep discounts to their market price. In this preferential lotment scam alone investors lost roughly Rs. 5,000 crore. The third andal of the decade was the disappearance of the companies during 1993-4. During this period, the stock market index shot up by 120 per cent and 911 companies that rose over Rs. 25,000 crore and disappeared with out arting business.

In this misdeed of companies, innocent investors had lost a lot of oney. During this artificial boom hundreds of obscure companies were lowed to make public issues at large share premia with their misleading ospectuses. Again the Plantation companies scam took place in 1995-96 llowed by non-banking finance companies scam in 1995-97. Yet another andal was the one in which BPL, Sterlite and Videocon price rigging ppened with the help of Harshad Mehta. The IT scam between 1999-000, the firms change their names to include 'infotech', and investors saw eir stocks run away overnight. The year 2001 witnessed yet another am in which Ketan Parekh resorted to price rigging in association with a ar cartel. This brings the evaluation of the corporate governance issue to the mainstream. It is strange but true that early initiative for better rporate governance in India came from the more enlightened listed mpanies and an industry association. This was quite different from the S or Great Britain, where the drivers of corporate governance were areholders' groups, activist funds and self-regulatory bodies within pital markets, or Southeast and East Asia, where it was the result of nditions imposed by the IMF and the World Bank in the wake of the ancial collapse of 1997-98.

What transpired in Satyam computers in 2009 culminating into the storic confession letter of former chairman B. Ramalinga Raju, admitting fraud of Rs 78 billion has caused the regulators and the investors erywhere to re-examine the corporate governance standards. The ultibillion dollar scam is unprecedented and idiosyncratic for more than e reason. The fact that company which was audited by one of the most estigious audit firms and adopted most advanced accounting and insparent IFRS accounting systems much ahead of time can penetrate such a colossal and a global fraud is clearly eye opening for corporat counsel worldwide. It was triggered with Satyam's bid to acquire Mayta companies for US$ 1.6 billion. This revealed the self aggrandizing policie of the promoters, which caused severe investor backlash. When Indi embarked on its corporate governance movement in 1996-97, the countr faced no financial or balance of payments crisis.

IMPACT OF GLOBALISATION AND PRIVATISATION

In the wake of global changes and globalisation of other developin economies, India started economic reforms in the early 1990s an integrated in to the global markets. The process of globalisation ha contributed much for the governance reforms. It is because of increasin the efficiencies of the corporates in different dimensions in order to attra the attention of foreign investors to lure more investments. Althoug emerging economies are generally characterised by weak corporat governance, foreign investors face higher standards of corporate governanc in their home countries. To preserve their global integrity, foreign investo need to maintain these higher standards of corporate governance in the home countries (Nandini rajagopalan et al, 2008). Further the foreig investors are more access to governance issues and ability to enfor governance codes. The investor's attitude towards the ability of th countries in managing global investments and business is that matter India is viewed as the world's most significant business process and services provider and a consumer market with long-term potenti (A.T.Kearney, 2004).The foreign direct investments in India tend to more skill intensive than capital intensive, the major motivation for Indi firms' corporate governance improvement is the need to attract talent fro a worldwide employment pool, a need that is further enhanced by glob product market competition (Nandini rajagopalan, 2008).

SEBI GUIDELINES POST-SATYAM SCAM' 2009

In the area of securities regulation, SEBI has made numerous chang in recent years including: revising and strengthening Clause 49 in relati to independent directors and audit committees; revising Clause 41 of t Listing Agreement on interim and annual financial results; and amendi other listing rules to protect the interests of minority shareholders, f example in mergers and acquisitions. SEBI brought out new rules February 2009 requiring greater disclosure by promoters (i.e., controlli shareholders) of their shareholdings and any pledging of shares to third parties. And in November 2009 it announced it would be making some further changes to the Listing Agreement, including requiring listed companies to produce half yearly balance sheets. More recently, in December 2009, the Ministry of Corporate Affairs (MCA) published a new set of "Corporate Governance Voluntary Guidelines 2009", designed to encourage companies to adopt better practices in the running of boards and board committees, the appointment and rotation of external auditors, and creating a whistle blowing mechanism. In the current corporate governance practices it is required to focus on particular corporate governance mechanisms. There are two types of mechanism that resolve the conflicts among different corporate claim-holders, especially, the conflicts between owners and managers, and those between controlling shareholders and minority shareholders. The first type consists of various internal variables, e.g. (1) the ownership structure, (2) board of directors (3) executive compensation and (4) financial disclosure. The second includes external mechanism with variables, e.g. (1) effective takeover market, (2) legal infrastructure and (3) product market competition. "Good corporate governance practices are a *sine qua non* for sustainable business that aims at generating long term value to all its shareholders and other stakeholders".

INDEPENDENT DIRECTORS

Nomination committee can be advisably established comprising solely of independent directors or a majority of independent directors empowered to appoint the board and evaluate its performance. Although evaluation of performance is not yet mandatory under the extent of corporate governance regime yet it might yield a better result and in further coarse of time it should be made compulsory.

There should be a fixed tenure beyond which an independent director should not be associated with a company. An aggregate limit of nine years has been prescribed under clause 49 VII (ii) of the equity listing agreement, but such a requirement is not mandatory.

AUDITORS

Compulsory rotation of auditors: Though there are views that periodic rotation of the audit firm may be enough to break the collusive links between the company and the auditors, The alternatives to rotation are joint audit, rotating of managing partners, harsh penalties for collusion and regulation will make it difficult for the companies to sack the auditors who insist on qualifying fudged accounts. SEBI released on September 14, 2009 on proposed changes to the Listing Agreement, one of the reforms suggested was the rotation of either audit firms or audit partners as a way to enhance their independence from clients. SEBI felt that the independence of auditors should be reviewed because, as it said in its discussion paper: "The quality of financials reported by companies and the true and fair view of the financial statements submitted by listed entities to the stock exchanges have, of late, come into sharp focus." Moreover, in India, there is no supervisory structure like the PCAOB in US which is an independent body which supervises the audit of public firms.... a similar structure should be mandated for Indian audits.

CORPORATE DISCLOSURE

The scope, depth, timeliness, consistency and formatting of corporate financial disclosure in India could be greatly improved. Certain reforms are needed to improve the quality and timeliness of corporate disclosure of most listed companies in India. Such reforms would provide investors with more useful information on which to make investment decisions and would strengthen the reputation of the Indian capital market.

All companies should, in effect, be required to produce audited annual results within three months of the year end and their full annual report within four, or at most five, months of the year end. The format of quarterly P&L statements is to be reviewed to require additional details regarding revenues. Listed companies are to be encouraged to provide both cash flow statements and balance sheets with their quarterly reports.

Corp Filing and EDIFAR should be merged into one database, with the structure following the organisation of EDIFAR, but with further thought being given as to how information could be even more easily accessible.

On November 9, 2009, the SEBI Board announced that it would amend the Listing Agreement in relation to three of these issues, namely:

- Allowing the voluntary adoption of IFRS by listed entities with subsidiaries;

- Requiring half yearly disclosure of balance sheets (which must provide audited figures, or non-audited figures with limited review); and

PREFERENTIAL WARRANTS

The scope for the misuse and abuse of warrants in India is considerable. Regulation of their issuance to promoters needs to be tightened. The issuance of preferential shares, warrants or other securities to promoters and other connected persons must be prohibited (as in other markets), except under the limited circumstances envisaged in markets such as Hong Kong (i.e., where the securities are part of a pro-rata entitlement made available to all shareholders on an equal basis, or as part of a shareholder-approved stock option scheme).

Companies are required to seek shareholder approval at their annual general meetings for the issuance, over the subsequent 12 months, of any new shares at a discount to a limited group of (non-controlling) shareholders. Strict rules should govern the size and discount of such offerings. Listed companies should review the way they use warrants and limit their application to forming part of a wider issue of debt or equity securities (i.e., where warrants act as sweeteners for investors).

CONCLUSION

The first major stimulus for corporate governance reforms was the Southeast Asian crisis of 1997-98 followed by the Enron debacle of 2001, which necessitated the need for ensuring better corporate governance practices, culminating in the enactment of legal measures like Sarbanes - Oxley Act of 2002 in the United States. In India no evidence of miserable corporate failures as in the west, such as Enron, Maxwell, WorldCom, etc. But in India interestingly a business association, not the government, has initiated to formulate and implement code of corporate governance at international standards. In India, the initial drive for better corporate governance and disclosure - perhaps as a result of the 1992 stock market scam and the fast emerging international competition consequent on the liberalisation of the economy that began in 1991, came from the Confederation of Indian Industry (CII) and the Department of Corporate Affairs. The Satyam incident, though unfortunate, exposed some big loopholes in the system. Just as the United States needed the Enron Scandal to clean up its act, perhaps India needed the Satyam fiasco to introduce sweeping changes in its own financial reporting system. It cannot be denied that the Satyam episode was a stark failure of the code of Corporate Governance in India.

CHAPTER-56

Corporate Governance in Indian Banks

Vandana Kulshreshtha

bru-blb@yahoo.com

INTRODUCTION

The term 'Corporate Governance' in a layman language relates to the set of laws,policies,procedures and actions as prescribed by the corporates with an aim to guide their future course of action.The CG guidelines ensure smooth and transparent operations of the organization,n the sense that the rolles and responsibilities of each party concerned is clearly defined and demarcated.

CG IN BANKS

Corporate Governance aims at the following three 'V's –

- Vision
- Values
- Visibility

Vision, here ,means the direction towards which the corporate is moving, value means the value orientation of the corporate, visibility means transparency, in terms of its performance and practices.

HISTORY

Banking dates back to 1786,when the first bank was established in India , then the nationalization of banks in 1969 and 1980 and recently the liberalization of the same since 1991.Banking in India has undergone many changes since independence.The liberalization,privatization and globalization moves have injected many drastic changes into the banking system .When 14 major banks were nationalized in 1969 and six more in 1980,they became wholly owned government enterprises, wherein the government protection was available to everybody associated with the banking system. But, the recent reforms have made these banks face a cut throat competition from the private sector banks .The competition is in terms of:

- Interest rates
- Service charges
- Service points
- Service time
- Availability of variety of products

This competition has reduced the margins of the banks as well. A large numbers of banks have come out with banking products which are absolutely based on customer preferences.

WHY CORPORATE GOVERNANCE IN BANKS ?

The role of the RBI has been very prominent in strengthening investor protection measures by laying down clear rules and guidelines for the appointment of directors and disclosure of both financial and non-financial information to the investors periodically.In order to reduce the possible fiscal burden of recapitalizing the public sector banks , a lot of importance is being given to CG in banks.The regulators of the banks should regulate and supervise these aspects so that the shareholders are not affected .The regulators must make the board accountable and should assess the effectiveness of the board. Transparency in banking operations should be ensured by them. Hence, the board, regulators and external auditors should keep a watchful eye on these manipulations to protect the interests of all stakeholders.

THE ICAI HAS ISSUED DIFFERENT GUIDELINES TO ALL ITS MEMBERS ON THE PROCESS OF

Of audit and the paper work to be followed in order to ensure that no corporate/board is able to defraud its stakeholders .The guidelines stipulate measures to prevent conflicts of interests in audit tasks. The guidelines regarding financial reporting clarify the format and the content of the reports to be disclosed.RBI,as the regulator, governs,the appointment and auditing of the banks through the central statutory auditors .The RBI and the government play a dominant role in the governance of banks .Both RBI and the governmentare strivingtowads making the boards of the bank accountable and transparent.

QUALITIES NEEDED FOR GOOD CORPORATE GOVERNANCE

Following are some of the requirements that are needed for effective implementation of CG-

- A clear system explaining the structure, roles and responsibility of the ajor players in the organizations.
- A clear vision statement,explaining princiles and rules on which the business development should take place.
- A clear system of management functions,such as planning, directing, organizing and controlling.

In India, the practice of CG is influenced to a greater extent by the Kumara Mangalam Birla Committee Report ,CII Committee Report on desirable CG practice and the NR Narayana Murthy Committee Report on CG.

CORPORATE GOVERNANCE IN BANKS

Banks follow a code of conduct that attempts to set forth the guiding principles on which the banks shall function and carry their daily business with the stakeholders, government and regulatory agencies, media, and others with whom they are conducted.The Code believes that a bank works as a trustee and custodian of money received from the public and in order to fulfill its fiduciary obligations and responsibilities, it has to maintain and continue to enjoy the trust and confidence of the public at large.

The bank should acknowledhe the need to uphold the integrity of every transaction it enters into.It should always keep in mind that honesty and integrity in its internal conduct would be judged by its external behaviour The bank should commit itself in all of its actions to the best interest of the countries in which it operates.The bank should always be conscious of the reputation it carries amongsts its customers and the public at large and should endeavour to do all it can sustain and improve upon the same in its discharge of obligations. The bank should continue to initiate policies, that are customer oriented and that are aimed at promoting financial prudence.

ROLE OF BOARD OF DIRECTORS OF BANKS

Following are some f the good CG practices to be followed by the board of directors-

- Participate in the meetings of board regularly and ensure that their participation is effective and contributory.
- They must study the reports submitted to them by the management team and enquire about follow up reports on definite time schedule .They should be actively involved in the matter of formulation of general policies.
- They should be familiar with the broad objectives of the bank and the policies laid down by the government and the changes in the various laws and legislations from time to time.
- They should not interfere in the day to day functioning of the bank.
- They should also ensure confidentiality of the bank's agenda papers ,notes and minutes of the meetings.
- They should be loyal to the bank and must remember that they should not reveal any information relating to any constituent of the bank to anyone.
- They should not sponsor any proposal relating to loans , investments, buildings or sites for bank's premises, enlistment or empanelment of contractors, architects, auditors, doctors, lawyers and other professionals etc.
- They should do only those things that are legal and acceptable.
- They should promote good and fair banking practice by setting proper benchmarks in dealing with customers.

The board of directors should promote good and fair banking practices by setting proper benchmarks in dealing with customers.

BASEL II AND CORPORATE GOVERNANCE

Basel II Accord ,especially Pillar 3, throws more light on CG practices .The key governance principles that would be relevant to banks have been enumerated in the Accord Basel II has listed several principles.Some of them are specified below:

- The board of directors will be composed of people of good character and integrity with expertise knowledge in areas, such as law, accounting, banking and risk management.The board will be a mix of both executive and non-executive members.
- The board will ensure that equal treatment is given to all shareholders.
- The board will determine determine and authorize clear strategies to deal with risks, risk profile and risk tolerance for the bank.
- The board will define the code of conduct for its management and staff.
- The board has the responsibility to finalize the investment plans.
- It will ensure that internal auditors and external auditors are independent.
- The management should promote a culture of trust, honesty and integrity within bank .The management is responsible to the board for protecting the interest of the stakeholders and is also responsible for the realization of plans and goals set.
- The management should consider the implementation of Basel II as a priority and communicate its process to the relevant staff.
- The staff should also possess skills and experiences with the complete knowledge of their authorities and responsibilities.

- They should avid disclosing internal information to external parties, without the consent of management.
- The management should design information systems that comply with regulatory requirements in reporting and public disclosures .
- Proper credit rating models, with periodic appraisals, should be developed by the bank that will evaluate Value-at-Risk (VaR) and Risk Adjusted Return On Capital (RAROC) techniques of the bank..The documentation should adequately inform customers and meet all requirements of public disclosure.Disclosure of risk profiles and risk management practices is expected under Pillar 3.
- Proper protection should be ensured to the cutomers and customer satisfaction should form an integral part of the corporate structure.
- The bank should ensure that it has adequate policies and procedures in order to identify, monitor and control risks in its international lending and investing activities and for maintaining necessary reserves to guard it from these risks.
- It becomes a responsibility of banks to respond positively to its regulators.Both banks and regulators should look into cultural changes that are needed to facilitate implementation of good risk management practices, as designed in Basel II.

CONCLUSION

The concept of CG is becoming an issue of serious concern in the current Business context.The organizational structure is relying too heavily on managers for creation of wealth.This dependence has given many opportunities to those managers to misuse their official position for personal gains and made them forgetthe reasons for their existence in the firm.In other words, they have ignored the concept of 'wealth maximization of shareholders'.The Satyam fiasco is a recent instance of good CG practices not being followed.The failure to adopt CG practices is one of the major causes of the current financial crisis. Transparency and accountability, the two basic constituents of good CG, were absolutely 'thrown to winds' by the investment banks as well as the commercial banks in the developed countries, leading to the financial crisis.It is high time that the regulators wake up and take firm actions before investors' confidence and psyche is irreparably damaged.

CHAPTER-57

NATIONAL CONFERENCE ON CORPORATE GOVERNANCE IN INDIA

Pardeep Kumar Soni

Lecturer, Deptt. Of Computer Sc.
Seth G.L. Bihani S.D. (PG) College, Sri Ganganagar

COUNTRY LEVEL RELATIONSHIP B/W CORPORATE GOVERNANCE QUALITY AND PERFORMANCE

Starting with the country level studies, one study found improvements in corporate governance quality in most countries, with convergence in corporate governance quality and a positive impact of these improvements on traditional measures of real economic activity. Another study showed that measures of financial openness, political risk, local banking sector and stock market development, and "push" factors together with equity market openness explain almost half of the variation in the degree of segmentation of equity markets. This finding suggests that corporate governance reforms can help emerging markets integrate with global financial markets and thereby lowers their risk-adjusted cost of capital. It relates to the theory paper of Yavuz (2007) that explains why the effects of investor protection on the cost of equity cannot be fully diversified even in integrated markets and why investor protection is different from other country-specific factors that affect the cost of equity. This paper not only justifies many previous empirical findings but also provides a new prediction: the effect of minority investor protection on the cost of equity is stronger in countries with larger GDP and higher GDP growth volatility.

FIRM-LEVEL RELATIONSHIP BETWEEN CG QUALITY, PERFORMANCE AND VALUATION

While country level evidence is useful to document broad patterns, such studies do not always identify the channels. Firm level studies can more directly find effects of corporate governance reform and enhanced corporate governance practices on valuation and operational performance, sources and ease of financing, and reduced level of expropriation. Such studies have shown that the channels through which corporate governance adds value include: (i) improved operating performance (productivity, return on assets, etc.), (ii) lower cost of capital and higher valuations, and (iii) better access to external finance. Many such studies exist for developed countries, but only recently has similar evidence been documented for emerging markets, transition economies, and other developing countries. Several of these studies were presented at the conference.

IMPORTANCE OF EASIER ACCESS TO EXTERNAL FINANCE

In addition to studies that address the first two channels (i.e., improved operating performance and lower cost of capital), some have focused on better access to finance as a third potential channel through which improved corporate governance translates into better economic performance. One such contributions is by Gugler and Peev (2007) who analyze the investment decisions of 25,000 firms in 15 transition economies over the period 1993-2003. They report that investment becomes less sensitive to the availability of internal funds over the transition years and that ownership changes induce further declines in this sensitivity. They also document hardening of the so-called soft budget constraints for state owned firms and more efficient investment by foreign companies, a finding which highlights the differences in the identity of owner categories.

The importance of external finance as a corporate governance channel is also documented for China by Du, Rui and Wong (2007) where the government-guided financial resource allocation favors large-scale state-owned enterprises (SOEs). Smaller SOEs and most non-state enterprises are at a disadvantage in securing external financing and thus have an incentive to acquire controlling stakes in listed companies, which have more access to external financing. Consistent with this motive to seek sources of financing rather than operationally based value adding synergies, the paper shows that the post-acquisition financing activities, in general, do not help to improve the operational performance of target companies and retard or even worsen the earnings performance. Corporate governance is also important for access to equity forms of finance. Kim, Sung and Wei (2007) show that international investors display a strong aversion to high-ownership-control disparity firms in Korea, highlighting a further channel through which bad governance practices hurt the availability of external finance.

DRIVERS OF CORPORATE GOVERNANCE

While the evidence that better corporate governance is associated with better outcomes from the perspective of countries and firms is mounting, there is still a suspicion that this relationships is due to other factors and merely reflects that better countries and better firms have better performance and better corporate governance (practices), but there is no causal relationship from corporate governance to performance. As such there is need for more evidence on how corporate governance reforms can lead to improvements in performance. And, most importantly, as also highlighted by the practitioners at the conference, there remain many puzzles on the lack of reforms by countries. And it is also surprising that many corporations do not yet adopt better corporate governance practices. It remains hard to introduce the legal and institutional changes which would enhance good governance, support efficient financial markets and protect minority shareholders. And many corporations do not see the rewards, in part because the domestic institutional environment and financial markets do not yet sufficiently support corporate governance. The reason that many emerging markets do not yet take steps to achieve the economic advantages should be sought in their political systems.

IMPORTANCE OF REFORMS

While large scale reforms can be blocked in many countries by insiders (managers and owners) of corporations, a number of papers presented at the conference show that reforms had substantially positive effects. Atanasov, Black, Ciccotello and Gyoshev (2006) analyzes the impact of changes in Bulgarian securities law in 2002 on two common forms of financial tunneling, dilutive equity offerings and below-market freeze-outs. After adoption of new laws in 2002 restricting both forms of tunneling, minority dilution via equity issuances virtually disappears, and the mean price of freeze-outs (measured by price/sales ratio) quadruples. Black and Khanna (2007) analyze India's adoption of major governance reforms (Clause 49) requiring among other things, audit committees, a minimum number of independent directors, and CEO/CFO certification of financial statements and internal controls. They document that reforms benefited more those firms that need external equity capital and cross-listed firms, suggesting that local regulation can sometimes complement, rather than substitute for firm-level governance practices. Beltratti and Bortolotti (2007) document a similar positive impact from improvements in the regulatory regime in the context of the Non-tradable Share Reform in China. Further evidence on the importance of the regulatory environment is provided by Farooq and Ahmed (2007) in the context of Pakistan.

MARKET PRESSURES

Changes are not just due to (lack of) reform. Much improvement in corporate governance has come about as a result of market pressures. But these can remain limited without some other legal or regulatory supports. An example of such market induced changes is provided by Dewenter, Kim and Lim (2007) who analyze the outcome of regulatory competition in the context of Korea's two stock exchanges KSE and KOSDAQ. They show that successive efforts to tighten the regulation of the delisting rules ended up with no clear winner. Other examples of market induced changes include voluntary adoptions of higher corporate governance quality by Brazilian firms joining Bovespa's New Market, the use of tag-along rights by Brazilian companies' controlling owners to increase investor protection for non-controlling owners, and decisions to cross-list in a better investor protection country. While these changes added value, they were also helped by legal and regulatory changes.

More generally, it is important to differentiate between firm-level and country-level corporate governance and to investigate whether there is substitutability or complementarity between rules and practices. Chhaochharia and Laeven (2007) find that many firms choose to adopt governance provisions beyond those adopted by all firms in the country, and that these higher corporate governance practices are positively associated with firm valuation. These results indicate that the market rewards companies that are prepared to adopt governance attributes beyond those required by laws and common corporate practices in the home country. Aggarwal, Erel, Stulz and Williamson (2006) also analyze the links between country-level and firm-level governance mechanisms.

THE LESSONS OF THE CONFERENCE

Besides the substance lessons, there are three lessons from the conference and the format that was followed.

- Networking among academics is very valuable to exchange methodology, data, and research experience. The large number of papers with authors belonging to different institutions in different countries and the lively discussions after academic and practitioner presentations confirm the importance of networking.

- Practitioners can add value as they can introduce real life perspectives and help guide research. The open discussion forum on boards was a good example of such an interaction. After Bernard Black's academic presentation on the issue of a causal link between board structures and firm performance, Paulina Beato gave examples from her professional life suggesting that the reason why most boards in emerging markets are not functioning well can be explained by the fact that they are not independent.

All in all, we believe that these factors demonstrate how the conference has filled a gap that other academic conferences would not be able to fill both in terms of the mix of papers selected for presentation and the involvement of practitioners.

CHAPTER-58

Data Leakage Prevention and Corporate Governance

Prabir Panda* **and GP Sahu**

Motilal Nehru National Institute of Technlogy, Allahabad (India)

Davesh Singh

Indian Institute of Information Technology and Management, Gwalior (India)

INTRODUCTION

Gabrielle O'Donovan (2003) defines corporate governance as 'an internal system encompassing policies, processes and people, which serves the needs of shareholders and other stakeholders, by directing and controlling management activities with good business savvy, objectivity and integrity. Sound corporate governance is reliant on external marketplace commitment and legislation, plus a healthy board culture which safeguards policies and processes'. O'Donovan goes on to say that the perceived quality of a company's corporate governance can influence its share price as well as the cost of raising capital. Quality is determined by the financial markets, legislation and other external market forces plus how policies and processes are implemented and how people are led. The internal environment offers companies the opportunity to differentiate from competitors. It is a system of structuring, operating and controlling a company with a view to achieve long term strategic goals to satisfy shareholders, creditors, employees, customers and suppliers, and complying with the legal and regulatory requirements, apart from meeting environmental and local community needs.

A TYPICAL "DEFENSE-IN-DEPTH" IMPLEMENTATION

The use of the Internet and networked computers has changed the computing environment significantly. While providing convenience, the systems are also more vulnerable to security threats. This article discusses actions that may be taken to enhance security. A comprehensive analysis should be conducted to identify resources that need to be protected. The resources should be classified according to the sensitivity level of information. A cost-benefit analysis should be performed to determine the level of security precautions that should be given to contingency planning and recovery. If security is compromised, the organization should be able to recover quickly and minimize damages (**Qureshi & Siegel, 2001**).

PROBLEMS IN EXISTING INFORMATION SECURITY SETUP

Information security (IS) management is both complex and challenging. The complexity stems from the pervasive and multi-functional nature of IS, first, to protect organisations' valued assets, in order to achieve secure and dependable information assurance, and second, to advance business relations for the organisation by creating platforms for trust, business alliance and collaboration. Further, the ever-growing dependence of organisations on technology to drive businesses and to create a competitive advantage makes IS management for organisations extremely challenging. These challenges facing organisations in managing IS are numerous and inherently diverse. A traditional approach in addressing these challenges includes the use of technical controls to treat risks. Whilst technical controls are helpful in protecting valued assets, unfortunately, technical controls alone are insufficient in providing dependable security and information assurance required in a contemporary global enterprise. (**Onwubiko & Lenaghan, 2009**). **Rishi & Goyal (2008)** brought out that strategic value of information systems and the impact of information technology on businesses have increased the need for effective Strategic Information Systems (SIS) development. But the available methodologies for the development of SIS stress different issues; hence there is no clear guidance available for SIS development. Also gap exists in the application of an integrated model for the development of SIS. **Williams (2007)** underlined the lack of threat realisation by the information consumers and suggested that security can be improved by those who are responsible for it. Apart from the end user/IS personnel awareness, management support is a critical success factor for information security adoption (**Reddick, 2009**).

The security hierarchy is prone to failures and inefficiency due to incompatibility between products/protocols. This happens because the same information is processed through multiple layers thereby making the system inherently inefficient and resource consuming. Following are the typical problems associated with multiple levels of security:

(a) **Encryption at multiple levels** : We have data encryption system available at virtually all layers of OSI model. These encryption layers may give a sense of satisfaction to the user but internally results in efficiency as it is more resource consuming, and has more network overheads. Further every layer of encryption adds its own header in the already existing TCP/UDP packet. Thus, with introduction of another layer of encryption, the overall data carried by a packet is reduced due introduction of additional encryption related information. Due to the fixed packet size, this may result in more number of packets being pumped into the network for the same amount of data during transmission.

(b) **Reliable over reliable protocol** : Popularly referred to as "TCP-over-TCP meltdown". Multiple reliable protocols operating over one another results in additional network overheads. Transmission control protocol (TCP) has various parameters (SYN, ACH, RTT) for setting retransmission times for the delivery of data from client to server in the event of packet loss. However, this repair and recover mechanism fails when encapsulated in a second TCP stream. If the encapsulating or Internet layer drops a packet (which is common even under ideal networking conditions) both TCP streams will attempt to correct the error and retransmit duplicate data. This exponentially queues up data transmissions and prevents the real private network data from promptly reaching its destination.

(c) **Anti-malware solutions** : A large number of antivirus solutions are available in the market that caters from individual PCs to large corporate networks. Installation of anti-malware solution is no more a luxury but is a necessity. However, antivirus systems come with their own set of problems. No antivirus solution is complete in all respect in the sense provides 100% protection. These antivirus engines are highly resource intensive and require regular update sometimes on a daily basis. This has now resulted in user being looser from both ends. If he does not install antivirus, he is vulnerable, and if he installs one he loses his system performance as the antivirus engine he is using is resource intensive. In addition, an anti-malware product may have built in firewall which is over and above the firewall provided by the operating system itself. The anti-malware software when not patched properly may in itself become an attack vector and open up the system to unauthorized access.

(d) **Wasteful expenditure**. Justifying security investments has been challenging for managers and executives alike for several well-published reasons. With the growing importance of security measures, companies are increasing the share of security investments in their overall Information Technology (IT) budgets (**Tallau, Gupta & Sharman, 2010**). Information security costs money and so do the products mentioned earlier. The expenditure incurred in these products is futile as they fail to thwart an insider attacker with reasonable amount of competence in information security.

HUMAN: THE WEAKEST LINK IN INFORMATION SECURITY SETUP

No amount of security can prevent a legitimate user with legitimate credentials to access the data intended for his use. Thus we can see that human is the weakest link in the complete security framework. Companies can spend thousands of dollars to setup security infrastructure but it can be easily penetrated if the humans controlling them want to. People let their guard down to attackers when they are tired or distracted by work. Some feel intimidated. Others just make honest mistakes. Social engineering is often what allows attackers to steal the information they desire. Firewalls, intrusion detection systems and antivirus software are just tools to improve security. But dealing with people is what's critical as most security breaches come from within an organization. Social engineering is the science of getting people to comply with your wishes and concentrates on the weakest link of the information security chain. Social engineering comes in many flavors. One kind may involve an attacker getting to know a person intimately and then using that knowledge to steal vital information. Sifting through garbage for sensitive information is another kind of tactic called dumpster diving. Combating social engineering requires educating employees about such techniques.

PROPOSED ARCHITECTURE

Having studied the problems of multi level security system one thing is clear that no amount of security can ignore the human in the chain as they still form the weakest link in the entire security infrastructure. Thus we propose an architecture which enforces data protection and encryption at the lowest level and ensures a buddy system for taking data out of the LAN in plain text. This architecture utilizes existing hardware solutions with little or no customization and management software to be custom made for the purpose.

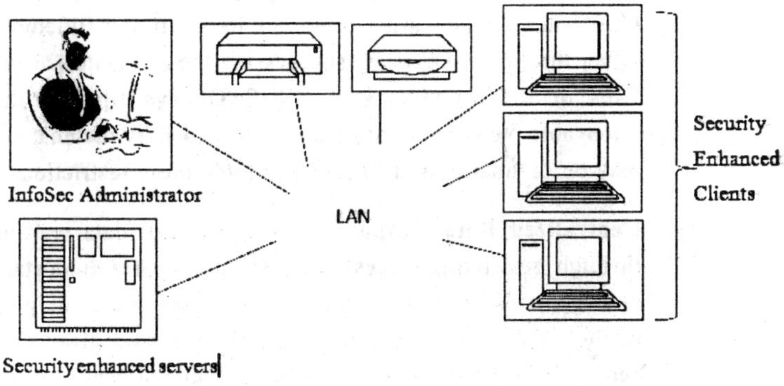

Figure 58.1: Deployment diagram

Preventing data leakage is not one magic wand solution but a combination of various tools; techniques and administration process all working together in tandem. Description of various components of the proposed architecture is elaborated below:-

(a) **Militarization of the sensitive LAN Segment**. A computer connected on network or on Internet is most vulnerable to attacks and data leakage. Even if the computer is installed with latest security tools, updated with latest security patches, it is still vulnerable to the next attack which will exploit the security hole not yet plugged by the installed security tool. A machine connected on the network or Internet is more prone to attacks from more number of attackers than the one which is standalone i.e. not connected to any network. The protected LAN segment be made fully militarized with no access to the Internet or outside world be permitted from either the clients or the servers placed in the segment. The BIOS password and system administration password of the clients would be required be maintained by the security administrator.

(b) **Port level security**. USB storage devices are the boon for data storage and transportation as they provide an un-parallel convenience to handle data. However the IT industry is facing their biggest challenge to control data leakage through USB storage devices. They are also one of the major contributors to virus menace. Therefore, it is prudent to block access to USB and communication protocols like wifi and Bluetooth either through BIOS or by suppressing the associated driver files or system files like USBSTOR.sys file for the removable media. Security features provided by the host OS may be optimally used to plug/reinforce these restrictions.

(c) **Centralized Data Output**. One may control data leakage through restricting access to USB ports. But important documents can still be printed and the hard copies may be mis-utilized. Therefore, printing facility should always be centrally controlled and should be available at central place so that it can be easily monitored. Further printing should be performed on special digital papers which are copy proof. In order to obtain data in unencrypted form for transfer out of the LAN environment, a user has to physically transfer (encrypted) data to a file server with requisite access control. This data would be decrypted by the security administrator using the portable keys in management console and given to the user on a copy protected CD/DVD. A proper record keeping would be ensured. **Gaur & Laxmi (2008)** presented development of a customised smart-card based system to transfer information securely from central server to identified client sites with information tamper protection. One of the primary aims of their system for secure information exchange was to make client reliably robust and inexpensive. They describe key-based generic but customisable encryption system that also incorporates tamper-proofing feature enhancing reliability. In the proposed process, both server and client can check if information has been tampered with and under such circumstances smart card is rendered useless. One area of application of such a system is pre-payment card based metering utilities as used in gas/water/electricity supply. These applications desire high reliability tamper proofing at low cost. To reduce installation cost, such meters need to be inexpensive and reusable. Smart card is used for reliable information exchange to/from client (meter) to server (company). Smart card can transfer information about consumption as well as time-varying tariff rates.

(d) **Encrypted Network Interface Card (ENIC)**. We can employ encrypted network interface card on the machine. This card is proposed to be modified for use in low level encryption of the entire HDD (using block cipher etc) of the clients as well as server using the system (PC) specific encryption keys stored in the flash of the NIC. The NIC would also contain second set of keys for the network wherein data would be encrypted using stream cipher. The keys would be managed and distributed using the central console. The ENIC can also exploit the facilities extended by TPM provided by Intel.

(e) **Trusted Platform Module (TPM)**. Trusted Platform Module (TPM) is a secure crypto processor embedded in the motherboard that can be used to authenticate a hardware device. Each TPM chip is unique to a particular device; it is capable of performing platform authentication. It can be used to verify that the system seeking the access is the expected system. A limited number of full disk encryption solutions have support for TPM. These implementations can wrap the decryption key using the TPM, thus tying the hard disk drive (HDD) to a particular device. If the HDD is removed from that particular device and placed in another, the decryption process will fail. Recovery is possible with the decryption password or token. Although this has the advantage that the disk cannot be removed from the device, it might create a single point of failure in the encryption

CONCLUDING REMARKS

Corporate governance deals with all organizational processes and attendant controls. These processes determine and specify the way business is conducted. In this digital era, the corporate secrets/business intelligence is stored in digital form. The cases of information pilferage can lead to lot of corporate embarrassment and loss of business. A case in point is flourishing Indian BPO sector that has learnt the value of including DLP as a part and parcel of corporate governance after suffering setbacks from leakage of customer data. Potential customers want to be sure that the data vested in the trust of a company is secure. In this digital era, DLP is an area of active research. This paper deals with an important, but often ignored issue, of safeguarding data against internal threat of a different kind.

CHAPTER-59

Corporate Governance in India: Constraining the Dominant and Protecting The Minority Shareholder

Paramvir Singh & Mona Singh

National Law University, Delhi

INTRODUCTION

India's growth rates have been amongst the highest in the world since its economic reforms in the 1980s. Its market infrastructure has advanced while corporate governance has progressed faster than in many other emerging market economies. This growth brings with it an acute need to understand the dynamics of corporate governance within an international context. An examination of corporate governance issues especially those concerning ownership structures and performance could yield important insights into the topic and provide a fresh perspective on what has become an increasingly international debate. The ethical climate of Indian organizations is soaring. The market dynamics and WTO led norms have led a new battle of consumerism on Indian Turf. No more considered to be a part of the third world country, India is rapidly moving the ladder to become super economic power. According to BRIC report (Global Paper 99) India has the potential to raise its per capita (US dollar) to 35 times in 2050 compared to its current levels thus making it one of the most attractive market for the FDI's and MNC's. Thus, there is a demanding urgency to resolve the conflicts in corporate sector through means best suited to Indian legal scenario.

PUBLIC SECTOR UNITS (PSUS)

The governance structures of PSUs date back to the days when they were typically wholly owned by the government and were merely an extended arm of the state. These structures allowed the administrative departments in the concerned ministry to exercise virtually complete control over the functioning of these enterprises. It is now evident that these structures are incompatible with the efficient and successful operation of the PSUs in an increasingly competitive and deregulated economy. It is to be noted that the Board has no role to play in any of the areas where US and UK reformers have sought to strengthen the Board. The Board has very little say in the selection of the CEO or in the composition of the Board. The government as the majority shareholder takes these decisions through the concerned ministry with the help of the Public Enterprises Selection Board. The Board cannot fire the CEO nor can it vary his compensation package. As far as audit is concerned, again the dominant role is that of the Comptroller and Auditor General (CAG). There is very little that an Audit Committee could add to what the CAG does.

In many PSUs, the Board may still be powerful on paper because the delegation of financial and operating powers to the CEO is very limited. Many operating decisions have to be brought to the Board for decision-making. This does not however make for an effective Board because it pushes the Board into "managing" rather than "directing". The current governance structure allows the Board to play a highly obstructive role if it chooses by opposing the CEO on operational matters. What it does not allow the Board to do is to play a meaningful strategic role since all strategic decisions are taken by the dominant shareholder through the concerned ministry. The more interesting issue which has not received much attention so far is the potential that exists for conflict between the dominant shareholder and the minority (public) shareholders

MULTI NATIONAL CORPORATIONS (MNCS)

Government regulations have required most MNCs in India to operate through subsidiaries which are not 100% owned by the parent. In the 70s, the government enacted a law limiting foreign ownership in most industries to 40% while allowing 51% in a few high technology areas. This law was liberalized in the 90s and now 51% is permitted in most industries while 74% or even 100% ownership is allowed in some cases. These regulations have created severe corporate governance problems in several key areas. In the 70s, MNCs were forced to issue shares to the Indian public to comply with the law. The controls that then existed on pricing of public issues meant that these issues were at substantial discounts to the market price.

Another corporate governance problem arises where the foreign parent has two subsidiaries in India in one of which it holds a higher stake (say 100%) while in the other it holds a smaller stake (say 51%). The manner in which the MNC structures its business in India between these two subsidiaries is riddled with problems as far as the minority shareholder is concerned. There have been allegations in some cases that the most profitable brands and businesses have been transferred from the long established 51% subsidiary to the newly formed 100% subsidiary at artificially low prices. This implies a large loss to the minority shareholders of the 51% subsidiary who have after all contributed to in equal measure to the investments that were made in the past to build up these businesses to their current dominant position.

Yet another problem is the payments that parent companies increasingly demand for all the services that they provide to their subsidiaries. One well-known example involves a company where the parent has recently started collecting royalties for the use of a brand. In this case, India is actually the principal market for this brand and the Indian company had assiduously cultivated the brand through decades of advertising paid for in part by the minority shareholders. Minority shareholders could only watch in dismay as the royalties knocked off a sizeable chunk of the earnings of the company.

CORPORATE GOVERNANCE & BUSINESS HOUSES

In India most large corporate houses are owned and managed by old business families. The widely discussed problem in contemporary corporate governance jurisprudence is that of accountability that management of the company owes towards its shareholders. Since a majority of the companies are family owned, and are the management of the company, the only conflict of interests that arises is between that of the controlling and the non-controlling shareholders. Firms in developing countries, especially in India, do not follow the widely dispersed ownership pattern found in US and UK. In addition, managerial control of these businesses are often in the hands of a small group of people, commonly a family, who either own the majority stake, or maintain control through the aid of other block holders like financial institutions. Their own interests, even when they are the majority shareholders, need not coincide with those of the other minority shareholders. This often leads to expropriation of minority shareholder value through actions like "tunnelling" of corporate gains or funds to other corporate entities within the group. Poor development of external financial markets also contributes to these ownership patterns. The state is an important party in some countries in Asia, notably India and China. The corporate governance mechanism and efficiency in state controlled companies are generally deemed to inferior.

Tax reforms coupled with economic liberalization have tilted the balance away from black money transactions. This is partly because tax rates are now lower, and partly because increasing scale economies make it more difficult to operate with the informal organizational structures and financial arrangements that black money entails. It is to be hoped that tax reforms, deregulation and competition would gradually reduce the role of black money to the point where it is confined to isolated cases of corruption. Another important corporate governance issue is that of mergers and restructuring of companies in the same group. There have been several instances where the valuation of two group companies for the purpose of merger has been perceived to be biased in favour of one of the companies. It has been alleged that in many of these cases, the promoters had secretly built up large positions in this company as a cheap means of acquiring shares of the merged company. The amorphous nature of the promoter group makes it very difficult to verify these allegations. Mergers are subject to approval by shareholder bodies of both companies as well as judicial review. But shareholder democracy is an empty defence against the dominant shareholder

REGULATORY RESPONSES

1. REGULATORY RESPONSE UNDER COMPANY LAW

Company law provides that a company can be wound up if the Court is of the opinion that it is just and equitable to do so. This is, of course, the ultimate resort for a shareholder to enforce his ownership rights. Rather than let the value of his shareholding be frittered away by the enrichment of the dominant shareholder, he approaches the court to wind up the company and give him his share of the assets of the company. In most realistic situations, this is hardly a meaningful remedy as the break-up value of a company when it is wound up is far less than its value as a "going concern". It is well known that winding up and other bankruptcy procedures usually lead only to the enrichment of the lawyers and other intermediaries involved.

Company law also provides for another remedy if the minority shareholders can show that the company's affairs are being conducted in a manner prejudicial to the interests of the company or its shareholders to such an extent as to make it just and equitable to wind it up. Instead of approaching the Court, they can approach the Company Law Board (now proposed to be renamed as the Company Law Tribunal). The Company Law Tribunal which is a quasi-judicial body can make suitable orders if it is satisfied that it is just and equitable to wind up the company on these grounds, but that such winding up would unfairly prejudice the members. In particular, the Tribunal may regulate the conduct of the company's affairs in future, order the buyout of the minority shareholders by the other shareholders or by the company itself, set aside or modify certain contracts entered into by the company, or appoint a receiver. The Tribunal could also provide for some directors of the company to be appointed by the Central Government, or by proportional representation.

Information disclosure and audit: Company law provides for regular accounting information to be supplied to the shareholders along with a report by the auditors. It also requires that when shareholder approval is sought for various decisions, the company must provide all material facts relating to these resolutions including the interest of directors and their relatives in the matter. Disclosure does not by itself provide the means to block the dominant shareholders, but it is a prerequisite for the minority shareholders to be able to exercise any of the other means available to them. Disclosure is also a vital element in the ability of the capital market to exercise its discipline on the issuers of capital.

2. REGULATORY RESPONSE UNDER SECURITIES LAW

Historically, most matters relating to the rights of shareholders were governed by the company law. Over the last few decades, in many countries, the responsibility for protection of investors has shifted to the securities law and the securities regulators at least in case of large listed companies. In India, the Securities and Exchange Board of India (SEBI) was set up as a statutory authority in 1992, and has taken a number of initiatives in the area of investor protection.

Information disclosure: The company law itself mandates certain standards of information disclosure both in prospectuses and in annual accounts. SEBI has added substantially to these requirements in an attempt to make these documents more meaningful. Some of these disclosures are important in the context of dealing with the dominant shareholder. One of the most valuable is the information on the performance of other companies in the same group, particularly those companies which have accessed the capital markets in the recent past. This information enables investors to make a judgement about the past conduct of the dominant shareholder and factor that into any future dealings with him.

Promoters' contribution and lock in: Another aspect of the SEBI regulations is that in most public issues, the promoters (typically the dominant shareholders) are required to take a minimum stake of about 20% in the capital of the company and to retain these shares for a minimum lock-in period of about three years. At first sight, it might appear to deal with a problem closer to the US and UK predicaments where the management has only a minuscule stake in the company. This however is not so at all. The SEBI regulations provide an exemption to those companies where there is no identifiable promoter group, that is to say, no dominant shareholder. In other words, if these regulations were copied by US and UK regulators, they would not make much of a difference to most of the companies in those countries as these companies would typically fall in this category of not having an identifiable promoter group. constitute 10% of the shareholders by number or by value. The powers given to the Company Law Tribunal are perhaps more effective remedies than the power of winding up which is vested in the Courts, though one may wonder whether these powers are too sweeping. However their scope is limited to very extreme cases of misgovernance where it is just and equitable to wind up a company.

Special majority: Another safeguard in the company law is the requirement that certain major decisions have to be approved by a special majority of 75% or 90% of the shareholders by value. This may not be an effective safeguard where the dominant shareholders hold a large majority of the shares so that they need to get the approval of only a small chunk of minority shareholders to reach the 75% level. Even otherwise, it may not be a sufficient safeguard if the process of conducting shareholder meetings is not conducive to broader participation by a large section of the shareholding public. The Indian system does not allow for postal ballots. Effective participation by small shareholders is possible only if there is a cost effective way of waging a proxy campaign. This would enable dissenting shareholders to collect proxies from others and prevent measures which are prejudicial to the minority shareholders. The SEBI regulations deal with a corporate governance problem very different from the US and UK problems. It affects those promoters who might have planned to have a very small equity stake and still be dominant shareholders because of large blocks of passive shareholders. Such promoters would be in the position to exercise effective control while having very little stake in the company itself. Most of their rewards would come not from dividends or from appreciation in share values, but from one sided deals which help them transfer profits to other entities owned by the promoters themselves. Apart from this category of promoters, the SEBI regulations may not be much of a constraint for most dominant shareholders. Many of them might even otherwise plan to have a stake of more than 20% (probably as high as 51%) to exercise unquestioned control.

Take-overs: Instead of directly exploiting all the privileges that his controlling block gives him, the dominant shareholder can choose to sell his entire holding to somebody else. In a well functioning market for corporate control, he can expect to get a premium over the marketprice equal to the present value of all the privileges that the dominant shareholder can enjoy in future. The take-over regulations in India require that a slice of this cake be shared with other shareholders. The acquirer of a controlling block of shares must make an open offer to the public for at least 20% of the issued share capital of the target company at a price not below what he paid of the controlling block. Of course, if more than 20% of the shareholders want to sell at that price, the acquirer is bound to accept only 20% on a pro-rata basis.

Discipline of the capital market: Corporate governance is such a burning issue for regulators that it is often forgotten that the capital market by itself exercises considerable discipline over the dominant shareholder. Minority investors may rarely attend shareholder meetings where the dice are loaded against them, but they are continuously voting with their wallets. They can vote with their wallets in the primary market by refusing to subscribe to any fresh issues by the company. They can also sell their shares in the secondary market thereby depressing the share price. A cash rich company with no foreseeable need for additional funds can be relatively unconcerned about this kind of action by minority shareholders. Even in this case, however, the dominant shareholder (unless he holds a clear 51%) faces the risk of being ousted in a take-over battle. A depressed share price makes the company an attractive take-over target. A well-functioning market for corporate control makes this threat more real. The most powerful impact of voting with the wallet is on companies with large growth opportunities that have a constant need to approach the capital market for additional funds. For these companies, shareholder disenchantment can be very expensive.

CHAPTER-60

Corporate Governance in India and CSR: An Empty Vessel

Nishant Sharma

Gujarat National Law University E4-GIDC, Gandhinagar, Gujarat, India.

The word governance is derived from the word 'Gobernare' which means to rule or steer. This though at the time of its origin had a very different meaning that what is propounded at the present time, it has acquired a special significance in the modern world. However modern Corporate Governance has several times been accused of either losing its way or it has been accused of not being strict in its following that has led to many violations of the same at many points of time.

Corporate Governance has caught the imagination of the entire corporate sector whether in India or abroad. Many of the larger corporate include a specific section on Corporate Governance in their annual report to throw light on what they have achieved. Corporate Social Responsibility is the new facade, and the Corporate heavily advertise their benevolent activities. Though governance can be said to have its roots in the early sixties and seventies, yet it was only later that these disparaged threads combined to form what we know as the phenomenon of Corporate Governance today. Thus is Corporate Governance only a smokescreen that has been put up so that consumers and stakeholders in general do not question the unethical practises that are used to dupe the consumer at every point of time or does it have a real chance of changing the scenario nowadays.

HISTORY OF CORPORATE GOVERNANCE

Whereas the seeds of modern Corporate Governance were probably sown in the US at the time of the Watergate scandal, where several major corporate organizations emerged to have certain political connection via bribes etc., hence highlighting the control failures that had emerged at that particular time. Hence Foreign Corrupt and Practises Act of 1977 came into place and established internal control to curb such acts in future.

This was later followed in 1979 with Securities and Exchange Commission of USA's proposal for mandatory reporting of the internal financial controls. Further a spate of collapses in the UK in 1980's and 1980's led to the stakeholders being unsure of investment and slowdown in the economy. This led to changes in UK. The 1997 East Asian crisis brought the faulty regulations to the fore in Asia, thus resulting in a renewed effort to better regulate the Corporates.

In India, Corporate Governance was a largely unheard term until about 1993. During the first flash of liberalisation, India's inability to deal with the difficulties that followed was exposed. The first was the scandals in several banks that led to the stock market nose-diving and was fondly termed as the 'Harshad Mehta Scam'. Later, multinational corporations started selling preferential equity shares to their controlling group at reduced prices, a mechanism that was used to avert any corporate takeovers that might take place. The Government had to step in and put an end to it in 1994. The third was the increase in the stock index by 120% which was caused due to 'disappearing companies'. These companies made public issues via obscure investment banks and misleading prospectuses and disappeared after luring enough unsuspecting customers. This had major implications as the shareholder had its confidence shattered and was vary of any sort of investment, thus virtually destroying any sort of market growth for the next six years.

These three episodes, while exposing the system and leading to major financial losses, also brought an invaluable concept to India known as Corporate Governance. What is particularly interesting to note, is that Corporate Governance did not come onto the fore due to nationwide or regional economic 'destruction' but due to the above three scams that resulted in huge individual losses but were a minor blip as compared to the whole economic structure in place at that time.

Thus, the Governance especially in the context of India means[2]:

- The exercise of political economic and administrative authority in the management of resources.[3]
- The capacity of government to formulate, execute and implement policies.

- Formal institutions and regimes empowered to enforce compliance.
- It comprises of mechanisms by which individuals can
  - Articulate their interests.
  - Exercise their legal rights.
  - Meet their obligations.
  - Mediate their differences.

Corporate Governance even after years of existence is still "ill defined and blurred at the edges".[4] It is still necessary for the Company to have to fulfil long term objectives and strategies, to show that they care for the employees, the shareholders and on a wider ambit the stakeholders, by taking into their needs and demands and trying to fulfil the same. To instil the confidence of the shareholder it needs to be shown that the board of directors are not only there to reap the rewards but are also accountable to the stakeholders.

WHETHER IT IS JUST AN EMPTY VESSEL

Corporate Social Responsibility in particular has come into being due to:

- The concerns from the citizens, consumers, public authorities and investors
- The fact that social criteria is influencing the investment decision of many individuals nowadays and thus what the Corporate give back to the society forms a major part of what people wish to give to the corporate. Now, it has become a two way street and neither is willing to let the other benefit without something in return.
- As stated before, the "disasters" for the society are economic disasters for the company as well, and they are stuck in between owning up to their fault and losing a huge sum of money, and denying their responsibility and end up being ostracised by the media and the gen-next for it.

Thus, Corporate are forced to show their responsibility instead of it being a personal choice for them. Further the twin faced bane for the

Companies being transparency and accountability which have caused the corporate to be more responsible to the citizens. But, the benefits of a strong CSR are also many as they not only bring:

- An improved image of the organization in the mind of the shareholders, but the stakeholders in general which includes the Government and also the society and the stakeholders.
- This improved image could very well result in increased sale and thus more revenue and profits.
- CSR does help the Companies but it also invariably helps the environment as better R & D research normally leads to environmentally friendly methods which should be deployed to make the world for our future generations sustainable.
- It leads to a better relationship with the customers that further helps in sales.
- Further, many young graduates prefer to join corporations that have a trail of such activity.

Though it might be said that there are several disadvantages to CSR as well, but then its advantages far outweigh the disadvantages.

Corporate now-a-days are making a difference to the common man, as can be seen by the efforts of the Life line Foundation and its trauma care centre. Tata has been a brand in corporate governance itself with work that includes establishment of hospitals and even the empowerment of the women through development of skills especially in rural India. The Akshaya Patra Foundation, has started the mid-day meal service for school students thus showing its strong resolution towards giving society back its due. However, as found out by the Karmayog CSR which stated that:

- 13 companies out of 500 tested scored 4/5 in the ratings and were described as very active.
- About 46% or 229 companies did not engage in any CSR activity at all thus proving true the existing fears that corporate governance and working for the stakeholders is only limited to the major market entities.

Thus it can be seen that Corporate Governance until now is only a namesake, and has never really been tested. Further, the Companies do not follow the practise at all. Only a handful of companies can be said to be interested in what they have to give back to the society. The rest are just empty vessels making a lot of noise. Thus, though Corporate Governance is not itself an empty vessel, but the Governance practise in India leaves a lot to be desired. The companies instead are the empty vessels and the value of Governance must be imbibed in them, as the Social responsibility is not only for the elite, but every company.

CHANGES REQUIRED AND RECOMMENDATIONS

Such activity for the society must not be restricted to the Corporate only but also to government and other services. Only a concerted and holistic effort shall result in any form of success. Even the most competent norms can be hoodwinked by the evil of corruption. Corruption and India seem to go hand in hand, thus curbing corruption would certainly help in better governance and lesser issues. The following reforms need to be brought in:

REFORMS IN THE BOARD

- Independence of the Board: Presently, the board is appointed by the controller and there is no real limit on the tenure of an independent director. This must be changed to ensure transparency in the system. The independence requirement must be increase and the directorships a number of a person can hold must be limited further.
- Mandatory Training: The director must be rained mandatorily with Corporate Governance reforms so that they can include and incorporate the same in their every day functioning.
- Increased Director Liability: As shown by the Satyam Scam, there is no real fear for the directors i.e. enough for them to stop their actions. Thus the liability of the directors must be increased to induce fear of their actions.
- RPT's: These require greater approval by independent entities and better disclosure.
- Audit Committees must have the power to pick auditors as otherwise the whole process would become fruitless.
- The liability of auditors especially when their negligence is proved should be increased as there is a huge burden of proof on them.

- Enforcement of these initiatives should be done at a better rate as Satyam has pointed out the issues. Criminal Sanction may be enough to curb the perpetrators and putting such cases through fast track may also be helpful.

- Eliminating the Regulatory Arbitrage: There must be elimination of such terms and their usage in the corporate scenario as the only weaken the governance actions.

- Revamping India's judicial system: As pointed out before it takes a lot of time and there are many procedural loopholes that are easy to exploit that result in the matters not being solved even after years of litigation. This must be changed. Every time some Corporate of allied matter comes to the fore, a fast track ad-hoc tribunal must be formed to efficiently deal with the matter in the fastest way possible.

- Ensuring compliance: Compliance by PSU's and by other sectors must be ensured by way of stricter sanctions that would help in the longer run.

- There should be some specific market changes and some particular regulations in India to deal with the issue better.

- Redefining the Laws: India's Corporate laws must be redefined and liberalized further to induce even more foreign investment as more competition and mandatory compliance can only result in better governance.

- The Bankruptcy laws must be implement in a more timely and efficient manner to better deal with the problems.

- The rights of whistleblowers must be expanded from the present stage so that more people can come out and disclose such practises.

- Embracing Corporate Governance in letter and in spirit:

- Shareholder activism must be increased as only that can lead to better regulation of the Corporate mechanism.

- India's Business Culture is at present focusing only on profits. Corporate Governance must be made the part and parcel of every company's activities. Only when management and governance are synonymous with one another can real progress take place.

Corporate Governance is not just an assortment of rules, it is a philosophy that must be followed to the core to become a success.

CONCLUSION

The word governance results in the corporate being committed to the stakeholders in every way. Though corporate governance as a concept has been slow to takeoff in India, yet it is expected to become the cornerstone or the yardstick for measuring the Companies development. It is expected that in the next few years there will be a lot of activity due to the increased competition that will drastically change the way business is done. It has led to overall positives as the companies that have survived through it are better than ever.

Further, it has been seen that the companies that are at the top of the Corporate chain are the ones that have laid great stress on accountability and transparency, which are the cornerstones of modern Corporate Governance. Even a phenomenal growth in market capitalisation has resulted in increased focus on governance. The investors are becoming smarter than ever and no longer have to rely on a company's name to make decisions on their behalf. They are more proactive than ever, and with an increase in their investment criteria, there will be resultant improvement in the Corporate world itself.

REFERENCES

1. Omkar Goswami, 'Legal and Institutional Impediments to Corporate Growth' in Charles Oman (ed.), Policy Reform in India, OECD Development Centre (Paris 1996), 124-25.

2. "*Conceptualizing Governance" National Human Development Report 2001, 115, Planning Commission, Government of India, March 2002*

3. Ibid.

4. Maw et al, Maw on Corporate Governance (1994) as cited by Sheikh ,Dr.Salim and S.K. Chaterjee 'perspectives on corporate Governance", Corporate governance And Corporate Control, Cavendish Publishing Ltd. London 2000 p.7.

CHAPTER-61

Current Issues in Good Corporate Governance

Prof. Nagachandra Rao. Ch

Krishnamuthy Institute of Management Edulabad, Ghatkesar, Hyderabad

INTRODUCTION

The **Organization for Economic Cooperation and Development (OECD)**, which in 1999 published its Principles of Corporate Governance offers a more detailed, definition of corporate governance as "*the internal means by which corporations are operated and controlled , which involve a set of relationships between a company's management, its board, its shareholders and other stakeholders. Corporate governance also provides the structure through which the objectives of the company are set, and the means of attaining those objectives and monitoring performance are determined. Good corporate gover nance should provide proper incentives for the board and management to pursue objectives that are in the interests of the company and shareholders, and should facilitate effective monitoring; thereby encouraging firms to use resources more efficiently.*"

Most definitions that center on the company itself (an internal perspective) do, however, have certain elements in common, which can be summarized as follows:

- **Corporate governance is a system of relationships, defined by structures and processes:** For example, the relationship between shareholders and management consists of the former providing capital to the latter to achieve a return on their (shareholder) investment. Managers in turn are to provide shareholders with financial and operational reports on a regular basis and in a transparent manner. Shareholders also elect a supervisory body, often referred to as the Board of Directors or Supervisory Board, to represent their interests. This body essentially provides strategic direction to and control over the company's managers. Managers are accountable to this supervisory body, which in turn is accountable to shareholders through the **General Meeting of Shareholders (GMS).** The structures and processes that define these relationships typically center on various performances management and reporting mechanisms.

Figure 1: The Corporate Governance System

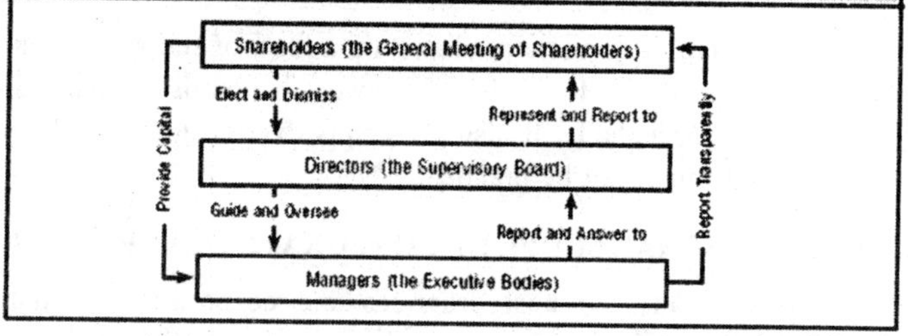

Source: IFC, March 2004

In recent years interest in corporate governance has exploded. There are a number of reasons for this but perhaps the most important is the corporate governance scandals that have occurred in the US, Europe, and elsewhere. But what exactly is corporate governance? One common way of using the term is based on the following narrow definition. This is how the term is typically used in Anglo-Saxon countries such as the US and UK. The standard mechanisms for ensuring that this occurs are (i) the board of directors; (ii) executive compensation; (iii) the market for corporate control; (iv) concentrated holdings and monitoring by financial institutions; and (v) debt. Underlying this narrow view of corporate governance is Adam Smith's notion of the invisible hand as the key principle that the organization of the economy is based on. Corporate governance reform has emerged as a critical business issue, thrust on the world stage by a number of high profile corporate failures. While many regulatory efforts are underway to identify and codify good governance practices to rebuild public and market trust, there are a parallel number of efforts to map out the social and environmental — non-financial — boundaries of corporate governance. The purpose of this study is to probe these issues further. What is the degree and nature of convergence of social, environmental and governance practices of corporations? What are the governance practices that exemplify best practice social and environmental performance and how fundamental are these governance practices to a company's effective financial and non financial performance? What are the factors driving these trends and will the social and environmental aspects of corporate governance grow in importance in the future?

Basic principles of Corporate Governence

1. oversight and management of risk
2. oversight and management of risk
3. oversight of the preparation of the entity's financial statements
4. Principles on the other hand are a form of self regulation. It allows the sector to determine what standards are acceptable or unacceptable. It also pre-empts over zealous legislations that might not be practical.

THE INTERNATIONAL SCOPE OF CORPORATE GOVERNANCE

Numerous codes of best practices and corporate governance principles have been developed over the last ten years. Worldwide, over 100 codes have been written in some 40 countries and regions. Most of these codes focus on the role of the Supervisory Board (or Board of Directors) in the company. A handful is international in scope. Among these, only the OECD Principles address both policy makers and businesses, and focus on the entire governance framework (shareholder rights, stakeholders, disclosure, and board practices). The OECD Principles have gained worldwide acceptance as a framework and reference point for corporate governance. Published in 1999 and revised in 2004, they were developed to provide principle-based guidance on good governance.

The OECD corporate governance framework is built on four core values:

- **Fairness:** The corporate governance framework should protect shareholder rights and ensure the equitable treatment of all shareholders, including mino rity and foreign shareholders. All shareholders should have the opportunity to obtain effective redress for violations of their rights.
- **Responsibility:** The corporate governance framework should recognize the rights of stakeholders as established by law, and encourage active co-operation between corporations and stakeholders in creating wealth, jobs, and the sustainability of financially sound enterprises.
- **Transparency:** The corporate governance framework should ensure that timely and accurate disclosure is made on all

material matters regarding the company, including its financial situation, performance, ownership, and governance structure. timely and accurate disclosure is made on all material matters regarding the company, including its financial situation, performance, ownership, and governance structure.

- **Accountability:** The corporate governance framework should ensure the strategic guidance of the company, the effective monitoring of management by the board, and the board's accountability to the company and shareholders.

CURRENT ISSUES IN CORPORATE GOVERNANCE

Financial economists have been interested in corporate governance for much longer and for more fundamental developments that have fundamentally changed the face and nature of international capital markets and financial systems over the last twenty years:

- Privatisations
- The growth of pension and other fund investment;
- Mergers waves and takeovers
- Deregulation;
- European and international capital market integration.

CONCLUSION

This thought leader study on the convergence between corporate governance and corporate social responsibility has been conducted during a period of great debate regarding the definition of good governance. The boundaries and definition of corporate governance are in a period of significant flux such that emergent CSR issues have made it on the radar of many companies and regulators around the world as never before. By and large the thought-leaders interviewed for their views on the convergence between corporate governance and corporate social responsibility were not a homogenous group. Their views differed fundamentally in a few areas and converged in others. To start, many of them do not use the term CSR, preferring corporate responsibility or other variations. While there was some dispute as to what was meant by convergence, they were unanimous in their view that CSR is an emergent area of risk in the broadening portfolio of risk management. No one really argued that the reclassification of risk to include the management of non-financial risks implied a convergence — though a number of interviewees advanced the view that CSR and governance are converging at the values level of governance, a result of the reclassification of the boundaries of corporate accountability to include non-financial stakeholder issues.

The function of developing and the implantation of an "ethics system" is difficult, because there is no clear, nor any singular decisive way that is able to be presented as a standard across the board for any organization – as due to each organization's own culture. Also, the implementation should be done accordingly to the entire areas of operations within the organization. If it is not implemented pragmatically and with empathic caution for the needs, desires, and personalities of the stakeholders, or the culture, then unethical views may be taken by the stakeholders, or even unethical behavior throughout the organization

Corporate governance is a young academic field characterized by partial theories, limited access to high–quality data, inconsistent empirics and unresolved methodological problems. Corporate governance affects the development and functioning of capital markets and exerts a strong influence on resource allocation. In an era of increasing capital mobility and globalization, it has also become an important framework condition affecting the industrial competitiveness and economies.

CHAPTER-62

A Full Blown Collapse of Integrity and Responsibility: Corporate Social Responsibility and Business Ethics in The Light of Recent Scandals

Mridushi Swarup

21, Priyanka Nagar, Risali, Bhilai, Chattisgarh -490006.

Ritika Banerjee

8B, Sevak Baidya Street, Kolkata – 700029.

INTRODUCTION

In the recent times, news of social irresponsibility like in the case of Enron or social misconduct like in the case of the delta in Nigeria has focused attention on ethics in business, government, business schools as well as professional bodies.[1]

Corporations are expected by society, not only to operate with the motive to make profit but also to adhere and comply with the laws and regulations put in place by the government within which that corporations operates in. Corporations are thus expected to achieve their goals and missions within the framework of the law. As oppose to legal responsibilities of CSR which embody norms about fairness and justice, ethical responsibilities duel on the activities that are expected or prohibited by society even though they are not codified into law. Ethical responsibilities embody what consumers, shareholders, employees, and the community regard as fair. In effect, ethical responsibility seems to be the most highly regarded value when it comes to consumers making decisions based on CSR.[2] The legal aspect goes hand in hand with the ethical aspect of corporate social responsibility. Ethical aspects embody basic notions of fair operations as established by our lawmakers.[3]

THE CONCEPT OF CORPORATE GOVERNANCE

Corporate governance is not a new phenomenon, yet it has gained attention in the last two decades in the wake of major corporate collapses in many parts of the world. The dam buckled with Enron's revelations in late 2001, and there has since been a national deluge of corporate malfeasance. Scandals at Adelphia, Arthur Andersen, Global Crossing, HealthSouth, Qwest, Rite Aid, Tyco, WorldCom, and Xerox have shaken investor confidence.[4] Disclosures of illegal practices at Wall Street's most venerable investment banks have tarnished once-sterling name brands.[5] Actions against mutual fund companies that engaged in improper trading have caused millions of investors to question the basic fairness of the financial institutions of their countries.[6] Instances such as these have made good corporate governance necessary.

Corporate governance stands for the management and the supervision of enterprises,[7] thus covering a wide range of topics related to company law and capital markets in the context of success-oriented management and responsible supervision of enterprises.[8] Farrar defines corporate governance as simply how companies are directed and steered[9]. This contrasts with a broader view by Du Plessis et al. as: "... the process of controlling management and balancing the interest of all stakeholders and other parties who can be affected by the corporation's conduct in order to ensure responsible behavior by corporations and to achieve the maximum level of efficiency and profitability for a corporation".[10] Redmond adopts a more legalistic approach by stating: "... Corporate governance refers to the complex of legal rules and constitutional provisions that regulate the internal affairs of the company as distinct from the external regulation of corporate behavior by the state and its agencies."[11]

The proliferation of publications by economists, organisation theorists, lawyers, sociologists, criminologists, and even political scientists, laying claim to its meaning, interpretation and applications, have tended to complicate matters with many competing claims. Thus, despite its rather fashionable use in modern times, a detailed definition of the globally-accepted term "corporate governance" does not exist.[12]

CORPORATE SOCIAL REPONSIBILITY – PART AND PARCEL OF CORPORATE GOVERNANCE

The totality of CSR can be best understood by three words: 'corporate,' 'social,' and 'responsibility.' In broad terms, CSR relates to responsibilities corporations have towards society within which they are based and operate, not denying the fact that the purview of CSR goes much beyond this.

Commentators have defined the term corporate social responsibility in a variety of ways. According to Keith Devis, "social responsibility begins where the law ends. Accordingly the term 'social responsibility' refers to both socio- economic and socio human obligation to others.[13]

Andriof and McIntosh[14]suggest that corporate social responsibility requires corporate leaders to understand that everything a company does has some flow-on effect either inside or outside the company, from customers and employees to communities and the environment. They suggest that these impacts have a ripple effect on society that can be divided into three broad overlapping areas. These are:

- Social – involvement in external social issues such as education, social inclusion, regeneration and employee volunteering.
- Economic – addressing issues relating to jobs, ethical trading standards and product value.
- Environment – consideration of emissions and waste control, energy use, product life cycle and sustainable development.

According to World Business Council for Sustainable Development "Corporate Social Responsibility is the continuing commitment by business to behave ethically and contribute to economic development while improving the quality of life of the workforce and their families as well as of the local community and society at large". Business for Social Responsibility (BSR)[15] defines CSR as "... operating a business in a manner that meets or exceeds the ethical, legal, commercial and public expectations that society has of business.

CSR is seen by leadership companies as more than a collection of discrete practices or occasional gestures, or initiatives motivated by marketing, public relations or other business benefits. Rather, it is viewed as a comprehensive set of policies, practices and programs that are integrated throughout business operations, and decision-making processes that are supported and rewarded by top management...".[16] And, finally the European Union defines CSR as "... the concept that an enterprise is accountable for its impact on all relevant stakeholders. It is the continuing commitment by business to behave fairly and responsibly and contribute to economic development while improving the quality of life of the work force and their families as well as of the local community and society at large..."[17]

Ethics is not definable; nor is it implementable, because it is not conscious.[18] Ethical behavior is doing what is best in enhancing the trust and confidence between two entities so that both the entities feel energized and enthused to work towards the betterment of the common good.[19] The framework for ethical behavior of the corporation is predicted on the ethical behavior of its owners, managers, employees and directors towards its stakeholders- customers, investors, employees and the society.[20] It is all about bringing in fairness and transparency to the whole system. The behaviour of a corporation is generally shaped by behavior of its CEO and other leaders.[21] Ethics is a mass of moral principles or sets of values about what conduct ought to be.

Business ethics concern the ground rules of individual company and societal behavior. It may be defined as an attempt to ascertain the responsibilities and ethical obligations of business professionals.[22] McNamara states that "Business ethics is generally coming to know what is right or wrong in the work place and doing what is right; this is in regard to effects of products/ services and in relationships with stakeholders." He further states that business ethics has come to be considered a management discipline, especially since the birth of social responsibility of business.[23]

CODES OF CONDUCT

The Securities and Investment Institute Code of Conduct states that:

"... [I]t is expected that the firm and its employees will act with integrity and will seek to avoid any acts ... which damage the reputation of the organisation ... which are improper ... and will promote high standards of conduct throughout the organisation."

To meet these standards, businesses design and implement—for the most part—codes of conduct or codes of business ethics and produce sustainability reports. By drafting their own codes, they ensure that the values or standards set are specific to their organisations, their needs and abilities.[24] This derives from the belief that businesses self-regulate themselves—a belief fed by the self-regulatory nature of the market economy outside the sphere of influence of governments. But the current crisis and other scandals have revealed the limits of this voluntary codification.[25]

Multi-stakeholder initiatives, meaning initiatives involving different players from different horizons, have bolstered these corporate initiatives and tried to address some of the limits of corporate self-regulation.[26] However, although these initiatives did tackle some of the limitations of corporate self-regulation, not all have been addressed.

CORPORATE SELF-REGULATION OR VOLUNTARY CODES OF CONDUCT

Every organization whether large or small it has its own corporate code. Corporate codes reflect the purpose of the company and guide the employee to behave in an ethical manner. For some years now, the topic of ethics has been gaining increased exposure across the ranks of the management community, its advisors and regulators.

A code of ethics express fundamental principals that guidance in cases where no specific rule is in place or where maters are genuinely unclear. A well-drafted code of conduct will be consistent with the primary code of ethics. However, it will provide much more specific guidance. In comparison to a code of conduct, a code of ethics will trend to;- Be more general, Contain fewer principles, Be expressed in term of 'ought' or 'should', Be directed to all personal affected, Provide general guidance in those where a code of conduct is silent and ambiguous or unclear.

Conscious that they had to embrace the discourse of corporate social responsibility, companies have defined new ways of doing business—an ethical way of doing business—but only on the condition that they would be in the driving seat: that they would define the terms of the change and that these terms would be favourable to their business.[27] Whether companies adopted these voluntary codes in response to accusations of bad behaviour or even in fear of bad reputation does not matter. What is noticeable is the trend to openly commit to embed CSR practices into their business.[28]

SUGGESTION AND CONCLUSION

CSR goes beyond the statutory requirements of corporations to include voluntary initiatives to improve the quality of life of stakeholders (consumers, employees and the local communities) and their environmental commitments as well.CSR actions are therefore not an obligation but rather ethical gestures corporations may wish to undertake for improve on the livelihood of her stakeholders.

Lasting solutions can only be found by transforming human consciousness through an inner discipline and higher moral reasoning. A company can build sustainable competitive advantage through ethics, values, excellence, quality, social responsibility and human development.

A transformed organizational culture which pays highest attention to ethical conduct and moral values will strengthen sustainable roots of the company. Transparency and effective auditing and regulatory checks through internal and external auditors and monitoring agencies will help establish long lasting credibility for any company. Companies should gather feedback, measure effectiveness, and continually improve their code of conduct.

REFERENCES

1. Jode S. Cohen and Greg Burns, *Can you teach a person ethics?*, Chi. Trib. (June 7, 2006).
2. Lawrence A. Crosby and Sheree L. Johnson(2006) Corporate Citizenship:It's the Brand.
3. Archie B. Carroll *The Pyramid Of Corporate Social Responsibility: Toward The Moral Management Of Organizational Stakeholders*, , Business Horizons /July-August 1991.
4. See *Scandal Scorecard,* WALL ST. J. B1 (Oct. 3, 2003).
5. Mitchell Pacelle, *Bankers Swear They've Repented and That Enron-Like Covenants That Fooled Investors Are Gone*, WALL ST. J. C1 (Feb. 2, 2004) (describing investment banks' recovery from "a punishing fire-and-brimstone treatment from prosecutors, regulators, politicians and investors"); See also Randall Smith, *Pay to Play? Companies Put a New Squeeze on Their Investment Banks*, WALL ST. J. A1 (Aug. 26, 2003) (chronicling improprieties at Morgan Stanley, Merrill Lynch, and UBS, among others).

6. Tom Lauricella, *Two-Tier System: For Staid Mutual-Fund Industry, Growing Probe Signals Shake-Up*, WALL ST. J. A1 (Oct. 20, 2003); See also Daisy Maxey, *It's "What Scandal?" in Fund Ads*, WALL ST. J. R1 (Mar. 1, 2004) (reporting that "the number of [mutual] fund firms and employees caught up in the [scandal] investigations grows longer by the day, and many operating rules are being rewritten for an industry that many had thought was a model for good business behavior").

7. Report of the Government Commission, *'Corporate Governance-Management of Enterprises-Modernization of the Stock Corporation Law,* Drucksache-Bundesrat 14/7515 (Aug. 14, 2001) (Aug. 16, 2010) *http://www.boersenzeitung.de/online/redaktion/buecher/b020302.html* ; German Corporate Governance Code (the "German Code"), (Aug.17, 2010) *http://www.corporate-governance-code.de/eng/download/DCG_K_E.pdf* See Neue Zeitschrift für Gesellschaftsrecht 273 (2002); Die Aktiengesellschaft 236 (2002).

8. T.P. GHOSH, STRUCTURE OF CORPORATE SOCIAL REPORTING IN INDIA, Vol. No. XLIII, Part IV, No. 165; R. Gray, *Social and Environmental Responsibility, Sustainability and Accountability, Can the Corporate Sector Deliver?* , Glasgow, Centre for Social and Environmental Accounting Research, University of Glasgow, (2001) (Aug.5, 2010) www.agenda-scotland.org/documents/Can%20business%20deliver%20Gray.pdf

9. J. Andriof & M. McIntosh, PERSPECTIVES ON CORPORATE CITIZENSHIP (Greenleaf Publishing, Sheffield) (2001).

10. (Business for Social Responsibility is a global non-profit organization that helps member companies achieve commercial success in ways that respect ethical values, people, communities and the environment. BSR member companies have nearly $2 trillion in combined annual revenues and employ more than six million workers around the world).

11. (Aug. 4, 2010) *www.bsr.org.*

12. *EU Green Paper: Promoting a European Framework for Corporate Social Responsibility* (July 18, 2001) (Aug. 6, 2010) *http://europa.eu.int/comm/employment_social/soc-dial/csr/greenpaper_en.pdf*

13. Rushworth M. Kidder, The Ethics Recession: Reflections on the Moral Underpinnings of the Current Economic Crisis (Institute for Global Ethics, 2009).

14. The Pope continues by saying that "the economy cannot function if it does not bear within it an ethical component". Letter of Benedict XVI sent to the Prime Minister dated March 30, 2009 and reproduced in Zenit (http://zenit.org [Accessed April 14, 2010]). Also in Simon Webley, Research Director of the Institute of Business Ethics, "Does doing business ethically affect corporate performance?" in Integrity at Work in Financial Services, A Practical Guide to Trust and Integrity

Dilemmas (Securities & Investment Institute, 2009), pp.85-91, at p.85.

15. Adam Smith, The Theory of Moral Sentiments (1759).

16. Longinos Marin,Salvador Ruiz,Alicia Rubio(2009),The Role of Identity Salience in the Effects of Corporate Social Responsibility on Consumer Behavior, Journal of Business Ethics (2009).

CHAPTER-63

SOCIAL RESPONSIBILITIES AND BUSINESS ETHICS

Manish Jha

(Asst.Professor - MBA)
Panipat Institute of Engineering & Technology

Amit Bansal

(Lecturer-MBA)
Samalkha Group of Institutions
01,SGI Campus, Hathwala Road, Samalkha-Panipat

INTRODUCTION

ETHICS

Ethics simply involves learning and understanding what is right or wrong, and then doing the right thing. "The right thing" is not as straightforward as conveyed in a great deal of literature. Ethicists assert that there is always a right thing to do based on moral principle, and others believe the right things to do depend on the situation-ultimately it is up to the individual. Many philosophers consider ethics to be the 'science of conduct'. Philosophers have been discussing ethics for ages now, since the time of Socrates and Plato. Many ethicists consider emerging ethical beliefs to be "state of the art" legal matters, i.e., what becomes an ethical guideline today is often translated to a law, regulation or rule tomorrow. Values which guide how we ought to behave are considered as moral values, e.g., values such as respect, honesty, fairness and responsibility. Statements around how these values are called moral or ethical principles.

WHAT IS SOCIAL RESPONSIBILITY

Social responsibility can be an example of ethical behavior. It is enhancing society in general. However, a business can't afford to go around doing good deeds if there is no potential payoff. If the business were to loose too much money, then it would cease to exist, hurt customers, and leave employees jobless. There are some that argue that social responsibility is shown only when companies go beyond what is optional, and really intend to create a benefit for others besides the company. Additionally, some companies may not benefit from some forms of social responsibility. These businesses should focus on what they do best as a business and give back what they can. Examples of socially responsible behavior range from projects that raise money for research on diseases, raising money for the needy, requiring workers to volunteer within the community, recalling products that may be dangerous, promoting recycling, and offering free services to the disadvantaged.

ETHICS AND SOCIAL RESPONSIBILITY

There are innumerable ethical dilemmas that may arise in a business setting. Some of them are more obvious while some of them are more obscure. There is a simple basis that helps keep decisions in perspective. Businesses should operate in a manner that is legal, profitable, ethical, and within social norms. By being within social norms means that you need to use society to gauge if your decisions are appropriate. Some cultures would define what is ethical differently from other cultures. Due to the fact that all businesses need to be profitable, sometimes there is an over emphasis on making more money. Social norms should govern what is appropriate to compensate individuals as well as to charge customers. Profit expectations and goals should not require a business to cut corners in an unethical way or to misrepresent or twist facts.

There are many things that an organization can do to facilitate good ethical behaviors. One of the best things to do is to make sure that the underlying culture of an organization promotes strong values. People should not be punished for coming forward with problems. As a matter of fact, workers should be allowed to communicate problems anonymously. Some organizations have a phone number to call or a suggestion box. Always allow employees to share any ethical concerns with authority above them when there are ambiguities about the right thing to do. Include a code of ethics as a written document for employees to read. Develop brochures, mission statements, and other media that express the company beliefs. Higher authorities within the organization should possess the beliefs and demonstrate the values that they want to see their employees have.

Another method for implementing ethical conduct is to make sure that unethical conduct can't occur. The ability to safeguard resources is an important function of internal controls. Examples of internal controls are to make sure that more than one employee works with cash and accounting related materials. This way there is more than one person who knows what is going on and can identify theft. Other methods are to require signatures, to lock up valuables, use security cameras, have employees rotate jobs, and randomly check employee work. The more secure your business is, the less likely that individuals within the organization will make unethical decisions.

CSR AND INNOVATION – WHAT IS IT?

Literature bringing together CSR and innovation has emerged gradually over the past decade. One interpretation of "social innovation" can refer to improvements in the CSR process. Examples could be improved social reporting tools or CSR management systems. In this review we do, however, not consider these kinds of improvements and instead focus mainly on product related social innovation. In the following we will discuss some of the main themes standing out from literature. Broadly speaking there are two schools of thought: The first line of publications deals with innovations aiming at social improvements (i.e. health, education, community development). Here the term social innovation can refer to product innovations with a social purpose. A subgroup of these types of innovations concerns "Base of the Pyramid" thinking. Social innovation is also used to refer to the process of starting and improving social enterprises. A second group of authors put environmental innovation at the heart of their work. These literature contributions have coalesced around the theme of eco-innovation, which more recently has spawned the discipline of clean-technology venturing.

REVIEW OF LITERATURE

There have long been conflicting expectations of the nature of companies' responsibilities to society. However, for those businesses that do undertake what might be termed "corporate social responsibility", what is actually socially responsible behaviour as opposed to management of corporate image management or other activity aimed predominantly at business benefits ***(Lance Moir, 2001).*** From the decision-maker's viewpoint, the success of a social responsibility program rests heavily on a corporation's ability to create links in the public consciousness between the CSR activities of an organization and its performance to different stakeholders ***(Navarro & Martínez, 2009).*** The social meaning of CSR includes ideas that to some extent mirror the conceptualization introduced by previous theoretical models (***Duarte et al., 2010***). The way in which CSR manifests itself determines consumer support. CSR can provide three forms of value to consumers: emotional, social, and functional. Each of these enhances or diminishes the overall value proposition for consumers ***(Green & Peloza, 2011)***. Benefits of CSR in profit based organizations are identified and compared with an example in a not for profit organization ***(Holme, 2010)***. Evaluating altruistic CSR from all major ethical perspectives – utilitarianism, rights, justice and care – leads to the conclusion that, for publicly held corporations, such activity is immoral. This is because altruistic CSR violates shareholder property rights, unjustly seizing stockholder wealth, and it bestows benefits for the general welfare at the expense of those for whom the firm should care in close relationships ***(Lantos, 2002)***. The favorable strategy towards stakeholders increases the corresponding corporate social responsibility towards them. The salience of all stakeholder groups also enhances the corresponding corporate social responsibility ***(Mishra, Damodar Suar, 2010)***. CSR triggers the corporate-image-building process and that its relationship to company success varies significantly based on company size, industry and marketing budget ***(Arendt, Malte Brettel, 2010)***.

IMPORTANCE OF ETHICAL AND CORPORATE SOCIAL RESPONSIBILITY

Being a good corporate citizen is increasingly crucial for commercial success. It is not good enough any longer just to be a good corporate citizen, you must also be seen to be. Corporate Social Responsibility has become increasingly important to businesses over the last few years. The case for demonstrating corporate responsibility is getting stronger. Expectations among key opinion formers, customers and the public are increasing, staying on top of and in front of this strengthening tide of opinion for company involvement is a challenge for all companies. Some are meeting it; others are failing to do so, and still others are scrambling to catch up with public expectations. Corporate Social Responsibility cannot be an additional extra - it runs to the core of every company's ethics (both abroad and at home), and its treatment of employees and customers. With more and more companies responding to stakeholders' calls for increased accountability, and many publishing Health, Safety and Environmental or Social reports, the wider issues of business ethics remain key for all large companies. In fact, the importance placed on these issues is borne out by consumer behavior three in ten of the British public tell us they have chosen - or boycotted - a product or company for ethical reasons in the past 12 months. That's million consumers acting on their concerns. Increasing numbers of consumers admit being influenced by their perceptions of companies' customer and employee care.

ETHICS AND CORPORATE SOCIAL RESPONSIBILITY POLICY

ADITYA BIRLA

In the Aditya Birla Group, reaching out to underserved communities is part of our DNA. Believe in the trusteeship concept. This entails transcending business interests and grappling with the "quality of life" challenges that underserved communities face, and working towards making a meaningful difference to them.

Vision is – "to actively contribute to the social and economic development of the communities in which we operate. In so doing build a better, sustainable way of life for the weaker sections of society and raise the country's human development index". (Mrs. Rajashree Birla, Chairperson, Aditya Birla Centre for Community Initiatives and Rural Development).

ANAND CORPORATE SERVICES LIMITED

Anand has a longstanding commitment to addressing the needs of the society, in view of its belief that for any economic development to be meaningful, the benefits from the business must trickle down to the society at large.Anand is of the firm view that the corporate goals must be aligned with the larger societal goals. 25 years ago, the SNS Foundation, an expression of Anand's corporate social responsibility, was born. The objective of SNS foundation was comprehensive community development. The Foundation has created programs in the fields of health, education, natural resource management and life skills training, only to make sure that fellow humans could breathe easy. The long term goal of Anand CSR is to implement concepts like 'Zero Tolerance Zone for Child Labour', 'Zero Waste Zone' using strategies like Reduce, Recycle and Reuse not only at Anand/SNSF locations but extend to Anand residential areas.

APTECH LIMITED

Aptech Limited, a leading education player with a global presence, has played an extensive and sustained role in encouraging and fostering education throughout the country since inception.As a global player with complete solutions-providing capability, Aptech has a long history of participating in community activities. It has, in association with leading NGOs, provided computers at schools, education to the underprivileged and conducted training and awareness-camps. Aptech students donated part of the proceeds from the sale of their art work to NGOs. To propagate education among all sections of the society throughout the country, especially the underprivileged, Aptech fosters tie-ups with leading NGOs throughout the country, including the Barrackpur-based NGO, Udayan, a residential school for children of leprosy patients in Barrackpur, established in 1970.The company strongly believes that education is an integral part of the country's social fabric and works towardssupporting basic education and basic computer literacy amongst the underprivileged children in India.

AVON CYCLE LIMITED

The poor and ignorant of India's rural population turn to nearest towns and cities for healthcare. They face indifference and exploitation. Hope gives way to despair. This gave inspiration to AVON for locating MATAKAUSHALYA DEVI, PAHWA CHARITABLE HOSPITAL. Mr. Sohan Lal Pahwa, AVON's Chairman and Principal Trustee of the hospital, spent a good part of his working life devoted to philanthropy. The hospital, in its 5th year of inception, has risen to serve a model healthcare facility boasting of some bold experiments in its very early years of existence. Its support since inception has been of the order of Rs. 3 crore to date and it continues uninterrupted. Reaching out to the needy farther a field, the hospital holds regular camps in surrounding villages to propagate scientific approach to healthcare. Recently the hospital took the social responsibility concept a step further and formulated a scheme titled 'Celebrated Female Child' to enable and inspire positive and enduring environment for society's all–consuming passion for 'sons only' to end.

CONCLUSION

Organizations are coming to realize the bottom-line benefits of incorporating sustainability into their DNA. It's beneficial for attraction and retention and it's the right thing to do. HR is a key organizational leader and can take the lead or partner with other executives to work cross-functionally to integrate CSR objectives into how business gets conducted. HR practitioners can act as translators of the organization's CSR commitment vertically and horizontally across departments. Most will find upon reading this report that they have many good practices underway. Many will find they have a new structure for their thinking hey can apply practically in the workplace. Some will believe the current conomic downturn will put these ideas on the backburner until the conomy rebounds, while others think that organizations which abandon heir CSR integration in the downturn will lose ground and breed cynicism n brighter times. Regardless of the point of view, all agree that effective HR leadership on CSR integration requires Board, CEO and executive commitment to be successful. Indeed, the roadmap is predicated on the assumption of this top level commitment

CHAPTER-64

CORPORATE GOVERNANCE AND BUSINESS ETHICS

M. Kavitha

M.Phil Scholar
Department of Commerce, Bharathiar University, Coimbatore – 641 046.
e-mail: kavi2686@gmail.com

INTRODUCTION

"The process and structure to direct and manage the business and affairs of the corporation with the objective of enhancing shareholder value, which includes ensuring the financial viability of the business."

Corporate Governance is the set of processes, customs, policies, laws, and institutions affecting the way a corporation (or company) is directed, administered or controlled. Corporate governance also includes the relationships among the many stakeholders involved and the goals for which the corporation is governed. The principal stakeholders are the shareholders, management, and the board of directors. Other stakeholders include employees, customers, creditors, suppliers, regulators, and the community at large.

There has been renewed interest in the corporate governance practices of modern corporations since 2001, particularly due to the high-profile collapses of a number of large U.S. firms such as Enron Corporation and MCI Inc. (formerly WorldCom). In 2002, the U.S. federal government passed the Sarbanes-Oxley Act, intending to restore public confidence in corporate governance.

NEED FOR CORPORATE GOVERNANCE IN INDIA

Post-liberalization period (1993-1995) was a boom period, Capital through Public issues, Many Fake companies came in, which are now here, Indian companies getting Global thus more transparency demanded by Foreign investors, Collaborators, buyers. Stories of Accounting Juggleries, Family owned business (family leaders appointed directors which are teeth less), Growing awareness towards Good Corporate Governance, Improving Ethical Climate, Shadow Directors.

CORPORATE GOVERNANCE NORMS

Corporate governance are the policies, procedures and rules governing the relationships between the shareholders, (stakeholders), directors and managers in a company, as defined by the applicable laws, the corporate charter, the company's bylaws, and formal policies.

Primarily it is about managing top management, building in checks and balances to ensure that the senior executives pursue strategies that are in accordance with the corporate mission. It consists of a set of processes, customs, policies, laws and institutions affecting the way of a corporation is directed, administered or controlled. Corporate governance governs the relationship among the many players involved (the stakeholders) and the goals for which the corporation is governed.

4 P'S OF CORPORATE GOVERNANCE

Corporate Governance is an integrated framework whereby people ormally organize themselves for a defined purpose, and they apply critical rocesses consistently to achieve predicted performance for sustainable evelopment.

Much debated principles of corporate governance like independent irectors, audit committees, control on related party transactions and nvestor protection cannot ensure corporate sustainability and hence orporate governance has remained a rhetoric only far from reality.

Recognizing the criticality of the theme, Life Development oundation (LifeDF) has redefined corporate governance and developed a omprehensive Corporate Governance System Standard based on 4Ps People, Purpose, Process and Performance) after an extensive research on orld greatest organizations, large Indian corporate, statutory bodies, ublic sector undertakings, trusts, societies, partnership firms, sole roprietorships and associations.

USINESS ETHICS

Business ethics (also known as corporate ethics) is a form of pplied ethics or professional ethics that examines ethical principles and oral or ethical problems that arise in a business environment. It applies all aspects of business conduct and is relevant to the conduct of dividuals and business organizations as a whole. Applied ethics is a field f ethics that deals with ethical questions in many fields such as medical, chnical, legal and business ethics.

Business ethics can be both a normative and a descriptive discipline. As a corporate practice and a career specialization, the field is primarily normative. In academia descriptive approaches are also taken. The range and quantity of business ethical issues reflects the degree to which business is perceived to be at odds with non-economic social values. Historically, interest in business ethics accelerated dramatically during the 1980s and 1990s, both within major corporations and within academia. For example, today most major corporate websites lay emphasis on commitment to promoting non-economic social values under a variety of headings (e.g. ethics codes, social responsibility charters). In some cases, corporations have redefined their core values in the light of business ethical considerations.

ETHICS IN CORPORATE GOVERNANCE

As part of more comprehensive compliance and ethics programs, many companies have formulated internal policies pertaining to the ethical conduct of employees. These policies can be simple exhortations in broad, highly generalized language (typically called a corporate ethics statement), or they can be more detailed policies, containing specific behavioural requirements (typically called corporate ethics codes). They are generally meant to identify the company's expectations of workers and to offer guidance on handling some of the more common ethical problems that might arise in the course of doing business. It is hoped that having such a policy will lead to greater ethical awareness, consistency in application, and the avoidance of ethical disasters.

Others believe that corporate ethics policies are primarily rooted in utilitarian concerns, and that they are mainly to limit the company's legal liability, or to curry public favour by giving the appearance of being a good corporate citizen. Ideally, the company will avoid a lawsuit because its employees will follow the rules. Should a lawsuit occur, the company can claim that the problem would not have arisen if the employee had only followed the code properly. Sometimes there is disconnection between the company's code of ethics and the company's actual practices. Thus, whether or not such conduct is explicitly sanctioned by management, at worst, this makes the policy duplicitous, and, at best, it is merely a marketing tool.

To be successful, most ethicists would suggest that an ethics policy should be:

- Given the unequivocal support of top management, by both word and example.
- Explained in writing and orally, with periodic reinforcement.
- Doable....something employees can both understand and perform.
- Monitored by top management, with routine inspections for compliance and improvement.
- Backed up by clearly stated consequences in the case of disobedience.
- Remain neutral and nonsexist.

BUSINESS ETHICS AND CORPORATE GOVERNANCE

Business world is, to an extent, a reflection of the country's social and cultural ethos. The unprincipled behaviour among people has become so commonplace that even the corporate world has been affected. It is; therefore, felt that unless companies look after the interests of their stakeholders and apply the ethical code of conduct in their dealings, they can at best gain only temporary benefits. Companies have begun to realize the importance of good Corporate Governance and Business Ethics.

GOVERNING BUSINESS ETHICS

In all the national codes of corporate governance the need for actively managing the ethical performance of companies is emphasized. The levels of detail with which these codes deal with the active management of ethics do, however, differ radically. All the codes recommend that the board of directors should ensure that a code of ethics is developed and that it is endorsed by the board. Most of these corporate governance codes also provide some guidance on the process of developing a code of ethics by either making reference to issues or topics that typically should be addressed in a code, or by outlining a process that could be followed in the process of code design or review. The code that is also fairly comprehensive in the way that it deals with the governing of ethics recommends that companies should issue a certificate at the end of every year in which they confirm that to the best knowledge of the board and management no employee of the company has been involved in, among others, corruption, money laundering, or the contravention of any national law or international convention.

CONCLUSION

This survey of the state of business ethics within the context of corporate governance made it clear that business ethics are considered an integral and essential part of good governance. From the various national codes of corporate governance that were analyzed, it is clear that standards of good governance are intimately intertwined with high standards of business ethics. The challenge that faces by enterprises is to translate this commitment to high standards of ethics into organizational practice. It is on this score that most codes of corporate governance fall short as they provide very little guidance on how business ethics should be institutionalized in enterprises. The second-generation codes of corporate governance that are now emerging tend to recognize this shortfall and address it clearly. This advance in combination with the new corporate governance developments outlined above might facilitate the process of institutionalizing ethics in organizations. It is, however, very important that these developments on the enterprise level should be unbreakable with governance reform on the regulatory and political level.

CHAPTER-65

E-Governance – A Modern Tool for Corporate Governance

Ms. Kanchan Bala

Lecturer, Faculty of Arts, Science & Commerce, MITS, Lakshmangarh

Ms. Ankita Babbar

Lecturer, Faculty of Arts, Science & Commerce, MITS, Lakshmangarh

Mr. Rajesh Yadav

Lecturer, Faculty of Arts, Science & Commerce, MITS, Lakshmangarh

Ms. Kiran Bala

Lecturer, APS Neighbourhood Campus, Punjabi Uni., Patiala

INTRODUCTION

"The Government would implement a comprehensive programme to accelerate e-governance at all levels of the Government to improve efficiency, transparency and accountability at the Government-Citizen Interface." – Hon'ble Prime Minister's Declaration on Independence Day - 15th August 2002."

The Government of India views electronic-Governance as a strategic tool for transforming Governance and improving the quality of services provided by the government to its people. E-governance has brought a new era in the quality of services delivered to citizens by computerizing the existing paper-based procedures. Several State Governments have taken various groundbreaking steps to boost e-Governance and have drawn up a guideline for IT implementation and on-line delivery of services to the citizens. Inefficiency in work; long queues; were some of the worst features of the working of the government departments. Consequently, a citizen visit to government department to make use of any service used to be a extremely painful experience. The awareness is rising amongst the citizen and they are getting better experiences from the private sector so the demand for better services on the part of government departments became more evaluated. The infusion of Information and Communication Technology (ICT) has played a prominent role in strengthening such a demand. ICT are being increasingly used by the governments to deliver its services at the locations convenient to the citizens.

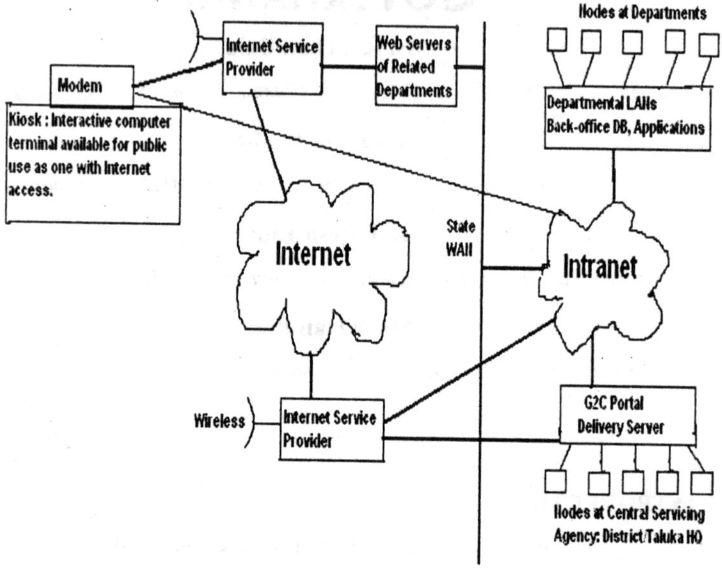

Figure : 65.1 ICT Infrastrucre for Rural Applications

The rural ICT solutions are normally offered through internet portals hosted on a delivery web server. The information flow between the delivery server and the other departments is fulfilled through Intranet/ LAN connectivity with servers of those departments (if exist). A number of stages involving several agencies fulfil the end-to-end connectivity between the central service providers and the citizens. Following table shows the stages, the technologies and agencies involved in offering the services.

Stages of Information Processing in Rural Applications			
Stage	**Connectivity**	**Technology**	**Agency**
1.	Related Departments to Central Servicing Agency	Manual or WAN / Intranet /LAN of individual departments	Individual departments of central, district administration and state.
2.	Central Servicing Agency to Delivery Server (web server)	LAN with or without Intranet	Coordination committee offering the service
3.	Deliver Server (web server) to Internet Service Provider.	Leased or Dedicated line /VSAT	Service deployment agency
4.	Central Servicing agency's ISP to Rural – ISP	ISP dedicated lines / BSNL /VSNL / Private Telecom	Internet Service Provider(s)
5.	Rural - ISP to Rural Kiosks	Dial up line / Wireless (WiLL)	Service Delivery Agents (Village Panchayats, Private Entrepreneurs)

PRIVATE PARTICIPATION

E-Government project champions have involved different private agencies for different tasks. These tasks include application development, software, population of data and content in the regional language, installation of networking and computer systems. Because of these arrangements the burden on the government is reduced. But one thing should be considered with great care that proper judiciary mechanisms will have to be worked out and to ensure that no injustice is done to the citizens by misuse of very sensitive and valuable data which is in the hands of the private agencies. R Chandrashekhar, joint secretary, department of information technology, government of India states that, "We welcome private participation in fulfilling the e-Governance initiatives of the Government of India. But this participation can only happen at the front-end level since the government is handling all the back-end work. For example, in the case of ICT kiosks, any private party can do the setting-up of a kiosk, but to run that kiosk the government will provide all support." The IT companies Microsoft, Sun, IBM, TCS, HCL Info systems and Adobe are placing a great roll in the e-governance projects.

SCOPE AND BENEFITS OF E-GOVERNANCE

It has following services which show the benefits of e-governance.

GOVERNMENT TO CITIZEN (G2C)

The goal of G2C service is to provide better services to the customers by talking with them. It provide them the services like better medical services to the citizen by linking of various hospitals in different parts of the country, license renewals, ordering of birth/death/marriage certificates, filing of income taxes, Ration Cards, Passports, taxes etc, Registration of motor vehicles, Issue of driving licenses, Tax and fee collection through Cash and Bank Challans and Control of Pollution, registration and transfer of the properties.

GOVERNMENT TO GOVERNMENT (G2G)

G2G service improves the government services by maintaining the database of criminals and policemen so that a detail of policeman regarding his skills, service record, family background etc can be easily traced which helps in the posting and promotion of policeman and criminal history can be easily received. Online filing of FIR's is also a big advantage. Online decisions of court based on the recorded fact of the case will reduce the backlog of cases. Linking of all the departments of the Government with various district headquarters and the state capital will easily exchange the information among them and will simplify the process of governance.

GOVERNMENT TO BUSINESS (G2B)

G2B transactions include various services exchanged between government and the business community like renewing licenses, registering businesses, obtaining permits, and payment of taxes, development of small and medium enterprises, an online government-supplier exchange for the purchase of goods and services by government.

SATE LEVEL INITIATIVES OF E-GOVERNMENT

Following are some of the key go-aheads taken in the country across some of the important citizen/business related departments.

BHOOMI PROJECT

The Revenue department in Karnataka State alleviated computerization of entire 20 million records of land ownership of 6.7 million farmers in the state. The software called "BHOOMI" is developed by National Informatics Centre, Bangalore. It has converted Record of Rights, Tenancy & Crops (RTC) into computer form which provides a printed copy of the RTC into only 15 rupees through kiosks. It helps the farmers in obtaining bank loans. It provides simplification of procedures, increased transparency and accountability in system, reduction in corruption, delays, harassment and victimisation of farmers.

E-SEVA PROJECT

E-Seva project is developed by Oracle partners, RAM Informatics Limited on the 25th of August 2001 by Andhra Pradesh. The aim of this project is to provide services like payment of utility bills for Electricity, Water and sewerage, Telephone, provision of birth and death certificates, registration of applications for passports, access to information like Transport Department Procedures, income verification, births and deaths records, land cultivation details, agriculture marketing, registration of small farmers, house numbering, occupation details of residents, drinking water details and irrigation sources, Reservation of APSRTC bus tickets, Reservation of water tanker, Reservation of tickets/ accommodation, Registration of new vehicles, Sale of passport application forms, Receipt of passport applications, Receipt of applications for new telephone connections, Sale of non-judicial stamps, Document writing service, Collection of small savings, Change of address of a vehicle own, Internet-enabled electronic payments, Filing of applications on the web, Cash withdrawals and deposits on ATM, Cell Phone Bill Payments etc. English as well as Telugu interfaces can be used for fulfilling these services. It has cut down the cost of travel and time, provides improved atmosphere, on line updating of data in server, accessibility of any service at any centre of city. The project is straightened by government to other parts of the state, including rural areas like the West Godavari district.

GYANDOOT PROJECT

The Gyandoot project was started in 1 January 2000 by doing conversation with the villagers regarding their problems and gram panchayats in the Dhar district of Madhya Pradesh. A GUI interface is used in Hindi language. Dial-up lines are used for the connectivity of kiosks with internet but in the near future it will be exchanged with wireless connections. These are handled by rural educated youth having matriculation and trained to work on the computer. It provides agricultural information in only Rs. 5, land records information in Rs. 15, e-mail system used for sending applications regarding income certificates in Rs. 10.

E-MITRA PROJECT

E-Mitra is introduced with the help of the State Bank of Bikaner and Jaipur and they got support from Rajasthan government. There are

1800-2000 e-Mitra kiosks in Rajasthan while Jaipur city alone has 180 such centres. The managing director, SBBJ, S.K. Bhattacharyya, said that "The facility would go a long way in resolving the problem of the common people of Rajasthan." It helps in Payment of electricity, water, telephone bills, and taxes through the bank's select ATMs. It is Implemented using a PPP (Public Private Partnership) model and provides the services like Ticket Reservations, Birth/death registration, Payment by cash/cheque/ credit card.

E-GOVERNANCE: KEY CHALLENGES

- Heavy investments for the purchase of hardware and software are required.
- To develop a great change in employees from manual mode to electronic mode is a difficult task which needs patience and some Workshops, seminars should be organized to spread consciousness among the employees.
- Kiosks works with the power so supporting infrastructures of power is required.
- Translators which translate English into other language Provides information to the public in their understandable language but this is a burdensome task so motivation should be provided.
- Interoperability of e-governance projects is required for providing benefits to the citizens.

CONCLUSION

E-Government is not about 'e' but about government. E-Government is not about computers but about citizens. E-Government is not about translating processes but about transforming processes. For successful implementation Standards, Infrastructure, Strategy all needs to be in place. E-governance has developed the rural areas electronically by providing them very important services. It has given a great opportunity to country to make the society more advanced and more efficient than ever before.

CHAPTER-66

Creating A Better India Through Corporate Governance

Sonal Aggarwal, *CA (Final)*

Dimple Aggarwal, *CA (Final)*

Shruti mundra, *CA (Final)*

Bihani S.D.P.G College, Sri Ganganagar(Rajasthan), India

INTRODUCTION

Corporate governance is one of the most talked about topics in business, indeed in society, today. Much more fraught, however, is the question: "Is it possible to resolve the Debates around the definition of CORPORATE GOVERNANCE?" It is clear that Corporate governance exists at a complex intersection of law, morality, and economic efficiency. Considering issues of executive compensation, financial scandals, and shareholder activism are all tied up with Corporate governance, its teaching is a topic worth investigation.

A well-defined and enforced corporate governance provides a structure that, at least in theory, works for the benefit of everyone concerned by ensuring that the enterprise adheres to accepted ethical standards and best practices as well as to formal laws. To that end, organizations have been formed at the regional, national, and global levels.

In recent years, corporate governance has received increased attention because of high-profile scandals involving abuse of corporate power and, in some cases, alleged criminal activity by corporate officers. An integral part of an effective corporate governance regime includes provisions for civil or criminal prosecution of individuals who conduct unethical or illegal acts in the name of the enterprise.

ISSUES IN CORPORATE GOVERNANCE IN INDIA

Corporate governance has been a topic of hot debate in developed countries like U.K. and U.S.A. for the last two decades. With the opening up of economies,it has also been a concern for developing country like India. This is because, opening up of economies has changed the scenario of Indian market i.e. on one hand, it has made the world market accessible to the Indian corporates & on the other hand, it has increased competition in the domestic market with the advent of the multinational companies..

Corporate governance is also important in Indian context because of the scams that occurred since liberalisation from 1991, for example the UTI scam, Ketan Parekh scam , Harshad Mehta scam & the latest & the biggest of them all the Satyam Fraud scam.

Another reason, is that it is believed that poor transparency and corporate governance norms were one of the main reasons for the Asian crisis in 1997. And also because such crisis have huge impact on the economy which can set a country several years back in its path to development.

A. SATYAM FRAUD SCAM

The biggest corporate scam in India has come from one of the most respected businessmen. Satyam founder Byrraju Ramalinga Raju resigned as its chairman after admitting to cooking up the account books. His efforts to fill the and quot; fictitious assets with real ones and quot; through Maytas acquisition failed, after which he decided to confess the crime. With a fraud involving about Rs 8,000 crore (Rs 80 billion), Satyam is heading for more trouble in the days ahead. India's fourth largest IT company lost a staggering Rs 10,000 crore (Rs 100 billion) in market capitalisation as investors reacted sharply and dumped shares, pushing down the scrip by 78 per cent to Rs 39.95 on the Bombay Stock Exchange. The NYSE-listed firm could also face regulator action in the US. and quot; I am now prepared to subject myself to the laws of the land and face consequences thereof, and quot; Raju said in a letter to SEBI and the Board of Directors, while giving details of how the profits were inflated over the years and his failed attempts to and quot;fill the fictitious assets with real ones. and quot; Raju said the company and apos;s balance sheet as of September 30 carries and quot; inflated (non-existent) cash and bank balances of Rs 5,040 crore (Rs 50.40 billion) as against Rs 5,361 crore (Rs 53.61 billion) reflected in the books. and quot;

B. INTRODUCTION TO THE "BIG BULL OF THE TRADING FLOOR". THE PIED PIPER OF STOCK MARKET. *HARSHAD MEHTA : THE SCAMSTER.*

He was known as the Harshad Mehta' Big Bull'. However, his bull run did not last too long. He triggered a rise in the Bombay Stock Exchange in the year 1992 by trading in shares at a premium across many segments. Taking advantages of the loopholes in the banking system, Harshad and his associates triggered a securities scam diverting funds to the tune of Rs 4000 crore (Rs 40 billion) from the banks to stockbrokers between April 1991 to May 1992. Harshad Mehta worked with the New India Assurance Company before he moved ahead to try his luck in the stock markets. Mehta soon mastered the tricks of the trade and set out on dangerous game plan. Mehta has siphoned off huge sums of money from several banks and millions of investors were conned in the process. His scam was exposed, the markets crashed and he was arrested and banned for life from trading in the stock markets. He was later charged with 72 criminal offences. A Special Court also sentenced Sudhir Mehta, Harshad Mehta's brother, and six others, including four bank officials, to rigorous imprisonment (RI) ranging from 1 year to 10 years on the charge of duping State Bank of India to the tune of Rs 600 crore (Rs 6 billion) in connection with the securities scam that rocked the financial markets in 1992. He died in 2002 with many litigations still pending against him.

C. THE FOLLOWER OF THE "BIG BULL" KETAN PAREKH

Ketan Parekh followed Harshad Mehta's footsteps to swindle crores of rupees from banks. A chartered accountant he used to run a family business, NH Securities.Ketan however had bigger plans in mind. He targetted smaller exchanges like the Allahabad Stock Exchange and the Calcutta Stock Exchange, and bought shares in fictitious names. His dealings revolved around shares of ten companies like Himachal Futuristic, Global Tele-Systems, SSI Ltd, DSQ Software, Zee Telefilms, Silverline, Pentamedia Graphics and Satyam Computer (K-10 scrips). Ketan borrowed Rs 250 crore from Global Trust Bank to fuel his ambitions. Ketan alongwith his associates also managed to get Rs 1,000 crore from the Madhavpura Mercantile Co-operative Bank. According to RBI regulations, a broker is allowed a loan of only Rs 15 crore (Rs 150 million). There was evidence of price rigging in the scrips of Global Trust Bank, Zee Telefilms, HFCL, Lupin Laboratories, Aftek Infosys and Padmini Polymer.

D. THE UTI SCAM.

Former UTI chairman P S Subramanyam and two executive directors — M M Kapur and S K Basu — and a stockbroker Rakesh G Mehta, were arrested in connection with the 'UTI scam'. UTI had purchased 40,000 shares of Cyberspace On September 25, 2000, for about Rs 3.33 crore (Rs 33.3 million) from Rakesh Mehta when there were no buyers for the scrip. The market price was around Rs 830. The CBI said it was the conspiracy of these four people which resulted in the loss of Rs. 32 crore (Rs 320 million). Subramanyam, Kapur and Basu had changed their stance on an investment advice of the equities research cell of UTI. The promoter of Cyberspace Infosys, Arvind Johari was arrested in connection with the case. The officals were paid Rs 50 lakh (Rs. 5 million) by Cyberspace to promote its shares. He also received Rs 1.18 crore (Rs. 11.8 million) from the company through a circuitous route for possible rigging the Cyberspace counter.

RECOMMENDATIONS

(a) SEBI should develop adequate expertise for analysing financial statements so that it is able to detect fraud in the financial statements in the future.

(b) The Institute of Chartered Accountants of India (ICAI)or the Government should encourage the development of a whistle-blowing committee so that anybody who finds anything doubtful or fishy about a company should report against the same immediately to the committee

(c) SEBI should reconsider its financial disclosure norms. A few years back SEBI suspended sending of printed copy of audited balance sheets to the shareholders as a cost cutting measure. In today's world , it can be done easily by uploading the same in the internet. Also Bankers & Rating Agencies can also then analyse the financial statements for detecting fraud.

(d) The ICAI should implement a rule, indicating that audit firms should be allowed to work as auditors of large companies for a period of two years on a rotation basis in order to avoid undue influence committed by the audit forms.

(e) The entire banking system & the Banking Secretary Act should be reviewed. In India, if one borrows one lakh rupees one is afraid of the bank while on the other hand if one had borrowed tweleve crore rupees the bank is afraid of the person. The Narasimham committee recommendation about putting some conditions at the time of issuing new loans addresses these problems to some extent.

CONCLUSION

Corporate Governance has become the latest buzzword today. Almost every country has institutionalized a set of Corporate Governance codes, spelt out best practices and has sought to impose appropriate board structures. Despite the 'Corporate Governance revolution' there exists no universal benchmark for effective levels of disclosure and transparency. There are several corporate governance structures available in the developed world but there is no one structure, which can be singled out as being better than the others. There is no "one size fits all" structure for corporate governance. Corporate governance extends beyond corporate law. Its fundamental objective is not the mere fulfillment of the requirements of law but in ensuring commitment of the board in managing the company in a transparent manner for maximizing long-term shareholder value. Effectiveness of corporate governance system cannot merely be legislated by law. As competition increases, technology pronounces the death of distance and speeds up communication. The environment in which companies operate in India also changes. In this dynamic environment the systems of corporate governance also need to evolve. The recommendations made by different expert committees will go a long way in raising the standards of corporate governance in Indian companies and make them attractive destinations for local and global capital. These recommendations will also form the base for further evolution of the structure of corporate governance in consonance with the rapidly changing economic and industrial environment of the country in the new millennium.

CHAPTER-67

Creating a Better India Through Corporate Governance

Gurjeet Singh

M. Com Final(ABST)
Maharishi Dayanand PG college
gurjeetdhiman6977@gmail.com

Inderjeet Singh

M. Com Final(ABST)
Maharishi Dayanand PG college
word_life56@yahoo.co.in

Anil Giri

M. Com Final(ABST)
Maharishi Dayanand PG college
anildygiri@yahoo.com

Corporate governance (CG) is one of the most talked about topics in business, indeed in society, today. A Google search revealed 513 news citations during a single week in June 2006. Most academics, business professionals, and lay observers would agree that CG is defined as the general set of customs, regulations, habits, and laws that determine to what end a firm should be run.

According to Sir Adrian Cadbury, "Corporate Governance is the system by which companies are directed and controlled............to do with Power and Accountability: who exercises power, on behalf of whom, how the exercise of power is controlled."

According to OECD the Corporate Governance structure specifies the distribution of rights and responsibilities among different participants in the corporation, such as, the Board, managers, shareholders and other stakeholders spells out the rules and procedures for making decisions on corporate affairs.

Yet another definition is "Corporate Governance is about promoting corporate fairness, transparency and accountability."

NEED, IMPORTANCE AND OBJECTIVES OF CORPORATE GOVERNANCE

In order to overcome the under noted serious concerns within the business community, there is a need to introduce a system of corporate governance that will ensure the transparency, integrity and accountability of Management including non-executive directors.

- Concentration of greater financial power and authority in a lesser number of individuals,
- Violations of foreign exchange rules and regulations,
- Large scale diversion of funds to associate companies and risky ventures,
- Preferential allotment of shares to promoters at low prices,
- Frequent changes in Board structures,
- Charging of royalty for use of brand name by the parent company by leading companies.

In an open financial market, investors choose from a variety of investment vehicles. The existence of a corporate governance system is likely a part of this decision-making process. In such a scenario, companies that are more open and transparent, and thus well governed, are more likely to raise capital successfully because investors will have the information and confidence necessary for them to lend funds directly to such companies. Moreover, well-governed companies likely will obtain capital more cheaply than companies that have poor corporate governance practices because investors will require a smaller "risk premium" for investing in well-governed companies.

Thus, in an efficient capital market, investors will invest in companies with better corporate governance frameworks because of the lower risks and the likelihood of higher returns. Good corporate governance practices also enable Management to allocate resources more efficiently, which increases the likelihood that investors will obtain a higher rate of return on their investment.

REASONS FOR CORPORATE GOVERNANCE FAILURES

If the Board is in awe of the family executive, it makes it difficult for the Board sometimes to ask tough questions or at other times the right questions at the right time in order to serve the interests of the shareholders better. As a result truly independent directors are rarely found in Indian companies. Serving on multiple boards is problematic because doing so can overburden directors, thus hampering their performance, and increase the potential for directors to experience conflicts of interest between the various corporations they serve.

It is admitted that contribution of the independent directors is limited because the average time spent in Board meetings by these directors is barely 14 to 16 hours in a year. In some cases, it has been found that no proper training and orientation regarding the awareness of rights, responsibilities, duties and liabilities of the directors is provided to an individual before appointing him/her as a director in the Board. Also there is unseen but the active participation of political class.

The directors on the board are largely reliant on information from the management and auditors, with their capacity to independently verify financial information being quite limited, while auditors, as this case suggests, have also been equally reliant on management information. The relevant issue here is the extent and the depth of auditors' effort in their exercise of due diligence. Excessive reliance on information from the management is symptomatic of the ownership or control of companies in India by business families, and that poses a particular challenge for corporate governance in India. The greatest drawback of financial disclosures in India is the absence of detailed reporting on related party transactions. In addition, poor quality of consolidated accounting and segment reporting leads to misrepresentation of the true picture of a business group.

Although India's investor-protection laws are sophisticated, litigants must wait a long time before receiving a judgment. Delays in the delivery of verdicts, high costs of litigation and the lengthy judicial appointment process in courts make the legal enforcement mechanism ineffective. According to the OECD, "the credibility and utility of a corporate governance framework rest on its enforceability."

In India, the two audit-related issues which are commonly recognized are that of auditor independence (which is a problem worldwide) because of the large if segmented market in accounting services, and the perceived powerlessness of auditors in the face of corporate pressure. In many cases, they are ill-equipped to handle the needs of large companies, because in the face of an audit failure, it is very difficult to discern whether the auditors were complacent or they were pressurized by the concerted efforts of the insiders.

REQUIREMENTS TO STRENGTHEN CORPORATE GOVERNANCE

- To promote or to increase awareness among entrepreneurs adoption of good corporate governance practices, which are the integral element for doing and managing business.
- To ensure the quality of audit that is at the root of effective corporate governance by making the Auditor accountable for the disclosure of financial information.
- To make the Board of Directors as well as the CEOs and CFOs accountable for the discharge of their duties with the proper use of their rights within the powers.
- To form an appropriate system in order to check the Directors independence in the board and to monitor the work of Audit firms.
- To pay special attention in the quality and effectiveness of the legal, administrative and regulatory framework.
- To increase the shareholder activism i.e. the exercise and enforcement of rights by minority shareholders with the objective of enhancing shareholder value over the long-term.
- To implement more robust Bankruptcy Laws which are a key component of any corporate governance system.
- To eliminate "Regulatory Arbitrage" i.e. to establish a clear mandate for each regulatory Authority for the enforcement of Clause 49 of the Listing Agreement, thereby improving India's corporate governance enforcement mechanism.
- To resolve the conflict between the dominant shareholders and the minority shareholders by improving the rights of minority shareholders.
- To make a statutory compliance for the listed companies to compulsorily obtain a report on Corporate Governance Rating (CGR) from a Credit Rating Agency in India.

FUTURE PROSPECTS FOR CORPORATE GOVERNANCE

To highlight the frauds and irregularities in the corporate sector the issues of governance, accountability and transparency in the affairs of the company, as well as about the rights of shareholders and role of Board of Directors have never been as prominent as it is today. With the integration of Indian economy with global markets, industrialists and corporations in the country are being increasingly asked to adopt better and transparent corporate practices. The degree to which corporations observe basic principles of good corporate governance is an increasingly important factor for taking key investment decisions. If companies are to reap the full benefits of the global capital market, capture efficiency gains, benefit by economies of scale and attract long-term capital, adoption of corporate governance standards must be credible, consistent, coherent and inspiring.

Hence, in the years to come, corporate governance will become more relevant and a more acceptable practice worldwide. This is easily evident from the various activities undertaken by many companies in framing and enforcing codes of conduct and honest business practices; following more stringent norms for financial and non-financial disclosures, as mandated by law; accepting higher and appropriate accounting standards; enforcing tax reforms coupled with deregulation and competition; etc. but we cannot eliminate the possibility of frauds and scams as seen in the recent Satyam case. Scams are an integral part of corporate history. They come to light only when the going gets rough. Only when the tide goes out we see all those swimming naked. Such scams are an opportunity for self-renewal; neither self-denial nor blame game. The frequency and scale of such scams has been far more in the West than in India. We need to take such types of scams as an opportunity in future for overhauling the system of corporate governance in India.

CONCLUSION

Good corporate governance may not be the engine of economic growth, but it is essential for the proper functioning of the engine. The investors both National and International would be loyal to invest in the Indian companies if they follow all the standards of corporate governance practices. Further, to nurture and strengthen this loyalty, our companies need to give clear-cut signal that the words "your company" have real meaning. That requires well functioning Board, greater disclosure, better management practices, and a more open, interactive and dynamic corporate governance environment. Quite simply, share holders' and creditors' support is vital for the survival, growth and competitiveness of India's companies. Effectiveness of corporate governance system cannot merely be legislated by law neither can any system of corporate governance be static. Thus, the essence of corporate governance is in promoting and maintaining integrity, transparency and accountability in the management of the company as well as in manifestation of the values, principles and policies of a corporation. In order to make an honest and objective assessment on corporate governance practices we do need more laws but better enforcement because the effectiveness and the utility of good corporate governance practices rest on its enforceability. Ultimately, good corporate governance practices in India will be shaped by our administrative and regulatory authorities like SEBI, MCA, etc. by implementing transparent and effective corporate governance laws.

CHAPTER-68

Corporate Governance Practices followed in India under Clause 49 of the Listing Agreement

Chhotelal Chouhan

Assistant Professor-in-Commercem, Sonamukhi College
(Affiliated to the University of Burdwan, Burdwan, West Bengal, India)

CORPORATE GOVERNANCE PRACTICES FOLLOWED IN INDIA UNDER CLAUSE 49 OF THE LISTING AGREEMENT

"The fundamental objective of Corporate Governance is the enhancement of long-term shareholder value while, at the same time, protecting the interests of other stakeholders."

- Kumar Mangalam Birla Committee Report on Corporate Governance, 1999.

Corporate governance has in recent years been a much-discussed topic in economics, management, business ethics, company law and other disciplines. Governance is a new buzzword in India as well as the world over. There is no well accepted definition of what Governance mean. As a result different people have came-up with different definitions that basically reflects their special interest in the field. Corporate Governance is the system by which business corporations are directed and controlled. The Corporate Governance structure specifies the distribution of rights and responsibilities among different participants in the corporations, such as, the board, managers, shareholders and other stakeholders, and spells out the rules and procedures for making decisions on corporate affairs. By doing this, it also provides the structure through which the company's objectives are set, and the means of attaining those objectives and monitoring performances. Corporate governance is concerned with holding the balance between economic and social goals and between individual and communal goals. The governance framework is there to encourage the efficient use of resources and equally to require accountability for the stewardship of those resources. The aim is to align as nearly as possible the interests of individuals, corporations and society (Adrian Cadbury, 1999).

Most important challenges faced by the corporate governance reforms in developing and emerging economies are establishing a rule-based system of governance (Arafat and Ugur, 2003). A main purpose of corporate governance is to protect the interest of a company's owners - the shareholders. The OECD principles on corporate governance pay special attention to the rights of shareholders and their equitable treatment. Corporate governance refers to how companies ought to be run, directed and controlled. It is about supervising and holding to account those who direct and control the management. It is believed that, good governance generates investor goodwill and confidence (Joshua Abor, 2007).

The most stringent enactment passed in corporate governance developments across the globe is the Sarbanes Oxley Act in the US in July 2002 after the corporate collapses of Enron, Worldcom and Xerox to restore trust in the public securities market. The "meltdown" of these companies has led to criticism of boards of directors and accusations that corporate boards aren't doing their jobs (Petra, 2006). Specifically, the US government enacted this law to protect investors by improving the accuracy and reliability of corporate disclosures made pursuant to the securities laws.

The recent Big Bang Scams are –

Company	Company	Company	Company	Company	Company	Company
Satyam Computer Services	Global Trust Bank	WorldCom	Xerox	Enron	Barings Bank	GrowMore Research and Asset Management
Person : B Ramalinga Raju	Person : Ramesh Geli	Person : Scott Sullivan	Person : Paul A Allaire	Person : Jeffrey Skilling	Person : Nick Leeson	Person : Harshad Mehta
Country: India	Country : India	Country: US	Country: US	Country: US	Country : UK	Country : India
Scam: Fudging accounts	Scam : Banking fraud	Scam : Accounting fraud	Scam : Accounting fraud	Scam : Accounting fraud	Scam : Future Trading	Scam : Bank securities misuse for stock
Amount : Rs. 3176 cr.	Amount : Rs. 812 cr.	Amount : Rs. 43650cr. ($9bn)	Amount: Rs. 29100cr. ($6bn)	Amount: Rs. 2866 cr. ($591m)	Amount: Rs. 6790 cr. ($1.4bn)	Amount: Rs. 4300 cr.
Year: 2009	Year : 2004	Year : 2002	Year : 2002	Year : 2001	Year : 1995	Year : 1992

Dollar converted to rupees on 7th Jan, 2009 exchange rate [Source – The Telegraph, page – 04, Calcutta (India), 8th Jan, 2009]

BOARD COMPOSITION

"Directors and managements must take upon themselves to improve accountability by setting a tone at the top", honoring the responsibilities that arise from the trust placed in them by investors. All directors and managements should implement their own best practices for corporate governance that promote integrity, transparency and accountability."

-Elisse B. Walter, Commissioner, U.S. Securities and Exchange Commission, remarks before the Practicing Law Institute, New York, February 18, 2009.

The minimum board size of all listed companies, as well as unlisted public limited companies with a paid-up share capital and free reserves of Rs.10 crore and above, or turnover of Rs.50 crore and above should be seven — of which at least four should be independent directors. However, this will not apply to: (1) unlisted public companies, which have no more than 50 shareholders and which are without debt of any kind from the public, banks, or financial institutions, as long as they do not change their character, (2) unlisted subsidiaries of listed companies. *(Report of the Committee on Corporate Audit and Governance -Naresh Chandra Committee, January, 2003, Para 4.3)*

REPORT ON CORPORATE GOVERNANCE

(i) There shall be a separate section on Corporate Governance in the Annual Reports of company, with a detailed compliance report on Corporate Governance. Non-compliance of any mandatory requirement of this clause with reasons thereof and the extent to which the non-mandatory requirements have been adopted should be specifically highlighted. The suggested list of items to be included in this report is given in **Annexure- I C** and list of non-mandatory requirements is given in **Annexure – I D.**

(ii) The companies shall submit a quarterly compliance report to the stock exchanges within 15 days from the close of quarter as per the format given in **Annexure I B**. The report shall be signed either by the Compliance Officer or the Chief Executive Officer of the company

COMPLIANCE

(1) The company shall obtain a certificate from either the auditors or practicing company secretaries regarding

compliance of conditions of corporate governance as stipulated in this clause and annex the certificate with the directors' report, which is sent annually to all the shareholders of the company. The same certificate shall also be sent to the Stock Exchanges along with the annual report filed by the company.

(2) The non-mandatory requirements given in **Annexure – I D** may be implemented as per the discretion of the company. However, the disclosures of the compliance with mandatory requirements and adoption (and compliance) / non-adoption of the non-mandatory requirements shall be made in the section on corporate governance of the Annual Report.

RECENT AMENDMENTS TO CLAUSE 49 OF THE LISTING AGREEMENT

SEBI has announced a complete revision of clause 49 in the listing agreement of stock exchanges vide circular dated October 29, 2004. This circular supersedes all other earlier circulars issued by SEBI on clause 49 of the Listing Agreement.

APPLICABILITY

The provisions of the revised clause 49 will be applicable to:

1. All entities seeking listing for the first time at the time of seeking approval for listing.

2. Existing listed entities having a paid up share capital of Rs. 3 crore and above or net worth of Rs. 25 crore or more at any time in the history of the company with effect from 1st April 2005.

SEBI has further extended the date for ensuring compliance with the revised clause 49 up to December 31, 2005 vide circular no. **SEBI/CFD/DIL/CG/1/2005/29/3** dated March 29, 2005.

Now the question is whether all the companies which is listed under Bombay Stock Exchange or National Stock Exchange or other stock exchanges followed SEBI guidelines' revised clause 49 of the listing agreement to protect the interest the stakeholders or not? For this purpose, comparative analysis has been made in between Public Sector and Private Sector units based on their reporting practices on corporate governance.

Over the years the UK has initiated a series of investigations into ways to improve the corporate governance of UK listed companies. These investigations have been high profile, lead by an experienced individual who has given his name to the final report. These are the Cadbury Report (1992), Greenbury Report (1995), Hampel Report (1998) and Turnbull Report (1999). Out of them the Cadbury Report and the Greenbury Report affected too much the corporate governance practices in UK. These reports are highlighted below –

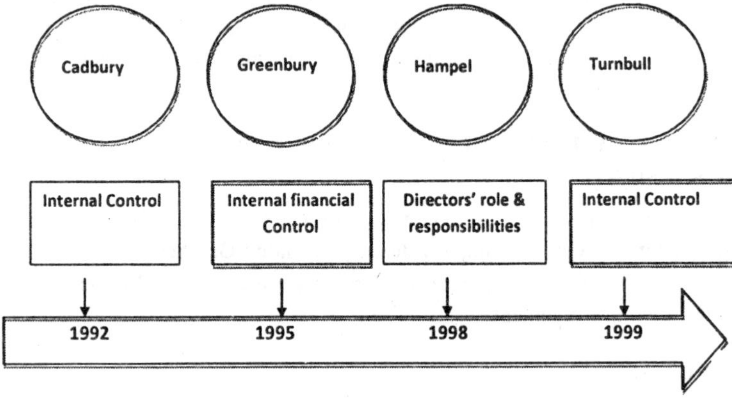

Fig. 68.1 : International Recommendations of various committees on Corporate Governance Practices

Over the years India has also initiated a series of investigations into ways to improve the corporate governance practices in Indian enterprises. The Securities and Exchange Board of India (SEBI), the chief corporate regulatory body in 'ndia, is entrusted with the task of overhauling the process of corporate governance practice in India. Over the last decade, SEBI has performed well and has formed various committees to look into the ways and means to regulate the corporate governance practice in India, at par with the above mentioned international practices. These are Kumar Mangalam Birla Committee (1999), Naresh Chandra Committee (2002), Narayan Murthy Committee (2003) and JJ Irani Committee (2005). The main objectives behind these committees are to promote corporate fairness, transparency and accountability in corporate governance and financial reporting practices.

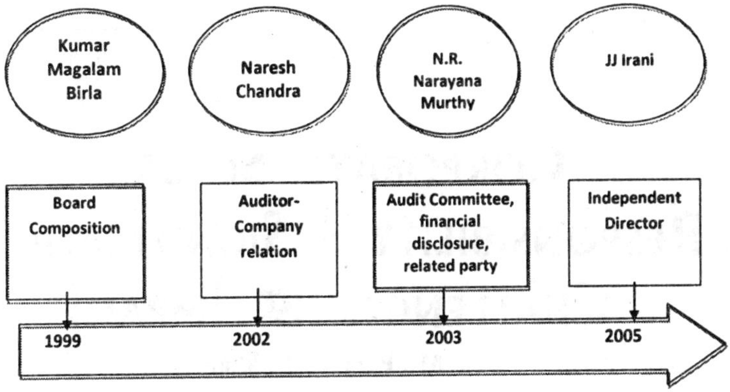

Fig. 68.2 Indian Recommendations of various committees on Corporate Governance Practices

Clause 49 of the Listing Agreement, which deals with Corporate Governance norms that a listed entity should follow, was first introduced in the financial year 2000-01 based on recommendations of Kumar Mangalam Birla committee. After these recommendations were in place for about two years, SEBI, in order to evaluate the adequacy of the existing practices and to further improve the existing practices set up a committee under the Chairmanship of Mr Narayana Murthy during 2002-03. The Murthy committee, after holding three meetings, had submitted the draft recommendations on corporate governance norms. After deliberations, SEBI accepted the recommendations in August 2003 and asked the Stock Exchanges to revise Clause 49 of the Listing Agreement based on Murthy committee recommendations.

CONCLUSION

Corporate Governance today is ineffective primarily because of the concentration of corporate power in the hands of management. A revolutionary approach to Corporate Governance is needed to rebalance or equalize this power, stop management fraud, promote accurate financial reporting, and thus regain the shaken confidence of the financial markets. This approach can be accomplished by recognizing the employees as key participants in the corporate process. The stock exchange is usually the primary regulatory institution concerning the quantity and quality of information disclosed by listed companies. The stock exchange and the other regulatory bodies can work to review and impose whether the information disclosure is sufficient and make changes when necessary.

CHAPTER-69

Corporate Social Responsibility - Significance, Challenges & Impact

1. Mr. Parveen Kukkar

Lecturer in A.V. Jain Girls College, Sri Ganganagar

2. Mr. Pankaj Kukkar

Lecturer in Aror Vansh Girls College, Sri Ganganagar

3. Miss Sveen Khungar

Lecturer in Aror Vansh Girls College, Sri Ganganagar

4. Sumit Bansal

S.D. P.G. College, Sri Ganganagar.

INTRODUCTION

In a global economy, increasingly organization have a responsibility to facilitate, demonstrate and promote corporate social responsibility (CSR). Long-term sustainability demands that organizations rethink their business goals and objectives from solely focusing on making profit to corporate citizenship.

- Company reputation and brand are greatly influenced by public perception.
- Open, reliable and regular reporting of a company's performance-known as accountability and transparency in CSR terminology-is quickly becoming a public issue.
- The rapid rise of socially responsible investment illustrates that corporate citizenship is becoming a key measure that investors consider when aligning ethical concerns with publicly hels corporations.

- With the anticipated labor shortage in the next 10 to 25 years, attracting, developing, motivating and retaining talent is, and will continue to be, very important. Correspondingly, CSR influences a company's competitive advantage today through two key value drivers: 1) company reputation and brand; and 2) human capital.

CHALLENGES TO THE BUSINESS CASE FOR CSR

- The business care for CSR is not necessarily a simple one. Among the challenges is that social and/or environmental impact differs across industries, complicated by the fact that the term CSR has different meanings to different industry sectors in different parts of the globe. Also, some may question if the message CEOs communicate about CSR is an add-an or part of company core business activities-or is it merely an insincere effort to boost public relations? In some organizations, CSR is still considered to mean compliance and philanthropyy, although some large companies are now placing CSR in a more strategic framework.

- There is the question of how to measure CSR. One of the largest obstacles noted was the lack of rigorous, credible business case backed up by performance indicators and metrics that can be quantified and benchmarked.

- HR leaders can help address this challenge by considering different options and developing creative approaches to CSR to present to their company. Below are recommendations to consider :

- Network with other HR Professional to learn aobut their organizations's CSR initiatives (ideas and information about progrms; what worked and lessons learned)

- Explore partnering with other organizations (e.g., co-sponsor a community event).

- Contact local business organizations, such as the chamber of Commerce, to learn what events they sponsor and how the compan may contribute.

- Solicit employee suggestions regarding CSR initiatives.

HR'S LEADERSHIP ROLE

With company reputation, viability and sometimes survival at stake, one of the critical roles of HR leadership today is to spearhead the development and strategic implementation of CSR throughout the organization and promote sound corporate citizenship. Attracting and retaining competent people is one of the primary business reasons for CSR.

Many HR leaders are already looking ahead to the future. According to the SHRM (R) 2004-2005 Workplace Forecast, key HR trends are (1) demonstrating HR's return on investment; (2) HR's role in promoting corporate ethics; and (3) building people management and human capital components into key business transactions.

- HR leaders can influene three primary standards of CSR-ethics, employment practices and community involvement.
- The impact of CSR is under close scrutiny. There are four primary areas of concern; (1) product responsibility; (2) strategies for sustainability : (3) the quality of CSR management; and 4) the future of CSR overall (30).
- A range of measures that include strategy, governance and stakeholder involvement show thest companies scoring an average of 24 out of 100 points with only five companies scoring more than 50% and only one U.S. company, Hwlett-Packard, placing among the 10 highest scorers. (35) Furthers, the level of effort that the worldwide community is putting into the achievement of the United Nations Millennium Declaration goals is less than half the effort necessary to meet any of the goals.

CONCLUSION

With the growing importance of human capital as a success factor for today's organizations, the role of HR leadership will become evermore critical in leading and educating organizations on the value of CSR and how best to strategically implement CSR policies and programs domestically and abroad.

■■■